# THE CROSSROADS
# OF CIVILIZATION

# THE
# CROSSROADS
# OF CIVILIZATION

## A HISTORY OF VIENNA

## ANGUS ROBERTSON

PEGASUS BOOKS

NEW YORK  LONDON

THE CROSSROADS OF CIVILIZATION

Pegasus Books, Ltd.
148 West 37th Street, 13th Floor
New York, NY 10018

First Pegasus Books cloth edition August 2022

ISBN: 978-1-63936-195-3

10 9 8 7 6 5 4 3 2 1

Printed in the United States of America
Distributed by Simon & Schuster
www.pegasusbooks.com

# Contents

Picture credits      vi

Introduction and Acknowledgements      vii

Maps      xiii

1   From Vindobona to Vienna      1

2   The Imperial Habsburg Capital      22

3   The Empire Strikes Back      51

4   Revolting French and Napoleon      87

5   The Glorious Moment: The Congress of Vienna      105

6   The Concert of Europe: The Age of Metternich      135

7   The Longest Reign      163

8   Nervous Splendour: Fin de Siècle      193

9   Waltzing to War      232

10   The First Republic to the Third Reich      269

11   Occupation, Intrigue and Espionage      306

12   Diplomatic Capital      329

Epilogue      363

Notes      367

Bibliography      399

Index      425

# Picture credits

# Introduction and Acknowledgements

This book focuses on Vienna as an international capital, a city that has been a pivot for diplomacy, culture, intellectual thought, music, art, design and architecture for hundreds of years.

Three high-profile funerals in the Austrian capital over the three last centuries illustrate the passing of different ages during this period. Charles-Joseph, 7th Prince de Ligne, died in December 1814 at the height of the Congress of Vienna, not long after famously saying: 'The Congress does not move forward, it dances.' One of the greatest characters of the age, he was a personal friend of the major figures of the 18th century, including the Austrian-born Queen Marie Antoinette of France, Tsarina Catherine the Great of Russia, King Frederick the Great of Prussia and Austria's Emperor Joseph II, as well as the leading thinkers and authors of the age, such as Rousseau, Voltaire and Goethe. Charles-Joseph's funeral on the Kahlenberg hill overlooking Vienna marked the passing of the *ancien régime*.

One century later, the funeral took place of Emperor Francis Joseph I, one of the longest-serving sovereigns anywhere, who reigned over Europe's second largest country from the 1848 revolutions to the First World War. In many ways his funeral in 1916 signalled the end of the Habsburg Monarchy, which had ruled for more than 600 years. Within two years the Austro-Hungarian Empire collapsed in defeat and disintegrated into eight successor states.

Almost another century later was the funeral of Francis Joseph's grandnephew, Otto Habsburg, the last ever heir to the throne. In a packed St Stephen's Cathedral in 2011, the old imperial anthem rang out and the Guard Battalion of the Austrian army followed the coffin in a procession through Vienna city centre. As the successors to the old imperial Trabanten Lifeguards, they marched behind its flag, proudly wearing insignia with the black eagle of the Austrian Republic superimposed on the golden eagle of the Habsburg Empire.

The timing and symbolism of all three Vienna funerals tell their own story about the preceding centuries, and how this city has played a central role in the events that have marked these ages. Vienna has been at the crossroads of European civilisations, continental trading routes, cultural developments and power relationships for more than two millennia. This began with the foundation of the Roman outpost of Vindobona, which developed over the centuries into the city we know today as the Austrian capital, especially since it became the city of residence for the up-and-coming Habsburg rulers in 1440.

For six centuries the blossoming of Vienna into a first-order international capital has been associated with the dynasty. 'Habsburg history is in both the particular and the general sense not national but European history. From its earliest origins the family was entrusted with the task of resolving the tensions between west and east, north and south. In their successes and frustration, the Habsburgs laid up an enormous store of European experience – a parallel to the collections of treasures created by artists all the European nations and put together by the connoisseurs of the family during the course of the centuries.'[1]

By 1600 the Holy Roman Empire was firmly in the grip of the Habsburgs, ruling from the Hofburg palace within Vienna's city walls. The empire had the largest population in Europe; it was bigger than France, Russia, Spain or England. With 50,000 people, Vienna itself still had a relatively small population compared to the likes of London, Paris and Moscow, but it held a key position as the dynastic hub of central Europe. 'In other countries dynasties are episodes in the history of the people; in the Habsburg Empire peoples are a complication in the history of the dynasty. The Habsburg lands acquired in time a common culture, and to some extent, a common economic character: these were the creation, not the creators, of the dynasty. No other family has endured so long or left so deep a mark upon Europe: the Habsburgs were the greatest dynasty of modern history, and the history of Central Europe revolves round them, not the other way round.'[2]

Vienna was a melting pot of nationalities from across central Europe and beyond, with visitors struck by its polyglot population and its burgeoning cultural scene, which attracted the finest composers, performers and artists from near and far. The city was also the Christian bulwark against two Turkish sieges, leading Catholic resistance to the Reformation and opposition to revolutionary and Napoleonic France. Bonaparte's foreign minister, Charles Talleyrand, stressed to Napoleon why Vienna's regional and international role was of such importance: 'Your Majesty can now eliminate the Austrian monarchy or re-establish it. But this conglomeration of states must stay together. It is absolutely indispensable for the future well-being of the civilised world.'[3]

Over the course of 20 years of warfare, Austria provided the most consistent continental opposition against revolutionary and Napoleonic France. Despite numerous defeats across Germany, Bohemia and Italy, the Habsburg forces continued to fight, handing Napoleon his first personal battlefield defeat at Aspern-Essling on the outskirts of Vienna. In the greatest battle before the First World War, an allied army under Austrian command took to the field at the Battle of Leipzig: half a million men from across Europe took part in this Battle of the Nations, where Napoleon met his real Waterloo. It took the Congress of Vienna to re-establish peace and stability across the continent.

During the 19th century, Vienna quadrupled in size to become one of the largest cities in Europe; the city walls were replaced by a wide boulevard around the old town centre, which became home to some of the grandest and finest buildings on the continent. While Austria's political relevance began to be eclipsed by the rising power of Prussia and a unified Germany, it remained one of the great powers. This ended with defeat and collapse in the First World War, a development that was even lamented by foes such as Winston Churchill, who described it as a 'cardinal tragedy': 'For centuries this surviving embodiment of the Holy Roman Empire had afforded a common life, with advantages in trade and security, to a large number of peoples none of whom in our own times had the strength or vitality to stand by themselves in the face of pressure from a revivified Germany or Russia . . . The noble capital of Vienna, the home of so much long-defended culture and tradition, the centre of so many roads, rivers and railways, was left stark and starving, like a great emporium in an impoverished district whose inhabitants have mostly departed.'[4]

Vienna's woes continued with the impoverishment of the 1920s, the Nazi Anschluss of the 1930s and the Second World War. Only after the re-establishment of the Austrian Republic and the end of four-power occupation in 1955 did Vienna begin to fully prosper and reinvent itself as the international capital. On the front line of the Cold War, only miles from the Iron Curtain, Vienna became the preferred neutral meeting place for world leaders from West and East. Today it is home to the third global headquarters of the United Nations, the Organization for Security and Co-operation in Europe (OSCE), the International Atomic Energy Agency (IAEA), the OPEC oil cartel and a myriad of international organisations. In becoming a world centre for diplomacy whilst retaining its status as a global city of culture, Vienna is, truly, the international capital.

*

Vienna was where, by pure good fortune, I spent my twenties after graduating from Aberdeen University in 1991 with a degree in Politics and International Relations. Originally an English teaching assistant at the Federal Commercial School on Polgarstrasse in Vienna's 21st district, I managed a lucky break into journalism that allowed me to work in one of the world's greatest cities for the best part of a decade. Following encouragement from the likes of Dr James Wilkie, a long-standing Scots expat working for the Federal Foreign Ministry and Chancellery at the Hofburg, I tried my luck with Austrian current affairs magazine *Profil*. Their foreign news editor, Georg Hoffmann-Ostenhof, graciously commissioned me to write an article, allowing me to show off 'my most recent journalistic work' at an interview soon afterwards with Tilia Herold of the Austrian Broadcasting Corporation (ORF). I was blessed to be given the chance to learn the skills of a radio journalist, newsreader and editor at Blue Danube Radio, the ORF's fourth national network, aimed particularly at the diplomatic and international community in Vienna.

Soon after I also began reporting for various BBC outlets, including the BBC World Service, and making films for BBC television with the talented Vienna-based producer and director Frederick Baker. Grandly described by the BBC as their Vienna correspondent – but paid as a stringer – I was able to report from Austria and neighbouring countries at a time of tremendous change following the fall of the Iron Curtain and during the war in the former Yugoslavia. I owe a debt of gratitude to all journalist colleagues from that time at BDR/FM4, ORF and the BBC.

My connection with Vienna continued for the best part of the two following decades while an elected politician in the UK, when I was Chairman of the Austrian All-Party Parliamentary Group in the British Parliament and a member of the UK delegation to the parliamentary assembly of the Vienna-based OSCE. It is a matter of considerable pride to have been honoured by President Heinz Fischer with the Grand Decoration of Honour in Gold for Services to the Austrian Republic for these efforts, which I would have happily done without any recognition.

Since 2017 I have been a guest lecturer at the Diplomatic Academy of Vienna, the oldest diplomatic academy in the world. I am particularly indebted to its director, Dr Emil Brix, the former Austrian Ambassador to London and Moscow, who is also a highly respected Austrian historian, for his encouragement, support and advice. I am also incredibly grateful for the assistance from members of the Vienna diplomatic community working in various missions and multilateral organisations, including the United Nations as well as the Austrian Federal Presidency, Federal Chancellery and Federal Ministry of Foreign Affairs, especially Ambassador Helmut Tichy.

My regular visits to Vienna have provided an opportunity to research this book at length in the Austrian National Library and Haus-, Hof-, und Staatsarchiv. To their staff, and those at the National Library of Scotland where I did much of the writing of this book, I would like to extend words of thanks, as well as to Hugh Andrew at Birlinn.

Over the years I have been extremely fortunate to meet a great number of people professionally and socially who have helped develop my knowledge and interest in Vienna and its remarkable history. There are too many to mention. But to you all: *Servus und vielen Dank*. I would like to dedicate this book to my wife Jennifer and daughters Saoirse and Flora.

The spelling of names and places is always a challenge, given there are some English-language versions for both and multiple different versions in the languages of the region. I have tried as far as possible to use the name versions that will be most recognisable to English-language readers, for example, 'Emperor Francis Joseph I' but 'Archduke Franz Ferdinand' despite their sharing the same first name. English-language versions are used for place names when they are common, for example, 'Vienna', 'Prague' and 'Budapest'. The common official German form is used when referring to places during imperial times, for example, 'Pressburg' rather than 'Bratislava/Pozsony', and national forms when referring to places after the end of the empire, for example, 'Sopron' rather than 'Ödenburg'. As far as possible, I have explained this throughout the text.

The Holy Roman Empire in the sixteenth century

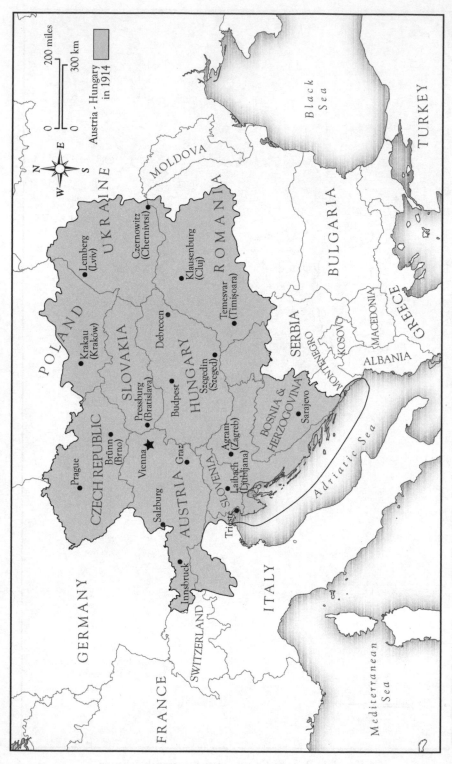

Austria-Hungary in 1914

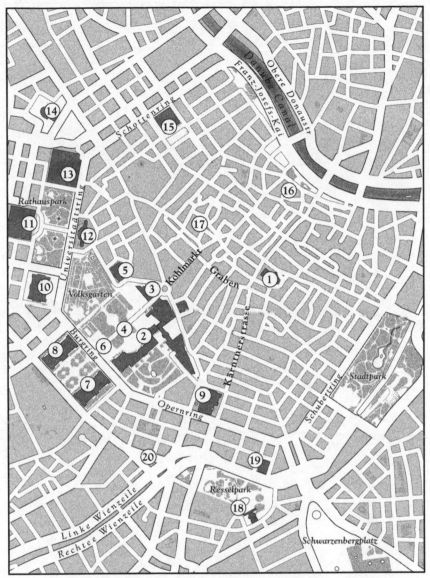

Vienna city centre

1. St Stephen's Cathedral
2. Hofburg Palace
3. Michaeler-Platz
4. Heldenplatz – Heroes' Square
5. Federal Chancellery – Ballhausplatz
6. Burgtor City Gate
7. Art History Museum
8. Natural History Museum
9. State Opera
10. Parliament

11. Rathaus – City Hall
12. Burgtheater
13. Vienna University
14. Votivkirche
15. Stock Exchange
16. Ruprechtskirche
17. Am Hof
18. Karlskirche
19. Musikverein
20. Vienna Secession

# 1

## From Vindobona to Vienna

'Look back over the past, with its changing empires that rose and fell, and you can foresee the future too.'

– Marcus Aurelius

For four centuries the River Danube was the front line between the Roman Empire and the barbarians beyond. From the North Sea to the Black Sea a heavily protected border separated Roman civilisation from the unknown; fortresses, walls, trenches and encampments defended the frontier along the Roman 'limes'. In the heart of the European continent the Roman provinces of Noricum and Pannonia bordered the Danube, from present-day Austria to Hungary and Serbia. Here the mighty river skirts the foothills of the Alps and the Pannonian Basin, the fertile, flat, open plains that stretch all the way to the Carpathian Mountains in the east.

For decades the borderlands along the Danube were stable, with the Romans at peace with the neighbouring tribes of Marcomanni, Quadi and Sarmatian Iazyges. This helped secure the region its status as an important trading centre at the meeting point of the east–west Danube Way (Via Istrum) and the north–south Amber Road, which brought the valuable gemstones from the Baltic to Italy.

Key to the Roman defences on the Danube was the legionary fortress of Carnuntum and the nearby camp of Vindobona. More than 15,000 people lived in the fortified garrison town after Emperor Claudius ordered the governor of Pannonia 'to have a legion with an auxiliary on the bank of the Danube', to deter any efforts to disturb 'the Roman peace', which was also protected by a Roman fleet based at Carnuntum.[1]

Invasions across the Danube by barbarian tribes during the reign of Emperor Marcus Aurelius (AD 121–180) led to major Roman counter offensives, which he commanded in person. He resided in Carnuntum for three years, during which time he also wrote the second book of his *Meditations* series on Stoic philosophy: 'Take care always to remember that you are a man and a Roman; and let every action be done with perfect and unaffected gravity, humanity, freedom and justice. And be sure you entertain no fancies which may give check to these qualities. This is possible, if you will but perform every action as though it were your last; if your appetites and passions do not cross upon your reason; if you keep clear of rashness, and have nothing of insincerity and self-love to infect you, and do not complain about your destiny. You see what a few points a man has to gain in order to attain a godlike way of living; for he that comes thus far, performs all which the immortal powers will require of him.'[2]

Over a number of years of conflict in central Europe Marcus Aurelius won the Marcomannic Wars and restored peace to the Roman Empire along the Danube border. After his death, which marked the end of the 'Roman Peace' (Pax Romana), Aurelius was deified and his ashes interred in Rome's Mausoleum of Hadrian.

Nearly two millennia after the death of Marcus Aurelius the final touches were being put on a new grand entrance to Vienna's Hofburg, the largest royal residence in Europe. St Michael's Gate, completed in the 1890s, faces north towards the original Roman camp of Vindobona. Built in the historicist Ringstrasse style, it is a homage to Roman design, style and symbolism, complete with pillars, cupolas and classical ornamentation. Four huge statues of Hercules hewn out of 25-ton stone blocks guard the entrance to the palace, while two large flanking fountains represent Austria's 'Power on Land' and 'Power at Sea'. The largest portal in the city, St Michael's Gate features the imperial coat of arms carried by spirits from Roman mythology and, above that, is the main entablature representing the virtues of justice, wisdom and strength. Triumphant imperial eagles sit atop golden globes on either side of the façade.

In the middle of St Michael's Square, under the watchful eyes of the Roman-inspired statues adorning the Hofburg palace of Holy Roman Emperors, is the preserved archaeological site of Roman remains from the time of Vindobona. Here in this one place is the direct physical connection between the reach of Roman imperial power and the power centre of one of Europe's greatest empires. That they should literally be in the same place is not a surprise. Vindobona was positioned on a key border, at the crossroads of cultures, trade and ideas. Over the next two millennia Vienna grew out of those very same dynamics to become the international capital.

*

Vindobona was named from the Gaulish *windo* ('white') and *bona* ('base' or 'bottom') and was previously a Celtic settlement. References were made to Vindobona by the geographer Ptolemy in his *Geographica* and, according to the historian Aurelius Victor, Emperor Marcus Aurelius died in Vindobona of an illness in AD 180 while leading his military campaign against the invading Germanic tribes. His connection to Vienna is marked by the street name Marc-Aurel-Strasse. More recent cultural references to Vindobona include the film *Gladiator*, with the lead character Maximus Decimus Meridius, played by Russell Crowe, asking his fellow gladiators if anyone had served in the army, to which one replies: 'I served with you at Vindobona.'[3]

Vindobona was a military complex covering nearly 50 acres where the central district of Vienna presently stands. Unusually for a Roman military camp, its layout was asymmetrical, and many of its original features determine today's street map, including Graben, Tiefer Graben, Naglergasse, Rabensteig, Rotenturmstrasse and Salzgries. Graben is one of present-day Vienna's grandest thoroughfares, but the word actually means 'ditch' and is thought to refer back to the defensive ditch of the Roman camp. The camp was surrounded by fortifications and towers and contained a command headquarters, houses for senior officers, soldiers' accommodation, workshops, stables and thermal baths.

The fort at Vindobona was established under Emperor Trajan (AD 98–117) with building work conducted by the XIII Legion. This was followed by postings for the XIV 'Gemina' Legion of heavy infantry and the X 'Gemina Pia Fidelis Domitiana' Legion, which became the house regiment at Vindobona until the end of the Roman presence in AD 400.[4]

The remains of the Roman camp have been found throughout central Vienna. As well as the excavations on display in St Michael's Square, parts of a canal system have been unearthed at Am Hof, and the remains of whole buildings under the Hoher Markt. An elaborate water supply system piped water to the camp from the Vienna woods nearly 11 miles away. The permanence of Vindobona over an extended period is supported by the discovery of thousands of stamped bricks, monuments and historic records, which show that a succession of Roman legions and other military units was based there.

Wars, administrative and military reforms in the third and fourth centuries, as well as devastating floods, led the population to retreat more and more into the military camp. The area lost its importance as a border region in the fifth century, and the local population lived within the former fortification.

\*

Roman rule was followed by the Migration Period (Völkerwanderung), which saw the wholesale movement of peoples, such as the Vandals, Ostrogoths, Visigoths and Huns, through present-day Austria. The invasion of the Huns led to the population of Vindobona largely abandoning the settlement, whose walls remained standing.

The period also corresponds with the emergence of Christianity and the name of one particular religious personality in the region: St Severinus of Noricum (AD 410–482). An evangelising ascetic, Severinus ate only once a day, went barefoot and slept on sackcloth wherever he halted for the night. Born into Roman nobility in northern Africa, he gave away his possessions to pursue a life of contemplation. While not much is known about his origins, the 'Apostle to Noricum' preached Christianity along the Danube, establishing monasteries, hospices and refugee centres for people displaced by the migrations. He also acted as a negotiator between the remaining Romans, local Christians and Germanic tribal chiefs, arguably making him Vienna's first diplomat.[5]

His disciple and biographer, Eugippius, described how Roman rule was disintegrating along the Danube and barbarian attacks were on the increase. Severinus himself prophesied the attacks on the region by Attila the Hun, and lived through incursions by German tribes: 'While the upper towns of riverside Noricum yet stood, and hardly a castle escaped the attacks of the barbarians, the fame and reputation of Saint Severinus shone so brightly that the castles vied with each other in inviting his company and protection; believing that no misfortune would happen to them in his presence.'[6]

Severinus established a monastery just outside Vindobona at the foot of the Kahlenberg hill and also later further upstream at Batavis (Passau). Throughout the region he preached, healed the sick and raised funds for the release of barbarian hostages held by the Romans.[7] His time on the southern bank of the Danube in present-day Austria and Bavaria corresponded with the final presence of Roman forces along the border with the barbarian lands to the north: 'So long as the Roman dominion lasted, soldiers were maintained in many towns at the public expense to guard the boundary wall. When this custom ceased, the squadrons of soldiers and the boundary wall were blotted out together. The troop at Batavis, however, held out. Some soldiers of this troop had gone to Italy to fetch the final pay to their comrades, and no one knew that the barbarians had slain them on the way. One day, as Saint Severinus was reading in his cell, he suddenly closed the book and began to sigh greatly and to weep. He ordered the bystanders to run out with haste to the river, which he declared was in that hour besprinkled with human blood; and straightway word was brought that the bodies of the soldiers mentioned above had been brought to land by the current of the river.'[8]

During the final decades of the Western Roman Empire in the fifth century, the border regions along the Danube became ever more unstable. Severinus established refugee centres for people displaced by the violence: 'After the destruction of the towns on the upper course of the Danube, all the people who had obeyed the warnings of Saint Severinus removed into the town of Lauriacum [Enns]. He warned them with incessant exhortations not to put trust in their own strength, but to apply themselves to prayers and fastings and alms-givings, and to be defended rather by the weapons of the spirit.'[9]

After decades of leading a spiritual revival in the Danube borderlands, Severinus foretold the date of his own death and reputedly died whilst singing Psalm 150: 'Praise ye the LORD. Praise God in his sanctuary.' He passed away from pleurisy in Favianae [Mautern], on the Danube to the west of Vienna. Six years after his death in AD 482, the last Romans were ordered to leave Noricum for Italy, where they were resettled.

In the centuries that followed, population change continued with the arrival of Lombards from the north, before they moved on to present-day Italy, then Pannonian Avars from the east and Slavs who lived under their rule. The expanding Frankish Carolingian dynasty secured the area around Vienna as border marchland under their Bavarian duchy in the eighth and ninth centuries. Throughout much of this period of unrest it is believed that a restored settlement remained within the original Roman walls of Vindobona, during which time the oldest remaining church in Vienna was constructed. St Rupert's Church was completed in the year 740.

*

Vienna emerged from the Dark Ages and assumed more importance during the rule of the powerful Babenbergs, which began in 976. The family, originally from Bamberg in northern Bavaria, were a noble dynasty of margraves and dukes who ruled over the eastern march of the Holy Roman Empire, an area roughly corresponding with the present-day region of Lower Austria.[10] Shortly after their rule began, the Old High German name for Austria – Ostarrîchi – was used for the first time.

The Holy Roman Empire was an elective monarchy, bringing together territories from across central and western Europe, where the crowned sovereign assumed power inherited from the emperors of Rome. The 'King of the Romans' was chosen by a small number of prince-electors to be crowned Emperor by the Pope, a tradition that continued until the 16th century. The Holy Roman Empire emerged in the ninth and tenth centuries from the coronation of the Frankish king Charlemagne as Emperor and continued for a millennium until 1806. At its largest in the 13th century, the Holy Roman Empire contained all of present-day Germany, eastern France, the Low Countries, Switzerland, Austria, Slovenia and northern Italy.[11] The empire was extremely decentralised with substantial powers resting in the hundreds of its constituent parts, made up of kingdoms, principalities, duchies, prince-bishoprics, free imperial cities and lesser units.

In Austria, what began as a lowly margraviate became a duchy and imperial state in the middle of the 12th century, as Emperor Frederick I Barbarossa (1122–1190) sought to restore order and peace to the Holy Roman Empire. He issued the Privilegium Minus, a deed that elevated the Bavarian frontier march to a duchy with an inheritable fief to the House of Babenberg, a right that unusually for the age allowed for female succession. At about the same time the Babenbergs made Vienna their capital by relocating from nearby Klosterneuburg. Henry II Jasomirgott (1112–1177) moved into a new residence built by the remains of the Roman town wall, an area known to this day as Am Hof ('At Court').[12] He also laid the foundations for some of the cities best-known landmarks with the completion of the first church on the site of the present-day St Stephen's Cathedral in 1147 and the calling of Irish monks to found the Scots Abbey (Schottenstift) and Scots Church (Schottenkirche), where Henry was buried. The naming of the Irish as 'Scots' relates to the use of Latin 'Skotti' for Gaelic-speaking, Hiberno-Scottish missions of monks who spread Christianity across Europe in the Middle Ages from both Ireland and western Scotland.

During Henry's time Vienna was first described as a 'metropolitan city' (*civetas metropolita*) and hosted its first diplomatic visit with the two-week stay of Frederick Barbarossa in 1165. Contemporary reports record the warm reception for the emperor and the abundant supplies of goods in the city, reflecting the fact that Vienna was becoming an important centre of trade, commerce and culture. The Babenberg court supported the two highest forms of medieval performing arts: heroic poetry such as the *Nibelungenlied*, and the Minnesang lyrical song tradition. Walther von der Vogelweide, the greatest of the Minnesänger in the Middle High German speaking-world, and who features in Wagner's *Tannhäuser*, was resident at the Babenberg court.

Emperor Barbarossa returned again in 1189 at the head of the Third Crusade on its way to the Holy Land. Despite being hosted and catered for by Henry's successor, Duke Leopold V (1157–1194), 500 knights are recorded as having to leave the crusader army because of their immoral behaviour and thefts in Vienna. The Third Crusade was ultimately a failure and was followed by a third, where Duke Leopold played a leading role as commander at the Siege of Acre in 1191. Legend has it that after the battle he took off the belt around his blood-soaked tunic leaving a white horizontal stripe in the middle, which became the Babenberg family colours and form the red-white-red triband flag of present-day Austria.

Leopold felt slighted after his victory when King Philip II of France (1165–1223) and King Richard I 'The Lionheart' of England (1157–1199) arrived and refused him equal rights and removed his ducal flag from over Acre. Richard foolishly returned from the crusades through Leopold's lands and was captured at Erdberg, just to the east of medieval Vienna. Despite being in disguise, Richard was identified by his signet ring, arrested and then imprisoned in Dürnstein Castle, overlooking the Danube west of Vienna. Detaining a fellow crusader was a serious offence and led to Leopold being excommunicated by the Pope. Richard was released only after the payment of a king's ransom of 23 tonnes of silver, an astronomic sum equating to more than three times the annual income of England at the time. Leopold split the ransom with Holy

Roman Emperor Henry VI and used his share to transform Vienna by filling in the old Roman defensive ditches along the Graben and building the city walls that stood until the 19th century.

In addition to consolidating their rule over Vienna and surrounding lands, the Babenbergs began to widen their territory with the acquisition in 1192 of the Duchy of Styria, which lies in present day south-eastern Austria and northern Slovenia. The next century saw the end of the Babenberg line, an interregnum and the ascendency of the House of Habsburg, which would rule from Vienna for more than 600 years.

The male line of the Babenbergs ended with Duke Frederick II 'The Quarrelsome' (1211–1246), who is best remembered for his disputes with the Holy Roman Emperor and the kings of neighbouring Bohemia and Hungary. He was killed in battle with the Hungarians in 1246 without any male heirs. During a nearly 30-year interregnum, King Ottokar II Přemysl of Bohemia (1233–1278), was installed as Duke of Austria and subsequently as Duke of Styria, Duke of Carinthia and Margrave of Carnolia. He married Frederick II's sister, Margaret of Babenberg, who was 30 years his senior, to legitimise his rule. While Prague was the power centre during his rule, Ottokar was regularly in Vienna and continued major Babenberg building projects, including St Stephen's Cathedral and the expansion of what became the Hofburg palace.

While Ottokar was consolidating his rule, a 'poor Swabian count'[13] with estates in Switzerland and south-western Germany was well placed for great things during the Holy Roman Empire's Great Interregnum, which ushered in centuries of Habsburg rule with Vienna at its heart. Rudolf, Count of Habsburg (1218–1291), was the first in a long line of his family to come to prominence in the Holy Roman Empire when he was surprisingly elected as Roman-German King in 1273 and crowned in Aachen Cathedral. The electors decided that Rudolf was neither too weak to allow continuing instability in the empire, nor too strong to dominate. However, his ambition was so striking that it led to a senior churchman to warn: 'Sit fast, Lord God, Rudolf will occupy thy throne.'[14]

This was all very far away from the Habsburg family origins. The name comes from Habsburg Castle, a modestly sized, 11th-century fortress overlooking the River Aare, a major tributary of the Rhine in the canton of Aargau in Switzerland. Whether it was named after a hawk (*Habicht*) or from the Middle High German *hab/hap* ('ford') is a matter of dispute among linguistic historians. Either way, Habsburg and von Habsburg stuck and seven generations later Rudolf and his family were set for a major promotion.

In an early and decisive power struggle, Rudolf clashed with Ottokar II, with their rivalry being decided at the Battle on the Marchfeld, north-east of Vienna, on 26 August 1278. More than 15,000 mounted knights and cavalry troops took part in what was one of the biggest medieval cavalry battles ever. Rudolf and his German and Hungarian army routed the Bohemian forces and Ottokar was slain, allowing Rudolf to take over Austria and the adjacent lands. After initial difficulties consolidating his rule, he invested his sons with the duchies of Austria and Styria. It was the beginning of Habsburg rule over what would grow and became known as the Habsburg hereditary lands (*Erbländer*). The Habsburgs raised the status of their duchies to archduchies and as a consequence their titles to archdukes. In time, the title came to be used by all senior members of the House of Habsburg.

In the 15th century the imperial crown was worn for the first time by a Habsburg when Frederick III 'The Peaceful' (1415–1493) became Holy Roman Emperor and the fourth member of his dynasty to be crowned Roman-German King, titles which were thereafter almost always held in conjunction. Frederick famously adopted the cryptic formula 'AEIOU', which he had stamped on his possessions, although its meaning is not certain. The most favoured interpretation is *Alles Erdreich ist Österreich untertan* ('All the earth is subject to Austria'), or in Latin, *Austriae est imperare orbi universo*.

\*

With their consolidation of power and wealth, the Habsburgs and their seat in Vienna grew in importance and prestige. As with all medieval ruling houses, the Austrian monarchical system was based on patronage with a nobility who owed their allegiances and position to the crown. This formed the heart of the court, the exclusive extended royal household that included senior aristocrats and courtiers who had day-to-day access to the monarch. The court involved elaborate hierarchy, rituals and rules of etiquette, which were supposed to highlight the majesty and power of the emperor. A strict order of precedence marked the different ranks of royalty, nobility and chivalry.

The only outside group which had guaranteed regular access to the court were diplomats, who were then all representatives of foreign monarchs at court. Throughout centuries of Habsburg rule, this status was taken literally, meaning they were accorded an exalted standing. Diplomats played a central role in the ceremony of court life, often to the chagrin of lesser-ranked Austrian nobles, an unhappiness that was easily noticeable to visiting diplomats and their spouses: ' . . . I am the envy of the whole town, having, by their own custom, the *pas* before them all. But, they revenge upon the poor envoys this great respect shown to ambassadors, using them with a contempt that (with all my indifference) I should be very uneasy to suffer. Upon days of ceremony they have no entrance at court, and on other days must content themselves with walking after every soul, and being the very last taken notice of.'[15]

The seat of the Habsburgs for the entire six centuries of their rule was the Hofburg (Court Castle) in Vienna. Originally built in the 13th century as a heavily fortified square castle with four turrets and a moat, it was massively expanded over subsequent centuries. This oldest part of the building is still at the heart of the Hofburg complex; it is known as the Swiss Court (Schweizerhof) and is accessed via the Swiss Gate (Schweizertor), both named after the Swiss mercenaries that formed the palace guard, just as the Swiss Guard continue to do at the Vatican to this day. The Swiss Court contains a gothic chapel dating from the 15th century; the treasury, which holds the imperial insignia of the Holy Roman Empire and of the Empire of Austria; and the Court Chapel, where the Vienna Boys' Choir

11

traditionally sing mass on Sundays. While the Habsburgs went on to adopt Schönbrunn Palace as their summer residence, and Laxenburg Palace as a country retreat, it was the Hofburg that remained at the heart of their dynastic rule until 1918.[16]

Originally hemmed in by the city wall, the Hofburg has expanded in all directions and now consists of 18 wings, 19 courtyards and 2,600 rooms. Nearly 5,000 people still live and work there, including the Austrian president, whose official residence and office is in the same wing as the apartments of Empress Maria Theresa (1717–1780). The diplomatic importance of the Hofburg over the ages is marked by the Ambassadors Stairs (Botschafterstiege) in the Swiss Court, which is adjacent to the present-day meeting place of the OSCE. Visitors to the Hofburg are still able to regularly see the pomp and ceremony that accompanies visiting heads of state and ambassadors handing in their credentials to the president. State guests arrive along a red carpet in the Inner Castle Court, past an honour guard of the Austrian army, who still fly an imperial flag and wear an insignia with both the eagle of the Austrian Republic and Habsburg Monarchy.

*

Early Renaissance life in Vienna was first described by the Italian Enea Silvio de Piccolomini (1405–1464), who worked as a secretary and diplomatic envoy for Frederick III. The account appears in the second and third editions of his *Historia Austrialis*, written around 1450. He describes Vienna as a rich, imposing city whose beauty is only diminished by the roofs of wood rather than tiles; a magnificent city with huge underground wine cellars, cobbled streets, beautiful churches and rich monasteries, but a poor university; a city that lives on the wine, which eats and drinks in vast quantities, where there are fights daily and murders are frequent; a city of newcomers, strangers, drinkers and prostitutes, with no attachment to tradition, morality and law, where women are free to choose husbands. Piccolomini's description is charged, vivid and deliberately subjective about the citizenry of Vienna. It was apparently a city of 'unlimited' opportunities in the 15th century, not only for men but also for women.[17]

'[Vienna] has important suburbs, which in turn are surrounded by wide ditches and ramparts. But even the city itself has a mighty ditch, and before that a very high wall. Behind the ditch come the thick and high walls with numerous towers and outworks, as they are suitable for the defense. The houses of the citizens are spacious and richly ornamented, but strong and solid in their layout. Everywhere you will find vaulted gate entrances and wide courtyards . . . and heated rooms, which are called "parlours" by them; because only in this way can you manage winter severity. Windows and glass let in the light from all sides, the gates are mostly made of iron. There are many songbirds . . . and horses and livestock of all kinds have spacious stables. The high front of the houses gives a magnificent sight.'

Piccolomini, who went on to became Pope Plus II from 1458 until 1464, was struck by the importance of religion in Vienna: 'The city has numerous churches with many reliquaries and other treasures, while the clerics have well remunerated sinecures. The city is in the diocese of Passau, although the daughter church is bigger than the mother church. Many houses have their own chapels and priests . . . the city has a university for the liberal arts, for theology and for church law . . . the population of the town has 50,000 communicants.'

The humanist, historian and prolific author detailed day-to-day life in the city, conjuring images redolent of Bruegel paintings a century later: 'It is hard to believe how much food is being made into the city every day. Carts are loaded full with eggs and crabs. Flour, bread, meat, fish and poultry are supplied in huge quantities; and yet, as soon as the evening breaks, you cannot buy any of these things . . . not a day goes by when not 300 wagons loaded with wine arrive twice or three times.'

Even the seedier underbelly of Vienna was detailed by Piccolomini: 'In such a large and important city, however many irregularities happen; with fights by day and night, even at formal meetings . . . rarely does a festivity go by without a homicide and murders are often committed. The common people indulge their bellies, are greedy ... a ragged, clumsy pack. Whores are in great numbers; seldom is a woman content with a man ... Most girls choose their husbands without prior knowledge of their fathers. Widows marry as they please during the mourning period. Few people live in the city whose forefathers know the neighbourhood; old families are rare, they are almost all immigrants or foreigners.'[18]

\*

Vienna's emerging economic and political importance in the 15th and 16th centuries was matched by the growing power of its Habsburg rulers and their desire to increase their international relevance and reach. This was especially true under the rule of Maximilian I (1459–1519), who developed the Habsburg tradition of wedding diplomacy, including his son Philip's marriage to Joanna of Castille in 1498, setting in train the Spanish Habsburg dynasty. Through diplomatic, military and marriage initiatives, he widened Habsburg influence in Bohemia, Hungary, Poland, Italy, the Netherlands and Spain. This involved the use of dedicated Habsburg diplomats like Johannes Spiessheimer (Cuspinian) (1473–1529) in Hungary, Bohemia and Poland; and Siegmund von Herberstein (1486–1566) in Russia and the Jagiellonian kingdoms. Their diplomatic missions continued under the rule of Ferdinand I (1503–1564), Archduke of Austria from 1521, which was a particularly fraught period in the region due to the growing threat from the Ottoman Turks.

At the start of the 16th century the Ottoman Empire included much of south-eastern Europe and was going through a period of expansion. This coincided with turmoil in Hungary, where the young monarch Louis II (1506–1526), King of Hungary, Bohemia and Croatia, was at the mercy of powerful magnates; his finances were in a precarious position and national defences were weakened by under-investment and disrepair. This was understood by the new Ottoman sultan, Suleiman 'The Magnificent' (1494–1566), who soon faced an incredibly foolish challenge by the inexperienced King Louis. On his accession to the Ottoman throne, Suleiman sent an ambassador to Hungary to collect the annual tribute the Hungarians were supposed to pay. Louis II chose to have the ambassador beheaded and returned the head to the sultan. It was an invitation to invasion and a calamitous miscalculation.

In 1521 the Ottomans declared war on Hungary and soon captured Belgrade as well as southern and central regions of Hungary before the crushing victory over the Magyars in the Battle of Mohács in 1526. In one of the most fateful battles in the history of central Europe the Hungarians were routed in a pincer movement and, in retreat, Louis II fell off his horse crossing a stream in full armour and drowned. He had no legitimate heir.

As a consequence, Hungary was divided between the Ottomans, the Habsburgs and the Principality of Transylvania. With the support of Hungarian nobles, Ferdinand of Austria assumed the crown of St Stephen from his brother-in-law Louis II and the territories of Bohemia, unoccupied western Hungary (or Royal Hungary, as it became known) and the Kingdom of Croatia in 1526. Meanwhile, the Ottomans supported the rival Transylvanian pretender, John Zápolya. Conflict continued unabated, with the end of the Ottoman–Hungarian wars leading to the Ottoman–Habsburg wars and the first siege of Vienna in 1529.

Whether the siege was aimed at consolidating Ottoman control over the whole of Hungary or was the prequel to further westward expansion is still debated to this day. What is beyond doubt is that Suleiman was serious in his intent to capture Vienna, with an army mustered in Ottoman Bulgaria between 120,000 and 300,000 strong. Unusually inclement weather caused significant problems for the large army, in particular its large siege cannons, which became bogged down in the sodden conditions during the march towards Vienna. Camels from the east of the Ottoman Empire, not used to cold and rainy conditions, died in large numbers. Casualties through ill health and sickness became a major problem amongst the sultan's janissary forces.

Having prior notice of the Ottoman advance, the Vienna city defences were strengthened in anticipation of a siege, which began at the end of September 1529. With the city walls holding firm, the

15

Ottomans sought to tunnel beneath them and explode mines. The defenders, who included effective German Landsknecht mercenaries, launched attacks on the tunnelling efforts and came close to capturing Ottoman military commander Ibrahim Pascha. After two weeks and four days, the besieging forces' last push to breach the walls was unsuccessful and, with their supplies depleted, they decided to withdraw. The retreat eastwards was made worse by wintry weather, which forced the abandonment of artillery and equipment.[19]

The Ottoman threat to the Habsburg lands was to continue for some time, but Ferdinand I consolidated his position by becoming Roman-German King in 1531, as part of arrangements with his brother Charles V (1500–1564), who was King of Spain. At this point in time the scope of the territory under control of the Habsburgs was immense, covering the Holy Roman Empire, the Low Countries, Spain, Naples, Sicily and Sardinia, as well as the Spanish territories in the Americas; it was genuinely global. Relations within the 'House of Austria' between Madrid and Vienna were extremely important under Charles V and his Spanish Habsburg successors, Phillip II and Phillip III. Resident ambassadors of increasingly high standing were sent to Madrid, including Adam von Dietrichstein (1527–1590), Hans von Khevenhüller-Frankenburg (1538–1606) and his nephew Franz Christoph von Khevenhüller (1588–1650), while Spain was represented in Vienna by the likes of the highly influential Íñigo Veléz de Guevara y Tassis, Count of Oñate (1566–1644).[20]

Meanwhile, heightened diplomatic efforts were similarly extended to the Sublime Porte in Constantinople,[21] including the dispatch of visiting envoys Benedikt Kuripečič von Obernburg (1491–1531), Johannes Leunclavius (1533–1594), David Ungnad von Sonnegg (1535–1600) and others. The first permanent resident Habsburg ambassador in Constantinople was Giovanni Maria Malvezzi in 1547, who spent two years in jail there because of an outbreak of hostilities. His replacement, Ogier Ghiselin de Busbecq (1522–1592),[22] secured a border treaty with the Ottoman Empire, but spent much of his Constantinople posting between 1554 and 1562 'under virtual house arrest in a building with barred windows'.[23]

In Vienna itself, the 16th and early 17th centuries saw a gradual increase in the number of ambassadors from different countries. One such was the English diplomat Sir Henry Wotton (1568–1639), best remembered for his oft-repeated quip: 'An ambassador is an honest gentleman sent to lie abroad for the good of his country.'

\*

While the Habsburgs were busy securing their realms from mounting external challenges from the Ottoman Empire, they faced a massive internal challenge at the same time from the Reformation. The emergence of Martin Luther challenged Catholic Church orthodoxy and he was ultimately made to answer to the Holy Roman Emperor Charles V about his teachings at the Diet of Worms in 1521. Although the Diet declared Luther a heretic and outlawed his teachings, the Reformation washed across Europe, including the Habsburg lands and Holy Roman Empire, where a growing number of princes and other rulers adopted the Protestant faith.

While under Ottoman pressure from the east, Ferdinand of Austria agreed to the Nuremberg Religious Peace in 1532, granting interim religious liberties. This was followed by the permanent Peace of Augsburg, signed in 1555 by Charles V with the Schmalkaldic League, the military alliance of Lutheran princes within the empire that aimed to end the religious conflict. The agreement established the principle of *Cuius regio, eius religio* ('whose religion, his realm'), allowing rulers across the Holy Roman Empire to choose between Lutheranism or Catholicism. Subjects of the local ruler were to share his faith or leave. In effect, it boosted Lutheranism in German states like Saxony, Palatinate, Hesse, Anhalt, Württemberg, Pomerania and Brandenburg, and imperial Free Cities like Augsburg and Frankfurt am Main.

While securing stability for some time, the exclusion of Calvinism, Anabaptism and other reformed traditions from the Peace of Augsburg stored up the potential for conflict, especially in places like Bohemia, which enjoyed religious freedoms reluctantly granted by Holy Roman Emperor Rudolph II (1552–1612). It was the threat to these religious freedoms that set off the Thirty Years' War, which ravaged central Europe between 1618 and 1648.

In one of the bloodiest conflicts in human history, more than 8 million people lost their lives, including 20 per cent of the population across German-speaking lands. A revolt in Bohemia marked the start of the conflict, when Protestants seized two Catholic Habsburg councillors and their secretary and threw them out of the windows of Prague Castle. The 'Defenestration of Prague', whose victims survived the 20-metre fall, was a reaction to the election of Archduke Ferdinand as crown prince and therefore next King of Bohemia. Without royal heirs, Emperor Matthias (1557–1619) was trying to ensure a managed Habsburg transition to the elective thrones of Bohemia and Hungary; however, Protestants in Bohemia were concerned about losing their religious freedoms and preferred an alternative king – the Protestant Frederick V, Elector of the Palatinate. What began in Prague soon spread in 1618 throughout the northern Habsburg lands of Bohemia, Moravia, Silesia and Lusatia. In 1619, further rebellions in Upper and Lower Austria threatened Vienna itself.

This period of tremendous uncertainty coincided with the death of Emperor Matthias and the election of his successor, Ferdinand II (1578–1637). In desperation he called on his Habsburg nephew, King Phillip IV of Spain, for support. Help was at hand in the early phase of the conflict, with Spain sending troops from Brussels and their ambassador in Vienna, Don Íñigo Vélez de Oñate, successfully persuading Protestant Saxony to invade Bohemia from the north and help crush the rebellion in exchange for the Lusatian region. Meanwhile, the Protestant Prince of Transylvania, Gabriel Bethlen, intervened in Hungary with the support of Ottoman forces. Bethlen sought a protectorate status for Bohemia from Ottoman Sultan Osman II, and a diplomatic initiative was launched between the rebellious Bohemians and the Ottoman Empire. Ambassadors were exchanged in 1620 and an offer was made by the Ottomans to provide significant military forces.[24]

At the same time, behind the scenes, Oñate also sought to undermine the new Calvinist Bohemian King Frederick V by transferring the

18

electoral title and rights from the Palatinate to Bavaria. In exchange, the Duke of Bavaria and the Catholic League would intervene in Upper Austria and Bohemia. United with imperial forces, they won the decisive Battle of White Mountain on 8 November 1620.

The battle immediately to the west of Prague had a profound impact on Bohemia, its people and the fortunes of its Habsburg rulers. It ended the Bohemian Protestant revolt and many of its leaders were executed while Frederick V fled and abdicated, having been on the throne for less than three months. His short-lived reign earned him the unkind epithet 'Winter King', and his Scottish-born wife, Elisabeth Stuart, the sobriquet 'Winter Queen'. The Habsburg victory led to a Catholic ascendency, including forced conversion and the expulsion of much of the Protestant aristocracy, to be replaced by German-speaking Catholic nobility; Bohemia remained firmly part of the Habsburg Empire for the next three centuries.

Further afield, what began effectively as a civil war in the Holy Roman Empire sucked in other powers, including the Ottoman Empire, France, Spain, Denmark and Sweden. Although the Thirty Years' War was largely concentrated over three decades in the German-speaking lands, there was conflict in the Low Countries, Italy, the Iberian peninsula and elsewhere. Not only did the Habsburgs become associated with the defence of Christendom against Muslim Ottoman incursion, but they also became recognised as the foremost dynastic defenders of Roman Catholicism.

The situation on the ground, however, was chaotic. Armies, often consisting of marauding mercenaries, marched back and forth across previously contested territories, confiscating supplies, destroying farms, villages and towns. Civilians were killed indiscriminately; famine and pestilence was widespread.

The conflict was brought to an end by the Congress of Westphalia, which is amongst the longest-running peace conferences in diplomatic history and is as complicated as the Thirty Years' War itself.[25] A number of particular challenges dogged the discussions. Papal diplomats wouldn't meet in an official capacity with Protestant envoys and wouldn't even negotiate in the same city. For that reason, the congress took place in parallel in Münster and Osnabrück, 30 miles apart. Ceremonial issues and matters of precedence were hugely consuming and, given that the congress brought together the greatest number of rulers and senior diplomatic representatives ever seen, it was a minefield. While the emperor's premier rank amongst ruling princes was universally recognised, Spain and France vied for second spot. Republics like the Dutch United Provinces and Venice, as well as imperial electors, insisted on an 'Excellency' title, to the chagrin of many monarchs. Titles and relative standing mattered particularly at ceremonial events and when anything was committed to paper, especially sensitive matters of dispute. These disputes meant that diplomatic interaction was often conducted indirectly via mediators, such as the Venetians and Danes.

Count Maximilian of Trauttmansdorff and Weinsberg (1584–1650) was the leading imperial ambassador at the congress. He was an extremely seasoned politician, having advised a whole series of sovereigns in Vienna: Rudolf II, Matthias, Ferdinand II and Ferdinand III. In addition to being a member of the Privy Council and Aulic Council, he had taken part in diplomatic initiatives including the 1622 Peace of Nikolsburg with Transylvania, the 1630 Treaty of Regensburg and the 1635 Peace of Prague. Suffering from worsening health, he only remained at the congress from 1645 until July 1647, after which Dr Isaak Volmar (1582–1662) became the leading figure in the imperial delegation.[26] Volmar was noted for his stubbornness in negotiations, and his diary is considered to be a 'central source for the congress, offering facts, dates and many official papers'.[27] He was joined by fellow diarist Johannes Maximilian, Count of Lamberg (1608–1682), who served as imperial ambassador in Osnabrück, and his junior ambassadorial colleague Johann Krane, who has the distinction of being the only diplomat of an important power at the Congress of Westphalia to actually come from Westphalia. Lamberg's diary suggests he was more focused on family and social life,[28] nevertheless he returned to Vienna with an original copy of the treaty, which he presented to the emperor and is still in the Haus-, Hof- und Staatsarchiv in Vienna.

Some 109 delegations were involved in reaching the Peace of Westphalia, which formalised the nation-state system that still exists today. At the heart of the agreement was 'Westphalian sovereignty', the acknowledgement that states have exclusive sovereignty over their own lands, which forms the basis of the modern international community of sovereign states. As Henry Kissinger wrote: 'The Westphalian peace reflected a practical accommodation to reality, not a unique moral insight. It relied on a system of independent states refraining from interference in each other's domestic affairs and checking each other's ambitions through a general equilibrium of power. No single claim to truth or universal rule had prevailed in Europe's contests. Instead, each state was assigned the attribute of sovereign power over its territory. Each would acknowledge the domestic structures and religious vocations of its fellow states and refrain from challenging their existence.'[29]

# 2

# *The Imperial Habsburg Capital*

'The Holy Roman Empire is neither Holy, nor Roman,
nor an Empire.'

– Voltaire[1]

The notion of Vienna as a capital city is complicated in that it
was actually more of a dynastic than a national capital. The terms
'Habsburg Monarchy' or 'Danube Monarchy' are both used to
describe a state that regularly changed in form and even name,
although Vienna remained the residence city of the dynasty.

In 1804, when the Austrian Empire was founded, Vienna had
already been the seat of the Habsburgs for more than 500 years,
during which time the dynasty mostly held imperial status as titular
head of the Holy Roman Emperor. Since 1276, the Habsburgs had
ruled the Duchy of Austria (essentially present-day Lower and Upper
Austria), with Vienna as its main population, administrative and
political centre, and the Hofburg palace as the pre-eminent royal and
imperial seat and nexus of government. Throughout the centuries, the
Habsburg dynasty grew in power and lands, famously by marriage:
*Bella gerant alii, tu felix Austria nube, Nam quae Mars aliis, dat tibi
regna Venus* ('Let others wage war, but thou, O happy Austria, marry;
for those kingdoms which Mars gives to others, Venus gives to thee').[2]

The Habsburgs had a sense of mission that would propel them
to global power status and their capital to a major world centre. At
different times over the ages Habsburg rule extended across much
of Europe beyond its heartland in central Europe, while the Spanish
Habsburgs had the largest empire in the world with their overseas

rule extending to most of South America, Central America and much of North America, the Caribbean, as well as territories in Africa, Asia and the Pacific.

While the scale and scope of Habsburg territories waxed and waned, even towards the end of the dynasty's rule the range was extensive, as reflected in the formal title of Francis Joseph I:

His Imperial and Apostolic Majesty, Francis Joseph I,

By the Grace of God,
Emperor of Austria,
King of Hungary and Bohemia,

King [of Lombardy and Venice] of Dalmatia, Croatia, Slavonia, Lodomeria and Illyria; King of Jerusalem etc., Archduke of Austria; Grand Duke of Tuscany and Cracow, Duke of Lorraine, of Salzburg, Styria, Carinthia, Carniola and of the Bukovina; Grand Prince of Transylvania; Margrave of Moravia; Duke of Upper and Lower Silesia, of Modena, Parma, Piacenza and Guastalla, of Auschwitz [Oświęcim] and Zator, of Teschen [Cieszyn/Těšín], Friuli, Ragusa [Dubrovnik] and Zara [Zadar]; Princely Count of Habsburg and Tyrol, of Kyburg, Gorizia and Gradisca; Prince of Trent [Trento] and Brixen [Bressanone]; Margrave of Upper and Lower Lusatia and in Istria; Count of Hohenems, Feldkirch, Bregenz, Sonnenberg, etc.; Lord of Trieste, of Cattaro [Kotor], and in the Wendish Mark; Grand Voivode of the Voivodina of Serbia etc. etc.[3]

As well as ruling over their hereditary lands, the Habsburgs were repeatedly elected as emperors of the Holy Roman Empire, an important and complex construct bringing together much of continental Europe under one imperial crown. Between the ninth century and its demise in 1806 the empire included present-day Germany, the Low Countries, Switzerland, Czech Republic, Austria,

Slovenia, eastern France and much of Italy. While power was dissipated amongst its electors, who decided whom the emperor should be, it was also shared by literally hundreds of rulers in its patchwork of various kingdoms, principalities, archduchies, duchies, earldoms, baronies, lordships, landgraviates, margraviates, archbishoprics, bishoprics, abbacies, bailiwicks, counties, cantons, imperial Free Cities and other realms. It was complicated, to say the least.

Despite the complexity, the Habsburgs managed to secure the imperial crown almost continuously between 1438 and 1806, by fair means or foul. While the Holy Roman Empire didn't have a formal capital city, it did have an imperial seat of residence and while a Habsburg wore the imperial crown that was mostly Vienna.

Diplomacy throughout this period was very far from what we now understand international diplomatic relations to be. Despite the difficulties of getting about, the emperor and his retinue would travel as an itinerant ruler with lavish progress ceremonies from one venue to the next, though not often in Italy: 'on average once a decade across the 14th and 15th centuries, but [the Habsburgs] made only one appearance between 1452 and 1496'.[4]

The Diet of Worms in 1495 saw reforms agreed to the Holy Roman Empire, including the enhanced importance of the institution of the Diet (Reichstag) itself. The nobles who gathered at Worms reached formal agreements to end feuding, and they created the Imperial Chamber Court (Reichskammergericht) and an imperial tax. More significantly, it was decided that the Diet would play a more important role as a deliberative body. From 1663 onwards it met in permanent session in Regensburg, Bavaria, and it functioned effectively as a gathering of ambassadors: 'All Imperial Estates sent envoys and agents not just to the Reichstag but to each other. The Empire defined their world. Only a few of the larger principalities maintained representatives at foreign courts by the 18th century.'[5] From the earliest records, it is clear that Vienna was a key diplomatic capital, hosting representatives from across the Holy Roman Empire and further afield. In the earliest published annual state handbook, nearly 200 states and territories are represented by diplomats of different ranks, such as papal nuncio, ambassador, envoy, resident, delegate, representative and agent. Foreign nations represented included Venice, Holland, England, Denmark and Sweden, while the rest were largely from throughout the empire. Smaller territories were often represented by a shared agent.[6]

After the demise of the Holy Roman Empire in 1806, Vienna was officially designated as the capital of the Austrian Empire and City of Imperial Residence (K.K. Haupt- und Residenzstadt). There were foreign missions and embassies from Denmark, France, Great Britain, Portugal, Russia, Sicily, Spain, Sweden, Turkey and the Vatican. German representation included Bavaria, Hannover, Hessen-Kassel, Hessen-Darmstadt, Prussia, Saxony, Saxony-Gotha and Würtemberg.[7]

\*

While the Holy Roman Empire cannot be thought of as a particularly bureaucratic or centralised organisation, its administrative and legal capacity did evolve over the centuries. The Diet acted more as a negotiating body than a legislative assembly. From 1489 its members were the Imperial Estates and were divided into three chambers: the College of Prince-electors (Kürfurstenkollegium), the College of Imperial Princes (Reichsfürstenrat) and the College of Imperial Cities (Reichstädtekollegium). Most important among the Imperial Estates were the prince-electors who formed the electoral college that elected the emperor. Three of the electors were ecclesiastical – the Archbishops of Mainz, Trier and Cologne – and four were secular: the King of Bohemia, the Count Palatine of the Rhine, the Duke of Saxony and the Margrave of Brandenburg, to which were later added the Elector of Bavaria and the Elector of Hanover. Prior to 1663 the Diet convened in 34 different cities before meeting permanently thereafter in Regensburg. The Imperial Chamber Court was first based in Frankfurt, then a series of other German towns, before being finally sited in Wetzlar, Hesse. One of the two senior judicial institutions in the Holy Roman Empire, it could hear cases brought from across the empire.

Vienna became an important administrative centre for the empire with the establishment of the Aulic Council (Reichshofrat) in the city by Maximilian I in 1496. It was the second of the empire's senior judicial institutions and is often seen as having been in competition with the Imperial Chamber Court. Not only did it have concurrent powers with its rival in Wetzlar, but it often had exclusive jurisdiction, including feudal cases, criminal matters and the affairs of the imperial government.[8]

From 1559 onwards the Imperial Court Chancellery (Reichhofkanzlei) became the key administrative body of the empire. Its function waxed and waned under different monarchs as it adopted and lost parallel responsibilities in its roles for the domestic Habsburg court and the empire. Theoretically, the chancellery operated under the aegis of the Elector Bishop of Mainz, who held the title of Archchancellor (Erzkanzler) and was the highest dignitary of the Holy Roman Empire. In practical terms, the daily leadership duties in the chancellery were exercised by the Imperial Vice-Chancellor in Vienna. The title is the origin of the modern-day Chancellor title used by the heads of government in both Austria and Germany.

The administrative functions of the Imperial Court Chancellery were conducted by a staff of fewer than 30 people. In the 17th century this included the Imperial Secretary, Lower Austrian Court Secretary, an articled Latin language clerk, a tax assessor, three registrars, a minutes secretary, 14 German language scribes, 4 Latin language scribes and two chancellery servants.[9] Over time, staffing levels increased and by the beginning of the 18th century the two-storey Chancellery Wing of the Hofburg was deemed too limited and plans were drawn up to build a new, taller, bigger and grander home for the Imperial Court Chancellery, which also included apartments for the Archchancellor and the most senior Habsburg courtier: the Lord Chamberlain (Obersthofmeister) and his offices.[10]

Design work and building of the Reichskanzleitrakt began in 1723 under court architect Johann Lucas von Hildebrandt (1668–1745) before being completed in 1730 by his great rival Joseph Emanuel

Fischer von Erlach (1693–1742). Erlach demolished the wing's new façade only just completed by von Hildebrand and replaced it with a new frontage. The five-storey baroque façade includes three projecting pilasters, and the oversized statues on the gateways at either end representing the Labours of Hercules are by Lorenzo Mattielli. The golden coat of arms flanked by two trumpet-sounding angels, is that of Karl VI, including the central crest with the Austrian triband on the left and tower of Castille on the right, a representation of his claim to the Spanish throne.

While the design of the wing aimed to highlight the majesty of the emperor, it also served to enhance the standing of the imperial institutions it housed, and provide purpose-built facilities for modern administration, including scores of offices for the chancellery, an archive and registry for the Aulic Council.

According to an 18th-century room plan of the Hofburg palace, the ground floor of the Chancellery Wing was taken up with coach stables and servants. The first floor (Controller Corridor floor) contained the chancellery offices and registry; the second floor (main floor) was the residence of the Imperial Vice-Chancellor, with connecting corridors to the state rooms of the emperor on the other side of the palace; the third floor had a further allocation of rooms for the Imperial Vice-Chancellor; the fourth floor comprised individual accommodation for female members of the imperial household.[11]

\*

The Holy Roman Empire was a feudal system demanding personal loyalty to superiors, all the way up to the emperor. This social and economic hierarchy had emerged in late antiquity and determined relative powers and legal rights. From the emperor down there was a mutual bargain: from the liege lord 'to shelter and protect' and for the vassal 'to assist and advise'. As the most senior liege lord, the emperor granted fiefs – heritable property, rights and titles – in return for personal loyalty, financial support and military service. In turn, crown vassal kings, dukes and other overlords dispensed feudal rights over their vassals, all the way down the ranks of nobility to the great mass of the rural population, who were often impoverished and indentured with precious few rights.

Symbolism and rituals were at the heart of medieval power relationships, and feudal vassals were expected to take part in an act of submissive homage and declare an oath of fealty at a commendation ceremony to their feudal masters. In a symbolic act the vassal would kneel in front of his overlord, placing his clasped hands between the hands of his feudal superior, followed by an oath of fealty on the Bible or a Christian relic. Attending court to take part in such ceremonies was still important in the 17th century, when official representatives were despatched in the place of their rulers. This is documented in the accounts of the 1660 diplomatic mission to Vienna by a delegation from Saxe-Weimar, following the ascension of Leopold I to the imperial throne. Secretary to the four-strong delegation was the 27-year-old Johann Sebastian Müller (1633–1708), who was responsible for sending reports back to his local ducal ruler. In a three-month long mission, the delegation took part in a commendation ceremony, officially resanctioning the feudal rights of the House of Wettin and their fealty to the emperor. The dynasty ruled territories in present-day Saxony, Saxony-Anhalt and Thuringia, and their agnates ascended the thrones of still-ruling houses in Britain and Belgium.

Greatest focus in Müller's *Diarium*[12] is reserved for the commendation ceremony itself, which is recorded over pages of minute detail, and reflects the importance of the representational act which (re)invested power and legitimacy on their rulers by the emperor. The account of the delegation also focuses on the city, its sights and inhabitants, including its Jewish population. As in the earlier English diplomatic account of Vienna by William Crowne,[13] Müller draws particular attention to the Jewish ghetto outside the city walls on the far side of the Danube, where he witnessed synagogue ceremonies and Jewish religious practice.[14] Only a decade later Leopold I expelled the Jews from Vienna, after which the area of the cleared ghetto was renamed Leopoldstadt.

In addition to its ceremonial feudal roles, the imperial court played an important legal role in disputed issues of aristocratic succession, such as the death of a local ruler without a legal heir. It was a matter of such importance that envoys were dispatched from far-flung parts of the empire to Vienna to resolve the situation. That is exactly what occurred in the late 17th century following the death of the ruling Duke of Saxe-Lauenburg, a small principality between Lübeck and Hamburg. While the duchy only amounted to 28 square miles of territory, with four towns, 27 estates and fewer than 30,000 inhabitants, succeeding to the title was a prize worth pursuing. The Duke of Anhalt-Dessau, whose territory was only 17 square miles, and contained eight towns, 100 villages and fewer than 30,000 inhabitants, thought he had the best claim. Despite competing interests from powerful neighbours in Denmark, Brandenburg and Saxony, it was decided to launch a diplomatic offensive to the Court Council and the emperor's advisors, counting on good connections to the imperial court in Vienna. The issues involved were highly complex, involving formal considerations of imperial law and international relations, as well as the complicated patronage relationships and internal politics of the Holy Roman Empire. In Vienna, there was also a wish for a diplomatic solution, to avoid potential unrest in the north of the empire.

As a small state, Anhalt-Dessau had traditionally relied on a diplomatic agent in Vienna, often a representative of lower standing than the larger states that had a dedicated but more costly diplomatic presence. On this occasion, Bernhard Georg Andermüller (1644–1717), a 55-year-old senior civil servant, was dispatched to Vienna as a *deputé* on a diplomatic mission that lasted four years. Unusually for diplomatic postings of the time, the details were preserved in more than 242 written reports, now held by the regional archive of Saxony-Anhalt. Andermüller also used his skill as a cartographer to produce a masterpiece birds-eye-view map of Vienna. As with so many diplomats, both before and after him, Andermüller made an enduring contribution to the understanding of the city.

Little is known about his personal life while living in the city. He lodged with the duchy's resident representative, and as a Protestant he had to worship at the reformed chapels hosted by the Danish,

Dutch and Swedish diplomatic missions. Much of his time seems to have been taken up with trying to arrange meetings with powerful decision-makers in the formal and informal legal and political power structures of the empire. He also notes the regular financial challenges in maintaining his lodgings, the important status symbol of his own coach and horses, paying taxes and also for the bribes that he had to offer. This was made even trickier by the irregular payments he received, some being years late, if paid at all.

Despite Andermüller's best efforts, a satisfactory resolution was not found for the Anhalt-Dessau claimants and the dukedom fell in 1716 to Elector Georg Ludwig of Hanover, who since 1714 had ruled in personal union as George I, King of the United Kingdom. Saxe-Lauenburg fell to Napoleonic France in 1804, then Prussia, Sweden and France again in 1810, before becoming part of Denmark in 1815. Fifty years later it went back to Prussia after the 1864/5 war with Denmark, and it remains part of the German region of Schleswig-Holstein to this day.

*

One of the earliest detailed city accounts of Vienna is by a member of a visiting Ottoman diplomatic delegation to the city in 1664–1665. Evliya Çelebi (1611–1682) arrived as part of a 300-strong deputation led by Grand Ambassador Kara Mehmet Pasha. Evilya's detailed observations and descriptions form part of his ten-volume travelogue, *Seyahatnâme*, which records his 40 years of exploration and travel throughout the Ottoman Empire and neighbouring regions. His portrait of the Austrian imperial city, where he stayed for nine months, is written with such 'charm and clarity' that it is assured a place of honour in the annals of Vienna'.[15]

Volume seven of his travelogue features his experiences in the 'Golden Apple', as Vienna was known to the Ottomans. His account of the city is peppered with references to the first Turkish siege, which occurred 136 years previously. He describes, for example, the delegation's visit to Neugebäude Castle, which was built on the site where the sultan had pitched his imperial tent.

30

While he noted the progress of the diplomatic mission, including the protocol disputes between the ambassador and the Austrian court, he was clearly more interested by the architecture of Vienna, with its churches and spires, and he was extremely colourful if not creative in his descriptions. For the noted historian of Islamic relations with Europe Bernhard Lewis, Evilya 'was indeed a great traveler but unfortunately also a great romancer. He does not hide from his readers that his purpose was to entertain rather than to instruct, and if a story was amusing did not greatly matter whether it was true.' Doubts about his presence 'have been proved false by a contemporary document attesting to Evliya's presence in Vienna. Most of what he says indicates firsthand observation, though his style and presentation are not always unduly serious.'[16]

For Evilya, St Stephen's Cathedral was particularly fascinating: 'This great church has four clock towers, one at each corner. Three of them are small. But the lofty tower next to this door on the right side are without compare in the inhabited quarter. If all the world's architects got together they could not place a single stone like it. Although it appears to be of black stone, it is actually an artificial concrete substance like gypsum. I examined it very closely and could not see where the stones were joined. The inside of this bell tower contains 27 stories and is filled with 1,000 monks.'[17] The cathedral's castrati and organ are described as an 'awesome, liver-piercing sound, like the voice of the Antichrist, that makes a man's hair stand on end'.[18]

Evilya paints a vivid picture of life in Vienna and its characters. His most detailed description is reserved for the Emperor Leopold, who was not famed for having good looks: 'One may almost doubt whether the Almighty really intended, in him, to create a man . . . his face is long and sharp like a fox, with ears as big as children's slippers, and a red nose that shines like an unripe grape and is as big as an eggplant . . . from his broad nostrils, into each of which he could stick three fingers at a time, droop hairs as long as moustachios of a 30-year-old swashbuckler, growing in confused tangles with the hair on his upper lip and with his black whiskers, which reach as far as his ears. His lips are swollen like a camel's and his mouth could hold a whole loaf of bread at a time. His teeth too are as big and as white as a camel's. Whenever he speaks, the spittle spurts and splashes over him from his mouth and camel lips, as if he had vomited.'[19]

While undoubtedly there was a lot of artistic licence and exaggeration to the description, it is true that Leopold inherited the Habsburg trait of prognathism, with a protruding lower jaw, something that was clear to see even on the coinage of the day. Leopold was also deserving of attention for Evilya because of the way in which he and other men in Vienna treated women, and the reason which he believed explained it: 'I saw a most extraordinary thing in this country. If the emperor encounters a woman in the street . . . he stands in a posture of politeness. The woman greets the emperor, who then takes his hat off his head to show respect for the woman . . . It is indeed an extraordinary spectacle. In this country and in general in the land of the unbelievers, women have the main say. They are honoured and respected out of love for Mother Mary.'[20]

Evilya's account also included a fascination for the advanced medicine practised in Vienna at the time, the ubiquity of mechanical and clockwork devices, and the linguistic similarities as he heard and imagined them between German and Persian languages. What was omitted from public accounts of the visit, which took place only two decades before the second Ottoman siege of Vienna, was the intelligence garnered about Vienna's defences, including detailed notes about the substantial city walls, bastions and trenches.[21]

It's not clear whether the description of Vienna's defences was seriously considered, but it certainly didn't put off Sultan Mehmet IV, who issued a flowery declaration of war against the emperor on 20 February 1683 with a temporal and spiritual claim to rival the greatness of the Habsburgs:

> Mahomet Son of Emperors, Son to the famous and Glorious God, Emperor of the Turks, King of Graecia, Macedonia, Samaria, and the Holy-land, King of the Great and Lesser Egypt, King of all the Inhabitants of the Earth,

and of the Earthly Paradise, Obedient Prince and Son of Mahomet, Preserver of the Towns of Hungary, Possessour of the Sepulcher of your God, Lord of all the Emperours of the World, from the rising of the Sun to the going down thereof, King of Kings, Lord of the Tree of Life, Conquerour of Melonjen, Itegly, and the City of Prolenix, Great Pursuer of the Christians, Joy of the flourishing World, Commander and Guardian of the Crucified God, Lord of the Multitude of Heathens.[22]

The capture of Vienna had been a long-term ambition of the Ottoman Empire, and already been unsuccessfully attempted in 1529. If Vienna fell, the major bastion resisting Ottoman enlargement would be no more and approaches into Germany would be clear, while strategic trading routes would fall under Ottoman control. In his declaration, Mehmet IV made abundantly clear this was to be a war of destruction and domination:

For I declare unto you, I will make myself your Master, pursue you from East to West, and extend my Majesty to the end of the Earth; in all which you shall find my Power to your great prejudice. I assure you that you shall feel the weight of my Power; and for that you have put you hope and expectation in the strength some Towns and castles, I have given command to overthrow them, and to trample under feet with either my Horses, all that is acceptable and pleasant in your Eyes, leaving nothing head after by which you shall make friendship with me, or any fortified places to put your trust in: For I have resolved without retarding of time, to ruin both you and your People, and take the German Empire according to my pleasure, and to leave in the Empire a Commemoration of my dreadful Sword, that it may appear to all, it will be a pleasure to me, to give a public establishment of my Religion, and to pursue your crucified God, whose Wrath I fear not, nor his coming to your Assistance, to deliver you out of my hands. I will according to my pleasure put your Sacred Priests to the Plough, and expose the Brests of your Matrons to be Suckt by Dogs and other Beasts.

You will therefore do well to forsake your religion, or else I will give Order to Consume you with Fire. This is enough said unto you, and to give you to understand what I have, in case you have a mind to know it.[23]

With a fifteen-month gap between the mobilisation of a mammoth Ottoman army and the invasion of Habsburg territory, the time was well used in Vienna to rally allies and pledges of support. Leopold I reached an agreement with King John III Sobieski of Poland to come to the aid of one another if attacked. Meanwhile, an appeal was made throughout the Holy Roman Empire for military assistance, and Pope Innocent XI called on Christian princes to rally to the defence of Vienna. The pontiff later played a key role in forming the Holy League to resist the threat from the Ottomans, bringing together the Papal States, the Holy Roman Empire, the Polish-Lithuanian Commonwealth and the Venetian Republic.

The siege of Vienna began on 14 July 1683 when more than 150,000 Turkish troops took up position around the city walls. Leopold I and tens of thousands of Viennese fled the city prior to the start of the siege, leaving 15,000 troops, 9,000 volunteer defenders and nearly 400 cannons, commanded by Count Ernst Rüdiger von Starhemberg. Having reinforced older parts of the city defences and cleared the open glacis area around the walls, there were no sheltered positions for the Turks to attack from. This delayed their assault on the city and forced them to construct an elaborate network of trenches and tunnels, especially near the southern sector of the wall by the Hofburg palace.

Meanwhile, a relief army under Sobieski approached on the northern side of the Danube, before crossing near Tulln to rendezvous with imperial troops and special contingents deployed from elsewhere in Germany, creating an army of 80,000. The coalition forces advanced downhill from the strategic heights of the Kahlenberg overlooking the city. With the Turks already being forced back, Sobieski ordered the largest cavalry charge in history, with 18,000 mounted troops, including 3,000 Polish Winged Hussars. This broke the Ottoman lines, and Vienna's defenders emerged from two-months of bitter fighting along the city wall to join the attack, hastening the invaders' retreat.

Descriptions of the victory were shortly being shared across Europe, including a pamphlet preserved in Oxford's Bodleian Library: 'The King of Poland having in the meantime with the greatest Vigour repulsed the Enemy on his side and put them to flight, leaving the Plunder of their Camp behind them, which consisted of a very Rich Tent of the Grand Visier, his Colours, Two Poles with the Horse Tails, their usual Signal of War, and his Guidon or Standard, set with Diamonds, his Treasure designed for the Payment of the Army, and in short, all his Equipage was possess'd by the Polanders. As for the rest of the Tents, Baggage, Artillery, Ammunition, and Provisions enough to load Eight thousand Waggons, was divided among our Army.'[24] Many of the spoils are now held at the Vienna Military History Museum, which has the largest collection of Ottoman artefacts on permanent display outside Turkey. Prominent pieces include lavish tents and weapons of all sizes, including ornate axes, daggers and swords, bows and arrows, rifles inlaid with mother-of-pearl, cannons and a flag with the Tawhid (verses on the unity of God) written on it.

The siege of Vienna made a particular impression on the city and its culture, which lasts to this day: its coffee-house tradition, for instance, which was developed using coffee beans left behind by the fleeing Turks. According to legend, the Polish diplomat and nobleman Jerzy Franciszek Kulczycki was responsible for this after helping break the siege, when he crossed the Ottoman lines in Turkish attire. Returning to the city he was able to confirm that relief was imminent, and the beleaguered defenders decided to carry on the fight. Grateful citizens rewarded his bravery with the gift of a house, and King John III Sobieski gave him large amounts of coffee from the captured Ottoman supplies. With this he opened a coffee house, Hof zur Blauen Flasche (House under the Blue Bottle), close to the cathedral on Schlossergassl. Kulczycki is memorialised with a statue on Vienna's Kolschitzkygasse, which is named after him.

What we now know as a croissant also goes back to the siege of Vienna. Legend has it that bakers in the city commemorated the victory with a pastry made in the shape of the half-moon Turkish flag, calling it *kipferl*: the crescent.

While Vienna was relieved from its besiegers in 1683, the war against the Ottomans continued for the next 15 years. Russia joined the Holy League, the first time it had taken part in an alliance of European powers, and together with the Holy Roman Empire, the Polish-Lithuanian Commonwealth and others defeated the Ottomans in a series of conflicts that became known as the Great Turkish War. Decisive victory was secured in 1697 at the Battle of Zenta, when Holy League forces commanded by Prince Eugene of Savoy (1663–1736) routed the Turks, leading to large-scale Ottoman territorial losses and Habsburg dominance in central Europe. It was the beginning of a glittering military and diplomatic career for Prince Eugene, whose equestrian statue dominates Heroes' Square in present-day Vienna. One side of the plinth is inscribed: 'To the wise counsellor of three Emperors.' On the other: 'To the glorious conqueror of Austria's enemies.'

\*

Prince Eugene of Savoy is without doubt one of the most significant statesmen, diplomats and military leaders in Austrian history, and earned the respect of friend and foe alike. Napoleon rated him as one of the seven greatest ever commanders.[25]

Over six decades, he served three Holy Roman Emperors, from the Siege of Vienna in 1683 and through a series of conflicts and diplomatic tussles until the War of the Polish Succession in the 1730s. Spurned from the military in his native France, perhaps because of his homosexuality, Eugene entered Habsburg military service, and then spent much of the rest of his life fighting France in the west and the Ottoman Turks in the east.

Eugene is best remembered for the crushing defeat of the Ottomans in the Battle of Zenta. The victory, in present-day Vojvodina in Serbia, led to the Treaty of Karlowitz, which ceded Transylvania, the Kingdom of Hungary and the Kingdom of Slavonia (Croatia) to the Habsburgs. Eugene's international reputation was enhanced further in the War of the Spanish Succession (1701–1714) with victories against the French together with the British Duke of Marlborough at Blenheim (also known as the Second Battle of Höchstädt), battles in the Low Countries and a series of engagements in northern Italy. He then commanded the imperial forces that decisively defeated Ottomans in the Austro-Turkish War (1716–1718) at Petrovardin and Belgrade. Austrian victory was sealed in the Treaty of Passarowitz, which brought yet more territory under Vienna's control: the Kingdom of Serbia, northern Bosnia as well as the Banat of Temeswar and Lesser Wallachia.

The later life of Prince Eugene was more focused on diplomacy than the battlefield. He became the governor of the Austrian Netherlands and signed the Treaty of Vienna (1725), which brought Austria and Spain closer together after the War of the Spanish Succession. Austria relinquished claims to the Spanish throne, while Madrid guaranteed the Pragmatic Sanction, paving the way for Maria Theresa's reign 15 years later. Eugene became President of the Imperial War Council and Chairman of the Secret Conference, which determined foreign policy together with the emperor, during which time he steered diplomatic relations with voluminous correspondence with Habsburg ambassadors at the courts of the continent.[26]

The high reputation of Prince Eugene has endured over the centuries, as has his personal stamp on Vienna with his summer and winter residences being two baroque jewels of the city. His city palais on the Himmelpfortgasse was built by both Johann Bernhard Fischer von Erlach and Johann Lukas von Hildebrand. The building, which has a twelve-bay baroque façade, also has an exquisite interior, including an extraordinary staircase, stone sculptures and frescoes. The building currently hosts the Austrian Finance Ministry.

Eugene's most famous residence was the Belvedere, a historic complex of two palaces and beautiful baroque gardens, just outside the city walls. Johann Lukas von Hildebrand designed and built the Lower and Upper Belvedere between 1712 and 1723. One of Europe's standout baroque landmarks, it is listed together with the rest of Vienna city centre as a UNESCO World Heritage Site. The Lower Belvedere, with its beautiful Hall of Mirrors, was the day-to-day summer home of Prince Eugene, while the Upper Belvedere was conceived with prestige and display in mind, positioned on a rise overlooking the middle of the capital with copper roofs. They were designed to resemble Turkish tents, an allusion to Eugene's victories over the Ottomans. The sumptuous grandeur of the interior includes Herculean figures supporting the vaulted ceiling of the Sala Terrena and the two-storey-high Marble Hall with its ornately painted ceiling.

The gardens between the Lower and Upper Belvedere are a baroque masterpiece in their own right and look down towards Fischer von Erlach's baroque Karlskirche, with its oversized flanking columns. Eugene had an intense interest in horticulture and nature, seeking out rarities and abnormalities. His menagerie was the second largest in Europe after that of King Louis XIV, numbering 43 species of mammals and 67 species of birds, including 'unheard of' species of the time. Eugene was also an avid collector of books and developed friendships with the leading international authors and thinkers of the age, including Gottfried Leibnitz, Jean-Jacques Rousseau and Charles-Louis Montesquieu. More than 15,000 books formed part of a world-class collection together with hundreds of manuscripts and prints, described as follows by Rousseau: 'The Prince's library is very extensive and consists of exceptionally fine books beautifully bound. But what is more remarkable is that there is scarcely a book in it that the Prince has not read or at least looked through. It is difficult to believe that a man who almost alone carries such a public burden for all Europe, who is Field-Marshall and the Emperor's Prime Minister, can find the time to read almost as much as someone who has nothing else to do.'[27]

When Eugene died in Vienna in 1736, aged 72 and without any close family, his niece inherited his properties and collections, which she sold almost immediately to the emperor. His book collection, bound in red, blue and yellow Morocco leather with gilt lettering and the arms of Savoy, takes pride of place today beneath the cupola of the beautiful, baroque State Hall of the Austrian National Library.

Prime Eugene's Belvedere Palace became an art repository in 1781, and one of the earliest public art galleries. Today, the Upper Belvedere houses the greatest collection of Austrian art, including the world's largest collection of Gustav Klimt paintings as well as works by Egon Schiele and Oskar Kokoschka. The Lower Belvedere is the Museum of Austrian Baroque Art. Throughout the last three centuries the Belvedere has hosted key diplomatic and representational events, including the wedding party of Marie Antoinette. It was the residence of the ill-fated Archduke Franz Ferdinand, and hosted the signing of the 1955 Austrian State Treaty that ended four-power occupation, with the famed declaration by Chancellor Leopold Figl: 'Austria is free!'

\*

One of the finest accounts of early 18th-century Vienna is by Lady Mary Wortley Montagu (1689–1762), the wife of the British ambassador to Constantinople, Edward Wortley Montagu. Her writings are best known for her accounts of when they arrive in Turkey: 'The very first example of a secular work by a woman of the Muslim Orient.'[28] However, Lady Montagu's letters also include detailed accounts of her three-month stop in Vienna from September to November 1716 and her experience of the city, society, its court and diplomatic life. In a letter to her friend the Countess of Mar, she writes about her arrival and first impressions of Vienna:

> We travelled by water from Ratisborn [Regensburg], a journey perfectly agreeable, down the Danube, in one of those little vessels, that they very properly call wooden houses, having in them almost all the conveniences of a palace, stoves in the chambers, kitchens, etc. They are rowed by twelve men each, and move with an incredible swiftness,

that in the same day you have the pleasure of a vast variety of prospects; and within a few hours' space of time one has the different diversion of seeing a populous city adorned with magnificent palaces, and the most romantic solitudes, which appear distant from the commerce of mankind, the banks of the Danube being charmingly diversified with woods, rocks, mountains covered with vines, fields of corn, large cities and ruins of ancient castles. I saw the great towns of Passau and Lintz [sic], famous for the retreat of the Imperial court when Vienna was besieged.

This town, which has the honour of being the emperor's residence, did not at all answer my ideas of it, being much less than I expected to find it; the streets are very close, and so narrow, one cannot observe the fine fronts of the palaces, though many of them very well deserve observation, being truly magnificent, all built of fine white stone, and excessive high, the town being so much too little for the number of people who desire to live in it, the builders seem to have projected to repair that misfortune, by clapping one two on the top of another, most of the houses being of five, and some of them six storeys. You may easily imagine, that the streets being so narrow, the upper rooms are extremely dark; and what is inconveniently much more intolerable, in my opinion, there is no house that has so few as five or six families in it.

Lady Montagu also describes living conditions inside the houses:

The apartments of the greatest ladies, and even of the ministers of state, are divided but by a partition from that of a tailor or a shoemaker: and I know nobody that has above two floors in any house, one for their own use, and one higher for their servants. Those that have houses of their own, let out the rest of them to whoever will take them; thus the great stairs (which are all of stone) are as common and as dirty as the street. 'Tis true, when you have once travelled through them, nothing can be more surprisingly magnificent than the apartments. They are commonly a suite of eight or ten large rooms, all inlaid, the doors and windows richly carved and gilt, and the furniture such as is seldom seen in the palaces of sovereign princes in other countries – the hangings the finest tapestry of Brussels, prodigious large looking glasses in silver frames, fine japan tables, beds, chairs, canopies, and window curtains of the richest Genoa damask or velvet almost covered with gold lace or embroidery. The whole made gay by pictures, and vast jars of japan china, and almost in every room large lustres of rock crystal.

... I never saw a place so perfectly delightful as the Fauxbourgs [suburbs] of Vienna It is very large, and almost wholly composed of delicious palaces; and if the emperor found it proper to permit the gates of the town to be laid open, that the Fauxbourgs might be joined to it, he would have one of the largest and best-built cities of Europe.[29]

It didn't take Lady Montagu long to be invited to the finest houses, including those of Johann Adam Prince Liechtenstein, Count Schönborn, 'the emperor's favourite' Gundacker Ludwig Count Althann and the salon of Madam Dorothea Elisabeth Rabutin: 'I have already had the honour of being invited to dinner by several of the first people of quality; and I must do them the justice to say, the good taste and magnificence of their tables . . . I have been more than once entertained with fifty dishes of meat, all served in silver, and well dressed; the dessert proportionable, served in the finest china. But the variety and richness of their wines is what appears the most surprising. The constant way is, to lay a list of their names upon the plates of the guests, along with the napkins; and I have counted several times to the number of eighteen different sorts, all exquisite in the kinds.'[30]

Lady Montagu visited both the opera and theatre, including a lavish outdoor opera performance of *Enchantments of Alcina* ('Angelica

Vincitrice di Alcina') by Johann Joseph Fux, the most important Austrian baroque composer of the age. The performance took place in the grounds of the then imperial summer residence, the Favorita Palace, and according to Lady Montagu cost the emperor €18 million in today's money, but 'nothing of that kind ever was more magnificent'.[31] The huge stage set was built over a pond, so the performance could include a naval fight of 'guilded [sic] vessels'. The event was clearly the place for high society to be and was also attended by the papal nuncio Monsignor Spinola, the French ambassador Comte de Luca and Venetian ambassador Cavaliere Grimani.[32]

'If their Operas are thus delightful, their comedies are in as a high a degree ridiculous. They have but one playhouse, where I had the curiosity to go to a German comedy,' Lady Montagu reports, having paid a gold ducat for a box in the Kärntnertortheater: 'I never laughed so much in my life.' The theatre, which stood right next to the city wall and its Carinthian Gate (Kärntnertor), was torn down in 1873 together with many other sites next to the old walls. It stood where today you find the world-famous Hotel Sacher at the rear of the State Opera.

One of the joys of Lady Montagu's letters is the colour and detail of her accounts. This is especially the case when she writes about her first visit to court:

> In order to that ceremony, I was squeezed up in a gown, and adorned with a gorget and the other implements thereunto belonging: a dress very inconvenient, but which certainly shews the neck and shape to great advantage. I cannot forbear in this place giving you some description of the fashions here, which are more monstrous and contrary to all common sense and reason, than 'tis possible for you to imagine.
>
> They build certain fabrics of gauze on their heads about a yard high, consisting of three or four storeys, fortified with numberless yards of heavy ribbon . . . it certainly requires as much art and experience to carry the load upright, as to dance upon May-day with the garland. Their whale-bone

petticoats outdo ours by several yards' circumference, and cover some acres of ground.

The visit to court by Lady Montagu was for an audience with Empress Elisabeth Christine, the wife of Emperor Charles VI. She was renowned for her delicate beauty and would become mother of the future Empress Maria Theresa. Accomplished in music, discretion, modesty and diligence, she was well regarded for fulfilling her representational role as empress, both within the Spanish court protocols of hunting and balls and amateur theatre, as well as observing the religious devotion days of *Pietas Austriaca* (Austrian Piety). She was an excellent shot, attending shooting matches and participating in hunting, and she and her ladies-in-waiting dressed in amazon attire and also played billiards.

Lady Montagu was 'perfectly charmed by the empress: I cannot however, tell you that her features are regular; her eyes are not that large, but have a lively look, full of sweetness; her complexion the finest I ever saw'.[33] The empress 'had the goodness to talk to me very much, with that grace so natural to her ... His imperial majesty did me the honour of speaking to me in a very obliging manner; but he never speaks to any of the other ladies; and the whole passes with a gravity and air of ceremony that has something very formal in it.'[34]

Time was spent playing cards (Quinze) and target shooting: 'The empress herself was seated on a little throne at the end of a fine alley in the garden, and on each side of her were ranged two parties of her ladies of honour with other young ladies of quality, headed by the two archduchesses, all dressed in their hair full of jewels, with fine light guns in their hands; and at proper distances were placed three oval pictures, which were the marks to be shot at ... all the men of quality at Vienna were spectators; but only the ladies had permission to shoot.'[35] Given that the female competitors laughed at Lady Montagu because she was afraid to handle a gun, it seems unlikely that she won the valuable first prize of a fine ruby ring set round with diamonds in a gold snuff box.

Lady Montagu didn't shy away from her more salacious experiences in high society: ' . . . getting a lover is so far from losing, that 'tis properly getting reputation; ladies being much more respected in regard to the rank of their lovers, than that of their husbands . . . Tis the established custom for every lady to have two husbands, one that bears the name, and another that bears the duties. And these engagements are so well known, that it would be a downright affront, and publicly resented, if you invited a woman of quality to dinner, without at the same time inviting her two attendants of lover and husband, between whom she sits in state with great gravity.'[36] Lady Montagu recounts how the 'belles passions are managed in this country' when a young Count suggests that she should engage in 'a little affair of the heart': 'Do me the honour of letting me know whom you like best among us, and I'll engage to manage the affair entirely to your satisfaction.'[37]

Lady Montagu's lively descriptions of her time in Vienna and Constantinople are credited as inspiration for subsequent travel writers, especially female writers, following her assertion that women travellers could gain an intimate view of foreign life not available to male counterparts. She also returned at the end of the diplomatic posting with an understanding of the Ottoman medical practice of inoculation against smallpox, which she introduced to Western medicine.

\*

The Habsburg court was one of the most powerful and grandest in Europe. Here the emperor was surrounded by the high nobility that owed him their allegiance, by senior advisors who helped manage the affairs of state and a small army of staff that maintained the court in the exalted manner it was accustomed to. Usually, the court was located at the Hofburg palace in Vienna, although it moved with the emperor to Budapest, Prague, Innsbruck and the main summer palaces of Schönbrunn and Laxenburg. Over centuries it adopted strict hierarchical traditions, including Spanish etiquette from their fellow Habsburg rulers in Madrid, and allowed few outsiders access except for visiting rulers and diplomats.

The four key positions in the Habsburg court were the Lord High Chamberlain (Obersthofmeister), Master of the Imperial Chamber (Oberstkämmerer), Lord Steward of the Household (Obersthofmarschall) and Master of the Horse (Oberststallmeister), all of whom had a black court uniform with intricate gold embroidery and bicorne hat.

The Lord High Chamberlain exercised wide-ranging powers across the court as its effective chief executive. His responsibilities covered the court administration, its finances and court services, including the running of court palaces, buildings, gardens and the royal hunt. As the effective protector and arbiter of court ceremony, he exercised great authority about precedence in the court: access to it, promotion and preferment. His importance was underscored in his ceremonial immediacy to the emperor, directly behind him in the likes of the Easter procession or announcing the entrance of the imperial entourage to court balls with a triple knock of his ceremonial staff.

The Master of the Imperial Chamber managed the treasury of the imperial family, its art collection, the Natural History Museum, Court Library and scientific organisations. The Lord Steward of the Household was the ultimate legal authority, dealing with matters such as inheritances within the Habsburg family, while the Master of the Horse was responsible for the imperial stables, riding school, coach and carriage collection.

The next most senior household positions were the commanders of the imperial guards, who were all leading noblemen, whose units were largely made up of aristocrats and included Royal Archers (Arcièren-Leibgarde), Hungarian Lifeguards (Ungarischen Leibgarde), Trabanten Lifeguards (Trabantenleibgarde), Horse Guards (Leibgardereitereskadron) and Hofburg Guards, later Foot Guards (Leibgardeinfanteriekompanie). Other senior household positions included Lord High Steward of the Kitchen, Lord High Steward of the Silver, Crown Equerry, Master of the Hunt and the Master of Ceremonies.

Right of presentation (*Hoffähigkeit*) was the highly guarded prerequisite to attend court, its ceremonies and events. This was automatic for the high Austrian nobility, whose lineage was exclusively from the upper levels of the aristocracy, possessing 16 quarters of noble ancestry. That meant being able to prove great-great-grandparents all of noble stock and no less high-status interlopers in between, to the satisfaction of the Lord High Chamberlain. At the top of the nobility were the 30 or so princely families, including the Sovereign House of Liechtenstein; the Mediatised Houses of Lobkowitz, Dietrichstein, Auersperg, Fürstenberg, Schwarzenberg, Thurn und Taxis, Colloredo, Khevenhüller, Hohenlohe-Langenburg, Starhemberg, Salm-Raitz, Orsini-Rosenberg, Schönburg-Hartenstein, Metternich, Windisch-Graetz, Trauttmansdorff; and the further Princely Houses of Dietrichstein, Lubomirski, Porcia, Lamberg, Kinsky, Clary, Paar, Czartoryski, Sanguszko, Rohan, Windisch-Graetz, Collalto, Sapieha, Montenuovo, Beaufort and Thun.

Members of these houses and also dukes, duchesses, counts and countesses formed the 'first society', the closed world of high-born aristocratic families, who did not mix with the 'second society' of lesser nobility (barons, knights, etc) and emerging mercantile and financial classes, including the Austrian Jewish families: Arnstein, Auspitz, Gomperz, Kuffner, Rothchilds, Todesco and others.

Access to court was guaranteed to members of an honorific order. These originally chivalric orders, which began in the 15th century, were created and granted by the monarch, with their neck insignia in the case of the most senior Order of the Golden Fleece, or with a sash and breast star in the case of the Military Order of Maria Theresa, the Royal Hungarian Order of St Stephen, Imperial Order of Leopold, Imperial Order of the Iron Crown, Imperial Order of Francis Joseph and the Imperial and Royal Decoration of Elizabeth and Theresa.

Senior noblewomen could receive the Order of the Starry Cross and Imperial Order of Elizabeth, while a host of 'palace ladies', often widows of high-ranking noblemen, were also received at court. All holders of Habsburg orders were of noble birth, except the Military Order of Maria Theresa, which was awarded for bravery to all ranks and included ennoblement if not already. All received an annuity.

Access to the court was also automatic to privy councillors (Geheimräte) and chamberlains (Kämmerer), the senior honorific court titles awarded by the emperor. The roles originated from the medieval times as advisors to the sovereign and keepers of the keys to the sovereign's quarters. Outer court positions included the ancient titles associated with formal court dinners: cup-bearer, carver and seneschal, where trusted nobles would serve the top table, as well as pages and heralds. The retinue included a small army of household staff available to the imperial family, including equerries, attendants, chaplains, personal physicians, pharmacists, painters, sculptors, musicians, actors and others; while below stairs a larger army of service staff kept the Hofburg and other palaces running, including cooks and kitchen staff, cleaners, firewood collectors, candle lighters, gardeners, farriers, coachmen, stable staff and many more.

While numbers varied, a study of the year 1847 showed there to be 2,228 servants and day labourers working for the household, in addition to its administrators, as well as 2,513 people listed as holders of Habsburg house orders and 2,136 who held imperial titles, from privy councillor to court chaplain.[38] The totals are complicated by honours often being held simultaneously, but the four most senior were limited in number: Order of the Golden Fleece (35), Order of Maria Theresa (123), Order of St Stephen (166), Order of Leopold (778). Honorary court positions included 242 privy councillors, 1473 chamberlains and 70 seneschals.

Relative importance between court attendees was underlined by who was allowed where and when, all of which was regulated in the ceremonial protocols issued by the Lord High Chamberlain. This included who was allowed in which state rooms on ceremonial days.

The one group of outsiders granted immediacy to the emperor or empress were diplomats, who as representatives of foreign heads of state (mostly fellow monarchs) took part in court events effectively as members of the 'first society'. Court tradition involved elaborate arrangements for their accreditation audience shortly after their arrival in Vienna, where the new ambassador was collected from their residence in a gala coach, a custom still conducted in London when new ambassadors are accredited at the Court of St James. Driven to the inner courtyard of the Hofburg, they ascended the Ambassadors Stairs towards the state rooms of the Leopold Wing, a route guarded by the five lifeguard formations all in different resplendent uniforms, which can be seen today at Vienna's Military History Museum.

The Arcièren Lifeguards, the noble archer bodyguards, were the senior guards formation, wearing a scarlet-red broadcloth tunic with horizontal bands of gold galloon and tassels, white buckskin breeches, thigh-high black leather boots with brass spurs, and a polished silver helmet with crowned gilt bronze double eagle mountings and white horsehair plume.

The Royal Hungarian Lifeguards, the joint senior imperial household formation, were made up exclusively of Hungarian noblemen. Members wore the classic hussar gala uniform, including a kalpak fur busby of dark green wool and fur brim, an elaborately braided red-wool Hungarian Atilla short coat and breeches decorated with silver embroidery, a fur leopard-skin cape with large silver buckles and Habsburg Hungarian heraldic crest, and yellow saffian leather boots.

Unlike the two senior formations, the Trabanten Lifeguards were open to junior officers, and they performed regular guard duty at the Hofburg and other Habsburg residences. They wore a spiked black-leather lacquered pickelhaube helmet with gilt brass and a buffalo plume, a red full dress tunic, white leather breeches with over-knee cuirassier boots. They carried a halberd during court duties.

The Horse Guards wore a black wool tunic, buckskin breeches and jack boots, while the Foot Guards wore a dark green tunic and green dress pantaloons. Both wore lacquered pickelhaube helmets with black horsehair plumes.[39]

The ambassador would pass the guards stationed on the stairs through the Hofburg's representative state rooms – the Trabanten Guard Room, Knights Hall, Ante-Chamber, Marble Hall and, finally, the Privy Council Room – led by the Master of Ceremonies to the middle of the ornately decorated room with parquet floors to await the sovereign. Both doors would be opened for the ambassador, who would then make a treble bow and present his accreditation, which was received by the emperor or chamberlain, depending on the status of relations with the ambassador's state.[40] Symbolically, only one of the double doors would then be opened for diplomats from the embassy to enter and be presented to the emperor, before leaving in reverse order without turning their backs.

The annual court calendar was largely focused on the first half of the year, beginning with a New Year reception, followed by carnival season with the two grandest balls: the Court Ball and the Ball at Court. The Court Ball, which included court society, was also open to senior representatives from politics, church and the military. With more than 2,000 guests there was hardly room to dance, but for many the evening was more about seeing and being seen. It began with a cortège of the imperial family and senior courtiers, then a welcome *cercle* for the diplomatic community, before the music started for the ball itself. The evening also included presentations to the emperor and empress for débutants, which was a prerequisite for 'coming out in society', the coming of age amongst adult nobility. Two weeks later the Ball at Court involved only the exclusive 'first society', where 700 members of the highest nobility attended.

> The court ceremonies are most pompous and most beautiful, and nowhere else can such a richness of colour be seen as at religious and State affairs in Vienna. So many races are represented on such occasions, producing a varying, ever changing assembly, different in features, complexion, gestures, garb and colouring. The hues of the different costumes are most gorgeous, some brilliant, others sombre, rich sable, silver fox and beaver, magnificent aigrettes of diamonds and other precious stones in fur birettas; or gold embroidering on uniforms, velvets fastened with priceless gold buckles beset with brilliants, leopard-skin attilas held together with heavy clasps of beaten solver, forming a lovely contrast to the bright scarlet uniform beneath; archbishops, bishops, and other church signatories in pompous robes, priceless laces, and with crowns shorn, all ever moving, only to give place to

new beauties of colour, high State officers in gorgeous gala uniforms, richly wrought in gold, their breasts bedecked with numerous decorations; Knights of the Golden Fleece and other Orders; army officers in their splendid array, others lower in rank in less vivid hue; everywhere this ever-changing, vibrating field of colour, moving onwards or interweaving itself, for a moment of dazzling the onlooker with the brilliancy of effect. And the nations represented are as bewildering as the colours; here a tall Austrian, there a stately Hungarian or a proud Pole, or a Moravian, shorter and thicker set than the others, as are also the Bohemians; every section belonging to the numerous Austrian dominions is represented.[41]

The ball season was followed by Ash Wednesday and Lent, when no dances were allowed. Church feast days became an important part of court life, underscoring the close relationship between the Habsburg dynasty and Catholic Church. These included the Corpus Christi procession through Vienna and the Maundy service, with its ceremonial washing of the feet of the poor. Throughout the Vienna season, higher society and the diplomatic community engaged in afternoon visits to one another's residences, coach trips to the Prater park, evening salons, dinners and banquets, as well as theatres and concerts. This came to an abrupt end in the summer months when the nobility left for their country estates, followed by autumn hunting season, before returning to Vienna and its whirlwind social calendar, which began anew after Christmas.

# 3

# *The Empire Strikes Back*

'Without money, without credit, without an army,
without experience, and finally without advice.'

– Empress Maria Theresa
at the beginning of her reign

Maria Theresa (1717–1780) was the only female Habsburg ruler and
one of the greatest European monarchs that ever reigned. Neither of
these facts was inevitable given the circumstances of the time, which
did not foresee or tolerate a female monarch on the throne. Given
that his only children were female, Charles VI (1685–1740) spent
much of his reign paving the way for this to happen. After issuing
the Pragmatic Sanction in 1713 to ensure that Habsburg hereditary
possessions could be inherited by a daughter, he and his chief diplomat, Johann Christoph von Bartenstein, worked for a decade to have
the edict accepted by courts across Europe. A series of concessions
had to be made for their agreement: France gaining the Duchy of
Lorraine, Spain the Duchy of Parma and Piacenza, Britain and the
Dutch Republic securing the end of international trade competition from Austria with the winding up of the Ostend Company
operating from the Austrian Netherlands. The Prussians gave their
approval too. However, as soon as Charles VI died without a male
heir, all bets were off.

Before his death in 1740 Charles VI had not been preparing 23-year-old Maria Theresa to take over the reins, despite the
Pragmatic Sanction. Born in the Hofburg in 1717, she spent much
of her childhood in the Favorita Palace, just outside Vienna's city

walls. Her education was patchy and more suited to that of queen consort rather than a ruling monarch, with her spelling and grammar wonderfully wild in German, and fairly eccentric in French.[1]

Maria Theresa was 19 when she married the 28-year-old Francis Stephen of Lorraine (1708–1765) on 12 February 1736 in the court church, St Augustin's, next to the Hofburg. The Holy See's ambassador to Vienna, papal nuncio Domenico Passionei, performed the ceremony and was paid a handsome 1,000 ducats for his services by the emperor, the equivalent of year's salary for a government councillor.[2] Not so fortunate was Francis Stephen, who had to pay a higher price shortly after the wedding by giving up his hereditary lands in exchange for the Duchy of Tuscany as part of the terms ending the War of the Polish Succession. The marriage between Maria Theresa and Francis Stephen founded the Habsburg-Lorraine line of the dynasty, which reigned until its end as a ruling house following the First World War in 1918.

Describing her own situation, the young monarch was brutally honest in acknowledging she was 'devoid of the experience and knowledge needful to rule dominions so extensive and so various because my father had never been pleased to initiate or inform me in the conduct of either internal or foreign affairs, I found myself suddenly without either money, troops, or counsel'.[3]

Maria Theresa's feet were hardly under the imperial table when her upstart northerly Prussian neighbour Frederick II (1712–1786) seized the moment to reject the Pragmatic Sanction and grab the wealthiest Austrian province, Silesia. This set off a chain of events that began conflicts on a number of continents, including the War of the Austrian Succession, which lasted from 1740 until 1748. While concentrated in central Europe with the First and Second Silesian Wars, there were also conflicts in Italy, the Mediterranean, the Netherlands, Scotland, North America, the West Indies and India.

While France, Bavaria and Spain used the opportunistic invasion of Silesia by Prussia as a chance to undermine Habsburg power and carve up its dominions, they were opposed by the maritime powers Great Britain and the Dutch Republic, as well as Sardinia and

Saxony. The conflict between the mercantilist powers of Britain, France and Spain involved military engagements on land and seas far away from the cause of the war and were a symptom of the commercial competition around their colonial interests.

For Austria, the perfidy of Prussia and the value of Silesia was underlined in the comments by Francis Stephen to the Prussian envoy, Kasper Wilhelm von Borcke: 'Better the Turks before Vienna, better the surrender of the Netherlands to France, better every concession to Bavaria and Saxony, than the renunciation of Silesia!'[4]

There were diplomatic efforts to halt the invasion of Silesia. Britain's ambassador to Vienna, Sir Thomas Robinson, was dispatched to meet King Fredrick and suggest the possibility of minor territorial concessions by Maria Theresa, which he dismissed as insufficient and without credible guarantees. 'Guarantees!' contemptuously rejoindered Frederick to the British ambassador. 'Who observes guarantees in these times? Has not France guaranteed the Pragmatic Sanction? Has not England guaranteed it? Why do you not all fly to her succour?' As Robinson recounts in his diplomatic dispatch to London, the king, with looks of high indignation, reiterated his demand for all Lower Silesia and said to the ambassador: 'Return with this answer to Vienna; they who want peace will give me what I want.'[5] With that, and a further failed attempt at shuttle diplomacy by Robinson, the war was well and truly on. There was no turning back.

After eight draining years of conflict, the war came to an end with the Treaty of Aix-la-Chapelle. Maria Theresa's position was much as she started with, namely the status quo ante bellum, with the loss of Silesia formalised to the now Frederick 'The Great'. The conflict marked the rise of Prussia as a serious power and was a foretaste of the wrangling for pre-eminence in the German-speaking world, which would take another hundred years before being settled at the Battle of Königgrätz in the Austro-Prussian War of 1866.

While the treaty effectively upheld the Pragmatic Sanction and Maria Theresa's rule, it left her with an abiding distrust and hatred for Prussia. This was captured in a letter to Frederick the Great shortly after the war's end by his ambassador to Vienna, Otto Christoph Graf von Podewils: 'She has, as you well know, a terrible hatred for France, with which nation it is most difficult for her to keep on good terms, but she controls this passion except when she thinks to her advantage to display it. She detests Your Majesty, but acknowledges your ability. She cannot forget the loss of Silesia, nor her grief over the soldiers she lost in wars with you.'[6]

The humiliation of losing Silesia and the precarious position of the Habsburg state caused Maria Theresa to try to solidify her rule and the finances of her realms, restore the military and rethink her alliances. During the War of the Austrian Succession, she had already begun the first moves to put Austria on a firmer footing.

While Vienna was in a panic at the outset of the conflict, Maria Theresa turned to the Hungarians for support, and started to consolidate her position, firstly by being crowned as King of Hungary – not Queen, as this was not possible. She wowed the burghers of Pressburg (Bratislava) with her regal arrival on barges 56 kilometres down the Danube from Vienna, and by wearing Hungarian national dress. She performed the horseback coronation ceremony pointing a sword towards the four compass points in a pledge to protect the kingdom of St Stephen, having practised her equestrian skills for months. As soon as was possible after being crowned by the Hungarians at St Martin's Cathedral, she pushed to be crowned Queen of Bohemia, which occurred two years later in St Vitus Cathedral in Prague.

It was not possible for Maria Theresa, as a woman, to become Holy Roman Emperor, so in a stroke of genius she secured her husband's elevation to the title after making him co-regent of the Habsburg dominions. Although she was never crowned as empress, she is widely styled as such owing to Francis Stephen becoming emperor, not that it made much difference in practice anyway, as it was she that decided matters of state.

Having inherited her father's aged, and in part incompetent advisors, she developed a game-changing skill: choosing trusted and talented advisors. These included the counts von Khevenhüller, von Tarouca, von Kaunitz, von Haugwitz and Gerard Van Swieten.

Johann Joseph von Khevenhüller-Metsch served as Habsburg ambassador to Munich, Den Haag, Copenhagen, Dresden and Warsaw before taking up the most powerful court positions under Maria Theresa: Grand Marshall of the Court (Obersthofmarshall) and then Grand Master of the Court (Obershofmeister). Don Emanuel Telles de Menezes e Castro, Count of Tarouca, was the son of the Portuguese ambassador to the court in Vienna and entered Habsburg military service before becoming the 'éminence grise' of Maria Theresa.

Wenzel Anton Graf von Kaunitz-Rietberg was the third generation of his family to serve as an Austrian diplomat and had been sent on special missions to Florence, Rome, Sardinia and Turin before being appointed Minister Plenipotentiary of the Austrian Netherlands, effectively the go-between Vienna and Brussels. He was then promoted to Austrian ambassador to the French court and was a key figure behind the Diplomatic Revolution that saw Austria pivot away from Britain as its traditional ally, in favour of France. He was appointed State Chancellor and Minister of Foreign Affairs in 1753 and held the offices for a remarkable 40 years, under Maria Theresa and her successors Joseph II and Leopold II.

Friedrich Wilhelm Graf von Haugwitz (1702–1765), originally from Saxony, was at the heart of administrative, economic and military reforms under Maria Theresa and was highly prized by her: 'He was truly sent to me by Providence, for to break the deadlock I needed such a man, honorable, disinterested, without predispositions, and with neither ambition nor hangers-on, who supported what was good because he saw it to be good, of magnanimous disinterestedness and attachment to his Monarch, unprejudiced, with great capacity and industry and untiring diligence, not afraid to come into the open or to draw on himself the unjust hatred of interested parties.'[7]

Gerard van Swieten (1700–1772) was of Dutch birth but moved to Vienna to become the personal physician of Maria Theresa. This position allowed him to play a transformational role, helping reform the Austrian health system and medical education. Less well known is his scientific and rationalist campaign against superstition, which included a mission to investigate the vampire myth that was widespread in parts of the monarchy's lands. He viewed it as a 'barbarism of ignorance' and his report *Discourse on the Existence of Ghosts* led to a decree being issued by Maria Theresa banning all traditional defences against vampires involving the desecration of graves, stakes, beheading and burning.

In addition to the cosmopolitan influx from across the Holy Roman Empire, the Habsburg Monarchy also benefited from a wave of immigrants from further afield: Ireland and Scotland.

*

Irish and Scots, often Catholics exiled from their Protestant-ruled homelands, served the Habsburgs for centuries. Richard Wallis, of Carrickmines, County Dublin, was one of the first Irish officers in imperial service in 1632. His son George Olivier, Count of Wallis, Freiherr von Carrighmain (1671–1743), went on to become a field marshal in the service of the Holy Roman Empire and the Kingdom of the Two Sicilies, and last regent of the Habsburg Kingdom of Serbia.

Irish officers infamously carried out the order of Emperor Ferdinand II in 1634 to bring back, 'dead or alive', Albrecht von Wallenstein (1583–1634), his most senior military commander, who had been accused of treachery. Irishmen Walter Devereux and Walter Butler, together with the Scots colonels Walter Leslie and John Gordon, performed the deadly roles in the Wallenstein assassination and were richly rewarded. Leslie (1607–1667), who originally hailed from Aberdeenshire, was appointed an imperial field marshal, Count of the Holy Roman Empire, a governor on the Croatian-Slavonian Military Frontier, and he became a high-powered diplomat as imperial ambassador to Naples and Rome in 1645 and to Constantinople in 1665–1666.[8]

The presence of the Irish and Scots in Vienna accelerated with the arrival of exiled supporters of King James VII/II, the last Catholic monarch of Scotland, England and Ireland. Collectively described as 'wild geese', they included the Hamiltons of Abercorn in West Lothian. John James Hamilton (Johann Jakob Graf von Hamilton, 1642–1717) began his Austrian service in the 1690s as 'diplomatic advisor'. His son Johann Andreas Graf von Hamilton (1679–1738) served as an imperial cavalry officer on many fronts and was promoted to General of the Cavalry and military and civil commander of the Banat of Temeswar in present-day Romania. Hamiltongasse in Vienna's 14th district is named after him.

A further Austrian military man of Scots descent was Sir Joseph Murray, 3rd Baronet and 1st Count Murray (1718–1802), who was commander-in-chief of the army in the Austrian Netherlands from 1781 until 1787 and also acted as plenipotentiary of the Austrian Netherlands. Rewarded for bravery with a knighthood in the Order of Maria Theresa, he was created a Count of the Holy Roman Empire as Graf von Murray by Emperor Francis I. His son Joseph Albert Murray (1774–1848), who succeeded as 4th Baronet and 2nd Count, served as a major-general in the imperial army.

Leading Irishmen in Austrian military service in the same century included Andreas Graf O'Reilly von Ballinlough (1742–1832), whose service extended through the Seven Years' War, the War of the Bavarian Succession, the Austro-Turkish War, the French Revolutionary Wars, and the Napoleonic Wars, in which he was military commander of Vienna.

The influence of the Irish in Austria is illustrated by the first ever St Patrick's Day diplomatic reception recorded anywhere in the world. What now is an important part of the Irish global diplomatic calendar, with annual St Patrick's Day embassy receptions, first occurred in Vienna on 17 March 1766 when the Irish-named Spanish ambassador to the imperial court, Count Demetrio O'Mahony, hosted a 'grand entertainment in honour of St Patrick to which were invited all persons of condition, who were of Irish decent, being himself a descendant of an illustrious family of that kingdom'.[9] Amongst the others at the event were: Count Francis Maurice Lacy, President of the Imperial Council of War; Irish-Austrian generals O'Kelly, O'Donnell, Browne, Maguire, McElligott and Plunkett;[10] as well as

dozens of others of Irish extraction serving as governors, privy councillors and in the army. The Annual Register for 1766 also noted that
all the principal officers of state, together with the entire court in
Vienna, wore Irish crosses to honour the day and 'shew their respect
to the Irish nation'.[11]

Only one year before, a note from Emperor Francis I had been
found saying: 'The more Irish officers in the Austrian service the better;
our troops will always be disciplined; an Irish coward is an uncommon
character; and what the natives of Ireland even dislike from principle,
they generally will perform through a desire for glory.'[12]

Amongst the most prominent Irish-Austrian families were the
Taaffe's of Carlingford, Corren and Ballymote, who played an outstanding role over generations in Habsburg military, diplomatic
service and political life.

Francis Taaffe (1639–1704), born in County Sligo, helped save
Vienna during the Turkish siege in 1683, becoming a field marshal
and member of the Order of the Golden Fleece. He was sent on
many diplomatic missions and, towards the end of his life, served
as Chancellor and Chief Minister to Duke Leopold of Lorraine.
Louis Graf von Taaffe, 9th Viscount Taaffe, was the Austrian
Minister of Justice during the revolutions of 1848 and President of
the Court of Appeal. Eduard Graf von Taaffe, 11th Viscount Taaffe,
served two terms as Prime Minister in the late 19th century and
held hereditary titles from two different countries: Imperial Count
(Reichsgraf) in the Holy Roman Empire and Viscount in the peerage
of Ireland.

Further prominent Irish-Austrians included the most respected
military officer of his age, Francis Moritz Graf von Lacy (1725–
1801), who was promoted ahead of jealous Austrian rivals to War
Minister and President of the Council of War. Writing at the time
of his appointment, Empress Maria Theresa said: 'I see no-one more
competent than Lacy.'[13] Serving as Minister of War for more than
20 years, he is remembered as 'the reformer of the Austrian Army,
the acknowledged European master of the science of supply, and for
Clausewitz the epitome of the spirit of eighteenth-century warfare'.[14]

His name was associated with the Austrian army for another century after his death, with the 22nd Infantry regiment named after him. His period in office coincided with another senior military man of exile stock: Baron Ernst Gideon von Laudon, who claimed kinship with the Scottish Earls of Loudon.

During the Napoleonic Wars the most famed commander of Irish ancestry was Field Marshal Laval Nugent von Westmeath, who captured Rome in 1815, for which he was made a prince by Pope Pius VII. The famed Irish connection continued into the 19th century, when Emperor Francis Joseph was saved by Maximilian Karl Graf O'Donnell von Tyrconnell (1812–1895) during an assassination attempt. The young adjutant struck down the Hungarian assailant on the Vienna city ramparts, saving the emperor's life. In thanks for the rescue, Europe's royal families contributed a votive offering to build a church near the site of the attack. The Votivkirche stands on the Ringstrasse close to the University of Vienna.

Military honours continued into the 20th century with Gottfried Freiherr von Banfield (1890–1986), the last living recipient of the famed bravery medal in the Order of Maria Theresa. The 'Eagle of Trieste', whose family was of Irish heritage, was the greatest Austro-Hungarian naval flying ace. He outlived the empire he served by 68 years.

\*

While Maria Theresa was consolidating her position through conflicts and reforms, she managed to bear 16 children, 13 of which survived infancy. Unlike many other monarchs who had little to do with their children's upbringing, Maria Theresa was a loving and attentive mother. At this time, she also made a striking impression on the outsiders who met her, such as the Prussian envoy at the Viennese court, Count Otto Christoph von Podewils, who penned the following description of the monarch in June 1746, when she was 29:

> Her figure is of over rather than under medium stature. It
> was very fine before her marriage, but the numerous births

she has undergone, together with her corpulence, have made her extremely heavy. Nonetheless, she has an easy gait and majestic posture. Her appearance is elegant even though she spoils it by the way she dresses. The little English hoop skirt she wears disfigures her. She has a full, round face and a clear brow. The well-shaped eyebrows are, like her hair, blonde, without any reddish sheen. Her eyes are large, lively and at the same time very gentle, to which the colour, which is pale blue, contributes. Her nose is small, neither curved nor turned upwards, her mouth is a little large but rather beautiful, her teeth white, her smile pleasant. Her neck and throat are well-formed. Arms and hands wonderful. Her complexion cannot be any less than this, to judge by what one can see, despite the scant care she has given it. She usually has a high colour. Her expression is open and cheerful, her way of addressing people friendly and graceful. One cannot deny that she is attractive.[15]

It didn't take long for Maria Theresa to begin to plan for her children's future, a matter of state policy, and the monarch doggedly pursued the traditional Habsburg marriage diplomacy: *Bella gerant alii, tu felix Austria nube* ('Let others wage war: thou, happy Austria, marry').

Her favourite was Archduchess Maria Christina, who was the only one of her children allowed to marry for love, in her case with Duke Albert of Saxony-Teschen. Every other brother and sister was married for advantageous dynastic considerations, especially to Bourbon offspring from monarchs on the thrones of Parma, the two Sicilies, Spain and, most importantly of all, France.

Archduke Joseph, later to become Emperor Joseph II, married Maria Isabella of Bourbon Parma. The wedding was such a big deal that a high-powered diplomatic mission was sent to Parma to escort the bride to Vienna. State ambassador Prince Wenzel von Liechtenstein was despatched as the proxy of Joseph to collect Maria Isabella from Parma in a golden state coach. The same coach, symbolising the glory and munificence of the Habsburgs, led the grand entrance to Vienna and is captured in a detailed series of large-scale paintings by court painter Martin van Meytens. More than 90 coaches took part in the ceremonial procession through the narrow streets of Vienna, so many that Meytens had to leave city-centre buildings out of the painting and create an imaginary square to fit all the ceremonial coaches of the nobility, diplomats and wedding guests into the vista.

The marriage in St Augustin's, the parish church of the court, was followed by a state banquet in the Hofburg. The event is shown in another Meytens painting with the imperial family sitting at the top table: Maria Theresa and Francis Stephen in the middle with the bride and groom to the left and right. Following old Spanish court traditions, members of the aristocracy wore black Spanish court dress and performed their honorary duties as royal stewards and cup bearers, serving the food and drink according to a strict choreography. If one looks closely at the Meytens painting, one can also see a young Wolfgang Amadeus Mozart immortalised on canvas sitting next to the musicians performing at the wedding supper.

Further dynastic weddings included Archduke Leopold, later Emperor Leopold II, with Princess Maria Ludovika of Spain; Archduke Ferdinand Karl with Duchess Maria Beatrice d'Este; Archduchess Marie Amalia with Duke Ferdinand I of Bourbon-Parma; Archduchess Maria Carolina with King Ferdinand I of the two Sicilies; and, most ambitious of all, the marriage of Marie Antonia, better known as Marie Antoinette, to the later King of France, Louis XVI.

As the union was a matter of state it was the French ambassador, Aimeric Joseph Marquis de Durfort, Duc de Civrac, who formally asked for the hand in marriage of Mademoiselle Antoinette on behalf of the French Dauphin. 'The wedding [in Vienna] was probably the most brilliant of a brilliant century. French and Austrian officials had laboured over knotty questions of mutual protocol for a solid year and finally given up in despair.'[16]

Marie Antoinette, just 14 years old, was married in the St Augustine's court church by the papal nuncio Antonio Eugenio

Visconti. The Dauphin wasn't at his own wedding, his place taken by a proxy bridegroom: his brother in-law, Marie Antoinette's brother, Archduke Ferdinand.

The wedding celebrations were opulent, including a masked ball for 6,000 guests at the Belvedere Palace, although testiness about social standing caused the French ambassador to stay away from the wedding supper as the seating plan gave preference to Duke Albert of Sachsen-Teschen. Two days after her proxy wedding in May 1770, Marie Antoinette left Vienna as the Dauphine of France. She never returned to Austria again before her execution by the French revolutionary guillotine in 1793.

*

During the reign of Empress Maria Theresa the massive baroque summer residence was completed at Schönbrunn. It rivalled Versailles for its splendour: built on the site of a royal hunting lodge southwest of Vienna's city walls, its scale and magnificence was designed to reflect the status and grand ambition of the Habsburgs.

Built to original plans from Johann Bernhard Fischer von Erlach and then finished by Nikolaus Pacassi in the rococo style, it had 1,441 rooms, including state rooms and imperial apartments, as well as exquisite gardens and palace grounds. At the top of sweeping steps at the front of the palace is the Great Gallery, which is 40 metres long and 10 metres wide, with tall windows, crystal mirrors, white-and-gold stucco and ceiling frescoes. Mozart performed there for the empress as a child, and three centuries later US President John F. Kennedy and Soviet premier Nikita Khrushchev were hosted there for a state dinner during arms control talks. The piano nobile also includes a Small Gallery, Hall of Ceremonies, Palace Chapel, Mirrors Room, East Asian Cabinets, Blue Chinese Salon, Vieux Laque Room, and a host of rooms for various senior members of the Habsburg dynasty, including the bedroom of Empress Theresa and Francis Stephen. It is today known as the Napoleon Room as Bonaparte stayed during his occupations of Vienna in 1805 and 1809. His only legitimate son died in the same room, aged 21.

The palace gardens lead from the south-facing side of the palace, with 32 sculptures of classical deities and virtues lining the Grand Parterre to the large Neptune fountain, which stands below the colonnaded Gloriette on a hill overlooking the palace. The grounds also contain the oldest zoo in the world, a Palm House, Orangerie, a Roman folly and palace theatre where Joseph Haydn and Mozart both conducted their works. The grand entrance to the palace passes two large fountains: on the left an allegorical representation of the rivers flowing from the west of the empire – the Danube, Inn and Enns; and on the right the eastern Kingdoms of Galicia, Lodomeria and Principality of Transylvania. The palace is painted in the famous shade of Austrian imperial yellow, known as Schönbrunn Yellow, the preferred hue of official buildings and hundreds of train stations across the empire, from the borders of Switzerland in the west to Russia in the east, and from Prussia in the north to the Ottoman Empire in the south.

The six-year-old Mozart and his sister performed for the empress and her family in the Hall of Mirrors, his father Leopold recounting: 'Now there is only time to tell you that we were so graciously received that as I tell it will be reckoned a fairy tale. Let it suffice that Wolferl sprang on the lap of the Empress, put his arms around her neck and vigorously kissed her. We were with her from three to six.'[17] The empress herself was less impressed by the prospects of supporting the Mozarts, writing to her son Ferdinand: '. . . you ask me to take the young Salzburger into your service. I do not know why, not believing that you have need of a composer or of useless people. If however it would give you pleasure, I have no wish to hinder you. What I say is intended only to prevent your burdening yourself with useless people and giving titles to people of that sort. If they are in your service it degrades that service when these people go about the world like beggars. Besides, he has a large family.'[18]

In addition to having Schönbrunn Palace renovated and completed, Maria Theresa was busily reforming her realms and their governance. An early change was the chancellery taking on responsibility for foreign affairs in 1742. Located just across the road from the

Hofburg, the baroque palais was designed by the favoured Austrian architect of the era Johann Lukas von Hildebrandt. The chancellery on the Ballhausplatz has been at the heart of Austrian governance, diplomacy and foreign policy ever since.

Its importance really took off with the appointment of the experienced diplomat Wenzel Anton Graf von Kaunitz-Rietberg as Chancellor and Minister of Foreign Affairs in 1753. Having returned from Versailles, where he had served as Habsburg ambassador, he played a leading role in the Diplomatic Revolution, which saw Austria's historic ally Britain move closer to Prussia, and Austria closer to France.

After London concluded the Westminster Convention with the Prussians, Maria Theresa gave a dressing down to Robert Murray Keith, the British ambassador in Vienna: 'I have not abandoned the old system, but Great Britain has abandoned me and that system by concluding the Prussian Treaty . . . why should you be surprised, following your example in concluding a treaty with Prussia, I should enter into an engagement with France.'[19]

Estrangement between Austria and Britain had in fact been developing for some time, and Maria Theresa had already dispatched Count Kaunitz to Paris to secretly sound out the French about a potential reset in their relationship. Kaunitz and the Habsburg ambassador at Versailles, Johann Georg Adam Graf von Starhemberg, managed important parts of the negotiations through Madame de Pompadour, the powerful court favourite and mistress of King Louis XV. It is widely believed that she intervened in support of the negotiations that led to the Treaty of Versailles, which effectively sealed the Diplomatic Revolution, realigning France with Austria and Russia against Britain and Prussia.

The diplomatic achievements with France led to Starhemberg being decorated with the title Ambassador to the Emperor, and shortly thereafter he became a knight in the Order of the Golden Fleece. But the Diplomatic Revolution did little or nothing to prevent conflict; in fact, it contributed to the start of what is generally described as the first genuinely global war: the Seven Years' War.

Escalating out of frontier clashes in North America between the British and the French, the war spread across five continents and involved all of the newly realigned allies on both sides. With Austria's loss of Silesia still unresolved, Prussia pre-emptively invaded Saxony, and most states across the Holy Roman Empire took Austria's side, declaring war on Prussia. The stage was set for a bloody drawn-out war across conflict theatres in Europe, North America, the Caribbean, West Africa and India. For Austria, the aim was the recovery of Silesia, which is why the conflict against Prussia is known specifically as the Third Silesian War. With most European states on Austria's side, including France, Spain, Russia, Sweden and the rest of the Holy Roman Empire, she had reason to be confident of success.

Initial progress by the Habsburg forces in 1756, which included retaking part of Silesia and blocking the Prussians from Bohemia, led King Frederick II to remark that he was not fighting the same Austrians as he had in the last war. A Prussian spring offensive into Bohemia led to a victory at the Battle of Prague and the siege of the city. However, defeat at the Battle of Kolin forced their withdrawal from Habsburg lands. Towards the end of the year, however, Frederick managed to regain the initiative after winning major strategic victories at Rossbach and Leuthen. On 5 November Prussian forces were outnumbered two to one by a joint force of French and imperial army troops near the Saxon village of Rossbach. Frederick's highly drilled forces were able to defy the odds with greater manoeuvrability and deploying flanking tactics, including 'oblique order', which concentrated attacking infantry on a particular side of the line. The battle marked a turning point in the war as it was the last time the French deployed against the Prussians, concentrating instead against the British in Spain and North America. Immediately after the victory at Rossbach, Prussian forces marched for 13 days to face the Austrians in Silesia, who had just taken the regional capital, Breslau. Again facing a force twice its size, Frederick deployed his favoured 'oblique order' at the Battle of Leuthen on 5 December 1757 and routed the Austrian army commanded by Prince Charles Alexander of Lorraine, the brother-in-law of Empress Maria Theresa.

The young captain Prince de Ligne from the Austrian Netherlands recounted the turning point of the battle: 'Our Lieutenant-Colonel fell killed almost at the first; beyond that we lost our Major, and indeed all of the Officers but three, three only . . . We had crossed two successive ditches, which lay in an orchard to the left of the first houses in Leuthen; and were beginning to form in front of the village. But there was no standing of it. Besides a general cannonade such as can scarcely be imagined, there was a rain of case-shot upon this Battalion of which I, as there was no Colonel left, had to take command; and a third Battalion of Royal Prussian Foot-guards, which had already made several of our regiments pass that kind of muster, gave, at a distance of eighty paces, the liveliest fire on us. It stood as if on the parade-ground, that third Battalion, and waited for us, without stirring.'[20]

The Prussian pursuit of the defeated Austrians was so speedy that King Frederick reportedly entered nearby Schloss Lissa, which was bustling with retreating Habsburg officers looking for accommodation, surprising himself and his enemies with bravura: '*Bon soir, messieurs*! Is there still room left, think you?' After showing him to the best quarters, they then made off sharpish.[21]

Frederick's cavalry chased the retreating Austrians back into Bohemia, leaving the Habsburg garrison in Breslau isolated. The fortified city was besieged for two weeks before surrendering. Frederick was now definitively 'The Great', and the Austrian hopes of regaining Silesia were dashed. Despite twice occupying Berlin during the course of the war and winning decisive battles against Prussia, including the Battle of Kunersdorf, Austria had effectively fought Prussia to a stalemate, and both states were financially and materially depleted. The withdrawal of allies Russia and Swedish from the war convinced Empress Maria Theresa that she could not regain Silesia, while her French allies lost badly to Great Britain in North America, the West Indies, India and at sea. On 15 February 1763, the Treaty of Hubertusburg ended the Third Silesian War between Austria, Prussia and Saxony. The treaty restored the pre-war status quo, confirmed Prussia's ascent to the status of a major power and underlined the continuing rivalry with Austria. The only silver lining for Empress Maria Theresa was the agreement she received from King Frederick that he would exercise his vote as Elector of Brandenburg to install the Habsburg heir Joseph II as King of the Romans, the precursor to becoming Holy Roman Emperor. Five days earlier the Treaty of Paris ended the conflict between France, Britain, Spain and Portugal, with Britain confirmed as victor and as the dominant imperial seafaring power.

*

Just over one year later, on 3 April 1764, the 'half-majestic, half-ghost-like world theatre' coronation of Joseph II took place. As Austrian historian Martin Mutschlechner described it:

> Archaic rituals were used to demonstrate the fictitious continuity of the Old Empire from the time of its myth-enshrouded origins under Charlemagne. Following a procession into the city, the coronation was then held, adhering to every minute detail of traditional formalities, and using medieval insignia.
>
> There then followed the coronation banquet in the Frankfurt City Hall, the Römer, where the leading figures of the Empire were supposed to perform their traditional 'arch-offices', i.e., symbolically serve the newly-crowned ruler at table. In order to avoid such personal submission before the ruler, however, most princes of the Empire were conspicuous by their absence, and their places at table remained empty, thereby emphasising the meaningless formulaic nature of the ritual in all its absurdity.
>
> The main protagonist, Joseph II, himself influenced by the rational ideals of the Enlightenment, evidently felt himself completely out of place amid this spectacle based entirely on long-established rites and medieval forms; in a letter to Maria Theresa, he described the whole affair as *une vraie comédie*.[22]

The coronation and subsequent celebrations were witnessed and vividly described by Johann Wolfgang von Goethe, who watched the day's events as a 15-year-old and recounted them in his autobiography, *Dichtung und Wahrheit* ('Truth and Poetry: From my own life'). The greatest German literary figure of the era saw the coronation procession from a balcony as it made its way through the packed streets of Frankfurt am Main. It included the bearers of the crown jewels, the electors, the ambassadors, richly dressed attendants and, under a richly embroidered canopy, the Emperor Francis Stephen in romantic costume, and, a little behind him, his son Joseph in Spanish dress. Goethe describes the faintly comedic aspects of the event, including the necessity of lining the imperial crown to fit Joseph's pate, but it 'stood out from his head like an overhanging roof'.[23]

After the crowning ceremony Goethe inveigled himself into the banquet by carrying a silver serving vessel and described the bizarre scene, with many electors absent: 'The buffets and tables of all the temporal Electors, which were indeed magnificently ornamented, but without occupants, made one think of the misunderstanding what had gradually arisen for centuries between them and the head of the Empire. Their ambassadors had already withdrawn to eat in a side-chamber; and if the greater part of the hall assumed a sort of spectral appearance, by so many invisible guests being so magnificently attended.'[24]

Within a year of Joseph's coronation as King of the Romans, his father Francis Stephen, the reigning emperor, died unexpectedly, meaning Joseph seamlessly became his successor and co-regent with his mother. While Maria Theresa continued to effectively reign over the Habsburg lands, the young Joseph began to rule in imperial matters, but as a subordinate in an often-fraught arrangement that led him to threaten his demission a number of times. His co-regency was influenced by the ideas of opening up to new thinking and trade, reducing the feudal burdens of the peasantry, religious toleration and constraining the influence of the Catholic Church. This stood in strong contrast to the traditional Habsburg role as defender of Catholicism in general, and Empress Maria Theresa's intolerance towards Protestants and Jews in particular.

Joseph II, 'whose education was heavily influenced by the works of Voltaire, the Encyclopédistes and philosophes, became one of the three leading enlightened monarchs of the age, together with Frederick the Great of Prussia and Catherine the Great of Russia. He strongly believed in the power of the state to deliver through reason, although his absolutist maxim remained: "Everything for the people, nothing by the people."'[25]

Unlike almost all previous rulers Joseph took the opportunity to get away from the court in Vienna and travel extremely widely across the empire and European continent. Around a third of his reign was taken upon by inspection and study tours of military, economic and social conditions. Most frequently he travelled in Bohemia, Moravia and Hungary, as well as Transylvania and Galicia. Internationally, he tended to travel incognito, without a great retinue, as Count Falkenstein. This included a trip to France where he saw his sister Marie Antoinette.

'He was a man,' a French noble said of him, 'more surprising than admirable, more singular than rare, more amiable than attractive, more brilliant than solid, and more extraordinary than great . . . in a word he possessed a thousand fine qualities which are of no use to kings.'[26]

Those qualities included self-deprecation and a dry wit rare amongst monarchs of the time. During his visit to France he was mistaken as servant in the imperial household and, asked what duties he performed for the emperor, he quipped: 'I sometimes shave him.' Pressed into service, again unrecognised, to act at a child's christening, he was asked by the priest for his name:

'Joseph,' he replied.

'Surname?' the priest continued.

'Second!'

'Occupation?'

'Emperor!'[27]

American President Thomas Jefferson used to enjoy telling the story of the monarch attending a Paris salon as Count Falkenstein: when conversation turned to the American Revolution, Joseph explained: 'I'm a royalist by trade.'[28] Joseph also travelled to Italy, where, without precedent for laymen, he and his brother Leopold, the Grand Duke of Tuscany, were present in the conclave in St Peter's in Rome that elected Cardinal Ganganelli, an opponent of the Jesuits, as Pope Clement XIV. The famous painting of the two brothers – then current and future emperors, and with St Peter's in the background – was completed during their two-week stay in Rome by Pompeo Batoni.

Joseph's travels were a matter of particular interest for court correspondents like Nathanial Wraxall: 'Among the characteristic features of Joseph, must be accounted his passion for travelling; scarcely any Prince of whom we read, having so minutely examined their own dominions. Adrian, in antiquity; and Charles the Fifth in modern ages, whose whole reigns were a perpetual journey, can alone be compared in this point of view to the present Emperor. He has visited nearly all the Courts of Italy; and when he went to Paris, two years ago, it was his intention to have prosecuted his tour as far as Madrid, if not to Lisbon. With that design he traversed the whole kingdom of France . . . Every part of Bohemia, Hungary and Transylvania, he has rode over, almost at a footpace: nor has he omitted to inspect the Sclavonian frontier, as far as Semlin, and to go in a boat upon the Danube, to the walls, and quite under the cannon of Belgrade.'[29]

Notwithstanding the enmity between Empress Maria Theresa and Frederick the Great, there were two meetings between Joseph II and the Prussian king, firstly at Neisse in Silesia in 1769, where Frederick had 30,000 troops assembled to parade in honour of the Habsburg emperor. They spent three days in one another's company and, writing to his mother afterwards, Joseph was both admiring and disparaging about Frederick: 'When the King of Prussia speaks on problems connected with the art of war, which he has studied intensively and on which he has read every conceivable book, then everything is taut, solid and uncommonly instructive. There are no circumlocutions, he gives factual and historical proof of the assertions he makes, for he is well versed in history . . . A genius and a man who talks admirably. But everything he says betrays the knave.'[30]

One year later Joseph reciprocated by meeting with the Prussian king at Neustadt in Moravia. Frederick and his entourage arrived on horseback wearing white uniforms, in the Austrian style as a mark of respect, and 'desirous of ingratiating himself with Joseph, whose consent and co-operation he wanted in the projected partition of Poland'.[31]

Both Prussia and Russia had designs on the territory of the Polish-Lithuanian Commonwealth, and, despite differences between Maria Theresa and Joseph II, Austria eventually joined them in the First Partition of Poland, which was agreed and ratified in Vienna in 1772. The empress disagreed with her son about the morality of the partition but acceded to the division. As King Frederick of Prussia caustically observed: 'She wept as she took, and the more she wept, the more she took.'[32] Austria gained the largest amount of territory and population, with lands totalling 32,000 square miles in Galicia and Lodomeria with a population of 2.5 million people. Three years later, Austria annexed the Bukovina from the Principality of Moldavia, and it became the easternmost part of the Monarchy. Joseph's aggrandising efforts continued later that decade, this time in the west with claims over neighbouring Bavaria, which led to the War of the Bavarian Succession. The incorporation of German-speaking Bavaria had been a preference for some time over maintaining faraway Austrian Netherlands and would link Bohemia and Tyrol in the west of the Monarchy, enhancing Habsburg influence in the German lands. However, with Prussia backing an alternative claimant following the death of the elector Maximilian Joseph without issue, the stage was set for another Prussian–Austrian conflict. Massive armies were mobilised on both sides, but casualties were largely caused by disease rather than fighting: the involvement of France and Russia, and Maria Theresa acting behind Joseph's back, led to a diplomatic solution before any battles took place. Known dismissively as the 'Plum Fuss' in Austria, and the 'Potato War' by the Prussians, it was the last of the 'cabinet wars' (wars between princes) of the European *ancien régime*, but Austrian-Prussian dualism continued to escalate in Germany over the next century.

In Vienna during the co-regency, Joseph and his mother lived separated lives, with the empress preferring Schönbrunn Palace and the Leopoldine wing of the Hofburg, now the official residence and workplace the Austrian president. Joseph, who preferred a residence in the Augarten park and Laxenburg Palace, was highly dismissive of court life and sought to avoid ceremony as much as possible: 'The Hofburg is an assemblage of a dozen old married ladies, three or four old maids, and twenty young girls, who are known as Ladies of the Court, seven archduchesses, an empress, two princes, [and] an emperor co-regent under the same roof – and yet no society at all, or at least none that is rational or agreeable, since they all keep themselves to themselves. The gossiping and squabbling between one old woman and another, lady and lady, archduchess and archduchess, keep everyone at home, and "What will people say?" prevents the most innocent gatherings or parties ... The intelligent, bored to death by the stupid women, eventually find an outlet for their intelligence, and then use it in unsuitable ways, whereas if they had the opportunity to deploy it in good company they would never contemplate such follies.'[33]

Eclipsed by his mother's power, Joseph's influence in Vienna during the co-regency was limited to a mostly symbolic level. Court ceremonial dress was reformed with the end of Spanish court dress and permission granted for the wearing of military uniform, which Joseph had himself adopted from King Frederick. Vienna's imperial parks at Schönbrunn, Prater and Augarten were opened to the public, and the Court Theatre beside the Hofburg became the German National Theatre. With Joseph's direct involvement, theatre pieces and operas would increasingly be performed in German rather than French and Italian, and serve an educational as well as entertainment purpose.

The co-regency period was particularly important as Vienna cemented its status as the world musical capital, as recorded by the foremost music historian Charles Burney (1726–1814) who visited

Vienna in 1772.[34] He went to performances, researched musical manuscripts and books at the imperial library, and met the leading musical figures of the day: the poet and librettist Pietro Metastasio (1698–1782), the leading writer of opera seria libretti; the hugely popular composer, singer and music teacher Johann Hasse (1699–1783), a composer of many operas and sacred music; and opera composer Christoph Ritter von Gluck (1714–1787), who together with the librettist Ranieri de Calzabigi (1714–1795) effectively revolutionised the dramaturgy of opera in Vienna. This led to Burney writing that Vienna is 'rich in composers and encloses within its walls such a number of musicians of superior merit'.[35]

*

Empress Maria Theresa made a lasting impression on the state with the professionalisation of the civil service, diplomatic service and military training. During her reign she repurposed Vienna's Favorita Palace into the Theresian Academy, an exclusive school to train young men for the civil service. The Theresianum, as it is known in Austria, remains one of the country's best-known schools to this day. Former pupils include Austrian and international political leaders, Nobel Prize winners, thinkers, writers and performers, including acclaimed actor Christoph Waltz.

One wing of the old palace now also hosts the Diplomatic Academy, the oldest institution of its kind in the world, which she established as the Oriental Academy in 1754. Originally founded to teach Turkish to young diplomats, it developed over time into the Consular Academy, and then the Diplomatic Academy. It moved in 1905 to a purpose-built building on Bolzmanngasse, which now houses the US Embassy, before returning to the Favorita in 1964. Its alumni include scores of Austrian and international diplomats and former UN Secretary-General Kurt Waldheim.

Also during her reign, the Theresian Military Academy (Theresianische Militärakademie) was founded to train military officers, and it remains amongst the oldest military academies in the world. No doubt its highly respected status was the reason behind the installation of the then Colonel Erwin Rommel as commander shortly after the Nazi Anschluss of Austria in 1938.

Under Maria Theresa the Austrian army celebrated its heyday, as she reformed and professionalised the branch of the state she had the keenest interest in. The success of the army came despite the linguistic diversity of the troops. 'No other army of the time could have produced a column of regiments chattering variously in German, Czech, French, Flemish, Rhaeto-Romance, Italian, Magyar, and Serbo-Croatian, and all passing in review under the eyes of a general who was cursing to himself in Gaelic.'[36] It was particularly striking how multinational the senior ranks were, with the officer corps recruited from both within and outwith the empire. During the Seven Years' War, there were 177 recipients of the Knight's Cross of the Military Order of Maria Theresa. Of them, 72 had German language names, 22 Irish or Scots, 21 French, 20 Italian, 18 Slavonic, 11 Magyar, 11 Flemish or Scandinavian and two Spanish.[37] The common sense of purpose against the Prussian threat, and common endeavour as the key branch of the Theresian imperial state, led the assertion by Prince de Ligne that in the Europe of that period the Austrian army was the 'sole national army, although made up of several nations'.[38]

The final summer of Maria Theresa's reign was witnessed by the famed travel writer Henry Swinburne, who arrived with his wife Martha in July 1780. Their first impression of the city wasn't overwhelming: 'Vienna is divided into towns and suburbs. The former is small, not above three miles round. It is hilly, but not much on a slope to a branch of the Danube, on which side the fortifications are not very considerable . . . There are eight ways out of the city. The gates are never shut. The streets are crooked, narrow and indifferently paved, with many disagreeable smells, as there are no sewers to carry off the dirt; but the scavengers are often at work. The houses are high, of brick stuccoed over, with heavy leaden ornaments, and iron bars as at Rome, to the lower windows.'[39]

Their international reputation as lovers of antiquity and as prominent Roman Catholics stood the Swinburnes in good stead in

Vienna with the chief literati and at the Habsburg court, and they were received by the leading noble personalities of the capital and both co-regents. 'The empress has a fine face, but is enormously fat and unwieldy,' Swinburne writes. 'A few days ago her chamberlain, Sinzendorff, waited on her with a petition from some part of her territories, which was very interesting to her. They were alone in the apartment, both standing whilst he read to her the document. Sinzendorff is a thin old man, stiff and erect, and troubled by rheumatic complaint, which has in some measure paralysed his frame. It happened that the paper fell to the ground. The empress bade him pick it up. "*Hélas! Madam,*" he said, "*il ya vingt années que je ne me suis courbé!*" [It is twenty years since I last bent down]. She would have stooped for it herself, but was too unwieldy; he was accordingly obliged to ring the bell for the purpose, and the groom of the chambers, on entering, found her imperial majesty in a violent fit of laughter.'[40]

The Swinburnes enjoyed four months in Vienna and, before their departure, the empress conferred on Mrs Swinburne the Order of the Starry Cross and Emperor Joseph stood godfather to their son of the same name.[41] In a long audience before they left, Maria Theresa said in conversation to Mrs Swinburne that 'she was sure her son the emperor would not live long, as he imitated the King of Prussia in everything and had not a constitution for it. She also told her she was certain she herself would soon die.' Within a few weeks, on 29 November 1780, the empress died, aged 63. Her son Joseph would only reign and live for a decade before his health failed, ruined on a military campaign that cost him his life.

*

At the accession of Joseph II it was by no means clear what course he would follow, even to seasoned observers like Sir Robert Murray Keith (1730–1795), who had already served as British ambassador in Vienna for eight years. 'It has been constantly remarked by every person of reflection in this country, that the Emperor has been at great pains to conceal as much as possible, the general principles of internal government, as well as the political views in regard to the other powers of Europe, which were to become the rules of his future reign.'[42]

Within weeks, however, concerns were being reported by the papal nuncio Count Giuseppe Garampi to Rome: 'His Majesty has principles that lead him to tolerate every religion, to restrict the jurisdictional rights of the Holy See, to enhance those of bishops and chapters, to diminish the number, property and revenues of the clergy in order to apply them to purposes he considers advantageous to the public ... He certainly will not act until he has maturely examined a question, but he will do everything so secretly and circumspectly that no one will have the least suspicion of his plans beforehand. There is little to be gained from audiences and conversations, since he has marvellous skill in sliding away from every argument or difficulty by witticisms and facetiousness ... and then, when his decision has been published, he allows no criticism.'[43]

By the end of 1781 Joseph had enacted edicts of tolerance for non-Catholic Christians and Jews, announced he would make ecclesiastical appointments in the Duchy of Milan, had begun a crackdown on Catholic contemplative orders and was considering the dissolution of monasteries. Over months the papal nuncio Giuseppe Garampi asked that his warnings and suggestions be passed on to the Pope. The threat posed by Joseph's reforming zeal was considered as big a threat to the Catholic Church as the Reformation.[44] Nuncio Garampi suggested that a special congregation be created in Rome to consider how to deal with the challenge, that the Pope should consider showing his disapproval publicly by withdrawing him from Vienna, and that he as papal representative at court might refuse to give communion to the emperor at Easter. The nuncio usually played a high-profile role at the traditional Maundy Thursday service at court where the emperor washed the feet of poor people. To refuse to give communion to the sovereign would be more than a major religious and diplomatic incident; together with considerations about excommunicating the emperor, it ran the risk of splitting the Church.

All of this caused such concern in the Vatican that Pope Pius VI became the first pontiff in two and a half centuries to journey outside the Papal States with a visit to Vienna. While Pius set off on the overland journey through northern Italy in early 1782, Joseph wrote about his intentions to his brother Leopold: 'However extraordinary his coming here, and although it is impossible to image in advance everything that he will propose, do and negotiate here, he will find me, I hope, a respectful son of the Church, a host polite to his guest, a good Catholic on the full meaning of the term, but at the same time a man above succumbing to mere phrases and tragic gestures . . . firm, secure and unshakable in his principles, and pursuing the good of the state as he sees it with conviction, regardless of all other considerations.'[45]

Despite Vatican plans to travel incognito and reside in the Nunciature on Am Hof square in the heart of Vienna, Joseph insisted that the papal party should stay at the Hofburg, in a suite formerly used by Empress Maria Theresa next to the emperor's own apartment. Despite an uncomfortable eye condition, Joseph extended the pontiff further respect by travelling more than 60 kilometres south beyond Wiener Neustadt to meet him, getting out of his carriage to walk towards the Pope and greet him in person before both returned in the emperor's carriage. According to Joseph, more than 100,000 people thronged the roadside back to Vienna. During a month-long stay, which included an extended series of one-to-one private meetings, the Pope was unable to persuade Joseph to go back on his reforms, but caused a sensation amongst the public with huge demonstrations of piety and Catholic observance.

The pomp, ceremony and religious fervour of the papal visit is captured in the correspondence of Sir Robert Murray Keith, who, although representing Protestant Britain, was much taken by the pontiff and his impact on Catholic Vienna: 'I witnessed one of the most extraordinary sights which this age has afforded, and which could not fail to make a strong impression on the mind of every man who has the history of former times fresh in his memory.'[46] Religious ceremonies were held in public and private, with throngs of people attending. It was a genuine sensation. 'The eagerness of the common people to receive his benediction amounted to a frenzy. The course of the Danube was fairly choked by the crowd of boats which bore the floods of pious pilgrims, and the great market-place was often found filled with shoes and hats lost in the scuffle by the assembled multitudes; who by twenty and thirty thousand at a time, passed into the streets leading to the Imperial palace at the balcony of which, repeatedly during the day, its illustrious guest was obliged to show himself, and distribute blessings to successive shoals of devotees.'[47]

Keith, who had been the British ambassador in Vienna for nearly a decade before the papal visit and was to remain for a further ten years, had the opportunity to meet Pope Pius together with other Protestant colleagues: 'I have just now paid my respects to the Pope . . . and [he] said in a quarter of an hour as many polite and flattering things of Britain, and the learned men of that country, as could be expressed in the time.' Clearly delighted with the meeting, Keith nevertheless wanted to signal a respectful distance to the head of the Catholic Church: 'He is comely, affable and easy, as any sovereign can be . . . We made our lowest and most respectful bows on inter-ring and retiring; but no kissings or genuflexion of any kind.'

During the visit, Pope Pius and Emperor Joseph held more than 30 hours of bilateral discussions with just the two of them present, running between two and three hours in length on different days. Joseph's 'journal' recorded accounts of the talks, church services and events undertaken by the pontiff.[48] Detailed accounts of the visit by the masterful biographer of Joseph II, Derek Beales, make clear that 'having received the pope, got to know him and stopped him from making any public criticism of his policies, Joseph could be reasonably confident of avoiding an outright confrontation with Rome and the schism that would follow – provided that he continued to acknowledge Catholicism as the dominant religion and that he should not seize the property of the Church and use it for secular purposes'.[49]

In 1783, Joseph hosted a delegation of ambassadors from Morocco. They stayed in Vienna for six weeks to conclude a commercial treaty with the Monarchy, 'attracting much curiosity and bringing the Court to life'.[50] Life at the court was much changed under Joseph, who massively reduced formality and etiquette as well as regular receptions and functions 'except during visits by such persons as the Russian grand duke, the pope, the duke of York or Marie Christine'.[51] Instead, he spent a lot of time holding audiences, literally for hundreds of thousands of his subjects, regardless of rank or background.

Meanwhile, he concentrated his efforts on public improvements, which in Vienna included the building of a model hospital, extending street lighting to the suburbs and further plans for their development, as well as improvements to the water course of the Danube and its crossings. In contrast, he did little to maintain his palaces, never bothered to visit many and didn't use Schönbrunn Palace at all.

Throughout his reign, Joseph was circumspect in his dealings with diplomats in Vienna, but there is evidence of him holding occasional friendly and wide-ranging conversations. In an 11-page 'Most Secret' account to the Foreign Secretary Francis Osbourn, the Marquis of Carmarthen, dated 7 August 1787, Sir Robert Murray Keith reported that he had passed on a message from George III on the Low Countries. The report is what Derek Beales describes as 'probably the fullest account we have of Josef talking'.[52] Laying hold of the ambassador's arm, the emperor said: 'His Britannic Majesty knows, by his own experience, that it is the unhappy lot of monarchs to see their upright intentions frequently misapprehended, their views wilfully misconstrued and their principles calumniated. He has seen the subjects of his distant dominions abandon their duty and allegiance, from false notions of liberty, and through the installations of factious, selfish, and artful men. What have they gained, – even by the success of their audacious enterprise? – only anarchy and confusion.' Drawing parallels between the emerging independent United States of America and growing rebellion in the Austrian Netherlands, he went on to damn the 'new-fangled dabblers in what they call patriotism'.[53] In uncompromising language that would no doubt have appealed to the British Foreign Secretary, who was extremely hostile to the newly independent USA, Joseph said he would deal harshly with pro-independence advocates: 'But, if any province of my monarchy should (which Heaven avert), ever wield against me the sword of rebellion, and I should succeed in reconquering it by the same weapon, I publicly declare that I should look upon the entire property of every individual, of every rank and condition, who had taken up arms against my government, as irretrievably forfeited to the Crown; and the whole laws, privileges, and institutions of that country, wholly and solely at my disposition and mercy.'[54]

Keith, who had largely been ignored by the emperor for much of his reign, was clearly delighted by the audience. However, it was transparent that Joseph wanted to secure British non-involvement in the Low Countries. When facing the loss of Habsburg territories, the emperor reached out to Britain in an effort to secure a defensive alliance, which was rebuffed.

*

Joseph's reign coincided with Mozart's move to the capital from Salzburg, where he had been unhappily employed at the court of the ruling Prince-Archbishop Colloredo. After years of travelling around Europe with his father, Leopold, seeking fame and financial support, the precocious composer and performer tried his luck in Vienna.

Gottfried van Swieten (1733–1803) played a key role in supporting Mozart, Haydn and Beethoven. The son of Maria Theresa's Dutch émigré physician and health reformer Gerard van Swieten, Gottfried served as a diplomat in Brussels, Paris, Warsaw and finally as Habsburg ambassador at the court of Frederick the Great of Prussia. Whilst in Berlin he was instructed to seek the return of the lost province of Silesia, which caused Frederick to say dismissively to him: 'That's the sort of suggestion you could make if I had gout in the brain, but I've only got it in my legs.'[55] His proposal was not successful.

Following his return to Vienna in 1777, where he was appointed head of the imperial library, van Swieten was better able to pursue his personal passion: music. While a keen amateur musician, his real strength was in his position and contacts, which helped him keep the company of the leading composers of the age, to whom he acted as patron and impresario. Described as 'stiff' by Haydn and by a Danish diplomat as having a 'pedantic appearance',[56] he did however make a more positive impression on other diplomatic peers like the British envoy to Berlin, James Harris, the Earl of Malsbury, who thought him to 'be greatly superior to the ordinary class of men'.[57] Van Swieten was interested in the Enlightenment ideas of the age, visiting Voltaire in 1768 and, in addition to his musical collection, he owned Johannes Vermeer's *The Art of Painting*, which shows an artist painting a woman dressed in blue in a studio with black and white floor tiles. It now hangs in the Vienna Art History Museum.

Under the rule of the reformist Joseph II, van Swieten prospered, becoming Councillor of State and director of the State Education Commission and also director of the new Censorship Commission. The music historian Volkmar Braunbehrens described his key positions in the Josephinian government as akin to being minister of culture, with supervisory powers over schools, universities and scientific institutions.[58] Throughout the period he remained responsible for the imperial library and introduced the world's first library card system for its more than 300,000 works.

Van Swieten, who had seen Mozart perform in Vienna as a child, met him again when he moved to the capital in 1781 as a young adult. Following a performance of his compositions at the salon of Countess Thun in front of van Swieten and other influential society figures, he received a commission for his first breakthrough opera: *Die Entführung aus der Serail* ('The Abduction from the Seraglio'). This was first performed in 1781 at the old Burgtheater, which stood at the St Michael's Gate entrance to the Hofburg and is commemorated by an innocuous plaque marking the former entrance to the theatre.

At this time Mozart was a regular visitor to van Swieten's home in his grace and favour apartments in the Augustinian wing of the imperial library.[59] Mozart played manuscripts of the German composers Bach and Handel, which van Swieten had collected in Berlin during his ambassadorial posting. Writing to his father in April 1782, Mozart said: 'I go every Sunday at twelve o'clock to the Baron van Swieten, where nothing is played but Handel and Bach. I am collecting at the moment the fugues of Bach – not only of Sebastian, but also of Emanuel and Friedemann.'[60]

Musicologists suggest that his exposure to Bach and Handel at this time had a big impact on Mozart and his musical development. Following the success of the sessions at his home, van Swieten started arranging concerts for his music-loving friends in the nobility. His Society of Associated Cavaliers (Gesellschaft der Associierten Cavaliers) organised private concerts in the palaces of the aristocracy, in the imperial library where he worked, and also in public at the Burgtheater and other venues. As founder and secretary of the society, he brought together 24 of the richest and most esteemed aristocrats to sponsor concerts and commission compositions, including the princes Liechtenstein, Esterházy, Schwarzenberg, Lobkowitz, Auersperg, Kinsky, Lichnowsky, Trauttmansdorff, Sinzendorf and Counts Czernin, Harrach, Erdödy, Apponyi and Fries.[61] In addition to conducting performances for the Caveliers, Mozart was also commissioned to rewrite Handel compositions for the concerts, including libretti translated from English into German by van Swieten.

Support for Mozart also came from the first permanent Russian ambassador to Vienna, Prince Dmitry Mikhailovich Golitsyn (German: Gallitzin) (1721–1793), who served at the Habsburg court for a remarkable 30 years, hosting concerts by Mozart at his city residence on Krugerstrasse, close to the present-day State Opera building. Mozart noted that Golitsyn 'placed his carriage at my disposal both going and returning, and treated me in the handsomest manner possible'.[62] Golitsyn's contribution is marked to this day, with one of the hills of the Vienna woods where his summer residence stood named after him, the Gallitzinberg, and the approaching road from the city is Gallitzinstrasse. Further support came from the diplomatic community, in the form of patronage by subscription to his concerts by the ambassadors of Spain, Sardinia, Holland and

Denmark.[63] The social and cultural importance of live music in the city was reflected on by Ottoman ambassador Hatti Effendi: 'They have in Vienna a playhouse, four or five storeys high, to present their plays, which they call comedy and opera. There men and women foregather every day, except days when they assemble in church, and most frequently the emperor and empress themselves come to their reserved boxes. The prettiest German girls and finest young men, in golden garments, perform various dances and wonderful acts; beating the stage with their feet, they present a rare spectacle.'[64]

Mozart's decade in Vienna from 1781 until 1791 was incredibly productive and it was where he composed his most famous works, including *Die Zauberflöte* ('The Magic Flute'); *Le Nozze di Figaro* ('The Marriage of Figaro'); *Don Giovanni*; the Serenade No. 13 in G major (*Eine Kleine Nachtmusik*); Symphonies 40 and 41; the Piano Sonata No. 11 ('Alla Turca'); Piano Concertos Nos. 20, 21, 23 and 24; the Clarinet Concerto in A major; the motet *Ave Verum Corpus*; and the *Requiem* in D minor. According to the chronological Köchel catalogue of Mozart's work, about half of his 626 main catalogued works were composed in Vienna.

Mozart died in 1791, and it was van Swieten who made the funeral arrangements and had a continuing loyalty to Wolfgang's cash-strapped widow, Constanze, and son, Karl. Van Swieten organised a fundraising benefit performance of Mozart's *Requiem* and helped arrange young Karl's education in Prague. Other financial support was forthcoming from the Prussian Embassy, which purchased copies of the *Requiem* and other musical manuscripts on behalf of King Frederick Wilhelm.[65]

During Mozart's last years, he struck up a friendship with gifted fellow composer Joseph Haydn (1732–1809,) from Rohrau in eastern Lower Austria, close to present-day Slovakia and Hungary. Haydn had for decades been employed as court musician by the wealthy Esterhazy family in Eisenstadt and Fertöd, south-east of Vienna. By the 1780s he was in the capital more often, playing music and spending more time with Mozart, becoming a Freemason in the Zur wahren Eintracht (True Concord) lodge, which Mozart also attended.

After a couple of two-year London journeys, where Haydn conducted hugely popular concerts and composed some of his best-known pieces, he returned to Vienna. While his friend Mozart had died in the meantime, Haydn picked up again with his mentor Gottfried van Swieten, who supported him through the Society of Associated Cavaliers and increasingly took on the role as his librettist. This collaboration included two of Haydn's best-known oratorios, *Die Schöpfung* ('The Creation') and *Die Jahreszeiten* ('The Seasons'), described by music critic Charles Rosen as 'among the greatest works of the century'.[66] Haydn also composed a series of instrumental pieces in Vienna, including his Trumpet Concerto, the last nine of his string quartets and the *Kaiserhymne* ('Emperor's Hymn'), which would become the Austrian anthem. Haydn had been impressed by the British anthem *God Save the King* during his time in London and was inspired to write a patriotic anthem at a time when Austria was threatened by Napoleonic France. Originally composed as a personal anthem to Emperor Francis II, it was first performed on his birthday, 12 February, in 1797. The melody is now more recognised as the *Deutschlandlied*, which was adopted as the German national anthem in 1918. For 120 years it was sung to different words in praise of the Austrian emperor: *Gott erhalte, Gott beschütze / Unsern Kaiser, unser Land!* ('God preserve, God protect / Our Emperor, our country!').

Different language versions of the anthem were sung by the various nationalities of the monarchy until its dissolution in 1918. The last time it was performed at an official event was at the 2011 funeral of Otto Habsburg, son of the last emperor, Charles, in Vienna's St Stephen's Cathedral. While sung with gusto by members of the Habsburg family, Austrian President Heinz Fischer and government ministers stood respectfully without joining in.

Van Swieten's patronage of Haydn was also extended to Beethoven (1770–1827), who had moved to Vienna from Bonn and studied composition with Haydn. As with both Mozart and Haydn before him, he was drawn into the musical scene which met regularly at van Swieten's residence, by then on Renngasse 3, close to the Freyung square and Schottenkirche: 'The evening gatherings at Swieten's home had a marked effect on Beethoven, for it was here that he first became acquainted with the music of Handel and Bach. He generally had to stay long after the other guests had departed, for his elderly host was musically insatiable and would not let the young pianist go until he had "blessed the evening" with several Bach fugues.'[67]

Beethoven felt indebted enough to van Swieten to dedicate his Symphony No. 1 in C major, Opus 21, and he dedicated his String Quartets Nos. 7–9, Opus 59, as well as his classic Fifth and Sixth (Pastoral) Symphonies to Russian ambassador Count Andreas Razumovsky. His famed choral work *Missa Solemnis* was first performed at a concert in St Petersburg organised by Prince Nikolai Galytsin, whose great-uncle had been Russian ambassador in Vienna and patron of Mozart.

Gottfried van Swieten died aged nearly 80 in 1803. In addition to the role he played promoting some of the all-time musical greats, he also helped changed attitudes about performing older music, in an age when the custom was to largely play newly composed works. The society of wealthy aristocratic musical patrons he had helped establish in 1786 was into its second incarnation by the turn of the century, and it endured until 1808, five years after van Swieten's death. The task of sponsoring concerts was soon taken up by the Society of Friends of Music (Gesellschaft der Musikfreunde), also known as the Music Association (Musikverein), a shift from predominantly aristocratic patronage to the wider involvement of bourgeois society. Founded in 1812 and best known for its concert hall, which is home to the Vienna Philharmonic Orchestra, it hosts the annual New Year's concert that is broadcast around the world. To this day, a box is reserved for diplomats accredited in Vienna.

The impact of Beethoven, Haydn and Mozart can be felt to this day on the cultural life of Vienna. Their homes are signposted and are major visitor attractions. The only surviving Mozart house is on the Domgasse, where he composed *The Marriage of Figaro*. The Haydnhaus is on the appropriately named Haydngasse in the former village of Gumpendorf in the 6th district. Beethoven's home in the 'Pasqualati House' still stands on the last ramparts of the Vienna city wall on the Mölkerbastei. Gottfried van Swieten is marked much less prominently. Van-Swieten-Gasse in the ninth district is named after his father Gerhard, whose bust is on display in the State Hall (Prunksaal) of the National Library.

The musical heyday of Mozart and Haydn in Vienna corresponded with the reign of Joseph II, who was portrayed two centuries later as a music lover in the multiple award-winning Miloš Forman film *Amadeus*. His reforming zeal as an 'enlightened despot' involved thousands of edicts and laws that caused massive conservative resentment and resistance across his realms. The later years of Joseph II's reign were also marked by unrest and warfare on multiple fronts. Habsburg forces were mobilised in 1788 against the Ottoman Empire because of treaty obligations to Catherine the Great. What began as the Russo-Turkish War soon also became the Austro-Turkish War with fighting across southern and eastern Europe. Major diseases would take a heavy toll on Austrian forces, including the emperor, who fell ill while spending time at the front and was unable to consolidate his domestic reforms at home: 'This war devastated his domestic economy. The next year the national debt soared to 22 million gulden, and in 1790 it reached 400 million. As food prices and taxes rose and a new conscription was implemented, the mood in Vienna turned ugly. Bread riots erupted after the bad harvest of 1788/89 and the emperor's popularity plummeted.'[68]

Meanwhile, at the opposite end of the Habsburg lands, an armed insurrection broke out in the Austrian Netherlands, fuelled in large part by opposition to Joseph's liberal reforms, which were seen as anti-Catholic. The Brabant Revolution temporarily overthrew Austrian rule in 1789 and highlighted the risk to the territory that neighboured France and was being rocked by its own revolution. The causes of the French Revolution were wide and deep-seated, but the unpopularity of the Austrian-born Queen Marie Antoinette was a contributory factor because of her lavish spending – which earned her opprobrium and the nickname 'Madame Déficit' – as well as widespread court intrigues, salacious rumours, Austrophobia and suspicions about her ultimate loyalties.

# 4

# *Revolting French and Napoleon*

'When you set out to take Vienna, take Vienna.'

– Napoleon Bonaparte

The French Revolution of 1789 led to a quarter century of instability and war across the European continent, with Austria providing the most consistent military and diplomatic opposition to revolutionary and Napoleonic France. Not long after the start of the revolution Emperor Joseph II died aged 48 and was buried in the imperial crypt. Having failed to deliver his reforming ambitions he asked that his epitaph read: 'Here lies Joseph II, who failed in all he undertook.'

His brother Leopold II (1747–1792) succeeded him and one of his first acts was to rescind the alliance with France entered into by his mother in 1756. Instead, he began diplomatic discussions with Britain to secure a counterweight to Prussia and Russia.

Leopold's sister, the French Queen Marie Antoinette, wrote regularly to her brother to report on her depredations and seek help. The emperor's first reaction to the revolution, while Louis XVI and Marie Antoinette remained on the throne as constitutional monarchs in Versailles, was not decisive or committed: 'We have a sister, the Queen of France. But the Holy Empire has no sister and Austria has no sister. I can only act according to the interests of my people and not according to my family interests.'[1]

This changed as revolutionary fervour increased and the French royal couple fled for the royalist fortress town of Montmédy near the border with the Austrian Netherlands. Here they were supposed to meet with émigré supporters and be protected by Austria. However,

87

they were arrested on the way and returned to Paris, where they were placed under house arrest in the Tuileries Palace. Within days Leopold issued a diplomatic note, the Padua Circular, addressed to other sovereigns across Europe, demanding their release:

> I am sure Your Majesty will have learned, with as much surprise and indignation as I, of the unprecedented outrage of the arrest of the King of France, of my sister the Queen, and of the Royal Family. I am also sure your sentiments cannot differ from mine with regard to this event which immediately compromises the honor of all sovereigns and the security of all governments by inspiring fear of still more dreadful acts to follow, and by placing the seal of illegality upon previous excesses in France.
>
> I am determined to fulfil my obligation as to these considerations, both as chosen head of the Germanic State, with its support, and as Sovereign of the Austrian states. I therefore propose to you, as I propose to the Kings of Spain, England, Prussia, Naples, and Sardinia, as well as to the Empress of Russia, to unite with them and me to consult on cooperation and measures to restore the liberty and honor of the Most Christian King and his family, and to limit the dangerous extremes of the French Revolution.[2]

While there was little interest by other European states in intervening in France, the circumstances brought Austria and Prussia closer together and led to the joint Declaration of Pillnitz calling on European powers to join in collective action should Louis be endangered. What was meant as a warning to the French revolutionaries was understood in Paris as a declaration of impending war. In these worsening circumstances Marie Antoinette wrote to her brother Leopold on 4 October 1791:

> My only consolation is in writing to you, my dear brother; I am surrounded by so many atrocities that I need all your

friendship to tranquillise my mind . . . A point of primary importance is to regulate the conduct of the émigrés. If they re-enter France in arms, all is lost, and it will be impossible to make it believed that we are not in connivance with them. Even the existence of an army of émigrés on the frontier would be enough to keep up the irritation and afford ground for accusations against us; it appears to me that a congress would make the task of restraining them less difficult . . . This idea of a congress pleases me greatly; it would second the efforts we are making to maintain confidence. In the first place, I repeat, it would put a check on the émigrés, and, moreover, it would make an impression here from which I hope much. I submit that to your better judgment . . . Adieu, my dear brother; we love you, and my daughter has particularly charged me to embrace her good uncle.[3]

By early 1792 French counter-revolutionary émigré forces had begun to form at the German town of Trier close to the border between the Austrian Netherlands and France. But Leopold died unexpectedly aged 44 after only two years on the throne. He is remembered as one of the first rulers to oppose the death penalty and 'one of the most shrewd and sensible monarchs ever to wear a crown'. [4] The eldest of his 16 children succeeded him aged only 24 as Francis II, the last ever Holy Roman Emperor. One of his first acts was to deploy 40,000 men to the Austrian Netherlands, 20,000 to the Rhine, and agree a treaty with Prussia 'to put an end to the troubles in France'. A 'dry, curt and formal note'[5] was sent to the French ambassador in Vienna, Emmanuel Marquis de Noailles, which named unrealistic restoration conditions as the only way to preserve the peace.

On 20 April 1792 the French Legislative Assembly declared war against Austria. It was the beginning of 22 years of conflict, where Austrian forces would be the largest power continually pitted against French revolutionary and Napoleonic armies. Despite suffering many defeats and setbacks, they rose time and time again to check French power and provided the largest contingent to the allied effort in Italy and Germany.

At the beginning, Habsburg forces joined other European monarchies in the War of the First Coalition, which lasted for five years. But the allies were hampered by splitting their forces on either side of the Alps. Despite early allied successes, the French began to gain the ascendency from the Low Countries to Italy, where the previously little-known General Napoleon Bonaparte won a series of battles and drove the Austrians out of most of the Italian peninsula. Vienna sued for peace after French forces crossed into Carinthia and were on the march towards the capital. The Treaty of Campo Formio was signed on 17 October 1797, ending the War of the First Coalition. It ceded the Austrian Netherlands to France while Austria received the city of Venice, Venetia, Istria and Dalmatia. The treaty formalised the end of fealty by Italian states to the Holy Roman Emperor and extended the borders of France to the Rhine. In the space of five years, nearly 100,000 Austrians had been killed in action, 100,000 had been wounded and 220,000 taken prisoner.

*

The French Revolution and Napoleon's military advances into neighbouring countries made Vienna a centre for exiles of all types. Foremost amongst them was Charles-Joseph Lamoral, 7th Prince de Ligne (1735–1814). An aristocrat from the Austrian Netherlands, he is one of the great characters of the 18th and early 19th centuries, befriending the leading figures of that age and, as a prolific writer, intellectual and raconteur, capturing the essence of European history and culture in 34 volumes of work. De Ligne was born a Habsburg subject in Brussels and raised in the family's country estate at Château de Belœil in the province of Hainaut in present-day Belgium. He served with distinction in the imperial military in the Seven Years' War, the War of the Bavarian Succession and against the Ottoman Empire at the Siege of Belgrade. Well-travelled across Europe as a diplomat in Russia, Prussia, Italy, France and England, he attended the courts and salons of the continent, and corresponded with the intellectual giants of the time, including Rousseau, Voltaire and Goethe. His personal friendships included Catherine the Great of Russia, Frederick the Great of Prussia and Emperor Joseph II. Losing his estate after the French Revolution, he moved to Vienna permanently in 1790.

Prince de Ligne rented a house on the Mölkerbastei, which literally stood on the western ramparts of Vienna, and one of the last visible sections of the city wall still standing today. Painted pink in the colours of the de Ligne family, the 'Hôtel de Ligne' was so narrow that there were ladders between the single rooms on each floor rather than stairs, which led to the house also becoming known as the 'parrot's cage' because of its curious dimensions. 'My little house, the colour of roses, like my ideas, is on the ramparts and is the only open house in Vienna. I have six dishes for dinner, five for supper. *Arrive qui veut. S'asseoit qui peut.* Sometimes when the sixty people who frequent it arrive or meet there, there are not enough of my straw chairs; people stand in flux and reflux, like in the stalls, until those most in hurry leave.'[6] Four doors along the Mölkerbastei, at number eight, was the Pasqualatihaus, the home of Beethoven. Over the next quarter of a century the de Ligne residence became one of the best-known addresses in Vienna, visited by the great and the good of Vienna society and international personalities. Not only did the prince have a lifetime of stories to tell, but his wit and repartee was famed for its good nature and humour.

Amongst de Ligne's friends were the Swedish ambassador Count Armfelt and the former Russian ambassador Count Razumovsky. Count Gustaf Mauritz Armfelt (1757–1814) was born in Finland, which at that time belonged to Sweden. Serving as a Swedish diplomat, general and courtier, including the posting to Vienna, his allegiances transferred when Finland became part of Russia in 1811. He is viewed to this day as one of the key father figures of Finnish independence, developing plans for the Grand Duchy of Finland to become an autonomous state within the Russian Empire. Armfelt became the highest representative of the Grand Duchy in St Petersburg as its Minister Secretary of State and then as Governor-General. De Ligne's other great friend amongst the diplomatic community was Count Andrey Razumovsky (1752–1836), who had been appointed as Russian ambassador to the Habsburg Court in 1792, a post he held until 1807, and then remained in Vienna. Razumovsky was a major patron of the arts in Vienna and commissioned Beethoven to write what become known as the three Razumovsky String Quartets Nos. 7–9, Opus 59, which are based on a Russian musical theme.

De Ligne hosted visiting diplomatic dignitaries, like the future British Foreign Secretary Henry Phipps, the 1st Earl of Mulgrave. While his special military mission to persuade the Austrians to retain troops in Switzerland was unsuccessful, he and de Ligne were able to continue their friendship, which had been forged 20 years earlier in the Low Countries. De Ligne also struck up new friendships with the likes of Sir Gilbert Elliot, 1st Earl of Minto, and Count Andrea Pozzo di Borgo, who arrived on a joint diplomatic mission to Vienna. Lord Minto (1751–1814) served as British ambassador to the Habsburg court, and Pozzo di Borgo (1764–1842) was a Corsican politician. The pair, who had been working together on the Mediterranean island, were in Vienna to encourage preparations for the next war against Napoleon.

Pozzo, who would eventually enter Russian diplomatic service, became a hit in the salons of Vienna, and Lord Minto a mainstay in the society life of the capital, which often included visits to Prince de Ligne, despite his quirkiness. Lady Harriet Minto wrote: 'He is very constant to us, very clever but too odd to be understood at first by everybody. I like the whole family . . . He has no money to live on but his pay; but they bear their misfortunes gently, and never grumble or complain.'[7]

The last years of the 18th century were a bleak time for the Austrians, suffering four major battlefield defeats at the hands of Napoleon, who also threatened invasion through the Alps. The only good news was delivered far away by British Admiral Horatio Nelson, who won a decisive naval engagement against the French at the Battle of the Nile, north-east of Alexandria. Haydn composed his *Missa in Angustiis* ('Mass for troubled times'), little knowing that Nelson would return from Egypt via Vienna and attend a *Te Deum* musical performance conducted by Haydn at Esterhazy Palace in Eisenstadt, sealing the soubriquet 'Nelson Mass' for what 'is arguably Haydn's greatest single composition'.[8]

Nelson stayed in Vienna at the Gasthaus zum Biedermänner (Inn of all Honest Men) on the corner of Graben and Habsburgergasse for a number of weeks, with contemporary accounts recording that crowds of well-wishers congregated outside the inn to see the famous admiral[9] and applauded him during theatre visits. Nelson had travelled to Vienna with the British ambassador to Naples, Sir William Hamilton, and his wife, Lady Emma, who was carrying Nelson's child at the time. The *ménage à trois* enjoyed the hospitality of Emperor Francis II and his second wife Maria Theresa of Naples-Sicily and the company of their exiled friend Queen Maria Carolina of Naples, who was a daughter of Empress Maria Theresa.

They also spent some of their time at the summer residence of Lord Minto in a former monastery in St Veit, not far from Schönbrunn Palace. Lady Minto described the visit by Nelson in a letter to her sister as follows: 'I don't think him altered in the least. He has the same shock head, and the same honest simple manners; but he is devoted to Emma; he thinks her quite an angel, and talks of her as such to her face and behind her back, and she leads him about like a keeper with a bear. She must sit by him at dinner to cut his meat; and he carries her pocket-handkerchief . . . he is a gig from ribands, orders and stars.'[10]

\*

Just a year after the end of the War of the First Coalition, hostilities were resumed with the War of the Second Coalition beginning after the French invasion of Egypt in 1798. Austrian armies again took to the field in Germany and Italy, with the first battles in 1799 seeing victories under the command of Archduke Charles at Ostrach and then at Stockach. In Italy, the Austrians were supported by Russian forces under the legendary Field Marshal Alexander Suvorov, one of the greatest ever military commanders, who never lost a single of his more than 60 battles. Allied victories at the battles of Magnano, Cassano and Novi effectively expelled the French from Italy. However, the defeat of a Russian army at Zurich before Suvorov could arrive caused Russia to drop out of the war, and momentum swung behind the French in 1800. Napoleon defeated the Austrians at Marengo in Piedmont while General Jean Moreau won a decisive victory at Hohenlinden in Bavaria over Austrian-Bavarian forces commanded by Archduke John of Austria. The losses on either side of the Alps led to Vienna to sue for peace, which was sealed in the Treaty of Lunéville on 9 February 1801, an agreement that largely mirrored the earlier Treaty of Campo Formio.

France was by this stage a military dictatorship under Napoleon, who adopted the Habsburg strategy of securing allies amongst neighbouring client states and territories, creating a buffer zone around France and creating a source for additional troops. What had previously been a strength for Vienna was turned into a weakness as the Holy Roman Empire began its final disintegration. In 1803 the Imperial Recess of the Empire proposed major internal consti-tutional changes, including the secularisation of states and abolition of imperial city status as compensation for German princes who had lost territories annexed by France to the west of the Rhine. The last significant law enacted by the empire presaged its dissolution and led Emperor Francis to change his own status, creating the title Emperor of Austria. For the first time in hundreds of years the com-posite Habsburg Monarchy was to have its own overarching imperial structure.

By 1803 the Third Coalition was formed against France, marking the beginning of the Napoleonic Wars, which lasted from 1803 until 1815. Early engagements were a disaster for Austria, with its main army north of the Alps forced to surrender at Ulm on 14 October 1805. One month later Napoleon interrupted the premiere of Beethoven's *Fidelio* by capturing Vienna. He spent two months in residence at Schönbrunn Palace.

The historical novelist Karoline Pichler (1769–1843), who led one of the foremost literary, musical and intellectual salons in Vienna, described Napoleon's arrival: 'The enemy was very close to the city. Our troops received the order to leave – the moment of separation has arrived – the battalion and rest of the military raced to the bridges to the other side [of the Danube]; meanwhile a deputation from the municipality and citizenry was dispatched to meet the approaching French Emperor, present him the keys of the city and commit it to his safekeeping.'[11]

Soon after the French arrival, Pichler and other Vienna residents had to provide quarters for the occupying forces: 'I bade them welcome in French and noticed how the sound of their native home had an immediately positive effect. The initial reception was pretty good as they were well behaved, the Major particularly refined. The Officers appeared for dinner and we had a not unpleasing lively conversation . . . This is how we experienced the pain! Our residence city, the home of the Emperor, that twice resisted the attacks of the Turks, was in the power of a foreign people – these Blues [colour of French uniforms], these children of a nation we have had antipathy towards since our childhoods were now the victors and our overlords.'[12]

The occupying troops were not in Vienna for long as French troops were mobilised northwards into Moravia to face the combined Austrian and Russian forces at the Battle of Austerlitz. On 2 December 1805 Napoleon secured what is considered his greatest tactical victory after feigning weakness against the larger enemy forces, abandoning the nearby Pratzen Heights and luring the allies into a fateful attack. The decisive Napoleonic victory led to the Treaty of Pressburg on 27 December 1805, which took Austria out of the war. Habsburg territories were ceded to France and her allies in Germany, including Vorarlberg and Tyrol, and in Italy: Venetia, Istria and Dalmatia. One small compensation was the Electorate of Salzburg. In recognising new kingly titles assumed by the Electors of Würtemberg and Bavaria, the Holy Roman Empire was all but dissolved. On the same day Napoleon issued a proclamation to the people of Vienna:

Inhabitants of Vienna! – I have signed a peace with the Emperor of Austria. As I am about to return to my capital, I must express to you the esteem I entertain for you, and the satisfaction I have felt at your conduct, during the time you were under my laws. I have given you an example, which hitherto has no parallels in the history of nations; ten thousand men of your national guards have remained armed, and have guarded your gates; your whole arsenal has continued in your power, while I have followed the uncertain fortunes of war. I have trusted to your honour, your sincerity, your integrity, and you have justified my confidence . . .

Inhabitants of Vienna, I have shewn myself little among you, not from contempt, or vain pride; no but not to diminish the feelings of esteem for that Monarch, with whom I was desirous to conclude a speedy peace. As I am now about to leave you, receive from me, as a present your arsenal, untouched, which, by the laws of war, had become my property; make use of it, for the maintenance of good order.

All of the evils you have suffered, you must ascribe to the calamities, inseparable from war; and every kind of indulgence with which my armies have treated these countries, to the esteem which you have deserved.

[Signed] NAPOLEON[13]

After Napoleon's return to Paris in early 1806, preparations were made for the establishment of a Confederation of the Rhine, involving French client states in Germany and forming a buffer between France and Austria and Prussia. Initially, 16 states were included, with Napoleon acting as hereditary protector of the confederation, which was officially established by treaty on 12 July 1806. The venerable Holy Roman Empire was formally coming apart with the secession of its constituent parts, and Napoleon threatened Francis with war if he did not abdicate as Holy Roman Emperor by 10 August. With fears that Napoleon might claim the august title himself, 'Habsburg officials feverishly prepared legal documents to enable Francis not merely to abdicate, but to remove the Empire entirely from Napoleon's grasp by dissolving it. Having been twice reminded by his ministers, Francis reluctantly signed the papers. On the morning of the 6th August an imperial herald in full regalia rode through Vienna to the Jesuit Church of the Nine Choirs of Angels. After climbing to the balcony, he summoned the inhabitants with a silver fanfare to announce the end of the [Holy Roman] Empire.'[14] A thousand years of Europe's history came to an end.

Having sat out the War of the Fourth Coalition of 1806–1807, Vienna decided to take the opportunity of Napoleon's Iberian distraction in the Peninsular War to launch the War of the Fifth Coalition in early 1809. Archduke Charles (1771–1847), the talented 38-year-old field marshal who had done much to reform the Habsburg army, commanded Austrian forces. He would do much to test Napoleon and proved the Corsican was not invincible in two large-scale battles within sight of the Austrian capital.

Charles had invaded Bavaria to take on Napoleonic forces there but was soon repulsed back along the Danube valley towards the Austrian capital. Napoleon reached the defended gates of Vienna in May 1809, took up residence in Schönbrunn Palace for a second time and let his artillery begin shelling the city. The population of all classes took to the basement of buildings for protection, including Beethoven, who spent the greater part of the time in a cellar in the house of his brother Casper, where he 'covered his head with pillows so as not to hear the cannons'.[15]

On learning that Francis' daughter, Archduchess Marie Louise, was still in the capital because of her ill health with smallpox, Napoleon ordered that the Hofburg should not be targeted, which was just as well as a year later he would marry her. After taking the city Napoleon issued a proclamation to his troops:

> One month after the enemy passed the Inn, on the same day and at the same hour, we have entered Vienna. Her landwehres, her levies in mass, her ramparts created by the

impotent fury of the princes of the house of [Habsburg-] Lorrain, have scarcely claimed your intention. The princes of that house have abandoned their capital, not like soldiers of honour yielding to the circumstances of war, but like perjurers, persuaded by their own remorse. In flying from Vienna they bade farewell to the inhabitants by murder and conflagration. Like Mandea, they have, with their own hands, slain their children.

Soldiers! The people of Vienna, according to the expression of a deputation of the suburbs, abandoned, widowed, shall be the object of our regard. I take its good citizens under my special protection; as to the turbulent and wicked, they shall meet with exemplary justice. Let us exhibit no marks of haughtiness or pride; but regard our triumphs as a proof of the Divine justice, which punishes, by our hands, the ungrateful and the perjured.[16]

While Archduke Charles marshalled his army north of the Danube from Vienna, Napoleon's pioneers built a bridge across the river for his forces to cross and meet the Austrian army on the left bank. Francis' younger brother rallied the nearly 100,000 troops under his command: 'Tomorrow or the following day there will be a great battle! The result of it will probably decide the fate of the monarchy and the freedom of every one of you. Between eternal disgrace and undying fame there is no middle way . . . this decisive battle will be waged under the eyes of our Kaiser and of the enslaved inhabitants of our capital who look for their liberation in the bravery of the army.'[17]

Over two days, 21–22 May 1809, the battle raged on the ground between the villages of Aspern and Essling. In his acclaimed memoirs, the French general Baron Marcelin de Marbot described the battle, including the turning point, when the Austrians started to gain the upper hand: 'The position was very critical. Compelled to act on the defensive, the Emperor [Napoleon] posted his army in an arc, having the Danube for its chord, our right resting on the river in the rear of Essling, our left in rear of Aspern. Under pain of being driven into the river we had to keep up the fight for the rest of the day . . . All along our lines the slaughter was terrible, but absolutely necessary to save the honour of France and the position of the army which had crossed the Danube.'[18]

The Battle of Aspern-Essling was extremely bloody, with more than 40,000 casualties, including Napoleon's friend and senior commander, Marshal Jean Lannes, who was hit by a cannonball. The Austrians won on the field, defeating Napoleon for the first time in a decade; however, Napoleon was able to withdraw most of his forces, denying Charles a decisive victory. Nevertheless, his success and personal bravery in rallying troops on the battlefield has been long celebrated and is commemorated with an equestrian statue on Heroes Square in Vienna. Napoleon later famously chided his brother-in-law and senior commander, Marshal Joachim Murat, saying: 'You did not see the Austrians at Aspern. Well you have seen nothing! Absolutely nothing!'[19]

After a six-week recovery period and with new reinforcements, Napoleon again crossed the Danube to face Archduke Charles at the Battle of Wagram, north-east of Vienna, on 5–6 July 1809. The battle was also particularly bloody, with more than 1,000 artillery pieces firing in excess of 180,000 rounds across the packed flat battlefield where the two massed armies faced each other. The historian Ian Castle concluded that 'Wagram had been the largest battle in history at that time. More than 300,000 men had fought for two days along a great front. Estimates for the losses sustained by the two sides vary greatly. For the Austrians, a figure of 23,750 killed and wounded, 7,500 prisoners and about 10,000 missing, many of whom returned to their regiments later, seems reasonable. In addition, the Austrians lost 10 standards and 20 guns. Estimates of the French losses also vary, but 27,500 killed and wounded, with an additional 10,000 for prisoners and missing, seems fair. It is interesting to note that the French lost slightly more trophies than the Austrians, twelve eagles or standards and 21 guns. After the battle, Napoleon was reported as saying that "war was never like this, neither prisoners nor guns. This day will have no result."'[20]

Defeated, the Austrians were forced to retreat into Moravia, where a follow-up losing battle took place at Znaim before an armistice was agreed. The senior French officer Baron de Marbot recalled the dramatic circumstances in which hostilities came to an end: 'As I was shouting "Peace! Peace" and with my left hand giving the sign for a halt, suddenly a bullet from the outskirts of the town hit me in the wrist. Some of our officers, understanding at length that I brought the order to suspend hostilities, halted their companies; others seeing the Austrian battalions within a hundred paces, were doubtful. At the same time an aide-de-camp from the archduke also came between the two lines, with a view of preventing the attack, and got a bullet through his shoulder, from the same quarter. I hastened towards him, and to make both sides see what purpose we had been sent, we testified it by embracing each other. At sight of this, the officers on both sides had no more hesitation about ordering a halt. Flocking round us they learnt that an armistice had been agreed on. There were mutual congratulations; the Austrians returned to Znaym [sic] and our troops to their former position.'[21]

While preparations were being made for a formal peace, Napoleon continued to stay at Schönbrunn, where he attended operas at the palace theatre and reviewed troops. This was the only public opportunity that the Viennese had of seeing the French Emperor, like Jakob Seidl, who described him in mixed terms: 'He is hardly taller than me, a little bit fatter, with a very puffy face and of seemingly good-character. His eyes and movements are lively, although his dark-yellow pallor doesn't seem healthy. He wears white breeches, waistcoat, a green uniform with red lapels and collar, quite simple without embroidery, with a small star and the Légion d'honneur in a buttonhole. His head is completely shorn and he is clean-shaven, his hat unbraided, without a feather, but instead a very small French cockade.'[22]

It was at one of these reviews during the peace negotiations that Napoleon survived an attempted assassination by the young German Friedrich Staps, who admitted his intention to kill the emperor with a knife. The next day, on 14 October 1809, the Treaty of Schönbrunn was signed at the palace. Its harsh terms included the territorial losses of Salzburg, its remaining Adriatic coastline, and lands ceded to both the Duchy of Warsaw and Russia. Austria lost 3.5 million of her population and had to recognise Napoleonic gains and rule across Europe, as well as pay a large indemnity and reduce its army to 150,000. As the treaty was signed at Schönbrunn, French and Bavarian troops were crushing a popular uprising in Tyrol led by the patriotic innkeeper Andreas Hofer, who was later executed and has since become a legendary folk-hero. With that, the last of Austrian resistance to Napoleon was extinguished.

International reports on this 'Carthaginian peace' were damning: 'We see through the whole of this instrument the humiliation of the weak and unfortunate Francis, who has preferred the resignation of his fairest territories to restoring to his vassals their liberties, and giving them that interest in the public cause which their valour would have known how to protect.—O, the brave and loyal, but, we fear, lost Tyrolese!'[23]

Napoleon left Vienna on 16 October, after which his would-be assassin Friedrich Staps faced a firing squad. Prior to the last French forces leaving the city on 20 November they blew up large sections of the city wall. Having survived his brush with death and conscious he didn't have an heir, Napoleon divorced his childless wife, Josephine, and decided that an Austrian or Russian bride would be fitting for the Emperor of France. He settled for Archduchess Marie Louise after the potential match was promoted by the new Austrian Foreign Minister, Prince Klemens von Metternich. Despite the 18-year-old daughter of Francis believing this to be 'an ordeal worse than any martyrdom imaginable', she acceded to his request, telling Metternich: 'I wish only what my duty commands me to wish. When the interests of the Empire are at stake, they must be consulted, not my feelings. Beg of my father to regard only his duties as sovereign, without subordinating it to my personal interests.'[24]

The proxy marriage took place with full imperial pomp and circumstance on 11 March 1810 at the court Church of St Augustine. Marie Louise gave her marriage consent at the altar to Napoleon, represented by Archduke Charles, who, until recently, had been his adversary. In a report back to France, the ambassador Marshal Louis-Alexandre Berthier described the ceremony:

> The marriage of His Majesty the Emperor with the Archduchess Marie Louise was celebrated with a magnificence that is hard to surpass, by the side of which even the brilliant festivities that have preceded it are not to be mentioned. The vast multitude of spectators, who had gathered from all quarters of the realm and from foreign parts, so packed the church, and the halls and passage-ways of the Palace, that the Emperor and Empress of Austria were often crowded. The really prodigious display of pearls and diamonds; the richness of the dresses and the uniforms; the numberless lights that illuminated the whole Palace; the joy of the participants, gave to the ceremony a splendor worthy of this grand and majestic solemnity. The richest noblemen of the country made a most brilliant display, and seemed to rival even with the Emperor. The ladies who accompanied the two Empresses, who for the most part were Princesses and women of the highest rank, seemed borne down by the weight of the diamonds and pearls they wore. But all eyes were fixed on the principal person of the solemnity, on this adored Princess who soon will make the happiness of our Sovereign.'[25]

Two days later, Marie Louise departed Vienna for France. On 20 March 1811 she gave birth to Napoleon François Joseph Charles Bonaparte.

*

Fatherhood did not distract Napoleon from his hegemonic aims and in 1812 he assembled the biggest army ever seen in European history and invaded Russia. The Grande Armée of 685,000 troops marched eastwards while the Russians evaded confrontation and lured the French further into the interior. After a narrow victory at the Battle of Borodino, Napoleon captured Moscow, which had been abandoned and was soon ablaze. Emperor Francis found himself awkwardly allied with his son-in-law against his traditional Russian allies; however, an Austrian corps operated far away from the main French forces. An understanding was reportedly reached between Vienna and St Petersburg that 'the Austrians would not seriously engage the Russians, nor would the Russians press the Austrian Corps more than appearances required'.[26] Meanwhile in Moscow the onset of winter and dwindling supplies forced the French to begin their retreat, at horrific cost. Only a fraction of the once grand army made it back with the French emperor. It was the beginning of the end for Napoleon, and only one year later the most devastating defeat would be inflicted on the French at the Battle of Leipzig.

Recent history had taught the European powers that only by standing together would they have a chance of defeating Napoleon. Metternich switched Austria's alliance with France to a position of neutrality, with a hope of securing an armed peace, but when that failed Austria declared war on France and joined the Sixth Coalition against Napoleon. Negotiating the command for the brilliant Austrian field marshal Prince Karl Phillip zu Schwarzenberg (1771–1820), Metternich also succeeded in getting all three main allied monarchs to follow Austria on the offensive. Schwarzenberg was greatly helped by his diplomatic skills, honed as the Austrian ambassador to Russia and Paris, where in the finest tradition of Habsburg marriage politics, he had helped negotiate the nuptials of Archduchess Marie Louise with Napoleon. The two men got to know one another well, with the French emperor holding him in high regard – while both countries were still allied, Schwarzenberg had commanded the Austrians during the doomed 1812 Russian campaign.

By 1813, however, with Austria now on the side of the coalition, it was Schwarzenberg who commanded the Grand Army of Bohemia and was senior general of the different forces ranged against Napoleon. The War of the Sixth Coalition involved a series of battles in Silesia, Brandenburg, Bohemia and Saxony and culminated in the decisive Battle of Leipzig. Known as the 'Battle of the Nations' in German, French and Russian it was to be the biggest battle in Europe until the First World War. More than 600,000 troops and 2,200 pieces of artillery were deployed in the battle of 16–19 October. As coalition forces gradually encircled the French Grande Armée, the Austrian Emperor Francis I, Russian Tsar Alexander I and Prussian King Frederick Wilhelm III watched from what became Monarchs Hill. It is the last time that so many heads of state would personally attend such a decisive battle.

Managing to break out of the coalition encirclement, Napoleon limped back to Paris, leaving more than 60,000 dead, wounded or captured troops. Previous allies, like the German states of the Confederation of the Rhine and the Netherlands, switched sides as coalition armies headed west towards the French capital, which capitulated in late March 1814. Schwarzenberg led the victorious forces into Paris, together with the Russian tsar and Prussian king. Napoleon, who was deposed by the French Senate, then announced his unconditional abdication and was sent into exile on the Mediterranean island of Elba.

On the 30 May 1814 the Treaty of Paris ended the war between France and the Sixth Coalition. Article 32 of the treaty gave two months for a final settlement to be agreed between the belligerents of the Napoleonic Wars. It was agreed that this should take place at the Congress of Vienna.

# 5

# The Glorious Moment: The Congress of Vienna

'The Congress does not move forward, it dances.'

– Charles-Joseph, 7th Prince de Ligne

The Congress of Vienna, which began in November 1814, established the Austrian capital as the pre-eminent diplomatic capital of the age. Aimed at securing a long-term peace settlement for Europe following the Napoleonic Wars, it was the first large-scale multilateral diplomatic conference to bring together the sovereigns and government ministers from across the continent.

Hosted by Emperor Francis I and managed by his brilliant foreign minister, Metternich, the other main congress participants included Russian Tsar Alexander I, Prussian King Frederick William III, British Foreign Secretary Robert Stewart, Viscount Castlereagh and French Foreign Minister Charles-Maurice Talleyrande-Périgord. They were joined by delegations from more than 200 states, ruling houses, cities, religious organisations and interest groups.

The arrival ceremony for Tsar Alexander and King Frederick William on 25 September 1814 gave an indication of the pomp for which the congress was to become famous. Emperor Francis rode out of Vienna to greet the monarchs and accompany them into the city, together with a military procession of Ulans, Grenadiers, Lifeguards and other troops. A 1,000-gun salute was fired from the city walls and the parade was watched by an estimated 100,000 people.[1] The meeting place of the three monarchs allied in defeating Napoleon, is commemorated today in Vienna's second district Leopoldstadt at Alliertenstrasse.

Vienna, which had a population of 250,000 at the time, swelled by 100,000 people. In addition to the monarchs, ministers, diplomats, their retinues and hangers-on, hosts of tradesmen, profit seekers, prostitutes and interested travellers all headed to Vienna. It has been described as the biggest ever gathering of monarchs and nobles in world history and attracted many an aristocratic parent trying to organise an appropriate marriage for their offspring. An exhausted Europe had suffered two decades of violence and privation, and the congress was set to chart a better future, although it was by no means clear how long this would take.

'Reasoned opinion predicted that all negotiations would be wrapped up in three or four weeks,' wrote David King, the author of the authoritative *Vienna 1814*. 'Even the most seasoned diplomats expected no more than six. But the delegates, thrilled by the prospects of a lasting peace, indulged in unrestrained celebrations. The Vienna peace conference soon morphed into a glittering vanity fair: masked balls, medieval style jousts, and grand formal banquets – a "sparkling chaos" that would light up the banks of the Danube.'[2]

The perception of diplomacy to this day involves dances, ballrooms and high society celebrations, images which all stem from the Vienna congress. 'You have come at the right moment. All Europe is here: and if you are fond of fêtes and balls you will have enough of them; the Congress does not move forward, it dances,' is how the great chronicler Charles-Joseph, 7th Prince de Ligne, famously described it.

The seemingly endless cycle of social events was recounted by Count Auguste de La Garde-Chambonas: 'The fêtes succeeded each other uninterruptedly; the time not given to pleasure was looked upon as wasted. Every week there was a grand reception and ball at the Court. Taking their cue from highest quarters, the foremost members of Austrian society also had their appointed days for welcoming in their drawing rooms the numberless strangers whom business or pleasure had brought to Vienna. On Mondays the Princesse de Metternich threw open her house; on Thursdays the Master of the Horse, the Prince de Trauttmansdorff, did the same, and on Saturdays the beautiful Comtesse Zichy followed suit. As a return for this gracious hospitality, the ambassadors and representatives of the great Powers on their side gave most brilliant entertainments. In virtue of this constant exchange of magnificent functions, the days went by without counting, and everybody appeared to have adopted the maxim – the first necessity of mankind is to be happy.'[3]

Vienna was the perfect host city of the time because of its standing as a musical centre of excellence (see Chapter 3). In addition, as the capital of a multinational empire with a cosmopolitan aristocracy, well connected across Europe, Vienna was well suited to accommodating and understanding the needs of the thousands of people drawn for the congress. English traveller John Morritt (1772–1843) reported the language skills of the Viennese: 'There is no town where languages are so much understood. Most people of fashion here understand four or five, and many more. Everybody speaks French and Italian amongst the tradesmen, even, and the higher ranks almost all speak English and perhaps Hungarian, Polish or Greek; for the Poles, Russians, Bohemians, and Carinthians, I believe, all speak different dialects of sclavonian [Slavic], a perfect distinct, and more ancient language than the German, I believe, and which, though I have heard that it is very difficult, certainly sounds far more soft and agreeable to the ear than that detestable gruntlng, for I cannot bring myself to bear German, and only wonder the language is not changed by agreement.'[4]

The allocation of accommodation was the immediate priority when the participants arrived in the city. Emperor Francis hosted crowned heads of state in the Hofburg, including Russian Tsar Alexander whose accommodation in the Amalienburg opposite the Swiss Gate is still known to this day as the 'Alexander Apartments'. The Kings of Prussia, Saxony, Bavaria, Württemberg and Denmark, as well as their retinues, were also accommodated in the Hofburg.

The British delegation initially took up residence in the Milchgasse, next to St Peter's Church, where Mozart once lived.[5] The apartment may have been well suited to Mozart, but it wasn't fitting for Foreign Secretary Castlereagh. He moved to new accommodation within weeks in Palais Dietrichstein-Ulfeld on the Minoritenplatz, adjacent to the chancellery of Metternich and the Hofburg. It is located on the square that today is home to the Austrian Foreign Ministry, Interior Ministry and State Archive. The same building housed the Spanish delegation, while the Sicilian delegation was based next door.[6]

The French delegation was accommodated just off Vienna's main street, Kärntnerstrasse, in the Questenberg-Kaunitz Palace on Johannesgasse. It was fitting for them to reside in the grand Palais Kaunitz, named after the Austrian diplomat and State Chancellor who had masterminded the Diplomatic Revolution of 1756, which brought France and Austria together as allies.

The Prussian head of delegation, Karl August von Hardenberg, took up an apartment on the Graben, while his assistant Wilhelm von Humbolt (after whom the Berlin Humbolt University is named) was nearby on the Bauernmarkt. Diplomats from smaller delegations, like Jacob Grimm (better known for his works as one of the Brothers Grimm) of the German state of Kurhessen, had to make do with lodging rooms and lesser accommodation.

The importance of delegations could be judged by whether they had a military honour guard posted outside the entrance to their accommodation. Participants in the congress were able to make use of a specially commissioned fleet of imperial liveried coaches. Examples can still be seen to this day at the Museum of Carriages and Department of Court Uniform at Schönbrunn Palace. On show are also the magnificent gold-braided court uniforms specially designed for the Congress of Vienna, which were worn by all imperial staff and servants.

It didn't take long for the inhabitants of Vienna to get the measure of the city's guests in a popular ditty of the day:

> Alexander of Russia: loves for all
> Frederick William of Prussia: thinks for all
> Frederick of Denmark: speaks for all
> Maximilian of Bavaria: drinks for all
> Frederick of Württemberg: eats for all
> Emperor Francis of Austria: pays for all[7]

From the start, the social side of the congress seemed as important, if not more important, than day-to-day diplomatic developments. Beginning with 'possibly the most spectacular party ever held',[8] the masked ball (or Redoute) in the Hofburg was attended by more than 10,000 guests, including Lulu, Countess von Thürheim: 'On the 2nd of October the Emperor hosted a monster masked ball in the Winter Riding School which had been decorated with ornaments and lights . . . offering a fairylike view into a sea of lights with beautiful bejewelled ladies and their flowers together with men in their gold braided uniforms.'[9]

Also at the ball was Friedrich von Schönholz: 'Every dais is draped in velvet, with red and gold the colours here, silver and blue beyond. A third, smaller, hall has been converted into an orange grove. There are canopies for the rulers and the mighty. Everywhere there are floating buffets with the most delicious refreshments, but everywhere, too, the most murderous crush, for your clever ticket collectors at the doors have resold the selfsame tickets immediately after, and at a handsome profit, too. Rumour has it that fully a quarter of the ten thousand silver spoons bearing the imperial crest, disappeared among the crowd.'[10]

The extravagance of the setting was matched by the culinary offering. Europe's leading chefs prepared a gigantic feast of 300 hams, 300 salted and 300 pickled ox-tongues, 300 capons, 300 poullards, 200 partridges, 200 pigeons, 150 pheasants, 60 hares, 40 rabbits, 20 large white turkeys and 12 wild boar. The bakery list included 650 cakes in 11 variations, 600 small brioche, 1,000 tarts and 2,500 smaller delicacies. The drinks list included 1,000 bottles of punch, 1,000 bottles of Hungarian Tokai, 3,000 bottles of Picolit dessert wine and thousands of other assorted wines. Nearly 6,000 candles were necessary for the evening.[11] The King of Württemburg, who according to the ditty famously ate for everybody at the congress, had such a 'monstrous paunch' a semicircle needed to be cut from his dining table so he could sit down to eat.

Food also played a less serious role at other social events, with top diplomats attending a dinner hosted by Talleyrand holding a best cheese competition. After the vote Talleyrand proclaimed that French Brie was the 'king of cheeses',[12] leading to subsequent quips that this was the only monarch that Talleyrand did not betray.

Concerts, balls and events at the Hofburg were to occur on a regular basis throughout the congress in 1814, establishing its reputation as a premier venue for diplomatic events for centuries to come. On 30 October, a special concert was conducted by Antonio Salieri, the court musical director. Best remembered unfairly by film fans as the bitter and inadequate rival of Mozart in the 1984 movie *Amadeus*, Salieri was in reality an accomplished conductor and composer. The 'monster concert' involved 100 pianists playing simultaneously, and it is recorded that the concert was more a statement of organisational rather than musical quality: 'In spite of the superior talent of the maestro directing it, was more like a huge display of strength and skill than a concert of good taste. This new surprise was nevertheless, such as might have been expected from a committee by the Court. To justify the confidence in it, it had ransacked its imagination for something unforeseen and unprecedented, something altogether out of the ordinary. It had succeeded to perfection.'[13]

The festival committee appointed by the emperor was said to be the hardest working part of the congress, organising one event after another. At its head was the trusted diplomat and former Foreign Minister Prince Ferdinand von Trauttmansdorff-Weinsberg (1749– 1827), who had been Lord Chamberlain since 1807. As master of ceremonies, he was in effective organisational control of the congress – and this control extended to overseeing one of the most developed spying operations seen ever, anywhere.

The Habsburg espionage service was already rated as one of the best in Europe, with a Secret Cabinet Chancellery (Geheime Kabinettskanzlei) based in the Stallburg imperial mews, an annexe of the Hofburg, and now home to the Lipizzaner horses of the Spanish Riding School. Its state-of-the-art Black Room operation was already expert at intercepting and opening wax-sealed communications, decoding and copying contents, and then resealing messages without any sign of tampering.

The Congress of Vienna presented a challenge to Chancellor Metternich and the police president, Baron Francis Hager von Allensteig of the Oberste Polizei- und Censurs Hofstelle, who wanted to know as much as possible about what was being said, by as many relevant people as possible. Located on Herrengasse,[14] the supreme police and censorship authority was based literally just round the corner from the Hofburg, not far from the present-day Austrian Interior Ministry.

From here, Baron Hager built a network of paid spies and informers who were to report on the comings and goings of persons of interest: who was meeting whom, conversations of note and any snippets of information about proceedings at the congress. Spies were recruited from all levels of society to give as complete a picture as possible; their reports would be filtered and daily reviews presented to Emperor Francis and Metternich. Raw intelligence was gathered as a full *rapporte* from a source, as an *interzept* of written communication or as a *chiffon*, literally a scrap of discarded communication in a bin or fireplace.

In high society there were a range of informants who attended the circuit of salons, dinners and entertainments with the visiting monarchs, their diplomats and delegation members. To this day many of their exact identities are still unknown, but their *rapporte* remain in the Austrian State Archive, complete with their secret code name. One, believed to be a senior aristocrat, reported a conversation with a senior French diplomat, who was inquiring about espionage at the congress. In his report to the head of the secret police, the anonymous informant put the Frenchman off the scent, claiming that the identity of the secret police chief was not widely known and that Baron Hager was not somebody who would be involved in espionage. More brazenly, he claimed that he had never heard of the Vienna secret police having spies in high society.[15]

The identity of other covert human intelligence sources has been established, including the Italian adventurer Chevalier Ludovico Freddi-Battilori, who had worked in the secretariat of the Papal Nunciature and spied on Spanish, Portuguese and Italians diplomats.

The German aristocrat Karl Christian, Count Benzel-Sternau, spied on the French, Bavarian and Württemberg delegations as well as his own aristocratic social circle. The Italian Giuseppe Carpani, who worked as a translator and musical biographer, and was a contemporary of Mozart, Gluck, Haydn, Salieri, Beethoven and Rossini, was also a prolific police source, signing his reports 'C-i' or 'Nota'. Herr von Neustädter, a civil servant from Hungary, ended his reports with the enigmatic symbol for infinity, '∞'. 'Herr H' was the poet and theatre critic Wilhelm Hebenstreit, who moved in high culture circles, allowing him to spy on members of the Prussian and Bavarian delegations. Further undercover informants are only recorded by their initials, including 'Count M', 'Count K', 'Herr von K', 'Herr von L', Herr von W', Herr von O' . . . the list goes on. All of these informants from higher society were rewarded financially and were on the payroll of Baron Hager.

There were many other Austrian sources, who provided information out of 'patriotic duty' or because they were encouraged to do so. Of particular importance were the locally hired servants and domestic staff employed by the embassies and delegations, as well as hoteliers and landlords.

It wasn't just the Austrians that ran espionage operations at the congress. The Russians collected information gathered by General Graf de Witt; Sir James Wylie, the Scots personal physician to the tsar; the Russian Princess Catherine Bagration, a major socialite who was the on–off mistress of Metternich; as well as the 'Graben nymphs', who plied their trade as prostitutes on the main Graben thoroughfare.[16]

With the widespread expectation that the congress would last no more than two months, the first weeks were absolutely packed with glittering balls, receptions, commemorative events, concerts, fêtes, parades, tournaments, hunts and excursions. The biggest celebration of the congress took place on 6 October, when between 18,000 and 20,000 members of the public attended the international peoples' festival in the Augarten, Vienna's oldest baroque gardens in the Leopoldstadt. The sovereigns watched from a specially constructed stage as 400 veterans of the Napoleonic Wars marched past behind a military band, before taking their place of honour at tables laden with food. A host of equestrian, acrobatic and martial shows entertained the guests, including a sharpshooting competition by Tyrolean marksmen, which was won by Andreas Hofer, the son of the venerated leader of the Alpine regions' resistance to Napoleon. The gardens were transformed, with a jousting enclosure and tiltyard, a Neptune grotto and copies of the Tsar Cannon monument in Moscow and Brandenburg Gate in Berlin. Performance groups from Bohemia, Lower Austria, Hungary and Tyrol, wearing brightly coloured regional dress, danced and sang folk songs. A hot-air balloon soared above the crowds and showered flags and crests of the states attending the congress. The festival ended with a firework display, and the public headed through streets specially lit with burning torches towards ballrooms in the city centre, while the sovereigns and nobility attended a ballet performance in the Kärntnertortheater. Star ballerina Emilia Bigottini wowed the audience at *Flore et Zéphire*, as she and other performers flew through the air on near invisible aerial lines.

On 10 October the tsar and Prussian king were taken by Archduke Karl for a battlefield visit to nearby Aspern on the northern side of the Danube, where he had famously commanded the victorious Austrian forces against Napoleon in 1809. After a joint dinner with their military retinues, they attended a performance of poetry and song at the Theater an der Wien by the German romantic author Ernst August Klingemann. Next day, the most important guests were treated to a performance of the comic opera *Jean de Paris* by François Adrien Boieldieu in the Schönbrunn Palace theatre. Two days later, the 124 guests were joined by the highest tier of Austrian nobility at the Hofball. Only those who were acceptable at court (*hoffähig*) were in attendance at the ball in the Ceremonial Hall of the Hofburg. A couple of days later, many in high society swapped their colourful ball gowns for the plain black and white of the chorus to sing the oratorio *Samson* by Handel. More than 700 mostly amateur choral singers and orchestral performers took part in the large-scale concert at the Riding School in the Hofburg.

On 18 October 1814, one year on from the decisive Battle of Leipzig, a grand celebration was held in the Prater park. Emperor Francis invited the 14,000-strong Vienna garrison, many of which had fought in the Battle of the Nations. They joined the congress guests in what was perhaps 'the first modern commemoration of war in history'.[17] Thousands of troops, both Austrian and from the other victorious powers, formed a massive square around a festive tent with pillars decorated with war trophies and Napoleonic military standards that fluttered in the wind. A draped altar with numerous candles stood in the tent above steps covered in red damask. The attending monarchs took part in the commemorative mass, which included cannon salvos, before reviewing a military march past. While the emperor and guests then ate in the Lusthaus, the summer house that still stands in the Prater, the soldiers enjoyed a lunch served on tables that ran the whole way from the Lusthaus to the Praterstern. They all received soup with dumplings, a pound of beef with sauce, three quarters of a pound of roast pork, three carp, three bread rolls and half a litre of wine. While they ate, grenadiers balanced their muskets in triangles, Cuirassiers and Ulans their armour and lances, while French weapons were arranged in displays of captured booty or holding up the handrails of pontoon bridges crossing the present-day Danube Canal. The prolific female Austrian historical novelist Caroline Pichler captured the positive feelings of those attending: 'Everything was lively, joyful, with high spirits and blissful hope for a better future.'[18]

Following the commemoration events in the Prater, Metternich held a 'peace party' for illustrious congress guests at his summer palais on the Rennweg, which is the current home of the Italian Embassy. Not to be outdone, the tsar hosted a celebration marking the last day of the Battle of Leipzig at the neoclassical palais of the wealthy Prince Andrey Razumovsky (1752–1836), ambassador to the Habsburg court and Russia's chief negotiator at the congress. Hundreds of guests attended the festivities in his opulent palace on the Landstrasse, lit by more than 6,000 candles. Only two months later, flames were to engulf the palace and burn a large part of it to the

114

ground, along with its valuable art collection. Church bells sounded the alarm as water pumps, troops and curious onlookers – from the emperor downwards – streamed towards the palace. Servants had little time to save much from the house, as its newfangled heating system, wax, oil and flammable tapestries helped the flames consume the interior of the building.

Two highlights at the end of November 1814 were the Carousel at the Hofburg and a gala concert conducted by Beethoven. The Carousel, held in the riding school, was an equestrian show featuring 24 knights dressed in the styles of the 16th and 17th centuries, with the addition of precious stones valued at more than 15 million gulden. The knights performed challenges such as lancing wooden rings, charging model heads of Turkish Saracens, and slicing apples in mid-air with their swords.

Beethoven's gala concert took place in the Redoute Wing of the Hofburg. It began with the composer's own *Wellington's Victory* or *The Battle Symphony*, celebrating the Battle of Vittoria, with stirring martial drums, trumpet fanfares, sounds of cannonades and recurring themes from *Rule, Britannia!* to *For He's a Jolly Good Fellow* and *God Save the King*. Next came the première of *The Glorious Moment*, specially composed for the congress by Beethoven, with four solo voices, a chorus of children, a mixed adult chorus and an orchestra. The role of Vienna was sung by a soprano soloist, a Prophetess by a mezzo-soprano, a Genius by a tenor and the Leader of the People by a bass:

*Chorus:*
Vienna!
Adorned with crowns,
favoured by gods,
city whose citizens serve monarchs, accept the greetings
of all peoples from all times
who may pass your way,
for now you are the queen of cities. Vienna! Vienna!
*Vienna:*

Within my walls shall
new times be established,
and all peoples will look on them with child-like trust
and loud rejoicing.

*All:*

Vindobona, hail and good fortune! World, your great moment![19]

The concert ended with a performance of Beethoven's recently composed Symphony No. 7 in A major, Opus 92. The symphony in four movements was regarded by Beethoven himself as one of his best compositions and dedicated it to the wounded troops of the Napoleonic conflict: 'We are moved by nothing but pure patriotism and the joyful sacrifice of our powers for those who have sacrificed so much for us.'[20]

Despite some criticism of the text of the *The Glorious Moment*, the concert was a massive hit and needed to be repeated twice, due to public demand. Contemporary reports draw particular attention to Beethoven himself, who by this time was largely deaf: 'As always all eyes were directed at the orchestra conductor Herr von Beethoven; every nuance of the notes seems to transfer into the muscles of his body. One estimates an audience of 1,500 in addition to the royal attendees and that Herr Beethoven earned 6,000 guilders in Viennese currency.'[21]

The outbreak of winter didn't hinder further socialising. In January 1815 a grand sledge party was organised with 34 large horse-drawn sledges setting off from the Hofburg towards Schönbrunn Palace accompanied by a brass band. Emperor Francis, who led the convoy, chose to be accompanied by the tsarina, followed by the tsar with the young widow Princess Maria Auersperg, then King Frederick VI Christian of Denmark with the Grand Duchess Maria of Weimar, then the King of Prussia and congress beauty Countess Julie Zichy. Lots were drawn to determine who would accompany whom in the following sledges. 'On this occasion there was a great display of *coquetterie et luxe*. The merry silver bells, the embroideries, the fringes, were all new, and glitteringly bright as the frost-bound snow. The cavaliers for the most part were beaux; les dames, without exception of course, *très-belles*, and all muffled up in ravishingly becoming velvets and furs,'[22] observed Count Otto Löwenstern.

*

The host of the Congress of Vienna was Emperor Francis (1768–1835) who was born in the then Habsburg-ruled city of Florence. He was the last of his kind amongst Europe's foremost royal family, reigning as the final Holy Roman Emperor from 1792 until 1806, and as the first Austrian Emperor from 1804 until 1835. The dissolution of the thousand-year-old Holy Roman Empire followed the crushing defeat by Napoleon at the Battle of Austerlitz and the Peace of Pressburg. As a consequence, Francis goes down in the annals of history as the one and only double emperor in history, including a two-year period when he was both at the same time, and is often titled Francis II (I). 'Good Emperor Francis', as he was known to his subjects, was affable, conscientious, unpretentious and virtuous, certainly by the standards of the day. Although a French speaker like the rest of the Austrian nobility, he preferred to speak Viennese German, which endeared him greatly to the inhabitants of the capital. He was described by the Swiss congress delegate Jean Gabriel Eynard as follows: 'The Austrian emperor has the most unprepossessing of figures. He looks decrepit and old, is small of stature, thin, round-shouldered, knock-kneed. His gala dress is ever the same: red trousers, white coat, black boots. In conversation he is bashfully shy. It is impossible to look less the sovereign and more the petty bourgeois than he does. The ruler is much beloved at court, and his praise is sung everywhere. His mien is indeed spiritual but shows no esprit.'[23] At the start of the congress he was 46 years old, although he seemed much older than the other great men of the period who were of a similar age, like Napoleon and Wellington. Francis had long and bony facial features with the prominent Habsburg jaw and white hair. He was of medium height and slim build as can be seen by his small uniform, which is on display in the Vienna Military History Museum.

Maria Ludovika of Austria-Este (1787–1816) was the cousin and third wife of Emperor Francis. Driven from her family home in Milan by Bonapartist forces, she was implacably opposed to Napoleon and became a leader of the war party in Vienna.[24] As chief hostess to the congress, she also played a significant role in the organisation of its social events, although her ill health became more serious, with tuberculosis claiming her life in 1816. She was only 28.

Russian Tsar Alexander (1777–1825) was 37 years old at the start of the congress and was for many as much a riddle as a powerful statesman who had done so much to defeat Napoleon. Raised in the Russian court as a French speaker, which was the norm for the age, he was also educated in English, which was very unusual at that time. Crowned after the regicide of his father, Alexander made early moves towards reform, including grand plans for a constitutional monarchy based on Enlightenment principles as well as significant changes to the state of the serfs. Neither of these reforms were realised. His early rule was dominated by the challenge from Napoleon, and he adopted foreign policy positions of neutrality, alliance and opposition to cope. The 1812 invasion of Russia by Napoleon was successfully repulsed by Alexander and the Russian winter. The tsar and his forces played a major part in the eventual defeat of Napoleon, including the Battle of Leipzig, and his troops occupied Paris in 1814 prior to the start of the Congress of Vienna. Alexander, who was a religious mystic, arrived in Vienna as the most powerful sovereign with a large standing army on Russia's western boundaries, having already made gains to his realm including Finland and the Caucasus, and he had his eye on further expansion in Poland.

It is noteworthy that many of Alexander's diplomatic team were not of Russian heritage. His Foreign Secretary, Count Karl Nesselrode, who couldn't even write or speak Russian, was a Baltic German like fellow Russian congress delegate and ambassador to Vienna Gustav-Ernst von Stackleberg. The multinational Russian delegation also included the German Freiherr Heinrich vom und zum Stein; the influential polish nobleman Prince Adam Czartoryski; Corsican Count Carlo Pozzo di Borgo; Corfiote Count Ioannis Kapodistrias, who would later become the first elected President of Greece; Swiss republican Frédéric-César de La Harpe; Alsatian Johann von Anstett; and the Scotsman Sir James Wylie.[25]

King Frederick Wilhelm III (1770–1840) led Prussia's delegation at the congress. He was crowned in 1797, meaning that the first half of his reign was dominated by the threat of Napoleonic France. Described as an 'apparition out of the armoury', his martial bearing included the Iron Cross decoration he introduced in 1813, famed since then as a symbol of German military bravery and of today's Bundeswehr. Frederick Wilhelm left the day-to-day diplomatic business to his chancellor and foreign minister, Karl August von Hardenberg, who was, however, outplayed by his Austrian opposite number, Prince Metternich.

Klemens von Metternich (1773–1859) was not just at the heart of the Congress of Vienna; he was at the centre of European affairs for the first half of the 19th century and the 'virtual inventor of modern diplomacy'.[26] The Austrian Foreign Minister from 1809, and State Chancellor from 1821, he was the effective chairman of the congress, and secured Austria's highest ever diplomatic standing with the 'Metternich System' of international diplomacy.

Given the title of prince for his services to Austria, Metternich was actually born into a minor noble family in the Rhineland of western Germany. The son of an imperial diplomat, he was educated in Strasbourg and Mainz and followed his father into the diplomatic service of the Holy Roman Empire. One of his first postings was to Dresden, where he met the publicist Friedrich Gentz, who would become his confidant, advisor and critic for the next 30 years. Metternich was appointed ambassador to Prussia and then to France, where he had extensive dealings with Napoleon and Foreign Minister Talleyrand. Aged 41 at the start of the congress, he was above average height, handsome, slim, with curly hair. Described as intelligent, suave, sophisticated and elegant, Metternich spoke better French than German, and had a confirmed reputation as a ladies' man.

Metternich was ably assisted throughout the congress by Friedrich von Gentz (1764–1832), who took to describing himself as its 'First Secretary'.[27] In many ways he was similar to the Foreign Minister: highly intelligent, well dressed, ambitious with impeccable manners, and his amours with women of the highest standing, were 'too numerous to record'.

Gentz was born in Silesia and educated in Königsberg in East Prussia under the philosopher Immanuel Kant, before becoming a Berlin-based writer and political polemicist. His essays and pamphlets were especially focused against the French Revolution, which led to both Britain and Austria supporting him financially. *The Origin and Principles of the American Revolution, compared with the Origin and Principles of the French Revolution* so impressed the US envoy to Berlin that he translated the book into English. Writing to Gentz, the US diplomat said: 'It cannot but afford a gratification to every American attached to the honor of his country to see his revolution so ably vindicated from the imputation of having originated, or been conducted upon the same principles as that of France, and I feel myself as an American citizen highly obliged to you for the consideration you have bestowed upon the subject, as well as for the honourable manner in which you have borne testimony to the purity of principle upon which the revolution was founded."[28] Twenty-five years later, Gentz's translator, John Quincy Adams, was elected as the sixth President of the United States of America.

Gentz also impressed the Austrian ambassador in Berlin, Johann Stadion, who helped secure him an introduction to Emperor Francis, the title Imperial Councillor and the beginnings of working life in Vienna. After Metternich took office as Foreign Minister, Gentz became Austria's 'unofficial propaganda minister'.[29] At the congress, he worked long hours, producing the drafts and documents for its key committees and participants.

Britain was represented at the Congress of Vienna by its Foreign Secretary, Robert Stewart, the 2nd Earl of Londonderry, better known as Lord Castlereagh (1769–1822). He was born in Dublin to a Northern Irish landowning family, whose Mount Stewart seat in

County Down is still home to a collection of delegates' chairs from the Congress of Vienna and the ornate table on which the Final Act was signed. During the congress, his brother Charles was British ambassador to Vienna, where he became the talk of the town for his loutish and drunken bad behaviour.

Stewart, who served in the Irish Parliament and then the House of Commons in London, played a significant role as Irish Secretary in resisting Irish self-determination and pushing through the 1801 Act of Union, which secured Westminster rule over Ireland. His parliamentary career blossomed with the cabinet office overseeing trade with the British colony of India, then as Minister of War and the Colonies and then in 1812 as Foreign Secretary. He was loathed in Regency Britain for his support of the bloody crackdown on reformists, which was immortalised by the poet Percy Bysshe Shelley: 'I met Murder on the way – / He had a mask like Castlereagh.' After a decade as Foreign Secretary, Stewart suffered a bout of mental illness and took his own life at the age of 53.

France was represented by the able but controversial Charles Maurice de Talleyrand-Périgord, who was aged 60 by the start of the congress. A great survivor, he had managed to serve in one senior political or diplomatic capacity or other for King Louis XVI, the French Revolutionary authorities, Napoleon, King Louis XVII and King Louis-Philippe. Marked since birth by a deformed foot and serious limp, his undoubted negotiating talents have made his name synonymous with deceitful, self-interested diplomacy. One recent reviewer described him as 'one of history's greatest, most repugnant, figures',[30] not for betraying every monarch and government he served, though he did, or his venality and corruption, which was monumental, but for his appalling personal relationships. As Metternich famously said: 'Men such as M. de Talleyrand are like sharp instruments, with which it is dangerous to play; but for great wounds great remedies are necessary, and he who has to treat them ought not to be afraid to use the instrument that cuts the best.'[31]

Arriving with a weak negotiating hand, Talleyrand brought a world-class support staff to wow the other delegates. These included the first internationally known celebrity chef and founder of the haute cuisine concept, Marie-Antoine Carême. Before departing Paris for Vienna, Talleyrand reportedly told King Louis XVIII: 'Sire, I need saucepans more than instructions. Let me do my work, and count on Carême.'[32] Talleyrand also took with him the peripatetic pianist and composer Sigismund Neukomm to play for his guests. Neukomm, who had been a pupil of Haydn, was born in Salzburg close to Mozart's birthplace, but in Vienna was considered a spy by Metternich, whose informers kept an eye on him.

Talleyrand also brought with him the renowned French painter Jean Baptiste Isabey. He painted the most famous group scene from the congress, which shows the main participants seated and standing in the same room, which in reality never occurred. The pen and ink with wash was commissioned by Talleyrand himself, and features the symbols of Truth, Prudence, Wisdom and Justice in the corners and the heads of rulers and arms of participating states in the border. Isabey, who was famed for painting Marie Antoinette and Napoleon, established an atelier in the Leopoldstadt and painted scores of portraits and miniatures on porcelain for the dignitaries. Another cultural ambassador brought with Talleyrand was the star dancer of the Paris opera, Emilia Bigottini. While the congress danced, its participants also were keen fans of dance performance, especially those by Bigottini at the two largest venues of the time: Kärntnertortheater and Theater an der Wien.[33] Centuries before 'cultural diplomacy' became a major priority or even properly understood, Talleyrand was pioneering the use of the arts, culture, cuisine and social events in diplomatic efforts.

In many ways the most interesting person at the congress was Charles-Joseph Lamoral, 7th Prince de Ligne (1735–1814), who famously said that 'the whole world is here'.[34] In his 80th year at the start of the congress, he was one of the great political and cultural characters of the preceding century (see Chapter 5). By the start of the congress he lived in genteel poverty in a rickety narrow house with one room per floor adjacent to the city wall on the Mölkerbastei, where he was visited by the great and the good, keen to hear from this leading light of the *ancien régime*. De Ligne was known for his legendary quips, even making one when he fell ill during December 1814, saying: 'Every kind of spectacle has been exhausted to amuse the Sovereigns; I shall furnish them with a new one – the funeral of a field Marshall.'[35] Days later he did just that, unintentionally underlining the congress as a break from the personalities and events of the previous century. His funeral service in the Schottenkirche (Scots Church), and the procession and funeral on the Kahlenberg hill overlooking Vienna, was indeed a huge spectacle, involving military pomp and ceremony. The funeral cortège from the city up into the Vienna woods to Prince de Ligne's summer house and burial plot included a riderless horse draped in black and a knight in black armour, symbolising chivalric princely values. It was the funeral of a passing age, at the exact spot from where the Siege of Vienna was broken with the cavalry charge of imperial forces from the Kahlenberg.

Another stand-out character at the congress was the British ambassador to Vienna, Charles Stewart, the 3rd Marquess of Londonderry (1778–1854) and half brother of Foreign Secretary Lord Castlereagh. Charles Stewart was an accomplished military man 'though decidedly maddish',[36] even in the estimation of his colleagues, and in no time he was 'regarded by the Congress as a wholly ridiculous figure'. A mixture of British imperial 'Flashman' derring-do matched with the social grace and diplomatic skills of Blackadder, Stewart bumbled from one diplomatic incident to another. He brought 40 dogs with him to Vienna for fox hunting, believing that Austrian hounds had to be inferior. He began his posting with a whirlwind of eccentricities and louche behaviour. After one drinking session he infamously picked a fight with a Vienna cab driver on one of the Danube bridges 'waving his arms like the sails of a windmill'.[37] He managed to punch the horse instead, before being flattened and beaten by the driver, who had no idea who he was. His appalling behaviour earned him a further beating after groping a young and beautiful countess during a crush on the grand staircase when leaving the theatre. She turned round in the crowded throng and belted him across the ears.

Stewart's diplomatic blunders included crass claims in public to a senior French diplomat that he had fought opposite him during the Napoleonic Wars, which was news to the Frenchman, who had never even been to Spain. All of these incidents were the talk of Vienna, regardless of rank or station, and are recorded in great detail by the contemporary chroniclers of the congress.

Within a few short months of partying at the British Embassy, more than 10,000 bottles of red wine had been consumed. Not only did Stewart pursue a string of affairs with the aristocratic ladies of Vienna, but his frequent brothel visits were trumped by turning his own embassy itself into a house of ill repute. Further incidents included riding drunk through the centre of town with his head (and that of his horse) garlanded with flowers, while the public stood and laughed.[38] It didn't take long for him to better known by the Viennese public as 'Lord Pumpernickel',[39] named after a comic character in a local box-office musical hit, or as the 'golden peacock'[40] because of his eccentric dress and overweening pride. In an age when it was normal to commonly wear many medals and orders, Stewart still managed to overdo even that and looked like 'a living book of heraldry'.[41] Ironically, none of this undermined his position as British ambassador, and he stayed on in Vienna until 1822. Long before that, however, he tried forlornly to sell his fox hounds, having realised that while hunting was extremely popular, fox hunting wasn't.[42]

*

Formal diplomacy and politics in 1814 was an exclusively male preserve. However, women were very involved in informal and highly influential ways: as unofficial advisors, hosts and communicators. According to the Austrian historian Hilde Spiel: 'Never before – or after – have a group of statesmen and politicians, assembled solely and exclusively to deal with matters of commonwealth interest, laboured so extensively under the influence of women.'[43] This was especially true given the informal nature of the congress, which never actually met in plenary, and where much of the interaction took place in what were notionally the social settings of salons hosted by women. Amongst the best attended was the Tuesday evening salon hosted by Fanny von Arnstein at her mansion on the Hoher Markt. Baroness von Arnstein, who was Jewish and 56 at the time of the congress, had a reputation for refined sociability and, notwithstanding widespread anti-Semitism, her house ranked 'amongst the first in Vienna'.[44] Her salons and other events involved up to 200 guests, including the leading ministers and diplomats from the participating nations but also less senior delegates with artistic interests, like the poet Friedrich von Schlegel, the budding writer Jacob Grimm and Carl Berthuch, who represented German publishers and book dealers. Her Christmas reception in 1814 involved the 'Berlin custom' of a Christmas tree: 'the first Christmas tree that Vienna had seen'.[45]

The most famous salons in Vienna were hosted by two women of the highest noble standing, who were at the heart of many intrigues, whispers and intelligence reports. They played leading unofficial roles in the congress as respected high society hostesses and also because of their romantic attachments with many of its top participants. Ironically, during the congress they both lived in opposite apartments at the top of the same baroque staircase in Palais Palm, close to the Hofburg, and both had romantic associations with Metternich.

Princess Wilhelmine Duchess von Sagan (1781–1829), the 'Cleopatra of Courland', was from a Baltic German noble family with lands in Bohemia and Silesia. Her regular salon in Vienna was attended by all of the key figures at the congress, including Metternich, her main lover. Sagan was described by those who knew her as having 'noble and regular features, a superb figure, and the bearing of a goddess', but even her lover Metternich was critical: 'She sins seven times a day and loves as often as others dine.'[46] He was followed by a dalliance with Tsar Alexander I and Austrian General Alfred I, Prince von Windisch-Graetz. The junior British diplomat Frederick Lamb, who would go on to become ambassador in Vienna, was followed by the then British ambassador Charles Stewart.

Princess Catherine Bagration (1783–1857) was a Russian aristocrat whose father had been minister in Naples. A young widow, she had been Metternich's lover before the congress and bore him a daughter, Marie-Clementine. Bagration was 'blonde with light blue eyes and pinkish white skin that one admirer compared to alabaster. Her scandalous evening gown, very low cut, earned her the nickname "the beautiful naked angel".'[47] The 31-year-old political salonnière and diplomatic figure in Vienna was the main lover of Russian Tsar Alexander I at the congress. Her affairs also included the Crown Prince of Württemberg, Saxon envoy Friederich von der Schulenberg and British ambassador and congress bad-boy Lord Charles Stewart.

Meanwhile Tsar Alexander paid close attention to the most attractive women in Viennese society: 'the coquettish beauty' Countess Caroline Széchenyi; 'the vulgar beauty' Sophie Zichy; 'the astonishing beauty' Princess Theresa Esterházy; 'the dazzling beauty' Countess Julie Zichy; 'the diabolical beauty' Countess Gabriele Saurau; and 'the virtuous beauty' Princess Gabrielle Auersperg.[48] The police reports sent to Emperor Francis and Metternich reveal the congress to be 'the most promiscuous in diplomatic history'.[49] According to Agent 'D': 'Russians lodged at the Burg, not content with keeping it in a filthy condition, are behaving very badly and constantly bringing in girls.'[50] One member of the Russian delegation used the classic sexist excuse that the bad behaviour was because of the 'unbelievable depravity of the female sex of the [Austrian] lower orders'. Intelligence reports detailed delegates who brought mistresses with them: Russian Prince Volonsky was visited in the Hofburg almost daily by his 19-year-old mistress dressed in disguise as a man, while Prussian delegate Prince Karl August von Hardenberg was reported to have with him a young actress from Paris named Jubille.

Excesses at the congress also included a roaring trade in bribery and corruption. Perhaps because he lived in a 'wretched little apartment' in the Seilergasse only a stone's throw from the Hofburg, Congress Secretary Friedrich von Gentz felt the need to accept financial inducements. In his diary he noted receipt of a *cadeau magnifique*'[51] of 24,000 florins in the name of the French king from Talleyrand, and that his finances were now looking up. Talleyrand himself had already enjoyed a highly profitable career, much of it questionable, including a significant profit share from the sale of Louisiana to the USA in 1803. In Vienna, he was well known to sell sensitive French national and military intelligence to the highest bidder.

With so much excess at the Congress of Vienna, largely at the cost of the host, Emperor Francis was heard to say, with tongue in cheek: 'If this goes on, I shall abdicate. I can't stand this life much longer.'[52]

The formal diplomacy at the congress ran largely through Metternich, who engineered progress with the different delegations and other power brokers. In a letter to his wife at the start of the congress he described the lobbying efforts of the key players: 'When I arrived in Vienna yesterday I found all Europe in my antechamber.'[53]

One of the first things to be settled was the common language for the congress, as reported by the Baltic German Count Otto Löwenstern: 'For the convenience of this réunion of nations, it has been found necessary to adopt a common language, and French is the chosen one, being the idiom most generally known – the only one, in fact, in which the English, the Russians, and the Poles can make them understood by the Germans. The ladies, too, declare that French is the language in which gallantry naturally expresses itself. Italian was at first, proposed, but for obvious reasons, its proposers were in a minority.'[54]

The settlement being negotiated aimed to restore a balance of power, which would secure relative peace for the next century but maintain a conservative order asserting the rights of autocratic monarchies.

The big winners against Napoleon all argued for their own interests, with Russia, Prussia and Austria all seeking territorial advantages. Britain wanted to restore the balance of power, secure independence of the Low Countries and protect its maritime interests. For many of the smaller actors, especially in Germany, it was about restoring their rule, riches and relevance. Meanwhile, France sought to emerge from its difficult position, as defeated aggressor, as the major European player it believed it should be, given its size and wealth.

In the course of the discussions, the main victors moved closer to their aims, with Russia eyeing control of Poland, Austria coveting northern Italy, and Prussia growing within Germany to include the Rhineland. For a while, however, the status of Saxony threatened to destabilise the search for peace: Prussia viewed the kingdom to its south as its right and prize; Russia feared Prussia becoming too strong; and Austria was concerned about losing this buffer state between its northern Bohemian lands and Prussia.

One of the most prominent experts on the congress, the former US Secretary of State Henry Kissinger, wrote his doctoral thesis at Harvard University on the negotiations. Subsequently published in 1954 as *A World Restored: Metternich, Castlereagh and the Problems of Peace 1812–1822*, his research identified five distinct phases in the Vienna negotiations: '(a) an initial period dealing with the essentially procedural problem of organising the Congress around the anti-French coalition; (b) an effort by Castlereagh to settle the outstanding problems, particularly the Polish-Saxon question, first by a personal appeal to the Tsar and then by attempting to rally the powers of Europe against him; (c) a complementary effort by Metternich to separate the Polish and Saxon problems and to create a combination of powers united by a consensus of historical claims; (d) the disintegration of the anti-French Coalition and Talleyrand's introduction into the Allied deliberations; (e) the negotiation of the final settlement.'[55]

While the title 'Congress' gives the impression of a large plenary format, with all the participants taking part, it actually functioned more through committees and working groups and official diplomatic events, although much of the business was conducted at the myriad of social functions – the salons, dinners and glittering balls.

Ten separate committees were established to deal with the business of the congress:

1. The German Committee
2. The Slave Trade Committee
3. Swiss Committee

4. Committee on Tuscany
5. Committee on Sardinia and Genoa
6. Committee on the Duchy of Bouillon
7. Committee on International Rivers
8. Committee on Diplomatic Precedence
9. Statistical Committee
10. Drafting Committee

In truth, the congress was directed by two separate bodies: the Council of Ministers, known as the 'Council of Four', and then the 'Council of Five' after the admission of Talleyrand for France. There were parallel meetings of sovereigns. The diplomats generally met during the mornings in the office of Metternich on the Ballhausplatz, while the allied sovereigns met every afternoon across the road in the Hofburg.

While Austrian Emperor Francis and Prussian King Frederick William were generally supportive of the diplomatic progress made in the morning, Tsar Alexander complicated proceedings as he 'regarded himself as his own sole plenipotentiary. In assuming this dual function of autocrat and negotiator he created a situation of extreme diplomatic complexity.'[56] A similar complexity would be repeated a century later when US President Woodrow Wilson acted both as a negotiator and head of state at the Paris Peace Conference in 1919.

Metternich and Castlereagh played key roles as master diplomats of the congress, agreeing to sufficient territorial concessions to Prussia and Russia, while not enough to ultimately threaten the restored balance of power. Although it's true that longer-term problems were built into the final agreement, especially the status of Poland under Russian rule and northern Italy under Austrian control, this wasn't of immediate concern to those at the congress. The growing influence of Prussia across the German lands and its potential dangers were also not yet apparent, given that the newly created German Confederation, under the chairmanship of Austria, had echoes of the weak Holy Roman Empire. This new set-up was crucially a confederation and not a federation, so its 39 states still had a say, while its new parliament in Frankfurt am Main was not strong. That left the future of Germany still largely to be determined by Prussia and Austria, a question that would only be finally answered in 1866.

The main territorial changes involved Russia receiving most of the Duchy of Warsaw and retaining Finland; Prussia taking over two thirds of Saxony; the Netherlands and present-day Belgium uniting in a monarchy; and Austria regaining Tyrol, Salzburg and the former Illyrian provinces, and receiving Lombardy-Venetia. In Italy, Habsburg princes resumed their control over Tuscany and Modena, the Papal States their historic territories and the King of Sardinia would rule over Piedmont, Nice, Savoy and Genoa. Hundreds of thousands of 'souls' were traded in the horse-trading at the 'conservative car boot sale that was the Congress of Vienna, which resulted in the denial of the Enlightenment and put most of the freedom won in the French and American revolutions on hold for a century'.[57]

Pretty much the only place that the Congress of Vienna forgot was Moresnet on the border between the new United Kingdom of the Netherlands and Prussia. Its 256 'souls' found themselves in a stateless no-man's land with a valuable zinc mine. 'Neutral Moresnet' was only 3.5 kilometres square, had three gin distilleries and was of particular interest for Esperantists who wanted to establish an Esperanto-speaking state called Amikejo (Place of Friendship) in the territory. One century after the Congress of Vienna, the Treaty of Versailles awarded Neutral Moresnet to Belgium, where it remains today as part of the country's German-speaking community.

The Congress of Vienna is best remembered for its Final Act, which restored peace, security and a conservative order. However, there were other important agreements reached, including support for the abolition of slavery, the neutrality of Switzerland, a boost to trade with the opening of river traffic on major European rivers and, importantly for the future of diplomatic relations, new regulations concerning the precedence of diplomatic envoys.

Next to the enduring neutrality of Switzerland, the changed rules on diplomatic relations have continued for the last 200 years and remain in place today. For the first time there was international agreement differentiating the importance of three categories of diplomats: full ambassadors, legates or nuncios; envoys or ministers who were accredited to heads of state; and, lastly, *chargés d'affaires*, who were accredited to the minister of foreign affairs. The rules agreed in Vienna ranked the members of the diplomatic corps by the date of their notified arrival. Centuries of sharp elbows, slights and bruised egos – about who was a more important diplomat than another, as shown by their order of precedence in a line-up, a procession or an official event – was all supposed to end. It would now be managed painlessly by the length of service at that foreign court and effective ceremonial equality. Custom and practice had previously afforded highest ranking to papal nuncios, and then representatives of the emperor of the Holy Roman Emperor, but even that was becoming outdated, especially with Protestant and republican courts. In Vienna, there was the additional problem that, owing to the Habsburg line of Spanish monarchs, the ambassador of Spain was always ranked higher than that of France, which literally caused centuries of ill feeling. A particular article of the new regulations disallowed any variance from the rules because of dynastic relations or family arrangements.

The Final Act included a declaration of the powers on the abolition of the slave trade, which upheld 'the principles of humanity and universal morality' as the basis for ending the trade. The slave trade was 'odious in its continuance' and the declaration called for its 'prompt suppression',[58] something that would still take some time to fully deliver. Meanwhile, free trade was to be boosted on the continent as the Final Act also included articles for the free navigation of the rivers Rhine, Necker, Mayne, Moselle, Meuse and the Scheldt.

Looking back at the conclusions of the congress, its secretary Friedrich von Gentz wrote: 'Never have the expectations of the general public been as excited as they were before the opening of this solemn assembly.' However, even he could see the extent to which it didn't deliver on more ambitious hopes: 'People were confident of a general reform of the political system of Europe, of a guarantee of eternal peace, even of the return of the golden age. Yet it produced only restitutions decided beforehand by force of arms, arrangements between the great powers unfavourable to the future balance and the maintenance of peace in Europe, and some quite arbitrary rear-rangements in the possessions of the lesser states, but not one act of a more elevated character, not one great measure of public order or security which might compensate humanity for any part of its long sufferings or reassure it as to the future.'[59]

While the congress was still meeting, Napoleon escaped from his exile on the island of Elba and began his return to Paris. The major powers, which were all in Vienna, declared him an outlaw and they committed to deploy 150,000 men each to end his comeback attempt.

Napoleon sought not just to regain power but also his Austrian wife, Marie Louise, and their son, who were living in Schönbrunn Palace. Writing to his father-in-law, Emperor Francis, he tried to rekindle relations with the Austrian court: 'My sole aim will be to consolidate the throne . . . so that I may leave it one day, standing upon unshakeable foundations, to the child whom your majesty has surrounded with paternal kindness. A durable peace being an essential necessity for this deeply desired end, nothing is nearer to my heart than the wish to maintain it with all the Powers, but above all with your Majesty. I hope that the Empress will come by way of Strasbourg, orders having been given for her reception on this route in my realm. I know your Majesty's principles too well not to feel confidence that you will be most eager, what-ever the trend of your policy may be, to do everything possible to accelerate the reunion of a wife with her husband, a son with his father.'[60]

Francis ignored the attempts at rapprochement, and Marie Louise had no desire to return to her husband. Napoleon despatched under-cover emissaries to Vienna, one of whom made it to the Austrian capital under the cover alias of an abbé using a passport from the Papal States. Comte Casimir de Montrond made contact with Talleyrand, Metternich, Nesselrode and other senior diplomats in Vienna, none of whom signalled any willingness to reach an understanding with Napoleon. Claiming to be a keen horticulturalist, Montrond gained entrance to Schönbrunn Palace gardens in the hope of getting close to Marie Louise, handing over letters from Paris and suggesting a plan to spirit her and her son back to France. Through an intermediary, it became clear that she had no desire to return to Napoleon: his letter had been burned.[61]

The Final Act of the congress was signed nine days before the final defeat of Napoleon at Waterloo on 18 June 1815. In what would mark the end of the Napoleonic Wars, the French army was defeated by the two armies commanded by the Duke of Wellington and Gebhard Leberecht von Blücher, Prince of Wahlstatt. The battle took place in present-day Belgium near Waterloo, and Napoleon hoped he would defeat the British-led allied army, which included Dutch and German forces, before turning to the Prussian army. This would buy him some time to recover before taking on the other major forces of the Seventh Coalition, with major Russian and Austrian armies heading towards France.

Napoleon had just 75,000 men at his disposal, while Wellington had 68,000 and Blücher 50,000. With repeated French infantry and cavalry attacks coming to a standstill, the arrival of the Prussian forces during the afternoon tilted the course of the battle. By the evening Napoleon gambled on a final attack by his elite Imperial Guard, which was beaten back, while the Prussians broke through on the right flank and the British-led forces counter-attacked in the centre.[62] Wellington later described the victory as 'the nearest-run thing you ever saw in your life'.[63] The defeat led to the abdication of Napoleon four days later and coalition forces occupying Paris. Napoleon was exiled to the island of St Helena in the south Atlantic, where he died in 1821, and the French First Empire came to an end. Now peace was to be restored to Europe on the basis of the Congress of Vienna.

'The congress established peace – a genuine peace that lasted much longer than any of the delegates would have imagined. Indeed, despite many of the tensions and hatreds that would long simmer in the age of nationalism and would result in numerous riots, rebellions, and civil wars, it is significant that no conflict would actually explode and drag all the Great Powers to war for a full one hundred years ... The Congress of Vienna would, indeed foster a spirit of cooperation that, in some ways, has still not been surpassed. No other peace conference in history can claim such a success.'[64]

# 6

# *The Concert of Europe:*
# *The Age of Metternich*

'The events which can not be prevented, must be
directed.'

– Klemens von Metternich

From the end of the Congress of Vienna in 1815 until the revolutions that rocked the continent in 1848, the figure of Klemens von Metternich plays an oversized role in both domestic Austrian and international European affairs. Relations between states were said to operate as part of the Metternich System (the Concert of Europe), while the era of his rule in Austria as chancellor has been dubbed the 'Age of Metternich'.[1] The importance of Austria and Metternich was acknowledged even by its sternest critics: 'Austria is no doubt, indebted to Metternich and his stratagems for its aggrandisement and its geographical arrondissement. Venice, Milan, and, above all, the Tyrol, Salzburg, and the territory which he prevailed on Bavaria in the most specious terms, to return, are important acquisitions. This empire constitutes now a compact body of kingdoms and provinces, with more than 30 million inhabitants, and a considerable sea-coast; – a monarchy which, if its interests were properly understood and managed might prove a match against the most powerful on the continent of Europe.'[2]

Immediately following the congress, the focus for Metternich remained international affairs and his role in them as mediator. 'It is impossible to converse with Prince Metternich and not see that his great ambition is to place himself at the head of politics of the

Continent,' is how he was characterised by the British ambassador to Vienna Henry Wellesley, First Lord Cowley. 'He considers himself, and wishes to be considered by others, as the champion of old systems, and the great opposer of innovation throughout Europe. He prides himself upon his dexterity in having got complete possession of the Emperor of Russia and the King of Prussia; and the Ministers of those Sovereigns, as well as the French Ambassador at this Court, are devoted to his politics, and to him personally.'[3]

Unity of purpose and action was Metternich's aim for the great powers, which convened in 1818 at the Congress of Aix-la-Chapelle (Aachen). The diplomatic summit formed an early part of the Concert of Europe, which would see conferences held over the next decades. At Aachen, representatives from the allied powers of Austria, Prussia, Russia and Britain met with France to arrange the withdrawal of troops from occupied France, finalise reparations and marked the full return of France as a European power.

The opening session on 1 October 1818 was attended by Emperor Francis I and Prince Metternich for Austria, Alexander I and counts Capo d'Istria and Nesselrode for Russia, King Frederick William III and Prince Hardenberg for Prussia, lords Castlereagh and Wellington for Britain and Duke de Richelieu for France. Outstanding arrangements for French reparations totalling 700 million francs were concluded and the occupation of France formally ended, with troops being withdrawn by 30 November.

The rehabilitation of France meant that the Concert of four now involved five powers, although the four that had defeated Napoleon secretly reaffirmed the Quadruple Alliance just in case. A proposal from Tsar Alexander for an entirely new alliance to protect the sovereignty and governing authorities of the signatories to the Vienna treaties, including the creation of a European army, with Russian forces at its heart, was rejected.

There followed a series of further congresses as part of the Metternich System, which aimed at maintaining the balance of power in Europe: the Congress of Troppau (1820), the Congress of Laibach (1821), the Congress of Verona (1822) and the Congress of London (1830).

The Congress of Troppau (present-day Opava) in Austrian Silesia and the Congress of Laibach (Ljubljana) in Austrian Carniola were primarily focused on cracking down on liberal movements in the Italian Kingdom of the Two Sicilies, while the Congress of Verona discussed revolution in Spain, and the Congress of London concentrated on the separation of Belgium from the Netherlands.

The 1820s saw particular challenges to the congress system, with revolutionary unrest in Spain, Portugal, Italy and Greece: there were demands for constitutional monarchies in the west and Greek independence from the Ottoman Empire in the east. The congress system mobilised troops to suppress revolutionary developments in Spain and Italy, and Metternich and Britain tried to protect stability by urging Russia not to side with the Greeks.

During this time Metternich also exercised his considerable authority within the German Confederation to restrict liberal forces. Created during the Congress of Vienna, the confederation brought together 39 states that had formerly been part of the Holy Roman Empire, with Austria and Prussia being the two most powerful members. In 1819 the Federal Convention (Bundesversammlung) of the confederation agreed to the Karlsbad Decrees, which had been initiated by Metternich at a meeting in the Bohemian spa town Karlsbad (Karlovy Vary). The decrees marked a crackdown on liberal and German nationalist activism, especially by student fraternities (*Burschenschaften*) and reform-minded academics, and also laid down harsh rules of press censorship. It marked the beginning of the repressive domestic reactionary political rule that Metternich would take forward as State Chancellor, which he became in 1821, in addition to remaining Foreign Minister. His effectiveness was the subject of much comment: 'The manner in which Metternich carries his measures into effect is certainly unique. To a perfect knowledge of all the leading characters with whom he has to deal, he unites an acuteness in selecting his instruments, not less astonishing. He has indeed collected a living gallery of Metternichians. His ambassadors are a sufficient proof of this fact. Like an immense spider, he has woven his net over the whole of Europe; has his spies in every capital . . .

thus wielding or rather resisting the destinies of Europe more than any other person. As a diplomatist and as a political intriguer, we may be allowed to say, he stands unrivalled; but there his power ends.'[4]

This assessment by the exiled Austrian Carl Anton Postl, who adopted the pen name Charles Sealsfield, acknowledges Metternich's impact but also hints at its limits. Another contemporary at close proximity to Metternich was the British ambassador to Vienna Henry Wellesley, who also wrote about the Austrian chancellor's early record: ' . . . He has been eminently successful. For by his counsels and vigorous measures, aided by the other German States, he not only put a stop to the efforts of the Propagandists in Germany, but by his promptitude and energy the timely employment of the Austrian forces in the Pope's dominions, put an end to the disturbance which had broken out there, and thereby prevented a revolutionary war in Italy which, had it broken out, would probably have spread itself over the whole of the Continent. If, therefore, Italy and Germany are at present in the enjoyment of peace, it is principle to be attributed to the wisdom, vigilance, and energy of the Austrian Cabinet.'[5]

The Metternich era is as known for its domestic repression as its international diplomatic successes: 'The greatest period of the Austrian secret police began after the Congress of Vienna. For more than three decades, Prince Metternich ruled with external isolation and internal repression, including censorship, snooping and arbitrary policing which all played a decisive role, especially in psychological terms, spreading the feeling of fear and powerlessness.'[6] The scale of state snooping was extremely significant, and even if some contemporary accounts are exaggerated, it felt pervasive: 'Since the year 1811 ten thousand "Naderer" or secret policemen are at work. They are recruited from the lower classes of the merchants, of domestic servants, of workers, nay even of prostitutes, and they form a coalition which traverses the entire Viennese society as the red silk thread runs through the rope of the English navy. You can scarcely pronounce a word at Vienna which would escape them. You have no defence against them and if you take even your own servants, they become within fourteen days, even against their own will, your traitors.'[7]

In addition to the snooping culture, the police followed international visitors to see who they might meet and tampered with mail, especially if it was destined for international delivery: 'On one occasion a certain English ambassador, who was something of a wag, aware that all his letters passed through the *cabinet noir*, conceived the idea of making a very slight alteration to his seal. The change passed unobserved, and his letters continued to reach their destination bearing the old seal. Encountering M. De Metternich at a reception one day, he said to him carelessly, "Oh, by the way, prince, you might mention to your people that we have altered our seal at the Embassy; they seem not to have noticed it." "Dunces!" muttered the Prince between his teeth, and marched off without a word.'[8]

One of the first US diplomatic representatives in Vienna wrote about the psychological impact of Metternich's police repression: 'The great object, however, of the system of espionage is not so much the information the spies are enabled to collect, which is generally not worth the cost of collection, but it is to keep down public opinion – to exercise a terrorism over the people, and thus effectively stifle the utterance of any liberal and consequently deemed injurious sentiments.'[9]

*

With the receding threat of further conflict after the Congress of Vienna, the physical and cultural face of Vienna began to see substantial changes. Trees were planted along the top of the bastions surrounding the city, making them a favoured place for citizens to promenade, as was the 'glacis', the open area between the walls and the suburbs beyond, including the new Volksgarten in 1823. A new city gate was constructed adjacent to the Hofburg, where Napoleonic forces had blown up a section of the city wall in 1809. The Neue Äussere Burgtor, which was opened in 1824, is the last of Vienna's city gates to remain standing.

The 1820s saw the rebuilding of the Theater an der Josefstadt, a new synagogue, the establishment of the now world-famous piano manufacturing company Bösendorfer, and the arrival of the first giraffe at Schönbrunn Zoo, a gift from the Egyptian royal family.

The Vienna era during the rule of Prince Metternich is also described by the term 'Biedermeier', a cultural period that affected the arts, music, design and style. During the decades of stability under Metternich, social factors such as industrialisation and the growth of the middle class and urban life impacted on particular trends in the arts. In a period of censorship, artists and middle-class consumers stayed on safe ground with a focus on home and family, and non-political or uncontroversial themes. The Biedermeier era – so-called after the pseudonym of a poet whose verses parodied the petit-bourgeois people of the times – describes the cultural period across much of the German-speaking and Habsburg world, but it has a particular resonance in Vienna. Many leading artists during the Biedermeier period lived in the capital and the subsequent particular creative movements developed in the city from them.

These included the emerging cultural greats like the dramatist Franz Grillparzer (1791–1872), with his first play *Die Ahnfrau* ('The Ancestress') premiering in the Theatre an der Wien in 1817; Johann Nestroy (1801–1862), the gifted singer, actor and playwright, first performing at the Theater an der Kärntnertor in 1822; and the actor and dramatist Ferdinand Raimund (1790–1836) whose first play was performed in 1823.

In literature, the Vienna author Adalbert Stifter (1805–1868) and poet Friedrich Hall (1806–1871) reflect the Biedermeier era. In the visual arts, which focused on themes like simple home life and *Gemütlichkeit* (meaning a sense of cosiness, similar to Danish *hygge*), the leading Vienna exponents included Ferdinand Georg Waldmüller (1793–1865), Moritz von Schwind (1804–1871), Friedrich Gauermann (1807–1862), Josef Kriehuber (1800–1876), Peter Fendi (1796–1842) and Joseph Anton Koch (1768–1839). Many of their works are featured today in Vienna's Belvedere Palace Museum.

The Biedermeier period also corresponds with the emergence of the two great romantic composers who popularised the waltz, which subsequently became synonymous with Vienna: Johann Strauss (1804–1849) and Joseph Lanner (1801–1843). Strauss (the elder) is best known for his *Radetzky March* and beginning the famous Strauss dynasty. Lanner, who was just as famous as Strauss in their heyday, was also known for his reworking of peasant waltzes and melodies into what would become the leading music and dance craze of the 19th century: 'Woe be to him who does not waltz, for tho' there is a blaze of beauty and the balls are quite lovely to look at once or twice, yet no girl will speak to a man who does not dance, and [the men say] very little to those who do. They dance uninterruptedly, and O what an exhibition it is. En attendent, strangers are stared at and, if not highly bred, quiz'd.'[10]

The early Biedermeier period also saw the passing of cultural greats better known from preceding decades, including Anton Salieri in 1824, Beethoven in 1827 and Franz Schubert in 1828. Salieri, who had been court composer and Kapellmeister of the imperial chapel, composed scores of operas and sacred works, as well as chamber music. A student of Christoph Willibald Gluck, teacher of Beethoven, Schubert and Liszt, he is sadly best remembered for his overdramatised rivalry with Mozart. Beethoven's death in 1827 followed three decades of severe hearing loss, which makes his later musical works all the more remarkable. Over 45 years he composed more than 722 works, across all forms of classical music. Contemporary reports describe a huge attendance at his funeral, which included an oration written by Franz Grillparzer. Just over one year later, Schubert died aged only 31, having already composed hundreds of *lieder* as well as a range of symphonies and other compositions, many of which were only discovered and performed after his death. All three were originally interred in suburban graveyards, but their remains were reburied next to fellow notables in the Central Cemetery (Zentralfriedhof) in the 1870s, which has since become one of the largest burial grounds in the world.

Vienna remained a key international cultural capital throughout the middle of the 19th century. The virtuoso pianist and composer

Franz Liszt (1811–1866), who composed the Hungarian coronation ceremony for Francis Joseph in 1867, received his musical education in Vienna in the 1820s from, amongst others, Salieri, and he met both Beethoven and Schubert. The Polish virtuoso pianist and composer Frédéric Chopin (1810–1849) was also in Vienna in the 1820s, as was the great violinist Niccolò Paganini (1782–1840), who gave 14 concerts in the Redoutensaal, setting off a veritable 'Paganini mania' with Viennese fans wearing Paganini hats and Paganini gloves, while the emperor granted him the title Imperial Chamber Virtuoso. According to a Vienna correspondent in the *Literary Gazette*: 'The great novelty and prodigy of the day is one M. Paganini . . . he is, without contradiction, not only the finest player on the violin, but no other performer, upon what instrument soever, can be styled his equal.'[11] Schubert, who gave his first and only concert in the hall of the Musikverein three days before Paganini, paid to see him twice.

Felix Mendelssohn (1809–1847) was in Vienna in the 1830s, while Giuseppe Verdi (1813–1901) conducted his *Nabucco* in 1843 and famous *Requiem* much later in 1875. The French romantic composer Hector Berlioz (1803–1869) wrote about his visits to Vienna in 1845 and 1846, when he followed in the footsteps of musical greats such as Beethoven: 'My knees were trembling when for the first time I stepped onto the stage on which his mighty feet once trod . . . The rostrum I was using had been his. This was the space occupied by the piano on which he used to improvise. The stairs here leading to the artist's room were the same he would go down after the performance of his immortal poems, when a few perceptive enthusiasts took pleasure in calling him back with their rapturous applause, to the great astonishment of the other listeners . . . '

Berlioz was impressed during his Vienna stay by the continuing high standard of musical performances in the city. In a letter of appreciation to the Gesellschaft der Musikfreunde (Society of Music-Lovers) he wrote that 'the wealth of vocal and instrumental talent that Vienna possesses . . . is enough to guarantee Vienna the musical supremacy over all the capitals of Europe'.[12]

In addition to conducting in Vienna and attending concerts,

another highlight of Berlioz's stay were the balls organised by Strauss in the Redoutensaal: 'The Viennese youth indulges there its sincere and touching passion for dancing, and this has led the Austrians to turn ballroom dancing into a genuine art . . . I have spent entire nights watching these thousands of incomparable dancers whirling around . . . Strauss is there in person, directing his fine orchestra . . . He is a true artist. The influence he has already exerted on the musical taste of the whole of Europe is not sufficiently appreciated.'[13]

The Vienna of Metternich's time was the subject of intense and vivid description by the accomplished Irish correspondent Martha Wilmot (1775–1873), who lived in the city from 1819 until 1829 while her husband, William Bradford, served as the chaplain to the British Embassy. In letters to her relatives and friends in Ireland and England she described life in the cosmopolitan city, including the much-feared police surveillance people were subject to: 'I suppose we never cough, sneeze, nor turn a child into the nursery to blow its nose without the events being reported to the Government!'[14]

With Vienna still squeezed into its ancient city walls, Wilmot was particularly struck by the number of people of all classes living cheek by jowl in the same multistoreyed buildings. In a letter to her sister Alice on 23 May 1820 she described the cramped conditions: 'Vienna is like a rabbit warren above ground, and that from the cellar to the garret, which includes 7 or 8 storeys, it is inhabited till every hole and corner is full, and that at an expense which was considerable always, but is this year increased. Well then, the shoe black and his Frow (wife) issue from the seller, the Hunter and stable men from the level of the street, the gentlemen and strangers from the first floor, the Princes of the Land from the second and third, the lovers of pure air and cheap lodgings from the fourth – Milliners and their train from the fifth – the Studious and sentimental from the sixth – and (ever the Muses) the poor starving poets from the seventh and eighth ! and these different classes meet to enjoy the same amusement in the same place, all nearly dress'd alike, for I do not exaggerate in saying that my kitchen maid sports eleven flounces of worked muslin at the bottom of her petticoat, and a gold cap on her head.'[15]

The amusement that Wilmot draws particular attention to is the Prater public park in the second Vienna district of Leopoldstadt. In the 19th century it was the place to go just outside the city walls to see and be seen: 'There we get out and walk about the lovely grounds which belong to that singular place, which is at once an exquisite retirement and the resort of all that is smart and fashionable in Vienna, for the grounds are so extensive that deer run wild in one part and there are walks without end in different directions under the shade of trees, and in another part hundreds or I believe thousands of carriages assemble as they do in Hyde Park, fill'd with beauty and rank, smart equipages and the most elegant style of dress. The evening, that is from five to seven o'clock, when all good Germans have eaten and drunken to their hearts' content, and their stomachs' surprise, is the fashionable time for repairing to this strife of vanity and display; from the Emperor down to the jew pedlar and the bearded Turk everybody assembles there and 'tis the most amusing sight that a stranger can possibly witness – 'tis a complete turn out of the town.'

With her husband attached to the British Embassy, Wilmot found herself at a number of court events of particular note, including the Maundy ceremony conducted by the imperial family:

A most curious ceremony which we saw just before Easter, which was the Emperor and Empress washing the feet of 12 old men and 12 old women, in imitation of our Saviour's acts to his disciples . . . The Ladies in Waiting took from the hands of the servants large dishes of meat, which they presented in succession to the Empress, and she with her own hands placed them on the table before the old women who eat most earnestly, and drank the same. This lasted a considerable timbering which the Empress stood, helping some with her own hands, removing dishes, replacing them by others, and in good earnest doing the service of the table. When their dinner and dessert were ended, the tables were removed, the grande Maitress tied a cambric apron around the Empresses waist, the Grande Maitre presented the Golden Ewer and Basin of water and a towel, she took the towel, kneeled down, and bone side washed and wiped the feet of each old woman (no doubt they had been well scrubbed beforehand), after which the Grande Maitresse took off the apron, and presented 12 little bags of money with long strings, one of which she placed with unaffected good nature and good humour round each of their necks, allowing each to kiss her hand, patting the forehead of the oldest and most infirm, and seeming personally acquainted with all.[16]

In 1825, efforts were being made by Metternich to improve relations with the powerful Hungarian magnates, with the calling of the Hungarian Diet and coronation of Emperor Francis' fourth wife, Caroline Augusta, on subsequent days in Pressburg/Pozsony (now Bratislava). Wilmot's husband attended the grand procession and opening of the Diet with the young embassy attaché Viscount Charles Ingestre, who would die tragically in a bizarre riding accident in the Prater only a few months later. The emperor addressed the Diet members from the throne in Latin, which was still in common use then in Hungary, and the ceremony was followed by great celebrations.

Next day, Martha joined her husband at the coronation in St Martin's Cathedral: 'So now fancy the flourish of trumpets, the magnificent Hungarian guard with their Huzar uniform more splendid than I can describe. Leopard skins hanging over one shoulder, fasten'd by chains of gold, and a clasp of precious stones. Then the Bishops, then Prince Metternich, head of the Civil, and Field Marshall Gelhard, head of the Military departments, the former in Hungarian costume quite resplendent, and amongst other things a diamond feather in his cap . . . after them came the Emperor as King of Hungary dress'd in the crown and robe of St Stephen, not the martyr of that name, but the 1st King of Hungary. The crown is a small snug-looking one, the robe old and ragged, but the Emperor look'd very stern and kingly in it. At each side of him walked a Bishop with high mitres on their heads, then came the Queen dress'd in an Hungarian costume of rich white tissue of silver embroidered. On her head was a crown, richly ornamented with diamonds of great value.'[17]

While the coronation clearly captured the imagination of Wilmot, the obvious highlight of her decade in Vienna was an 1826 fancy dress ball organised by the British ambassador Henry Wellesley to mark the end of that year's carnival season. No ordinary ball, it involved Austrian high nobility, diplomatic staff and their children dressing up in themed costumes from popular romantic literature of the time, most notably Sir Walter Scott. The event was of such international note that a special commemorative book was published in London, featuring a full running order of all costumed participants, and coloured plates of the leading characters: 'The grandeur of the whole, the high rank of the co-operating persons, the assemblage of the flower of the highest nobility, of female beauty, and noble manly forms, the brilliant weapons and armour, the succession of characters of the East and West, of history and romance – all served to heighten the impression of this extraordinary fête, which can never be erased from the memory of those who had the good fortune to be present. Thus terminated at Vienna the Carnival of 1826, with an exhibition, which eclipsed all of the kind that have gone before, and will scarcely be equalled by any that shall succeed it – an exhibition, splendid and noble as the place and the persons by and for whom it was instituted, and which affords a new proof, if more were wanting, of the taste and wealth of the Austrian nobility.'[18]

\*

A curious fascination following the defeat of Napoleon and the Congress of Vienna was that his son and heir was living in Vienna as part of the imperial family, his mother being Napoleon's wife, Marie Louise of Austria, the daughter of Emperor Francis. Napoleon François Joseph Charles Bonaparte (1811–1832) was born in the

Tuileries Palace in Paris in 1811 as the Prince Imperial and given the title of King of Rome as the heir apparent. When Napoleon was defeated in 1814, Marie Louise and her young son left France and returned to Austria; within days Napoleon abdicated in favour of his three-year-old son, who became Napoleon II for just two days before his father fully renounced all rights to the throne, including his descendants. This did not reduce the fears amongst some that he was the legitimate heir for Bonapartists, who might seek to restore him to the French throne.[19]

Before their departure for Vienna, Napoleon senior said: 'As far as I am concerned I would rather that my son was strangled than see him brought up as an Austrian prince in Vienna.'[20] The latter, however, is exactly what happened, with Franz (as he became known) being tutored as a German speaker, granted the suitably Austrian-sounding title Duke of Reichstadt by his grandfather Emperor Francis and raised as most young Habsburgs: with a view towards military service. All the while he was the object of fascination for both the Viennese and visitors alike, who wanted to see the young Napoleon, or 'Eaglet' (L'Aiglon), in person.

Nearly six feet tall by the time he was 17, he made a striking impression in his white Austrian uniform, but he was still a source of concern for both Metternich and Emperor Francis. He rebuffed efforts to use him for leverage with France, and refused requests to serve with the military far removed from Vienna. This led to a growing estrangement from his mother and his Austrian family, who he felt were controlling him and using him as an object to reduce the risk of embarrassment or international political intrigue.

His understandable interest in his father was finally assuaged following a chance meeting at a British Embassy ball in January 1831 with Marshal Auguste Marmont, who had previously served as aide-de-camp to Napoleon senior before becoming one of his senior military commanders. Marmont spent considerable time with the young Napoleon at the Hofburg, meeting no less than 17 times to go through the rise of the French emperor and his military campaigns, with the help of maps spread out on long tables. 'Metternich had hoped that contact with Marmont would leave the Prince with an unfavourable picture of France and discourage him in his ambition of sometime ascending the French throne. But in this he had over calculated. Far from quieting the Duke's inner excitement, it brought the [French] Imperial epic to life within him with a vividness it had never had before.'[21]

Who knows what might have become of the young Bonaparte-Habsburg, as his ill health overtook the situation. 'My birth and my death – that's the whole of my story,' is how he reacted when it became clear that he wouldn't recover.[22] He died, aged just 21, of tuberculosis on 22 July 1832 in the same Schönbrunn Palace bedroom that his father occupied after the battles of Austerlitz and Wagram.

Perhaps because of his military admiration for Napoleon and his hatred of the Habsburgs, Adolf Hitler ordered that Napoleon II's remains be returned from Vienna to Paris in 1940, where they remain interred in Les Invalides, where his father has pride of place. But his heart and intestines remain in Vienna, having been buried separately after his death in the Ducal Crypt of St Stephen's Cathedral, according to Habsburg tradition.

Another international diplomatic curiosity of the period relates to the Habsburg role in the independence of Brazil, which followed an approach to Metternich from Rio de Janeiro for a royal marriage with the exiled Crown Prince of Portugal Pedro Bragança. 'For Prince Metternich this enquiry opened up some interesting new prospects. To send one of Emperor Francis I's daughters to Brazil to marry meant that Austria could send an expedition to this then still largely unexplored exotic land, thereby re-establishing Austria as a powerful nation in the fields of science and art. Metternich proposed Archduchess Leopoldina Josepha Carolina as a suitable candidate, since it was her turn to be married.'[23]

The fifth child of Emperor Francis was promptly married by proxy and despatched across the Atlantic on an 81-day voyage, after which she met her husband for the first time. In addition to a very difficult new life with her dissolute husband, nine pregnancies and extreme homesickness, Leopoldina found herself in the middle of moves towards independence from Portugal, and Pedro being crowned Emperor of Brazil. When in need of international recognition, it was Leopoldina who petitioned her father-in-law, Dom João VI, in Lisbon to ratify the independence constitution and wrote to her father Emperor Francis in Vienna to form an alliance:

Dearest Papa,

. . . the size of Brazil is of maximum interest for the powers of Europe, especially in respect of trade. It is my duty to speak on behalf of the noble Brazilian people.

Now I have nothing more to wish for, but that you, most worthy Father, step forward as our true friend and ally. As to myself, dearest Father, you may be sure that I shall always remain wholeheartedly Brazilian, for this is my duty as a wife, a mother, and one who is thankful to a worthy people, who, when we were abandoned by all the powerful nations, were willing to support us, and did not shrink from the greatest sacrifices and perils.

I kiss your hands again and again and remain always, with the deepest filial love and most profound respect, dearest Papa, your obedient daughter

Leopoldina.[24]

Three years after declaring independence, and with intense international lobbying, Brazil's sovereignty was recognised on Leopoldina's name-day: 15 November 1825. To this day the Brazilian flag and national football strip is golden yellow, the colour of the Habsburg dynasty, and Leopoldina is feted as a great Brazilian patriot.

*

The Metternich years were closely watched and documented by the man of letters and Baden diplomat Franz Xaver von Andlaw-Birseck (1799–1876). As legation secretary for the Grand Duchy of Baden in Vienna from 1826–1830 and 1832–1835, and as the head of mission from 1846–1856, he wrote at great length in his *Erinnerungsblätter aus den Papieren eines Diplomaten* ('Reminder Notes from the Papers of a Diplomat') of 1857 and his two-volume diary of 1862. One aspect of his memoirs was the changing nature of court life under Emperor Francis: 'The court became plain and simple, like the emperor himself, with quiet domesticity replacing the former splendour and great hospitality during the Congress times with rarely any festivals or ceremonies. After a busy life the Emperor longed for peace and undertook only necessary business. Representative duties and noisy court pleasures were not to his taste, and even the once common formalities, like church going, excursions and gala days disappeared more and more ... high society and the diplomatic corps had less contact with the court and often months would pass without coming close to their majesties.'[25]

Emperor Francis, like Metternich, was not interested in liberal reforms. His creed was 'the most narrow-minded absolutism'.[26] When his personal physician examined him for a cold and said there is nothing like a good constitution, the emperor famously replied: 'There is no such thing as a good constitution. I have no constitution and will never have one.'[27] He had a reputation for kind-heartedness and was known as 'the good Kaiser', accessible to all subjects, but that did not extend to dissenters and political prisoners.

Francis died of a sudden fever in the 43rd year of his reign, aged 67, on 2 March 1835. He was the last Holy Roman Emperor and first Austrian Emperor, the first double emperor in history. It took three days for thousands of members of the Viennese public to file past his coffin before he was laid to rest in the imperial crypt at the Capuchin Church in central Vienna. Before his death he left clear instructions for his eldest son, who succeeded him as Ferdinand I (1793–1875): 'Do not disturb the foundations of the edifice of state; rule and change nothing; stand fast upon the fundamental principles by the constant observation of which I have steered the Monarchy, not only through the storms of difficult times ... Honour acquired rights; ... Vest in Prince Metternich, my truest servant and friend, the trust that I have devoted to him over such a long succession of years. Do not come to any decisions about public affairs or people without having listened to his opinion on them.'[28]

The advice to Ferdinand was in part because of his poor health, which massively impacted on his life and reign: he was a severe epileptic with hydrocephalus and a speech impediment. It was not uncommon for him to endure 20 seizures a day, draining him of energy and the ability to manage the affairs of state. History has been unkind to him, recalling his more bizarre statements: 'I am the Emperor, and I want dumplings!' Or his question to Metternich about rioters at the start of the 1848 revolution: 'But are they allowed to do that?' During his reign, government business was largely steered by a state conference consisting of his uncle, Archduke Ludwig, Prince Metternich and his great rival Count Franz Anton von Kolowrat-Liebsteinsky. Ludwig supported the absolutist policies of Metternich, which would continue for another 13 years.

The later Metternich period was witnessed by one of the best foreign travel writers, the English novelist and writer Frances (Fanny) Trollope (1779–1863). Spending eight months in Vienna during the 1830s, she recounted her experiences and observations in her two-volume *Vienna and the Austrians*, capturing much of the city and life in Vienna, including its society and diplomatic life. Amongst her highlights was a dinner hosted by the British ambassador Sir Frederick Lamb with Prince Metternich: 'The prince is of middle height, rather thin than otherwise, with handsome and regular features, his hair quite grey, and the prevailing expression of his countenance that of mild benevolence; but in his light blue eyes there is a character of deep and earnest thoughtfulness that is exceedingly remarkable. His person and manners are eminently dignified and graceful; and there is moreover such an air of calm philosophical tranquility in his aspect, that had I been told, out of a hundred gentlemen chosen at hazard, to select the one who for twenty-five years had held a steady and unvacillating course, while all beyond the circle of his influence had blundered and tottered, I am very sure I should have made no mistake.'[29]

While reporting on high society life, she also noted the ubiquity of the waltz craze and music of Strauss and Lanner, although she was clearly not its biggest fan: 'A pretty waltz, well played, has great charms; but . . . I am weary of it, and would much rather have visited Vienna when every garden, every theatre and every salon breathed the rich strains of Mozart.'[30]

One of the most striking aspects of Trollope's Vienna account is the unvarnished anti-Semitism of the age, which she shared. She didn't like attending some of the best parties because of the prospect of meeting Jews; she thought it better for Christians and Jews to live separate lives, and she was distrusting of Jewish converts to Christianity.[31]

The later Metternich era has a curious connection with its early years at the Congress of Vienna through French representative Talleyrand, whose illegitimate son went on to serve as French ambassador in Vienna from 1841 until 1848. Charles, Comte de Flahaut (1785–1870), was a dashing general and aide-de-camp to Napoleon during a series of army campaigns, including a time in Austria when he also acted as his courier and envoy to Emperor Francis. Promoted to Lieutenant General and Count of the French Empire, he was wounded nine times in combat over 15 years of active military service. After a romantic liaison with Queen Hortense of Holland, who bore them a son, he went on to marry the Scottish heiress Margaret Mercer Elphinstone,[32] the Baroness Keith and Nairne (1788–1867), who was the daughter of the British Royal Navy Admiral Viscount Keith.

Flahaut and Margaret took up residence in the suitably grand Palais Starhemberg on Minoritenplatz, one of the oldest baroque palaces in Vienna. Commissioned in 1667, the palace had played a major part in the affairs of state and international relations long before Flahaut arrived in 1841. The defence of the city during the second Turkish siege was commanded from the residence of Count Starhemberg in 1689 and had been the British Embassy and residence during the Congress of Vienna in 1815. It presently houses the Austrian Ministry of Science and Research as well as the Ministry of Education, Arts and Culture, and it shares the square with key government departments including the Austrian Foreign Ministry, Interior Ministry, Federal Chancellery, State Archive and Ministry for Civil Service and Sport.

Flahaut and Margaret both recorded developments during their Vienna posting, which turned out to be the final years of Metternich's rule: 'Prince Metternich hopes to spend his few remaining years in peace and quiet. He is constantly saying that there are no problems of foreign policy in Europe today, and that if any should arise, they must instantly be suppressed. This is the motive behind all of his actions. He regards himself as a kind of patriarch, with a duty to preserve the peace and he cordially dislikes anyone whom he suspects of being adventurous or likely to cause trouble.'[33]

By the later 1840s, however, trouble was brewing for Metternich and his autocratic government, which was losing touch with the threats to its future existence. Flahaut recorded at the start of 1848 that 'the Austrian government has so many pressing affairs on hand that it cannot decide which is the most urgent'.[34]

*

The 1840s, in the run-up to the revolutions towards the end of the decade, were marked by agricultural failures leading to famine and near-famine conditions across much of Europe. In 1845 it was a potato crop failure, followed by a poor grain harvest and food supply problems in 1846. This was followed by an economic downturn, recession and growing social and political tensions. Even Metternich knew that the writing was on the wall, telling a Prussian diplomat: 'I am no prophet and I know not what will happen: but I am an old practitioner, and I know how to discriminate between curable and fatal diseases. This one is fatal; here we hold as long as we can, but I despair of the issue.'[35]

The touchpaper for the 1848 revolutions was lit in Paris, where demonstrations in February led to the abdication of King Louis Philippe and set off demonstrations across the continent. Within a month, protests escalated in Vienna with demands for the resignation of Metternich. With Austrian forces preoccupied in suppressing revolutionary uprisings in northern Italy, order broke down in the capital. The Lower Austrian Diet joined calls for Metternich to resign – which he did on 13 March, before fleeing to exile in Britain.

In many respects, Vienna was the capital of the 1848 revolutions, including as it did the different reform movements – social, democratic-liberal and national – and, like in no other state, the Habsburg authorities in Vienna had to manage competing national aspirations. It was the closest the Habsburg Empire came to dissolution before the First World War. While anger had been aimed against Metternich personally, insurrections were largely not directed against the ruling dynasty. As an example, Czech historian, patriot and politician František Palacký (1798–1876), who has been described as the 'Father of the Nation', said: 'Indeed, if the Austrian state did not exist we should have to create it in the interests of Europe and humanity.'[36] It was also the case that reform efforts were energised by developments elsewhere in the empire.

Protesters in Vienna were inspired by calls from Hungarian leader Lajos Kossuth (1802–1894) for political reform, including a constitution for Austria and parliament for Hungary. Emperor Ferdinand acceded to demands by a Magyar delegation including Count Lajos Battyány de Németújvár that a Hungarian government should be supreme in 'the lands of the Crown of St Istvan', including Transylvania, Slovakia and Croatia.[37] Within days, a government was in place with Battyány as Prime Minister, Kossuth as Finance Minister. The March Laws, passed and approved by the emperor, made Hungary a nation state, with a national guard, national finances and foreign policy.

The emperor also sanctioned elections to a Croatian national assembly, while the noted general Count Josip Jelačič (1801–1859) was appointed Ban of Croatia (viceroy) – a precursor to military action in opposition to the Magyar revolutionary movement and in the furtherance of independence from Hungary. His Croatian forces would go on to play a large military role in Hungary and Vienna in defence of Habsburg interests.

In Italy, revolutionary events were inspired by calls for political reform and Italian unification, with the ending of Austrian rule in the north. In a first stage of insurrection, the Kingdom of Sardinia was joined by Italian nationalists in attempts to force out the Habsburgs in the Austrian-ruled Kingdom of Lombardy-Venetia, especially in Milan and Venice. The Italians were beaten on 24 July 1848 by the octogenarian Austrian Field Marshal Joseph Count Radetzky von Radetz (1766–1858) at the Battle of Custoza, which was followed by a truce.

Meanwhile, in Vienna, pressure for reform led to a series of liberal governments being appointed by Emperor Ferdinand, but tensions around demands for democratic elections to the German Confederation set off nationality conflicts in different parts of the empire, especially Bohemia. Freedom of the media was introduced, along with freedom of association and elections for constituent assemblies that should draft constitutions. But differences between reformists and revolutionaries in the heated political environment led to a breakdown of law and order.

In Bohemia, the tensions between Czech and German nationalists grew, leading to a boycott of elections to the new German National Assembly. While the 1848 revolutions had stirred great democratic hopes for a unified Germany, this was not widely welcomed by Bohemia's Czech nationalists, like František Palacký. In his famous 'Letter to Frankfurt' (*Psaní do Frankfurtu*) he refused, as a Czech of Slav descent, to take part in the inaugural meeting of an all-German parliament. Instead he attended a Slav congress in Prague to discuss the reorganisation of the Austrian Empire. Clashes broke out on the streets of the Bohemian capital between the public and troops under the command of General Alfred I, Prince of Windisch-Grätz (1787–1862). His military victory was followed by a clampdown, the dissolution of the Slav congress and the arrest of Czech nationalists.

The revolutions at the end of the 1840s were closely observed by William Henry Stiles (1808–1865), the US *chargé d'affaires* in Vienna, who became an active participant as a go-between for the imperial authorities and Hungarian revolutionaries, as well as a chronicler of events. His two-volume *Austria in 1848–49*[38] has been described as 'an American classic because of the light it sheds on the principles and practice of the United States towards foreign revolutions, national self-determination, and the European balance of power, at a time when Americans were fighting a controversial war with Mexico and nearing a showdown over slavery'.[39]

Stiles, who hailed from an aristocratic slave-owning planter family in Savannah, Georgia, served as a Democratic member of the US Congress before his diplomatic sojourn. His conservative views on state rights and social privilege, and opposition to widening the franchise, gave him a natural sympathy with middle-class reformers in Austria and Hungary, but a strong fear of revolutionary 'mob rule'.[40] His early reports to the State Department showed he had pretty clear sympathies: 'The [Hungarian] party in opposition to the [Austrian] government holds the superiority both in talent and numbers';[41] Austria was 'in the most deplorable condition of any European state. Miracles can save her from dismemberment and miracles only. Hungary is dissatisfied and demanded a constitution herself.'[42]

As unrest continued into 1848, things were looking increasingly ropey for the Habsburgs, who at one stage fled the capital for the safety of Innsbruck before beginning to reinstate control with the help of the military. On 3 October the Habsburgs declared war on the democratic Hungarian government of Lajos Kossuth. This, however, led to the Vienna October uprising, when students, workers and mutinous military personnel sought to stop troops leaving the city to help put down the Hungarian rising. The stand-off between the military and crowds sympathetic to the Hungarians developed into street battles in the city centre. Minister of War Count Theodor Franz Baillet von Latour, who had ordered the Hungarian troop deployment, was hanged from a lamppost by a lynch mob outside his ministry on Am Hof square. Revolutionaries then stormed the military arsenal and plundered weapons, leading to the imperial family fleeing Vienna for a second time, this time to Olmütz in Moravia.[43] With the city now in revolutionary hands, the Habsburgs launched an offensive to regain control, with the northern Austrian army under Prince Windisch-Grätz and the Croatian Army under

Count Jelačič. Over a number of days, Vienna was under cannon fire and loyalist imperial troops fought their way past street barricades into the city centre. At the same time, an army of inexperienced insurgent Hungarian forces reached Schwechat, the location of today's Vienna International Airport. Outnumbered and outgunned by the imperial troops of Windisch-Grätz and the Croats of Jelačič, the Hungarians withdrew after a limited engagement. The Battle of Schwechat on 30 October coincided with the end of the 1848 revolution in Vienna, which in the following days was finally crushed with the execution of its revolutionary and democrat leaders.

Not long afterwards, a letter from Lajos Kossuth was couriered through the military lines to Stiles: '. . . we gladly avail ourselves of this opportunity to call upon the feelings of justice of the representative of the United States, inviting you to initiate the negotiations of an armistice for this Winter between the two armies standing on the frontiers of Austria and Hungary and so stop the calamities of a war so fatal to the interests of both countries'.[44] Stiles immediately contacted the new Austrian Foreign Minister, Prince Felix Schwartzenberg, and told him: 'I had no disposition to interfere between the Austrian government and one of its provinces, and that I would only take such action or pursue such a course in the matter as might be agreeable to the imperial government.' Schwarzenberg, however, responded that 'matters had progressed too far – that they could enter into no negotiation with rebels, and that nothing short of unconditional surrender could now be submitted to by the government'.

Stiles reported on the Hungarian appeal and his reply to Kossuth in a report to US Secretary of State James Buchanan: 'I frankly stated, on that occasion, the difficulties which such a step suggested to my mind, arising from the fact that it was a domestic quarrel between the government of the Austrian empire and one of its dependencies, and with which no foreign power could properly have any concern . . . that it was a subject which the United States had ever regarded with peculiar jealousy, and that I could not, therefore, reconcile it to myself to be in any manner instrumental in committing her; that, besides, so extensive, as I understood, had been the preparations made by the imperial government for the subjugation of Hungary, that it was scarcely to be expected that it would, at this eleventh hour, listen to any proposals of settlement short of the unconditional submission to imperial authority.'

The go-between diplomacy pursued by Stiles also included a visit to Prince Windisch-Grätz, who was leading the military campaign against the Hungarians. 'I can do nothing in the matter. I must obey the orders of the emperor,' he told the US diplomat. 'Hungary must submit. I will occupy Pest with my troops, and then the emperor will decide what is to be done. I have received orders to occupy Hungary, and I hope to accomplish this end – I cannot, therefore, enter into any negotiations. I cannot consent to treat with those who are in a state of rebellion.'[45]

The authorities in Vienna were aware of the contents of the communications between Stiles and Kossuth the whole time because the locally employed US consul in Vienna, J.G. Schwarz, was an Austrian police informer and his report was shared directly with Prince Schwarzenberg.[46] This led to Schwarz's eventual replacement and a decision by the US Congress that non-US citizens should no longer be able to act as consuls.

The foremost international observer who witnessed the events in Vienna in the summer of 1848 was Karl Marx. The journalist, author and revolutionary spent ten days in the city, where he gave three lectures during the height of the turmoil. Just prior to his arrival, workers had taken to the streets to protest against wage cuts and large-scale protests continued after he left. Writing in the *Neue Rheinische Zeitung* under the headline 'The Victory of the Counter-Revolution in Vienna', Marx lambasted the bourgeois revolutionaries in the city and the intervention of the Croatian Habsburg loyalist Jelačič:

> Croatian freedom and order has won the day, and this victory was celebrated with arson, rape, looting and other atrocities. Vienna is in the hands of Windischgratz, Jellachich

and Auersperg. Hecatombs of victims are sacrificed on the grave of the aged traitor Latour [Habsburg defence Minister lynched by revolutionaries].

For a while we hoped Vienna could be liberated by Hungarian reinforcements, and we are still in the dark regarding the movements of the Hungarian army.

Treachery of every kind prepared the way for Vienna's fall. The entire performance of the Imperial Diet and the town council since October 6 is a tale of continuous treachery. Who are the people represented in the Imperial Diet and the town council?

The bourgeoisie. A part of the Viennese National Guard openly sided with the camarilla from the very beginning of the October revolution. Towards the end of the October revolution another part of the National Guard in collusion with the imperial bandits fought against the proletariat and the Academic Legion. To which strata do these groups of the National Guard belong? To the bourgeoisie.

Writing on 9 November 1848, Marx hoped that 'for all their pious resignation the struggle in Austria will assume gigantic dimensions such as world history has never yet witnessed'. It didn't turn out how he wished.

While the military situation was deteriorating for the Austrians in Hungary, it was improving in Italy following the breakdown of an earlier truce. During his second Italian campaign, Field Marshal Radetzky secured his legendary status with victory at the Battle of Novara on the 23 March 1849, which led to the abdication of King Charles Albert of Sardinia. While the first campaign in 1848 lasted 134 days, the second in 1849 lasted only 100 hours. Radetzky's victories were immortalised by Johann Strauss senior with his popular *Radetzky March*, the jaunty melody featured at every New Year's Concert from Vienna, which in turn inspired the classic Austrian novel of the same name by Joseph Roth. Radetzky's biographers are in agreement that he is one of the most significant military figures of the 19th century: he 'without doubt, twice saved Austria and Europe from revolutionary success and radical geopolitical change. His defeat of Napoleon meant that not only had Europe been liberated from the scourge of French military rule but that America, the Caribbean, the Near East, and India also escaped whatever fate Napoleon at the head of a united Europe would have had in store for them. Likewise in 1848, but for him, a united Italy, and enlarged and revisionist Hungary and a united Germany would have soon been locked in conflict with either France or Russia or both. It is far too simplistic to deny him real world-historical significance.'[47]

Having secured victory in Italy, the Austrians could move their troops to Hungary to deal with the insurrection there. Meanwhile, William Henry Stiles received further instructions from Washington and praise for maintaining the US policy of non-interference: '. . . I am gratified that your prudence and ability were equal to the occasion. In our foreign policy, we must ever be governed by the wise maxim not to interfere with the domestic concerns of foreign nations; and from this you have not departed . . . You were placed in a novel and embarrassing position by the application of Mr Kossuth to undertake an intervention for the settlement of the differences existing between the Imperial Government and Hungary . . . you acted wisely in becoming an intermediary. The President entirely approves your conduct.'[48]

That, however, was only half the story, as the US was actively considering the possibility of recognising Hungarian independence, should the insurrection succeed. President Zachary Taylor despatched roving US diplomat A. Dudley Mann to Hungary, with instructions from new Secretary of State John M. Clayton: 'If it shall appear that Hungary is able to maintain her independence she has declared we desire to be the very first to congratulate her and to hail with a hearty welcome her entrance to the family circle of nations . . . Should the new government prove to be in your opinion firm and stable, the President will cheerfully recommend to Congress at their next session the recognition of Hungary. The President would in that event be gratified to receive a diplomatic agent from Hungary in the United States.'[49]

Mann didn't actually manage to make it to Hungary as events overtook his mission, with the involvement of Russia in support of the Austrians. Following an appeal from Vienna, the tsar's forces intervened in 1849 to assist their Holy Alliance partners and defend absolutist rule. Together, they tipped the military balance, with Russian forces totalling nearly 190,000 men and 600 guns.[50]

The Hungarians became desperate for international support and even US envoy Mann reported over-optimistically back to Washington about the prospects of other European powers, including Great Britain, recognising Hungary. But he underestimated the desire in London to protect stability by maintaining the integrity of Austria.[51] This was underlined by British Foreign Secretary Lord Palmerston, who told the House of Commons: 'Austria is a most important element in the balance of European power. Austria stands in the centre of Europe, a barrier against encroachment on the one side and invasion on the other. The political independence and liberties of Europe are bound up, in my opinion, with the maintenance and integrity of Austria as a great European power, and therefore anything which tends by direct or even remote contingency to weaken and to cripple Austria, but still more reduce her from the position of a first-rate power to that of a secondary state, must be a great calamity to Europe and one which every Englishman ought to deprecate and try to avoid.'[52]

Without any international support, the Hungarians capitulated on 13 August 1849 and the Austrians began a brutal crackdown, including the execution of Hungarian generals and Prime Minister Count Lajos Batthyány de Némétújvár, as well as the declaration of martial law across the country. Writing about the failure of the Hungarian uprising and the success of the Austrian counter-revolution, US diplomat Stiles clearly showed where his sympathies lay: 'Had Hungary established her independence, Austria must inevitably have sunk into a third or fourth rate power. Had she been able to establish a free Constitution, and, absorbing Croatia, opened to herself the ports of the Mediterranean, the future consequences to the freedom of Europe can not be overrated. The struggle, when once commenced, was one worthy of the utmost effort; and this was not wanting. The labors of Kossuth were Herculean; and, assisted by the most gallant people of Europe, no contest more worthy of the poet and the historian has ever been waged between the opposing spirits of freedom and tyranny, of good and evil, that have immemorially divided the world.'

Defeat of the Hungarians led to exile for Kossuth and his many allies who fled to the US at the same time as Stiles was recalled home. A great number of them went on to serve with the Union Army during the American Civil War, while William Henry Stiles raised the 60th Georgia Infantry for the Confederates and served as its colonel.

In Vienna, the counter-revolution was complete and had been delivered with a new young emperor who was prepared to do what was necessary to maintain absolutist Habsburg power.

# 7

# *The Longest Reign*

'I am the last ruler of the old world.'

– Emperor Francis Joseph[1]

Francis Joseph became the new Austrian Emperor aged only 18 because dynastic change was the only way to regain the initiative at the height of the 1848 revolution in Vienna after the court fled to Olmütz.

Preparations were made and agreed to replace Emperor Ferdinand with his young nephew by new Minister-President and Foreign Minister Prince Schwarzenberg, military leaders Field Marshals Radetzky and Windisch-Grätz, and the power behind the throne, Princess Sophie, the mother of the new emperor. Named Francis Joseph I, to raise hopes that his would be a more liberal monarchy like his pro-reform predecessor Joseph II, the intention, however, was very different: to restore Habsburg power and the old absolutist order.

Francis Joseph I (1830–1916) would remain on the throne for nearly 68 years, one of the longest reigns in history, and he almost lived to see the end of his dynasty and empire at the close of the First World War. Francis Joseph took over just as the Austrian Empire seemed destined to go under, owing to insurrections in Vienna, Italy and Hungary. In these, his darkest days, he turned to his Holy Alliance partner, Tsar Nicholas I of Russia. In his first foreign visit he travelled to Warsaw in Congress Poland to meet his fellow autocratic monarch and appeal for his support. In a sign of submissiveness on their meeting, Francis Joseph bowed and kissed the hand of the

Emperor of all the Russias. He reported the details of their meeting in a letter to his mother: 'He received me exceptionally graciously and cordially, and at 4 o'clock I dined with him tête-à-tête. We travelled very fast, and the Russian railways are especially outstanding for their good organisation and smooth ride. Altogether everything is so pleasantly orderly and calm here.' Nicholas was also impressed with his young visitor, writing to his wife, the tsarina: 'The more I see of him and listen to him, the more I am astonished by his good sense and by the soundness and rectitude of his views.'[2]

Not only was Francis Joseph indebted for the thousands of Russian troops who helped secure victory over insurgent Hungarian forces, he was personally honoured by the tsar who awarded him the Russian Imperial Order of St George, 4th Class. The bravery medal for leading troops across a burning bridge into Raab (Győr) was worn on his tunic throughout his long reign, even after war was declared against Russia in 1914.

The effects of the victory and crackdown in Hungary might have taken a further dramatic turn, with an assassination attempt on Francis Joseph by a lone knife attacker in 1853. While walking on the city bastions close to the Hofburg, the young emperor was attacked from behind by the dagger-wielding Hungarian apprentice tailor János Libényi. The emperor was saved by his adjutant, Count Maximilian O'Donnell, and passers-by, and suffered only superficial wounds. His attacker was led away shouting 'Long live Kossuth' in Hungarian; he was executed a week later for attempted regicide.

The domestic impact of the revolutions had not been surmounted before Francis Joseph faced his first major international crisis: the worsening conflict between Russia and the Ottoman Empire, which led to the Crimean War. What started as a dispute about access to religious sites in the Holy Land escalated as Russia flexed its muscles as the protector of Orthodox interests, while France and Britain supported the weakening Turks, fearing that Russia would control access from the Black Sea and potentially threaten their trade routes. Austria was in a difficult position as the first Russian military moves in July 1853 involved occupying the Danubian

Principalities, in present-day Romania, to put pressure on the sultan in Constantinople. By doing so, the tsar was doubling the length of his border with Austria, thus undermining a key Habsburg security buffer zone and threatening to become a major rival in the Balkans as Ottoman power was receding. But, having been saved by Russian troops only a few years before in Hungary, there was an expectation from the tsar that Austria would show its gratitude by siding with him. However, that would pit Austria against France, a situation that would undermine Austrian interests in Italy. If, on the other hand, Austria sided against Russia, most of the fighting would take place along its border and it would lose its main security backer and undermine its position against France in Italy and Prussia in Germany. It was a lose–lose situation for Austria. Instead, Francis Joseph dispatched Foreign Minister Count Karl Ferdinand von Buol-Schauenstein (1797–1865) to try and find a diplomatic solution.

A conference in Vienna on 24 July 1853 led to the Vienna Note, drafted by Buol-Schauenstein and agreed by Britain, France, Prussia and Austria. Its main points were that the tsar should withdraw from Moldavia and Wallachia, but, as the protector of the Orthodox Church, Russia should exercise nominal protection of Orthodox Christians in the Ottoman Empire and the Holy Places. The Note effectively confirmed the status quo ante, with neither Russia nor France gaining anything, but face would be saved and war averted. However, with only minimal support from Britain and no military commitment to enforce the peace, the Ottomans sought revenge and declared war on Russia.[3] The tsar dispatched his trusted senior envoy, Prince Alexey Orlov, to Vienna in early 1854 on an unsuccessful mission seeking Austrian neutrality on Russian terms. Buol-Schauenstein continued to try to find a peaceful solution, but, as this became a faint hope, he began to argue for an alignment with the West to secure Russian withdrawal from the Danube Principalities.[4]

In the midst of the international crisis, 23-year-old Francis Joseph was preparing for his nuptials with 16-year-old Elisabeth Wittlesbach, the daughter of Duke Maximilian of Bavaria. The Belgian ambassador to Vienna noted the emperor had had to cut short a visit to Bavaria because of developments: 'The seriousness of the situation forces the Emperor to hasten his return . . . the political situation causes him much anxiety.'[5] Less charitable was the assessment by the Russian ambassador to Vienna, Peter von Meyendorff: 'For some time now, he is no longer called "the Emperor", but increasingly the "young gentleman". Some even say: "this is a child". Really, he thinks of his wedding more than anything else, he writes long and frequent letters to his bride, and while Buol signs infamous protocols, the emperor is hunting grouse and in the evening you can often see him at the circus.'[6] Nevertheless, he advised the tsar to maintain contact with Vienna and not give up hope.

Elisabeth travelled down the Danube aboard the aptly named steamship *Francis Joseph*, before arriving at Nussdorf on 22 April 1854, where she was met at the quayside by her royal fiancé and throngs of well-wishers. VIPs and diplomats had an excellent grandstand view of the arrival while military bands played and cannon salvoes thundered for the state entry to the capital. Much effort had been made to deck out the city with flags and bunting and spruce up public buildings and aristocratic residences: 'Several nobles have gone to an enormous expense in the external decoration of their palace. The Papal Nuncio has taken advantage of the festive occasion and had his palace whitewashed, of which kind attention it has been in very great need for many long years.'[7]

Over two days of ceremonial receptions, introductions and dinners, the first signs of fatigue with court ceremony were already apparent with Elisabeth before the wedding day itself. It took two hours for the bride's coach to drive along streets packed with sightseers in a procession of the high nobility and court office holders and military from the Theresianum to the Hofburg court church. The Archbishop of Vienna, Joseph Othmar von Rauscher, and 70 mitred bishops and prelates conducted the royal wedding in the church lit by 15,000 candles and with nearly 1,000 present. According to Swiss diplomat Johann Jakob Tschudi: 'Except for the Congress, such extraordinary splendour was never yet seen.'[8] The Belgian ambassador reported to Brussels: 'In a city where the revolutionary spirit has recently caused so much destruction, it was not unhelpful to deploy the whole monarchical beauty.'[9]

A reception followed immediately afterwards, with the victorious generals from 1848 – Radetzky, Windischgrätz, Nugent and Jelačič – first to be formally received, before the assembled diplomatic corps were individually introduced by Buol-Schauenstein in the Audience Room. Next, in the Hall of Mirrors, came introductions to the ambassador's wives, court officials and palace ladies, which caused Elisabeth to suffer a panic attack.[10] It was a sign of what was to come as 'Sisi' struggled to come to terms with the strict court protocol. This didn't yet detract from Francis Joseph's personal happiness, and he used the wedding as an occasion to improve the monarchy's standing in the empire. The immense sum of 200,000 florins was gifted to church charities in different crown lands, 380 political prisoners received an amnesty from the emperor, and martial law came to an end in Lombardy-Venetia. For the first time since the revolutions four years previously, senior Hungarian nobility took part in court events.

Hardly any time passed after the royal wedding before Francis Joseph had to deal again with the Near East crisis. In June 1854 Vienna called for Russia to evacuate Wallachia and Moldavia or face conflict with entering Austrian forces, accompanied by the wholesale mobilisation of 11 army corps – amounting to 327,000 men – in Transylvania and Galicia. The tsar relented, withdrawing his troops across the River Pruth, which marked the border. For a moment it looked like a diplomatic masterstroke: occupying the principalities without war. But it didn't stop a wider conflict, with Russia fighting against Turkey, Britain, France and Piedmont-Sardinia.

While the Austrians remained neutral, allied troops landed on the Crimean peninsula in September 1854 and began a siege of the Russian fortress at Sevastopol that would last a year. Major battles were fought within months at Alma River, at Balaclava (including the famous Charge of the Light Brigade) and at Inkerman. An appalling 650,000 casualties were caused amongst the 1.5 million men that took part, largely because of disease.

After the fall of Sevastopol, Russia sued for peace, leading to the Peace of Paris in 1856, which ensured the Black Sea became a demilitarised neutral territory. It was a big setback for Russia, but as European diplomatic historian A.J.P. Taylor argued, it was even worse for Austria: 'The Crimean War forced the Habsburg Monarchy to the crisis of decision; and the contradictory decisions then taken determined her ultimate fate. Unable to opt for either east or west, Austria remained thereafter in a state of suspended animation, waiting for extinction . . . Thus the Crimean War left Austria without friends. Russia ascribed her defeat to the Austrian threat to join the allies; the allies believed that Russia would have withdrawn without war if Austria had joined them at the beginning.'[11] For Paul Schroeder, the historian and author of *Austria, Great Britain and Crimean War*, the chief lesson for Austria was that 'a conciliatory foreign policy and an effort to internationalise dangerous questions cannot by itself compensate for the failure to solve internal problems and meet the challenge of modernisation'.[12]

One major sign of modernisation was, however, taking place in Vienna, with the order by Francis Joseph to demolish the city walls. As only an autocrat could, he signed a proclamation written in the first-person plural to Interior Minister Alexander von Bach on 20 December 1857 that would pave the way towards the modern metropolis we recognise to this day: 'It is our desire that the extension of the inner city of Vienna should be undertaken as soon as possible, that at the same time it should be linked to the suburbs, and that in doing the improvement and embellishment of Our residence city and capital should be a matter of concern. For this purpose We grant the use of the area of the ramparts and fortifications round the inner town and the moats around these . . . The erection of public buildings should also be taken into account, namely a new building for the general staff, an office for the town commandant, an opera house, a national archive, a library, a town hall, as well as the necessary buildings for museums and galleries.'[13]

The Ringstrasse would be just over five kilometres long and 57 metres wide – too wide for street barricades, which was a priority after the 1848 revolutions. Security considerations included the construction of three major military installations nearby, in case troops needed to be mobilised: the Francis Joseph Barracks, Crown Prince Rudolf Barracks and the Arsenal.

In a novelty for the time, there was a public competition for the design, the best of which would receive 2,000, 1,000 and 500 gold ducats respectively. A master plan was completed by April 1859 and a City Expansion Commission appointed to see through the huge project. While the municipal authorities were responsible for road construction, amenities, parks and the new city hall, the cost of the public buildings was to be offset by income from private developers building expensive blocks of flats. Between 1860 and 1870 most of the Ringstrasse had been built and fortifications removed; 190 exclusive apartment blocks were completed, with another 200 on the way. The public buildings were completed towards the end of the century.

Just as change was in the air in Vienna at the start of the municipal transformation in the late 1850s, Austria faced its biggest challenge in Italy, a region of the empire that was hugely important to the Habsburgs. Much of southern Italy, including Sicily and Naples, had been ruled by the Spanish Habsburgs and was then handed over to Vienna's control, together with Sardinia, at the end of the War of the Spanish Succession. The Grand Duchy of Tuscany, with its capital Florence and cities including Siena and Livorno, came under Habsburg-Lorraine rule after the last Medici of the ducal line died in 1737. The Kingdom of Lombardy-Venetia was not just amongst the wealthiest parts of the Habsburg Empire, it was one of the wealthiest regions of Europe. Habsburgs had ruled over the Duchy of Mantua, the Habsburg-Este cadet-branch of the dynasty were Dukes of Modena and Reggio, and Habsburg Archduchess Marie Louise ruled the Duchy of Parma. Lombardy-Venetia, which was ruled in personal union by the Austrian Emperor, had a population of 5 million and cities including Milan, Venice, Bergamo, Brescia, Mantua, Padua and Verona. Prior to 1848, around 60 per cent of the monarchy's manufactoring output was from Lombardy, while the tax yield of the northern Italian provinces totalled 30 per cent of the empire's overall tax revenue.[14]

As the First Italian War of Independence had shown in 1848–1849, there was growing support for the unification of the different Italian states. The Risorgimento was particularly focused on ending Austrian rule in the north of Italy, which had been resisted by the Austrian military successes of commanders like Field Marshal Radetzky, Field Marshal Laval Nugent von Westmeath, Archduke Albrecht and a young Colonel Ludwig von Benedek, of whom we will hear more later. By the late 1850s the temptation to displace Austria led to a verbal agreement between Piedmont-Sardinia and France, known as the Plombières Agreement. The agreement was made between Chief Minister of Piedmont-Sardinia Camillo Benso, Count of Cavour, and Napoleon III on 21 July 1858. The secret deal, arranged in the back of a horse-drawn carriage that circled round the small Vosges spa-town of Plombières for four hours, paved the way for French troops to support Piedmont-Sardinia against the Austrians in return for the territorial transfer of Nice and Savoy to France.

The first wind that Austrian diplomats received of the brewing military threat was months later at the New Year diplomatic reception at Tuileries Palace in Paris. Emperor Napoleon caused a minor diplomatic incident, when in conversation with Austrian ambassador Baron Alexander von Hübner: 'I regret that our relations are not as good as I desire that they be, but I beg you write to Vienna that my personal feelings for the emperor are always the same.'[15]

What started as understated sangfroid, soon fed wild rumours of impending crisis and even led to a sharp drop in the stock market. On learning about the alliance and military manoeuvres near their border, the Austrians issued the Ultimatum of Vienna on 23 April 1859, demanding the demobilisation of Piedmont-Sardinia. This was refused, leading to a declaration of war. This satisfied France's desire for it to appear that its involvement was only due to 'Austrian aggression'. In the first example of large-scale military deployment by train, the French assigned more than 170,000 soldiers, 2,000 cavalry and 300 artillery pieces to the campaign against Austria, joining 70,000 Sardinian troops, 3,000 cavalry and 90 canons. The conflict would be the first to see the deployment of rifled field artillery. On paper, the Austrians were superior in number, with 220,000 infantry, 22,000 cavalry and more than 800 pieces of artillery under Field Marshal Ferenc Gyulay de Marosnémethi et Nádaska, who was the Austrian governor of Lombardy-Venetia. Instead of taking out the weaker Sardinian forces before the arrival of French reinforcements, Gyulay vacillated and suffered defeat at the Battle of Magenta on 4 June 1859, which led to his recall to Vienna and replacement as commander by Emperor Francis Joseph himself.

The war was decided a few weeks later at the Battle of Solforino, the last large-scale military battle in history under the personal command of the monarchs of the combatant nations. On the 24 June 1859 the forces of King Victor Emanuel II of Sardinia and Emperor Napoleon III of France met the Austrians under 29-year-old Francis Joseph at Solforino, a small town 10 kilometres south of Lake Garda in Lombardy. In the largest battle since the Battle of Leipzig in 1814, more than 300,000 men fought in three main engagements over nine hours of particularly brutal fighting. The horrific scenes were described by Swiss businessman Jean-Henri Dunant: 'On the heights as well as in the ravines, the dead lie piled up. The Austrians and the allied armies march one against the other, killing each other above the blood-covered corpses, butchering with gunshots, crushing each other's skulls or disembowelling with the sword or bayonet. No cessation in the conflict, no quarter given, the wounded are defending themselves to the last. It is butchery by madmen drunk with blood.'[16] The conditions were so appalling that they led to Dunant founding the Red Cross and the development of the Geneva Conventions. Dunant received the first ever Nobel Peace Prize.

After a full day of fighting at Solforino, the Austrians yielded the field, granting the French and Piedmontese forces a tactical victory.

Emperor Francis Joseph and his troops withdrew to the safety of the Austrian 'Quadrilateral' of fortresses at Verona, Peschiera del Garda, Mantua and Legnano.

Writing after the battle, Francis Joseph told Sisi about his order to retreat: 'This is the sad history of a terrible day on which much was achieved, but fortune did not smile on us. I have learnt much from what I have experienced, and I know what it feels like to be a beaten general. The grave consequences of our misfortune are still to come, but I put my trust in God and do not feel myself to blame for having made any faulty disposition of troops.'[17]

Hostilities were ended shortly thereafter with the Armistice of Villafranca on 12 June 1859, with costly consequences for Austria: the loss of Lombardy to France, which was promptly ceded to Piedmont – which within a year transferred Nice and Savoy to France. The Piedmontese also pressed their advantage, taking over the Habsburg satellites in the Grand Duchy of Tuscany, the Duchy of Parma and the Duchy of Modena and Reggio, going a long way to build momentum for a unified Italian nation state. This left Austria with a much-diminished foothold of Venetia in northern Italy; however, this would only remain part of the empire for another seven years.

The late 1850s were also the time when Empress Elisabeth's melancholy caused her to flee Vienna and seek sanctuary in travel. Initially her visits were within the empire: in 1855 to Tyrol and Carinthia; in 1856 to Venice and Verona; in 1857 to Buda in Hungary, where her first child, Sophie, died aged just two; followed by a six-month trip to Madeira. Her sister Queen Marie of Naples and brother-in-law Archduke Maximilian both suggested she visit the Portuguese island, which she did aboard the British Royal Yacht *Osborne*, which was lent to her by Queen Victoria (1819–1901), who also invited her to visit on her way. In official dispatches the British ambassador Lord Blomfield described an audience with the empress, who looked 'frail and pale'. She expressed her thanks for the use of the yacht but declined the personal invitation because of her ill health and travelling incognito. During her trip she also stopped at Cadiz and Seville in Spain, the British colony of Gibraltar and the Greek island of Corfu, where she would later build her Achilleon villa at Gastouri, before returning via the Austrian port of Trieste.

The day after her return, Lord Blomfield reported to the British Foreign Office: 'The accounts of the Empress are definitely improved, but she continues to be very excitable.' It was followed by another report: 'The Empress continues to cough a great deal and I hear her health has not derived any serious good from her winter in Madeira.' Later, the Prussian Minister in Vienna reported: 'There is some talk of the Empress spending the winter in the south.' However, her attendance was cancelled at her own sister's wedding in Munich, 'on account of her mortal illness'.[18]

*

While other European powers were busily colonising other parts of the world in the 19th century, the Austrian Empire was more focused on protecting its position in Europe. Austria did have global ambitions, in particular a desire to join the other great powers in discovering other parts of the world, or at least demonstrating its reach. This is best illustrated by the Austrian imperial expedition to circumnavigate the Earth. Early in the reign of Emperor Francis Joseph I the SMS *Novara*, a three-masted, six-decked frigate of the Austrian navy with 30 cannons, set off for a voyage that lasted two years and three months. On 30 April 1857 seven scientists joined 345 officers and crew in setting sail from Trieste on behalf of Archduke Maximilian and the Imperial Academy of Sciences in Vienna. Under the command of Captain Bernhard von Wüllerstorf-Urbair, the mission included famed scholars from the Austrian Academy of Sciences, including botanists Eduard Schwarz and Anton Jellinek, geographer Ferdinand Hochstetter, ethnographer Karl von Scherzer and zoologist Georg Ritter von Frauenfeld. Its aim was to collect and research botanical and zoological samples, complete geological mapping and oceanographic research.[19]

The route of the SMS *Novara* took it to Gibraltar, Madeira, Rio de Janeiro, Cape Town, Île Saint Paul, Ceylon (today Sri Lanka), Madras, the Nicobar Islands, Singapore, Batavia (Jakarta, Indonesia), Manila,

Hong Kong, Shanghai, Puynipet Island (today part of Micronesia), Stewart Island (today called Sikaiana), Sydney, Auckland, Tahiti, Valparaíso (Chile) and Gravosa (Gruž, Dubrovnik), before returning to Trieste on 26 August 1859 having travelled 51,686 sea miles.

Much has been written about the scientific accomplishments of the expedition, including the collection of 26,000 botanical and zoological specimens, and the introduction of coca plant leaves which made it possible to isolate cocaine in its pure form for the first time in 1860. Many of the exhibits can be seen at Vienna's Natural History Museum. The expedition also returned with ethnographic objects, which can be viewed today in the World Museum in Vienna, formerly the Museum of Ethnology. So much material was collected on the expedition that the final report on the results had to be published in 21 volumes by the Viennese Academy of Sciences, entitled *Journey of the Austrian Frigate Novara around the Earth*.

What is less well known is that the expedition returned to Austria with two New Zealanders. Wiremu Toetoe and Hemara Te Rerehau (or Wilhelm Toetoe and Samuel Rerehau, as they were known in Austria) were the first Maoris to ever visit central Europe and did so of their own free will. They also kept a diary of their stay in Vienna, where they were given work in the state printing works and had an audience with Emperor Francis Joseph:

> These words are set down in praise of the Austrians. They are a good people, the most generous people we visited in the land of the Europeans. The buildings are beautiful, the food and the beverages delicious. Hard liquor is not found amongst them, nor did we see one drunk on the road during the nine months of our stay and we did not see anything bad in that land. They are undoubtedly a people of the highest standing in the world.
>
> They have paper money which is unlike the English. Money varies from people to people and theirs is Austrian money. It only costs one penny for a meal in a restaurant, whereas in England it is more than two schillings.

We began our stay in this country in the month of September 1859, and were taken to a leading chief of the land who was to arrange the place of our stay. He did so and we were made welcome at the printing house of that great gentleman. And here these two Maoris stayed until it was near the time for them to return to their homeland, when a visit to the Emperor was to be arranged.[20]

The journal details how the two prepared themselves, tidying their clothes and shoes, before arriving at the palace for their audience on 16 February 1860, and processed past the honour guards and were announced to Francis Joseph: 'These men are from New Zealand; they are chiefs from that land. They are Wiremu Toetoe and Hemara Rerehau who came on the Novara. They wish to speak to you in their own language and the chamberlain will translate it into German for you.' Wiremu was then invited to speak in the Maori language 'loudly and with emphasis', which he did:

We greet thee, we greet thee, Francis Joseph, Emperor of Austria. Great has been our desire to see thee, and that is the reason of our journey to this country. We desired to see thee, Emperor of Austria; we desired also to see the country of the foreigner. The commander of thy ship of war, the Novara, said to the Governor of New Zealand that he would allow us to sail with him in order that thou mightest see New Zealanders. The Governor and all the chiefs of the Maoris assented to the wish of the commodore. That is the reason of our journey to this country. All the chiefs of the Maoris said to us, "Go, that you may see the foreign country; go, that you may see the king of the foreigners." We greet thee, king of kings, lord of lords, thou that hath above all others rulest, we praise thee and thy name evermore. A strong sceptre is the sceptre of thy kingdom. We greet thee, we greet thee, Francis Joseph, Emperor of Austria: we greet thee, we greet thee, Empress of Austria. We shall inform all people of thy splendour when we shall have returned to New Zealand. These are our words to thee.[21]

They seem to have been taken aback by the emperor's reaction: 'For a long time the Emperor gazed upon us, his cheeks aglow: then he said "I have never heard such well chosen words as these two have said: their address was very excellent."'[22]

Shortly thereafter they left Vienna and Austrian newspapers printed a farewell message from the two Maoris:

Dear friends and people of Vienna, we greet you. We two men from New Zealand have come here on your frigate Novara to see your land and the white people who live there; now we have seen it all. This city is very beautiful, so are the houses and the streets and the fountains and the fishes in the fountains, so are the gardens and the sculptured heads; all things are very beautiful in Vienna, very beautiful.

We have seen the State Printing Works where we are staying, to learn your language and the craft of printing; we have seen the treasury and the great Stephanskirche as well as the very beautiful new church in Lerchenfeld. We climbed the tower of the Stephanskirche and also visited the garden in Schoenbrunn, belonging to the emperor of Austria. There we saw all the animals; it gave us great pleasure to see the animals about which we heard the English talk to us in New Zealand—the lion, the tiger, the elephant, the wolf, the reindeer, the fox, the bear, the giraffe, in short all animals and birds of which we had seen pictures in New Zealand.

Our teachers in New Zealand had also told us about your kings of old – how brave the Germanic kings used to be and how powerful were their armies. During our stay we saw the garments of those kings and their arsenals and afterwards we saw their effigies in the vaults of a church; the pakehas of New Zealand had talked about all these things, and how beautiful they were. We have seen your country; it is very good. There is only one evil thing and that is the abundance of snow and the harshness of the wind for the biting of the wind hurts our eyes, and also the great cold. In New Zealand it is not cold; snow in New Zealand lies only on the tops of mountains and only little of it; and the snowy mountains are far away, nowhere near the town. We greet you all, dear friends and people of Vienna.[23]

Before leaving Vienna, both men were asked by Archduke Maximilian what they would like as a parting gift. They requested a printing press and type, which was subsequently shipped to New Zealand. The printing press was put to use producing the Maori newspaper *Te Hookioi e Here Atu Na* ('The Far-Flying Hookioi of New Zealand'), which took a stance against British settlement and was seen as 'stirring and exciting the Maori to declare their independence'. The early versions of *Te Hookioi* included the declaration 'printed with the loving gift of the Emperor of Austria to the Maori people'.[24] The printing press is on display in the Te Awamutu Museum, in Waikato, North Island, the home region of the first two Maori men who ever visited Austria.

*

Born during the middle of the Congress of Vienna, Otto von Bismarck (1815–1898) had a profound impact on his native Prussia and on Austria. As the dominant political figure leading towards German unification, the Prussian junker pursued the Lesser Germany solution (Kleindeutschland) that would in time exclude Austria altogether, and see it eclipsed as the leading German-speaking power by its northern neighbour. Bismarck began his political career in 1847 as a conservative member of the newly created Prussian legislature, where he quickly earned a reputation as a gifted speaker who actually argued against German unification, as he believed it would end Prussia's independence. That changed after 'the humiliation of Olmütz', where Austria exerted its still dominant diplomatic position over Prussia in the German-speaking world: with the gifted diplomacy of Chancellor Felix zu Schwarzenberg, the restoration of the German Confederation was agreed under Austrian leadership. It was a humiliation for Prussia, which had sought to unify Germany under its leadership in the Erfurt Union. With the support of its absolutist ally Russia, whose forces had just defeated the Hungarian insurrection, Austria was able to dictate terms to Prussia in the Punctation of Olmütz, named after the Moravian town where the agreement was signed in November 1850. In Prussia, it became a synonym for defeat: 'a second Olmütz'. While Austria dictated strong terms, Vienna was not powerful enough to push through its own plans for 'Greater Austria', which would have seen the entire Habsburg Empire join an enlarged German federation as the dominant player. Also known as the Schwarzenberg Plan, it echoed moves by Austrian Trade Minister Karl Ludwig von Bruck to establish an enlarged customs union covering the same territories. At this stage, neither Prussia nor Austria was strong enough to deliver their plans. This would change under the Prussian leadership of Bismarck, who in 1851 became the Prussian envoy to the Diet of the German Confederation in Frankfurt. During his eight-year-long diplomatic posting, his views evolved, and he became convinced that Prussia had to improve its relations with other German states in reaction to the restored Austrian position. Bismarck's diplomatic skills were further honed with ambassadorial postings to Russia and France, while he remained closely informed and personally connected with political developments in Prussia.

In 1861 Bismarck was recalled from Paris by the new King Wilhelm, who appointed him Prussian Minister-President and Foreign Minister. Together with the modernising Minister of War Albrecht von Roon and Chief of the Prussian General Staff Helmut von Moltke, they would dominate Prussian fortunes and force Austria's decline in the 1860s. Before departing Paris, Bismarck spoke with Austrian ambassador Richard von Metternich (the son of the former chancellor) about the leadership role he would seek for Prussia, 'by any means without scruple'. And shortly after taking up his post in Berlin, he told the Habsburg ambassador Count Alois Károli, a Hungarian magnate, that the time had come 'for Austria to shift her centre of gravity from Germany to Hungary',[25] and, if not, then Prussia would side with France in any future crisis. The warnings were not taken seriously enough in Vienna.

The German question regained momentum in the decade after Austria had lost the 1859 Italian War and with it the wealthy Lombardy region. In 1863 Emperor Francis Joseph invited fellow rulers to attend the Congress of Princes (Fürstentag) in Frankfurt to discuss reforms to the German Confederation. He proposed a five-strong directory at the head of the confederation under his own chairmanship, with a federal council and an advisory assembly of delegates from the 38 state diets, as a sop to reformist democrats. Given that Austria could count on the support of the smaller German states, its majority would be secured in both the directory and assembly. Addressing his fellow monarchs at the beginning of the congress, the 33-year-old Emperor Francis Joseph said: 'Let us . . . agree speedily and readily to the details. Let us with federal good faith, allow to the power of Prussia what is due to it, and let us hope that, with God's blessing, this example of our unity may have a deep effect on all German hearts. For my own part . . . it will be a source of the greatest satisfaction to me, to have contributed my best efforts to consolidate the German bond of unity and to elevate the Confederation, by which we form a united power, to the highest point of its destiny, important for Germany and important for Europe.'[26]

Despite Francis Joseph travelling in person to Gastein, near Salzburg, where King Wilhelm and Bismarck were vacationing, to persuade Prussia to take part in the congress, they did not. Instead, a rival plan was issued which would have seen an alternating presidency of the confederation between Prussia and Austria, a right of veto over war powers and a German parliament elected with a general suffrage. While the heads of state at the congress largely accepted the Austrian plan, subject to Prussian approval, this would never be forthcoming. The die was cast, according to a historian of the assembly: 'The failure of this attempt placed the destiny of Germany in the hands of Prussia and Bismarck with the incalculable consequences of authoritarianism and militarism of a virulent type. The old-fashioned, inoffensive, and localised type of monarchy represented by Austria gave way to the modern industrialised and efficient Prussian type, with its dreams of pan-Germanism, sea power, and world conquest. The meeting may therefore be considered an event of considerable importance in the history of Germany and the world.'[27]

On his return trip to Vienna, Emperor Francis Joseph stopped to visit Queen Victoria, who was residing in mourning at Rosenau Palace, the German birthplace of her husband and consort, Prince Albert of Saxe-Coburg and Gotha (1819–1861). In the first of a number of meetings over their long reigns, and three days after she had hosted King Wilhelm for lunch, she agreed with Francis Joseph that it had been a mistake for the Prussians to boycott the Frankfurt Congress.[28] Describing him as 'very quiet, simple and unaffected, not talkative, but very dignified',[29] she tried to encourage cooperation between Austria and Prussia.

That is exactly what happened within a few short months, when events overtook efforts to reform the German Confederation, with the death of King Frederick VII of Denmark. It set off a hugely complex and convoluted dispute, about the Danish succession and the future of the Duchies of Schleswig and Holstein, which was famously described by British Prime Minister Lord Palmerston: 'The Schleswig-Holstein question is so complicated, only three men in Europe have ever understood it. One was Prince Albert, who is dead. The second was a German professor who became mad. I am the third and I have forgotten all about it.'[30]

In a war from February to July 1864, Prussia and Austria jointly battled the Danes on the Jutland peninsula, most famously in April at the Battle of Dybbøl, and in May at the naval Battle of Helgoland, the last of its kind between wooden ships.

With Bismarck steering towards Prussian annexation of the duchies, the victorious monarchs and their foreign ministers met on 22 August at Schönbrunn Palace. Austrian Foreign Minister Count

Johann von Rechberg und Rothenlöwen (1806–1899) was prepared to allow a Prussian takeover in return for guarantees over Austria's north Italian and Balkan possessions. In the end, the October 1864 Treaty of Vienna concluded that Holstein would be administered by the Austrians, and Schleswig by Prussia. The follow-up Gastein Convention, signed by Austria and Prussia on 14 August 1865 in the Alpine Austrian spa-town, was 'papering over the cracks',[31] according to Bismarck – the first time the expression was put to use. The treaty favoured Prussian interests and, in early 1866, Austria referred the issue to the German Confederation in Frankfurt, which Bismarck viewed as a breach of the treaty and a hostile act. Within months Austrian and Prussian military forces were on a heightened state of readiness on both sides of their common border. At the same time, Bismarck reached an agreement with Italy, setting the challenging conditions for Austria to face a two-front war. Rather than just concentrate their armed forces against the Prussians in the north, they had to mobilise in the south against the Italians at the same time. Austria still had many allies amongst the smaller German states, and when on the 14 June the German Diet voted to mobilise troops against Prussia, the Prussians responded the next day by invading Saxony, Hannover and Hesse. Within days, Italy declared war. France remained neutral, in accordance with secret arrangements with Austria, while Colonel Merlin, the French military attaché to Vienna, failed monumentally in his assessment, advising Paris that 'Bismarck would not dare overthrow the German Confederation in 1866 for fear that he would trigger a punitive strike at Prussia'.[32] The stage was set for a conflict conducted in Bohemia and northern Italy. It lasted just over a month and determined the future of Germany and Europe.

Prussia's political leadership had been preparing for war for some time, to secure its leadership in Germany. In his most famous speech Bismarck told the Prussian parliament in 1862 that 'the position of Prussia in Germany will not be determined by its liberalism but by its power . . . by iron and blood'.[33] At the same time, the Prussian armed forces were being reformed, with major changes to conscription, training, tactics and armaments. Not only were Prussian forces better drilled but they also used a bolt-action rifle, the Dreyse needle gun, capable of much more rapid rates of fire than the muzzle-loading Austrian Lorenz musket. They were also in a better position to concentrate their forces in the optimal offensive location in northern Bohemia. As Chief of the General Staff Helmuth von Moltke explained in a memorandum, the Prussians could mobilise quickly to take the fight to the Austrians: 'One advantage for us, which cannot be overstated, is that we can advance our army on five railroad lines and thereby have it essentially concentrated on the Saxon-Bohemian border within 25 days. Austria has just one railway leading toward Bohemia, and allowing for the troops it already has in Bohemia and Galicia, and assuming further that its cavalry is already on the march, it requires 45 days to assemble 200,000 men.'[34] In comparison to the professional brilliance of the Prussian military leadership, the Austrians were led by Ludwig von Benedek, a commander popular with his troops and who preferred concepts of service and heroism rather than 'complicated calculations'.

While the two sides were converging in Bohemia in June 1866, the war had already started in Italy, where things started well for the Austrians with victory at the Battle of Custoza on 24 June under the commanded of Archduke Albrecht. Later the Austrians would also go on to win the naval Battle of Lissa under Admiral Wilhelm von Tegetthoff, despite being outnumbered and outgunned by the Italians. The Austrian naval forces won the engagement with minimal losses off the Croatian island of Vis in what was the first major naval battle to include ironclads.

In Bohemia, the Prussians' invading forces had to advance through separate mountain passes, which is where they first encountered Austrian resistance. Opening engagements on 27 June saw Prussian advanced units repulsed the Austrians at Náchod, while at the Battle of Trautenau the Austrians were victorious at great cost. In both engagements the Austrian casualties were three to four times that of the Prussians, whose routes of advance remained open. Unable to defeat the deploying Prussian forces before they converged, Benedek telegrammed Francis Joseph: 'Beg Your Majesty most urgently to make peace. Catastrophe unavoidable for the army.' The emperor replied: 'Impossible to make peace. If unavoidable, I authorise an orderly retreat. Has the battle already taken place?'[35] Interpreting the last sentence as an order not to retreat before fighting a major battle, Benedek deployed his forces between Sadowa and Königgrätz.

On 3 July 1866 the Austrian army of 215,000 clad in white stood opposite two of three Prussian armies in dark blue totalling 124,000. It would be the biggest battle in Europe between the Napoleonic Wars and the First World War. Despite a superiority of numbers and also field position, with their capable artillery on raised heights, the Austrians were rocked by a full-frontal Prussian assault with devastating breech-loading rapid-fire infantry rifles followed by a flanking manoeuvre. Austrian corps commanders unsuccessfully requested reinforcements and a counter-attack before the arrival of the third Prussian army, which occurred at 2.30 p.m., tipping the scales with an additional 100,000 men. At 3 p.m., Benedek ordered the retreat and informed the emperor that the catastrophe had come to pass. The consequences of the Battle of Königgrätz would be as calamitous. In one day the Austrian General Staff accounted for Austrian casualties totalling 1,313 officers, 41,499 men and 6,010 horses, compared with the Prussians' 359 officers, 8,794 men and 909 horses.[36] In the military context of the age, it dwarfs the bloodiest single-day battle of the US Civil War at Antietam in 1862, where there was a joint total of 23,000 men killed, wounded or missing.

A Russian military observer at the battle, Major General Dragomirow, said later: 'It wasn't the needle gun by itself that won the victories of 1866, but the men who carried it,' while the French military attaché in Berlin, Colonel Stoffel, believed that the superiority of the Prussian high command made the difference, and even if the Austrians had possessed breech-loading rifles it wouldn't have made any difference.[37]

With the benefit of hindsight it seems scarcely imaginable that the outcome might have been different; however, it remains one of the great 'what ifs' of history: 'Had the Austrians won the war, the Prussians could have expected no mercy . . . Vienna would have stunted Prussian's economic growth by a debilitating schedule of reparation payments, the amputation of industrial provinces like Silesia, Lusatia and the Ruhr, and by the forcible attachment of the Austrian Empire to the Prusso-German Zollverein. With its north German rival thus constrained and diminished, great, wobbly Austria may have continued to exercise its rather harmless leadership of the multistage German Confederation.'[38] The consequences may also have been profound further afield: 'The history of Prussia, of Germany, of Europe, and now we may say even Asia Minor – even of Asia – would have been different.'[39] It wasn't to be.

Ironically, it was a Vienna-based American who was in the cockpit of events throughout much of the Austro-Prussian conflict, owing in large part to an unusual friendship going back to university days. John Lothrop Motley (1814–1877) studied at university in Göttingen and Berlin during the 1830s with the young Bismarck, with whom he retained a life-long friendship. Motley, who hailed from Massachusetts, became a historian and was a stout defender of the Union during the American Civil War. Perhaps because of this and his fluent German, he was appointed by President Abraham Lincoln as the US senior diplomat to Vienna in 1861, a posting that lasted until 1867. Together with other European-based US diplomats, a large part of Motley's efforts was taken up with preventing recognition or support for the Confederacy. Details of his friendship with Bismarck and events during the worsening Austro-Prussian crisis while at his Vienna posting have been saved for posterity in two volumes of *The Correspondence of John Lothrop Motley*, which was published in 1889.

Writing to Lothrop in English, Bismarck asked him: 'Why do you never come to Berlin? . . . Let politics be hanged and come to see me. I promise that the Union Jack [Stars and Stripes] will fly over our house, and conversation and the best old hock shall pour damnation upon the rebels.'[40] The two met in 1864 at Motley's residence at 20 Favoritenstrasse, the details of which Motley shared with his mother: 'My friend Bismarck . . . is at present Prime Minister of Prussia and is here to negotiate a peace with Denmark. We were very intimate in our youth, and have always kept up the association, having renewed our old friendship six years ago in Frankfurt, where he was Prussian envoy at the Diet. He dined with us yesterday en famille asking me to have no one else except Werther, the Prussian Minister here, so we might talk of old times and be boys.'[41] In correspondence to his eldest daughter shortly after the Battle of Königgrätz, Motley explained the perilous situation facing Austria: 'This has been the most lightning-like campaign in all military history . . . Observe the position and shape of Prussia when the campaign opened. She has swept down from Schleswig, Pomerania and Silesia. In a week or two of battles she has captured, Saxony, Bohemia, Moravia and is looking grimly across the Danube into the very window of the Emperor's palace. With her right wing, if we consider the whole mighty army as one, she has demolished Bavaria and the other south-western states and she has occupied Frankfurt. All Germany is in her grasp or at her feet.'[42]

The consequence of the Austrian defeat was its exclusion from German affairs, as Prussia replaced the German Confederation with the North German Confederation as the first step to full unification, which occurred after the Franco-German war of 1870. On 18 January 1871 the German Empire came into being, with Prussian King Wilhelm as German Emperor and soon thereafter Bismarck as German chancellor. Motley visited his old friend Bismarck at Varzin, his Pomeranian country estate, for a week in 1872 and recorded his opinions about the peace that followed the Prussian victory of 1866: 'The military opinion was bent on going to Vienna after Sadowa [Königgrätz]. Bismarck strongly opposed this idea. He said it was absolutely necessary not to humiliate Austria, to do nothing that would make friendly relations with her in the future impossible . . . I asked him if he was good friends with the Emperor of Austria now. He said Yes, that the Emperor was exceedingly civil to him.'[43]

*

One of the first consequences of the Austrian defeat and exclusion from German affairs was the necessity to improve relations with

185

Hungary within the monarchy. Things had remained strained since the 1848 revolutions and the military defeat of the Hungarian independence movement. Now it was necessary to try and find a new way forward and discussions had already started during the Austro-Prussian war between Emperor Francis Joseph and the leading Hungarian politician Count Gyula Andrássy (1823–1890). He and fellow Hungarian statesman Ferenc Deák (1803–1876) played the major part in securing a fundamental restructuring of the state as an effective grand bargain that delivered Hungarian self-government while protecting the position of the Habsburgs.

The 1867 Austro-Hungarian Compromise saw the Danube Monarchy reorganised as a 'personal union', with Francis Joseph reigning as Emperor of Austria in an Austrian half of the empire, and as King of Hungary in the other. Both halves would have their own parliaments, prime ministers, domestic laws and citizenship. Only in the areas of foreign affairs and defence would there be common policies under the direction of the monarch in this new 'dualist' system. A joint finance ministry was responsible only for the imperial and royal household, and the common army, navy and diplomatic service. A common ministerial council included the monarch, the three common ministers and both prime ministers, while two delegations of parliamentarians from Vienna and Budapest decided on the joint financing, which became a major area of dispute when reviewed every decade. Funding responsibilities began in 1867 with the Austrian half bearing 70 per cent of the costs and the Hungarian 30 per cent.

The two states of Austria-Hungary were known as Cisleithania and Transleithania, from the Leitha river, which demarcated the border between the two halves. Cisleithania, or the Kingdoms and Lands Represented in the Imperial Council, with its capital in Vienna, was in effect the west and north of the empire, including most of present-day Austria and South Tyrol, as well as Bohemia, Moravia, Silesia, Galicia and Lodomaria, Bukovina, Carnolia, Dalmatia and the Austrian Littoral on the Adriatic. Transleithania, or the Hungarian Lands of the Crown of St Stephen, with its capital in Budapest, consisted of the Hungarian Kingdom and the Kingdom of Croatia, Slavonia and Dalmatia, including regions in present-day Hungary, Croatia, Serbia, Slovakia, Romania and Ukraine. Vienna remained the imperial city of residence, the seat of the shared defence and foreign ministries, and the embassies of countries with a diplomatic presence. Austria-Hungary remained the second largest country in Europe after Russia, with the third largest population after Russia and Germany: around 50 million people.

Rapprochement between Francis Joseph and Magyar leaders came after strong interventions by his wife, Empress Elisabeth, who had developed a keen interest in Hungary after a stifling existence at court in Vienna. For years, Sisi had endured the machinations of her mother-in-law, Archduchess Sophie, and suffered bouts of depression. After first visiting Hungary in 1857, she fell in love with the country, made major efforts to learn its language and spent an ever-growing amount of time there with her children. Sisi became an admired advocate of Hungarian claims by Magyar leaders, including Gyula Andrássy whose demands she sought to promote with her husband during the compromise negotiations: 'I have just had an interview with Andrássy. He set forth his views clearly and plainly. I quite understood them and arrived at the conclusion that if you would trust him – and trust him entirely – we might still be saved, not only Hungary, but the monarchy, too ... I can assure you that you are not dealing with a man desirous of playing a part at any price or striving for a position; on the contrary, he is risking his present position, which is a fine one. But approaching shipwreck, he, too, is prepared to do all in his power to save it; what he possesses – his understanding and influence in the country – he will lay at your feet. For the last time I beg you in Rudolf's name not to lose this, at the last moment.'[44]

As progress was being made with the Hungarian question and peace with Prussia and Italy, another Habsburg diplomatic crisis had been developing, involving the emperor's younger brother, Maximilian. After a career in the Austrian navy, which he ended up commanding, he also served as Viceroy of Lombardy-Venetia before the region was forfeited and he retired to Miramare Castle near Trieste. Lost without a defined role, he was soon proposed as a potential Emperor of Mexico, with a degree of legitimacy as a Habsburg, given Spanish Habsburgs ruled over much of the Americas. The establishment of a Mexican monarchy followed an armed intervention in the country by France, Spain and Britain, and Napoleon III sought to maintain French influence in the country. All the while, ousted Mexican republicans resisted international interference, but Maximilian was assured by the French there was popular support for the proclamation of an empire. A Mexican delegation headed by diplomat José María Gutiérrez de Estrada travelled to Miramare Castle to offer Maximilian the Mexican throne, which he accepted in October 1863. Travelling to Mexico aboard SMS *Novara* with his wife Charlotte, they arrived in May 1864 and took up residence in Mexico City. It soon became clear that there was ongoing resistance to foreign-imposed imperial rule, and French and locally recruited troops were required to maintain Maximilian's position. His rule became even more precarious as he tried to balance the interests of his wealthy, conservative, landowning supporters with the liberal reforms of the preceding republican government. When the American Civil War ended in 1865 and the US government again focused on regional developments, it recognised the ousted Mexican government and pressured France to withdraw support from Maximilian. A crackdown on republican supporters led to thousands of summary executions, but further weakened his position. Empress Carlota, as Charlotte was known in Mexico, left on a tour of European capitals to seek support just as France withdrew their troops. Facing a worsening security situation, Maximilian refused to abdicate or surrender, instead enduring a last stand and siege at Santiago de Querétaro in May 1867 where he was captured by republican forces.

This was the situation just as preparations were being made for the crowning of Francis Joseph and Elisabeth as King and Queen of Hungary in Budapest. According to Hungarian tradition, a coronation was essential to become king; if not, the nation was 'orphaned', laws could not be approved or royal prerogatives exercised. A magnificent ceremony was organised for 8 June 1867, which would combine Magyar patriotism and pomp. Days beforehand Vienna-based diplomats, international guests and journalists travelled by train or down the Danube to Budapest. All suitable accommodation was reserved for the nobility, and all hotel rooms were fully booked; ordinary Hungarians who travelled from across the country had to make do if they wanted to see the colourful five days of celebrations culminating in the coronation itself.

Volleys of cannon fire woke the city at 4 a.m. and guests and onlookers began to make their way to the parade route and Mathias Church on the western side of the Danube. Throngs of guests in their finest national costumes packed the Romanesque Church of the Assumption of the Buda Castle and the surrounding square as Ferenc József and Erzsébet set off in a grand procession from the Royal Palace, the order of which was detailed in the London *Times*:

1. A squadron of Liechtenstein Hussars in dark blue and yellow facings.
2. Two mounted officers of the Court in an old-fashioned uniform which looked like gold lace with small pieces of blue on it.
3. The Imperial Royal footmen and the Court trumpeters and kettle-drummers in their most gorgeous liveries.
4. Two mounted officers of the Court, equally splendid.
5. The Imperial Royal pages in cocked hats, knee breeches, and silk stockings, with their Governor mounted, some 10 or 12 in number.
6. The Court purveyor, quite a glory of finery, mounted.
7. Noblemen and Chamberlains mounted.
8. The Magnates, Privy Councillors, Barons of the Realm, and Ministers, mounted.
9. Knights of the Imperial Royal orders, according to their rank, mounted.
10. Knights of the Golden Fleece, mounted.

11. The President of the Ministry, Count Andrássy, mounted.

12. The Halberdier Guard, mounted.

13. The Royal Bohemian and the Archducal Austrian herald, the Royal Hungarian between the two Imperial Royal Heralds, mounted.

14. The Royal Hungarian Grand Chamberlain with his staff of office, mounted.

15. The Imperial and Royal Archdukes, mounted.

16. His Majesty the Emperor and Apostolic King, preceded by a bishop on his right with the Apostolic Cross, and on his left proceeded by the Royal Hungarian Master of the Horse, uncovered, carrying the drawn sword of State followed by the Captains of Body Guard and Lord Chamberlain.

17. Her Majesty the Empress and Queen in a state carriage drawn by eight horses, three running footmen, uncovered, on each side, and followed by her Marshall of the court, the chamberlain on duty, and four pages.

18. The mistress of the robes in a state carriage, drawn by six horses, a running footman, uncovered on each side.

19. Four state carriages, drawn by six horses, in each three ladies of the bedchamber, two running footmen uncovered to each carriage. The carriages, some of them dated from the time of Maria Therese, were most splendid.

20. The Hungarian Body Guard.

21. The Gendarmes of the Guard.

22. A company of infantry.

23. A Squadron of Hussars.

On reaching this church His Majesty, who was in his uniform of Field Marshall, was assisted from his horse by the Lord High Chamberlain, while the Mistress of the Robes assisted Her Majesty to descend from the carriage of state which was of singular magnificence and richness. Within the church, where the Magnates, Deputies, Ministers and diplomatic body were assembled, their majesties were received by the Primate and the officiating prelates and clergy.[45]

In an elaborate ceremony conducted in Latin by János Simor, the Archbishop of Esztergom, Primate of Hungary, Francis Joseph took the oath of office in front of the altar, then lay prostrate during the litany and was anointed before having the ancient royal mantle of St Stephen placed solemnly over his shoulders and being ceremonially presented the sword of state. Finally, while Francis Joseph was bowed on one knee at the top step of the altar, the archbishop and Count Andrássy placed the 11th-century Byzantine-made crown of St Stephen on his head and he took his place on the throne. The church then broke out into three traditional Magyar hurrah cries of *Éljen*. A similar crowning ceremony then followed immediately for Elisabeth. In the second high point of the day, Francis Joseph, wearing the Hungarian crown and regalia, rode on horseback to the top of a coronation mound and, pointing the sword of state to the four points of the compass, swore to protect the kingdom and its subjects. With that, Francis Joseph was officially King of Hungary as well as Emperor of Austria and had solemnised the newly reformed Austro-Hungarian state. In a message of reconciliation, he handed back a valuable financial coronation offering so it might support the widows and orphans of the Hungarian uprising, while Elisabeth said: 'Were it in our power to do so, we two would be the first to recall Lajos Bathyány and the martyrs of Arad to life.'[46] Gödöllő Palace, east of Budapest, which Sisi had coveted from her husband, was gifted to them both by the Hungarian state as a coronation present, and would become her favourite residence.

Immediately after the coronation, the royal couple and their children took a vacation at their country retreat at Bad Ischl. Whilst they were there, on 19 June 1867, Maximilian was executed by firing squad in Mexico after uttering his last words: 'I forgive everyone, and I pray that everyone may also forgive me and I hope that my blood which is about to be shed will bring peace to Mexico. *Viva* Mexico, *viva la independencia!*'[47] It took a week for the news to arrive in Europe. Three and a half years after arriving in Mexico, the SMS *Novara* was back to collect the body of Maximilian, who died aged only 34. Returning to Vienna via Trieste, he was buried with imperial obsequies next to his Habsburg ancestors in the Capuchin Crypt. His wife Charlotte suffered a serious breakdown after his death and was scarred with mental illness for the rest of her life. She died in 1927. The rumour persists that she gave birth to an illegitimate child in 1867: Maxime Waygand, who would go on to become the French military commander during the First and Second World Wars.[48]

# 8

# *Nervous Splendour: Fin de Siècle*

'The Streets of Vienna are paved with culture, the streets
of other cities with asphalt.'

– Karl Kraus[1]

During the last decades of the 19th century, record numbers of
international visitors and dignitaries from different countries visited
Vienna, including Japan. After centuries of being shut off from the
rest of the world, largely feudal Japan opened up, keenly aware that
it could learn much from industrialised nations about technological
and economic development as well as their forms of government.
In 1871 the new administration of Emperor Meiji dispatched the
Iwakura Embassy, a high-level delegation, for an epic tour of the US
and Europe led by Prince Iwakura, a senior member of the Japanese
court and government minister. He was joined by high-ranking
decision-makers and a 108-strong delegation, including 45 commis-
sioners and clerks. The secretary to Prince Iwakura was the young
scholar Kume Kunitake (1839–1931), who wrote the official report
of the tour, which has been described as 'an outstanding piece of
work containing shrewd analysis and compelling observations'.[2]

The Japanese delegation spent eight months in the US, travelling
by train from San Fransisco to Washington, then on to Europe for a
full year, starting in Britain before visiting Paris and northern France,
Belgium, the Netherlands, Berlin and Prussia, St Petersburg and
Russia, Denmark, Sweden, Italy, Austria-Hungary and Switzerland.
They returned to Japan from Marseilles through the recently opened
Suez Canal. Their extended travels included meetings with US

President Ulysses S. Grant, Queen Victoria, Otto von Bismarck and Emperor Francis Joseph.

Arriving from the south, the Japanese were impressed by the beauty of the railway journey and the engineering of the route as they crossed the Semmering Pass towards the Austrian capital. In his report, Kunitake sought to explain to Japanese readers the difference between Austrians and Prussians: 'It has been argued that both . . . are circumspect and slow, but they deserve praise for their natural aptitude for intricate craftsmanship. Because they spend their lives on the cold, bare plains of the north, the Prussians nurtured their spirit in poverty, practised perseverance and elevated their morale; thus, they excel at war and often engage in harsh practices. Of late they have been victorious in war against four of their neighbours and the mood in Berlin is fierce. Austria, by contrast, enjoys good soil and a milder climate and has long been used to civilised ways of its famous capital city; it has learnt to live with riches and has steeped itself in urban elegance; the people are discriminating and fond of the arts. The two seem to be opposites; yet they both share the phlegmatic character of the German people.'[3]

Kunitake was 32 at the time of the visit, which corresponded with the eclipse of Austria by Prussia: 'At present Prussia is on the rise and Austria is in decline, and everybody lauds the military culture of the Prussians. Military skills are not one of Austria's strengths, but its literary arts are truly amongst the finest in Europe. It is a leader in politics, law, science and engineering, and in medicine it is virtually without equal.'[4]

The first stop of their tour in Vienna was at the Arsenal building, which is now home to the Military History Museum, where the military hardware did not impress the visitors: the weapons 'did give the impression of being 40 years behind the times, the same as its constitutional arrangements'.[5] The tour continued with audiences with the emperor, empress, and 'several princes', a visit to the treasury with its 'astounding items', observing the Corpus Christi procession and washing of the feet of the poor: 'all Catholic ceremonies, remnants of old religious practices'. The delegation visited the Foreign Ministry, attended a military tattoo, and viewed the World Exposition a number of times. The 1873 World's Fair in Vienna was located in the Prater Park and drew visitors from around the world: 'The enormous size of the Rotunda at the centre was enough to astound the visitor. The dome of this structure was 250 feet in diameter and 370 feet in height . . . and the apex was so high that one could not see it clearly. The doors and windows were glazed. At the top of the Rotunda there was a replica of the jewelled crown of Austria. Above this flew the country's flag. Seen from a distance, it seemed to rise into the very clouds . . . Every section was filled with treasures; at each step one discovered marvels. If one walked without stopping, taking in something new at every step, at the end of a day one would still have seen only a fraction of the exhibition.'[6]

Hosting the 1873 World's Fair in Vienna was a major effort by the Austrian government to boost its international image after its major setbacks in Italy and Germany and the recent compromise arrangements with Hungary. The silver anniversary year of Francis Joseph's reign was also deemed as opportune to showcase the economic progress of the empire and the largest urban reconstruction project of anywhere in Europe. Not only was the urban redevelopment around Vienna's Ringstrasse proceeding apace, but large-scale regulation works were under way on the River Danube. While the Danube Canal continued to flow next to the city centre, the main body of the river was subject to major engineering works to straighten its course and reduce the risk of regular flood events. Half a million cubic feet of excavated gravel from the riverbed was used to construct the site of the World's Fair in the Prater park between the main channel of the River Danube and the Danube Canal.[7]

The Vienna site was five times larger than the preceding fair in Paris, with so much exhibition space for different participating nations that the organisers constructed separate Palaces of Industry, Machinery, Agriculture, and Art in addition to the main exhibition rotunda, which was the largest structure of its kind ever built, with its dome twice the diameter of St Peter's in Rome and weighing 4,000 tonnes. Between 1 May 1873 and 2 November 1873,

7.2 million visitors viewed the displays in 194 pavilions from 35 different countries involving 53,000 exhibitors.

It was not all plain sailing for the exhibition, however, as Vienna was rocked nine days after the official opening by a stock market crash, which followed feverish speculation on projects such as the massive Ringstrasse building development. The crash amounted to 'a tremendous setback for the city and caused a rash of suicides among financiers and speculators. A severe financial depression gripped the city and country and caused widespread unemployment.'[8]

The summer also saw an outbreak of cholera in the city, which claimed the lives of more than 2,000 people. Visitor numbers never reached their targets, in part because of rampant profiteering by the city's hotels, restaurants and cab drivers, which discouraged even the wealthy from attending. All of this contributed to the exhibition running at a loss of 15 million gulden and earning it the dubious accolade of being 'one of the greatest financial failures of the nineteenth century'.[9]

Nevertheless, the exhibition was a success as a national and international society event of the highest order, and as the backdrop to a number of high-level diplomatic meetings and agreements. During the six months it was open, it was attended by visiting foreign government ministers and delegations, 33 ruling princes, 13 royals next in the line of succession and 20 princes from the Vienna court. In addition to top Austro-Hungarian attendees, like Crown Prince Rudolph and Foreign Minister Count Gyula Andrássy, international visitors included King Leopold II of Belgium, King Victor Emanuel II of Italy, Prussian Crown Prince Frederick III, Prince Albert of Saxony, Edward Prince of Wales, Crown Prince Frederick of Denmark, Prince Nicolas I of Montenegro and scores of diplomats.[10] A particular international high point was the visit of the Shah of Persia Naser al-Din, which was considered so exotic that 40,000 visitors attended in the hope of seeing him. According to the official British report on the exhibition: 'It may well be doubted whether the practical and the picturesque, the modern and the medieval, the East and the West will ever again mingle in one harmonious whole, with such equal aid from art and nature, as on the Prater of 1873, in the Buildings in the Park.'[11]

The exhibition also served as a backdrop for meetings and agreements between the Emperors of Austria-Hungary, Germany and Russia – Francis Joseph I, Wilhelm I and Alexander II. The Three Emperors' League (Dreikaiserbund) effectively resurrected the Holy Alliance, and followed the Schönbrunn Convention signed earlier in the year between Russia and Austria-Hungary. The monarchs even had their own meeting place, where their three empires physically met one another – Three Emperors' Corner, which became a minor tourist attraction. The spot lay at the confluence of the Black and White Przemsza rivers, not far from Oświęcim in present-day Poland, more widely known internationally as Auschwitz.

The aim of the league was to protect peace in Europe after recent wars, on the basis of a balance of power. The newly united Germany was concerned about the potential for aggression by its neighbours, including Austria where Chancellor Count Friedrich von Beust had been 'impatient to take his revenge on Bismarck for Sadowa [Königgrätz]',[12] but newly strengthened Hungary used its new position in the dual monarchy to effectively block it. Bismarck pursued the agreement as a way of cutting the risks for Germany, reducing the rivalry between Austria-Hungary and Russia in the Balkans and excluding France. Vienna would, in future, have a predominant sphere of influence in the western Balkans, Moscow further east.

The first article of the league secured the key German priority in relation to France: 'In case one of the High Contracting Parties should find itself at war with a fourth Great Power, the two others shall maintain towards it a benevolent neutrality and shall devote their efforts to the localisation of the conflict.' Concerns over conflict in the Balkans were addressed in the second article: 'The three Courts, desirous of avoiding all discord between them, engage to take account of their respective interests in the Balkan Peninsula. They further promise one another that any new modifications in the territorial status quo of Turkey in Europe can be accomplished only in virtue of a common agreement between them.'[13]

Despite the publicly avowed hopes for the league, it would be tested to destruction by events over the next decades, which led ultimately to the First World War. 'Though the three emperors talked of their conservative principles, none of them would make any sacrifices for these principles. The League was supposed to keep Europe at peace; in reality it could exist only so long as Europe remained calm. It was a fair-weather system as the Holy Alliance had been before it. A new conflict between France and Germany, a new twist of the Eastern Question, would destroy it.'[14]

It didn't take long for the first challenge to emerge, with the out-break of the Great Eastern Crisis of 1875–1878, beginning with a series of localised rebellions against Ottoman rule in the Balkans, which in turn sparked the intervention of the major powers and the Russo-Turkish War of 1877–1878. In the Ottoman province of Bosnia-Herzegovina, peasants were refusing to pay taxes following a bad harvest, and threats of armed resistance were brutally repressed. Thousands of Christian peasants began to flee across the border to Austria-Hungary, an exodus that within a year would total between 100,000 and 250,000 people, while 5,000 people were killed and many local villages destroyed.

The dangers for Austria-Hungary were significant if receding Ottoman control fed Pan-Slavism, irredentism and growing Russian influence in the Balkans. Andrássy raised these concerns with Emperor Francis Joseph at an extraordinary Crown Council meeting in January 1875: 'Turkey possesses a utility almost providential for Austria-Hungary. For Turkey maintains the status quo of the small Balkan States and impedes their [national] aspirations. If it were not for Turkey, all these aspirations would fall down on their heads . . . if Bosnia-Herzegovina should go to Serbia or Montenegro, or if a new state should be formed there which we cannot prevent, then we should be ruined and should ourselves assume the role of the "Sick Man".'[15]

On 25 July 1875 the Russian ambassador to Vienna Yevgeny Novikov proposed that the Three Emperors' League powers make a joint intervention to end the uprising. He suggested that, together with Foreign Minister Andrássy and German ambassador Hans Lothar von Schweinitz, they should seek to alleviate the situation for the insurgents. Despite efforts by Andrássy to limit involvement, the initiative soon grew to include France, Britain and Italy with a mission involving consuls from all six countries deploying to Bosnia-Herzegovina to make an on-the-ground assessment and meet with both the local Ottoman authorities and insurgents. The mission to seek de-escalation failed after Ottoman forces treacherously attacked rebels who had just met with the consuls; however, not before the consuls had witnessed the scale of destruction and heard from the locals about the fundamental lack of trust in the Ottoman authorities and the prospects for fair treatment. Both the British and Austro-Hungarian consuls reported that only European intervention could solve the problem of the appalling chaos and anarchy they had seen.[16]

In addition to the Bosnia-Herzegovina uprising, there were revolts against the Ottoman occupiers in Bulgaria, and Serbia and Montenegro declared war against the Ottoman Empire. On 8 July 1876 the emperors of Austria-Hungary and Russia, Francis Joseph and Alexander II, met in person at the Reichstadt Palace in Bohemia to discuss the ongoing crisis and reach a common understanding for the future of the Balkans. The Reichstadt Agreement proposed a carve-up, with Russian control of Bessarabia and gains in the Caucasus, while Austria-Hungary would have Bosnia-Herzegovina, although its status was not defined. The understanding also supported greater independence for Balkan Christians but would not lead to the creation of a large Pan-Slavic state in the region.

While Ottoman rule was being challenged by the uprising in Bosnia-Herzegovina, revolutionaries in Bulgaria also took up arms. Turkish forces put down the rebellion with brutal force, including massacres that claimed the lives of tens of thousands of civilians. The Ottoman atrocities caused a surge of international revulsion, especially in Russia where there was a wave of sympathy for their Orthodox neighbours and outright support for Bulgarian independence. At the same time, the principalities of Serbia and Montenegro took their opportunity to declare their independence from Ottoman influence and declared war on the Sublime Porte. The conflict lasted from 1876 until 1878, during which time Russia also declared war on the Ottoman Empire.

The Russo-Turkish War took place in the Balkans with a force of 185,000 troops, and in the Caucasus with 75,000 soldiers. Together with Romanian, Bulgarian, Serbian and Montenegrin forces in the Balkans, the Russians eventually pushed the Ottomans back to within 11 kilometres of Constantinople at San Stefano, where hostilities were ended. Had it not been for a five-month siege of Ottoman fortifications at the Battle of Plevna, however, the Russian-led forces might well have had the momentum to take Constantinople before the involvement of the Great Powers, who sought to secure a wider diplomatic agreement for the region at the Congress of Berlin.

Representatives of six great European powers – Russia, Germany, Austria-Hungary, France, Great Britain and Italy – were joined at the Reich Chancellery in Berlin by the Ottoman Empire and four Balkan states: Serbia, Montenegro, Romania and Greece. Bulgaria was not formally represented as it was not a sovereign country, but it did secure greater independence as a result of the congress. Bismarck, who chaired proceedings, sought to re-establish peace in the Balkans but had to balance the competing interests of the different states as the Ottoman Empire receded, while protecting the League of the Three Emperors.

The headline results were: the establishment of an independent Bulgarian principality formally under Ottoman suzerainty; Romania became fully independent, as did Serbia and Montenegro; Austria-Hungary took over Bosnia-Herzegovina; Great Britain received Cyprus; and Russia secured territorial gains in Bessarabia, in present-day Moldova, but not 'Greater Bulgaria' including Eastern Rumelia and Macedonia, which had been agreed in the preceding Treaty of San Stefano and would have allowed Russian access to the Mediterranean. By granting the larger states some of what they wanted, but not all, tensions in the Balkans were not resolved, just postponed, with calamitous consequences at the beginning of the 20th century.

The Treaty of Berlin was signed on 13 July 1878, including article 25 on the future of Bosnia-Herzegovina: 'The provinces of Bosnia and Herzegovina shall be occupied and administered by Austria-Hungary. The government of Austria-Hungary, not desiring to undertake the administration of the Sanjak of Novi-Pazar, which extends between Serbia and Montenegro in a South-Easterly direction to the other side of Mitrovitza, the Ottoman administration will continue to exercise its functions there. Nevertheless, in order to assure the maintenance of the new political state of affairs, as well as freedom and security of communications, Austria-Hungary reserves the right of keeping garrisons and having military and commercial roads in the whole of this part of the ancient vilayet of Bosnia. To this end the governments of Austria-Hungary and Turkey reserve to themselves to come to an understanding on the details.'[17]

Two weeks after the treaty was agreed, Austro-Hungarian troops began to occupy Bosnia-Herzegovina in what Foreign Minister Andrássy predicted would be an unopposed 'walk with a brass band'. Instead, eight whole infantry divisions were mobilised in two waves, with more than 153,000 troops, thousands of horses, and hundreds of cannons to secure the mountainous province the size of Bohemia and with a population of 1.1 million.[18] While the 18 per cent population of Bosnian Croats welcomed the prospects of joining their fellow Croat co-religionists under Habsburg administration, the same couldn't be said for the 39 per cent Bosnian Muslims, who feared losing their status, and the 43 per cent Bosnian Serbs, who viewed Austrian rule as a block on closer ties with Serbia proper and had already been fighting the Ottomans for two years. The Austrian general staff estimated that their forces faced 79,000 insurgents, who were being supported by 13,800 regular Ottoman troops. In a three-month campaign, which involved a number of pitched battles and numerous guerrilla attacks, the Austro-Hungarians were finally victorious after besieging the capital, Sarajevo, which involved shelling the city and house-to-house combat. Casualties amongst the occupiers totalled 5,000 men, while no statistics were collected for insurgents or civilians.

The growing influence of Austria-Hungary in the western Balkans was not universally domestically popular, especially in Hungary, despite the Treaty of Berlin being negotiated by two Hungarians, Andrássy and ambassador to Berlin Count Alajos Károlyi de Nagykároly. The French Ambassador to Vienna Melchior de Vogüé summed it up as follows: 'Particularly in Hungary the dissatisfaction caused by this "adventure" has reached the gravest proportions, prompted by that strong conservative instinct which animates the Magyar race and is the secret of its destinies. This vigorous and exclusive instinct explains the historical phenomenon of an isolated group, small in numbers yet dominating a country inhabited by a majority of peoples of different races and conflicting aspirations, and playing a role in European affairs out of all proportions to its numerical importance or intellectual culture. This instinct is today awakened and gives warning that it feels the occupation of Bosnia-Herzegovina to be a menace which, by introducing fresh Slav elements into the Hungarian political organism and providing a wider field and further recruitment of the Croat opposition, would upset the unstable equilibrium in which the Magyar domination is poised.'[19]

The potential imbalance to the nationalities in the dualist state led to the province being administered for the next thirty years as a condominium by the joint Finance Ministry. Having at least protected their prestige and interests in the western Balkans in the unavoidable circumstances of Ottoman decline, Austria-Hungary had secured a degree of stability for the remainder of the 19th century. This was enhanced with a secret bilateral treaty with Serbia that guaranteed its dominant diplomatic, security and trading position, in return for recognition and support of the ruling Obrenović dynasty as Kings of Serbia.[20] It followed agreements on the construction of the Vienna–Constantinople railway (which would carry the Orient Express) as well as a trade treaty guaranteeing dominant Austro-Hungarian market arrangements for Serbian agricultural exports. The agreements also effectively tied Serbia to the Triple Alliance that Austria-Hungary signed with Germany and Italy in 1882 guaranteeing support for one another in circumstances of attack by another power.

*

As the Belle Époque period developed across Europe, peace, growing prosperity and urban and technological progress could be felt in Vienna too. 1879 was a year of jubilee celebrations marking the 25th anniversary of the marriage of Emperor Francis Joseph and Empress Elisabeth. At its heart was a historic inspired pageant around the Ringstrasse with more than 14,000 participants. It was organised by Hans Makart, the most popular Vienna artist of the age. Although the *via triumphalis* was formerly opened in 1865, it would take a number of years for the first main buildings to be erected and further decades to be completed. All were designed in the historicist architectural style, inspired by historical eras thought to be fitting to their modern function: a Hellenic temple from the home of democracy for the parliament, Renaissance palaces for the museums, Roman grandeur for the imperial residence, Flemish urban splendour for the municipal government.

The first public building completed on the new Ringstrasse was the Vienna Court Opera (now State Opera) in 1869. The Neo-Renaissance-style building, which accommodates a seated audience of 1,700, with room for another 500 standing guests, is one the foremost opera houses in the world. At the time of its construction, however, it was very controversial, which led to one of the architects, Eduard van der Null, dying by suicide. Over the years, Gustav Mahler and Herbert von Karajan have been among the many leading conductors of its opera company and orchestra, which provides the musicians for the Vienna Philharmonic Orchestra. The Vienna State Ballet is based at the State Opera, which also hosts the annual Vienna Opera Ball.

The other major performance venue on the Ringstrasse is the Court Theatre, which opened in 1888 and is the largest theatre in the German-speaking world. It replaced the old court theatre, which had been an annexe to the Hofburg, and it retains that connection in its current name: the Burgtheater. Built directly opposite the new Vienna city hall in the historicist style, its main influences are from the Italian High Renaissance and it also includes ceiling paintings by Gustav Klimt and his brother Ernst.

Vienna City Hall (Rathaus) was completed in 1883 and built in a neo-Gothic style, inspired by Flemish and Brabant public buildings like Brussels Town Hall. Its central tower is nearly 100 metres high and topped by the Rathausmann, a knight in armour who has become a symbol of the city of Vienna. The giant municipal building boasts more than 1,500 rooms over six floors, including the grand meeting rooms of the city council and senate as well as a series of halls and a ballroom.

The Austrian Parliament Building stands next to the City Hall and was also opened in 1883, with sweeping ramps accessing the main Corinthian colonnaded portico entrance. Inspired by Athenian architecture and the Greek origins of democracy, the building is fronted by a massive fountain statue of Athena, the Greek goddess of wisdom, and female figures representing executive and legislative power. The design, by the Dane Theophil Hansen, has at its centre a Hall of Pillars with the two chambers of the Imperial Council of the Cisleithanian half of the empire on either side. The lower chamber remains in its original form and is used for special sessions of the current Austrian parliament, including the inauguration of the president. The chamber of deputies was famed for its disorderly proceedings, with repeated disputes about language rights and proceedings in a time before simultaneous translation. Members of the last parliament before the dissolution of the empire included a political generation that played a leading role in the successor states of the empire, including Karl Renner, who became Austrian Chancellor and President; Tomáš Masaryk, the first President of Czechoslovakia; Karel Kramář and Vlastimil Tusar, both future Prime Ministers of Czechoslovakia; Wincenty Witos, who served three times as the Prime Minster of Poland; Alcide De Gasperi, who became Prime Minister of Italy; Anton Korošec, a later Prime Minister of Yugoslavia; and Yevhen Petrushevych, who became President of the Western Ukrainian People's Republic after the First World War, along with Kost Levytskyi, who became the head of the government.

On the outer side of the Ringstrasse from the Hofburg palace are the Natural History Museum and the Art History Museum, which opened in 1889 and 1891 respectively. The two large buildings, which face each other, are of identical construction in the historicist style, with differing exterior designs featuring statues of leading figures from the fields of natural science and art. Both museums began with the collections of the Habsburg household and have grown since to secure their status amongst the leading museums in the world. Some 100,000 objects are on display in 39 rooms in the Natural History Museum from a collection totalling 30 million objects. The picture galleries of the Art History Museum include masterpieces by Breughel the Elder and Younger, Rubens, Rembrandt, Vermeer, Dürer, Arcimboldo, Titian, Michelangelo and Velásquez. The main staircase of the building interior itself was painted by Gustav and Ernst Klimt, Franz Matsch, Hans Makart and Mihály Munkácsy. The museums were part of a wider symmetrical plan to extend the Hofburg with two giant wings flanking Heroes Square, but the Kaiser Forum plan never came to full fruition as only one of the two proposed wings were completed: the New Castle (Neue Burg), which was finished in 1913. It today houses the Hofburg Congress Centre, Austrian National Library, Museum of Austrian History and the World Museum. In 1938 Adolf Hitler made his infamous speech from the main balcony announcing the Anschluss to Nazi Germany.

Further representative buildings around the Ringstrasse include the Vienna University main building, which was designed by Heinrich von Ferstel and completed in 1884. Constructed around a central arcade with the busts of its academic greats, the building includes scores of university departments, lecture theatres, seminar rooms and the original library. Vienna University is the oldest in the German-speaking world, founded in 1365, and it is also the largest, with more than 90,000 students. Next to the university is the neo-Gothic Votive Church, also designed by Ferstel, which was consecrated in 1879. The only spiritual construction on the Ringstrasse, the church was built to commemorate the failed 1853 assassination attempt on Emperor Francis Joseph. Close by on the inner side of the Ringstrasse is the Stock Exchange which was one of the first completed buildings on the Ringstrasse and opened in 1877. The historicist-inspired design was built on an 8,000-square-metre site by Theophil Hansen, who also planned the parliament building. Other public buildings of the age include the Palace of Justice, the Academy of Fine Arts and the Museum of Applied Arts.

The last major buildings to be completed on the north-east of the Ringstrasse were the Post Savings Bank and War Ministry at the beginning of the 20th century. The Postsparkasse is one of the most famous Jugendstil (Youth Style) buildings in Vienna and opened in 1906. The art nouveau design by Otto Wagner is regarded as a classic of the Vienna Secession school and remains in its original condition today, including its famous counter hall. Close by is the mammoth War Ministry, with a 200-metre-long façade, 1,000 rooms and 2,500 windows. It was opened in 1913 and is fronted by a statue of Field Marshal Radetzky and features a massive bronze imperial eagle with a 16-metre wingspan. The building was designed by Ludwig Baumann, who also designed the building for the Consular Academy, which is the current home of the US Embassy.

In addition to the built-up sections along the Ringstrasse, major park areas were incorporated, continuing the tradition of the former city walls and glacis as a place to walk and socialise, including the Burggarten, Stadtpark, Volksgarten and Rathauspark. The Ringstrasse itself fast became a fashionable place for the middle classes to promenade, visit its many coffee houses or see the visiting guests staying at plush new hotels, like the Imperial. The main social promenade, the 'Corso', extended on the city centre side from the Court Opera to Schwarzenbergplatz, the large square on the Ringstrasse dominated by the equestrian statue of Karl Philipp, Prince Schwarzenberg, the military hero and diplomat.

The urban redesign of Vienna and mushrooming of new representative buildings around the new Ringstrasse gave an impetus to the development of a diplomatic quarter, to the south-east of the city centre in the grounds of former Chancellor Metternich's residence. His son, Richard, who had served as Austrian ambassador to Paris and inherited the property, lost badly in the financial crash of 1873 and began to sell off parcels of land for development.

Both the British and German ambassadors took the opportunity of the downturn and commissioned architects to design appropriate buildings opposite one another. The UK Embassy was commissioned in 1873 and completed within a year on the corner of Jauresgasse and Metternichgasse. It was the first purpose-built UK embassy in the world and was presented as a fait accompli to the UK Treasury by ambassador Sir Andrew Buchanan, who made local construction and lease arrangements within his allocated mission spending limits.[21] The three-storey building was designed by Viktor Rumpelmayer, who had already built Sigray-Saint-Marsan Palace (now the Iranian Embassy). He would go on to build Hohenlohe-Bartenstein Palace (now the Belgian Embassy), and he became a popular architect of the late-historicist Ringstrasse school, with strong Italian and French influences. Public rooms were accessed via a grand staircase and included one large and a number of smaller reception rooms, a dining and large entertaining room. The ambassador had a work study and library as well as four chancellery rooms. Private residence rooms were on the second floor, while servants' quarters and stables were accommodated at the back of the building. As the recollections of later ambassador Sir Horace Rumbold show, there was distinct 'embassy envy' in the diplomatic district: 'Besides our own Embassy, there stands the splendid house built by the German Government for the use of their Ambassador – which was immediately opposite to, and sadly overshadowed ours – and beyond it, the charming petit hôtel that had been purchased by the Russian Government from the Duke of Nassau. Having, however, recounted the deficiencies of our new official residence, I am bound to add that we succeeded in making it very habitable, and we were able in it to do our duty by the Vienna world, and that it had left in my mind none but the pleasantest associations.'[22]

That positive view was not the impression left by Lady Walburga Paget, the wife of his predecessor Sir Augustus, for whom the interior design left much to be desired: 'I had a severe shock when I entered this house, which appeared to me to be a cross between a Café Chantant and a second-rate railway hotel, vulgar and commonplace

in the extreme, much worse than our predecessors had described it . . .
I sat down in my bedroom and wept.'[23]

The German Embassy was inspired by the purpose-built British Embassy, with the same architect Rumpelmayer drawing up the plans. Its costs were the subject of political controversy and a 169–133 vote in the Berlin Reichstag about the purchase of the plot. Ambassador Schweinitz argued in a memo to Bismarck that, by building an embassy palace, Germany was sending a signal about continuing good relations after Austro-Prussian War, and that wider impressions matter in the Austrian capital: 'Vienna is alone amongst all capitals where a rich aristocracy maintains a socially popular and important political position, and a fitting building is required for the Ambassador's residence and Chancellery, so that everyone passing through can see that the business of a powerful empire is conducted there.'[24]

The plot for the German Embassy was four times the size of the British Embassy on the other side of the road and was meant to impress. The entire first floor was designed for representational functionality, where guests could circulate and make their way through the public rooms without returning to the initial reception room. The plans included a ballroom, a throne room, a dining room with capacity for 36 guests, a number of salons, including a music room, a ladies' room, a billiard room and a smoking room. A Kaiser Apartment was included for the eventuality of a visit by the German emperor, although he never stayed there.

The Russian Embassy is located in the Reisnerstrasse, only a stone's throw from the British and German embassies. Originally constructed as a town palace for the wealthy banker Israel Simon, it became the residence of the Duke of Nassau before Russian ambassador Prince Aleksey Lobanov-Rostovsky secured the prestigious building as an embassy in 1891, as well as neighbouring properties. The Russian Orthodox Cathedral of St Nicolas was built on the embassy's grounds two years later, while the religious needs of the expatriate English community in Vienna was similarly provided for with the building of an Anglican church across the road from the British Embassy.

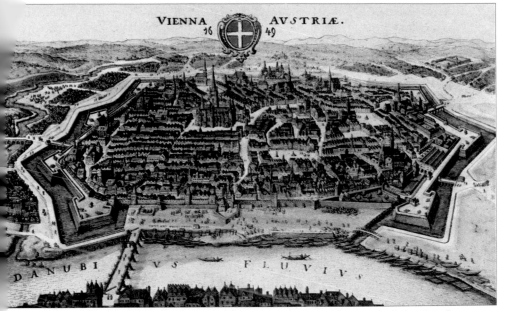

Vienna view featuring the city wall and battlements, river Danube, St Stephen's Cathedral and Hofburg Palace. Copperplate engraving by Matthaus Merian, c.1649.

kish siege of Vienna, 1683. *The Battle of Kahlenberg*, painted by Frans Geffels, 1688.

*Right*. Imperial Crown of the Holy Roman Empire, 10th–11th century

*Below*. Austrian Crown Jewels: Imperial crown, orb and sceptre, 17th century. Both at the Imperial Treasury, Hofburg palace, Vienna.

Empress Maria
Theresa (1717–80).
The only ever female
Habsburg monarch
and one of the most
successful Austrian
rulers.

Emperor Joseph II
(1741–90). A leading
enlightened absolutist
and over-ambitious
reformer.

Emperor Francis II and I (1768–1835). The last-ever Holy Roman Emperor, first Emperor of Austria and host of the Congress of Vienna.

Emperor Francis Joseph I (1830–1916). His 68 years on the throne are amongst the longest in history anywhere.

Ottoman traveller and diarist Evliya Çelebi (1611–82) visited Vienna in 1665.

Lady Mary Wortley Montagu (1689–1762), the trailblazing woman travel writer, was in Vienna in 1717.

Gottfried van Swieten (1733–1803), Habsburg diplomat and patron of Mozart, Haydn and Beethoven.

The Congress of Vienna (1814–15), where peace and stability was restored to Europe after the Napoleonic wars.

Prince Klemens von Metternich (1773–1859), Austrian Foreign Minister from 1808 and Chancellor from 1821 until the 1848 revolutions. Painting by François Gérard, 1830.

Robert Stewart, Viscount Castlereagh (1769–1822). British Foreign Secretary, 1812–22.

Charles Maurice, Prince de Talleyrand Périgord (1754–1838). French Minister of Foreign Affairs at the Congress of Vienna.

Russian Tsar Alexander I (1777–1825). He thwarted Napoleon's invasion of Russia and joined Austria after his defeat in suppressing national and liberal movements.

ıcess Wilhemine, Duchess of Sagan (1781–1839).

Princess Catherine Bagration (1783–1857).

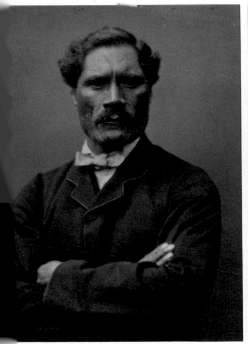

ri emissary Wiremu Toetoe Tumohe, who lled from New Zealand to Vienna aboard .ustrian frigate *Novara* in 1859.

Fellow Maori emissary Hemara Rerehau Te Paraone.

Lady Walburga Paget (1839–1929).

Julia Dent Grant (1876–1975), daughter of the US minister to Austro-Hungary and debutante at the Habsburg Court.

dolf Hitler announcing the Anschluss in 1938 from the balcony of the Hofburg, overlooking Heroes Square,
ding Vienna's status as a sovereign capital city, and ushering in the persecution and extermination of the
ty's Jewish population.

ning of the Austrian State Treaty, 1955, confirming independence of the alpine republic and the end
he post-Second World War occupation by the Soviet Union, Britain, France and the United States.

US–USSR Vienna summit, 1961. US President John F. Kennedy and Soviet leader Nikita Khruschev were hosted by Austrian President Dr Adolf Scharf at the Schönbrunn Palace.

Middle East Peace Talks, Vienna, 1978. Chancellor Bruno Kreisky hosts discussions between Egyptian President Anwar al Sadat and Israeli Labour Party leader Shimon Peres.

Stephen's Cathedral, Vienna's premier landmark, located at the heart of the city centre.

The Hofburg,
St Michael's Gate.

The Hofburg,
New Castle Wing
on Heroes Square.

The Hofburg,
the largest royal
palace in Europe.
Pictured from the
air, with Heroes
Square in the
foreground.

...lskirche at dusk. The 18th-century St Charles Church is one of the city's baroque masterpieces.

Secession building, with its motto: 'To every age its art, to every art its freedom.'

The Schönbrunn Palace, the former imperial summer residence, Vienna.

The Austrian National Library, with statue of Emperor Charles VI.

The Spanish Riding School, with its Lipizzaner horses, located in the Hofburg palace, the oldest of its kind in the world.

Karlsplatz station, a Jugendstil classic designed by Otto Wagner.

Belvedere palace, with St Stephen's Cathedral and Vienna city centre behind.

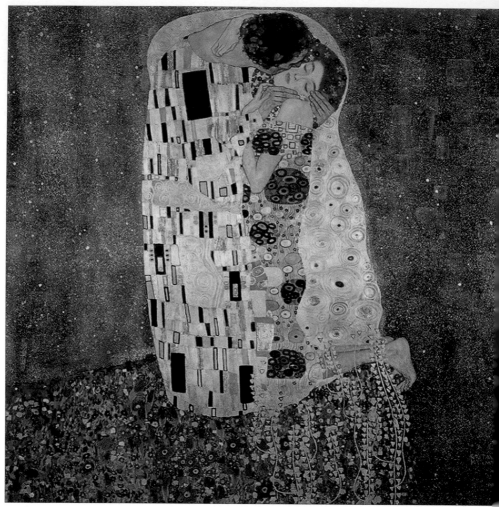

*The Kiss* by Gustav Klimt. The iconic art-nouveau painting is on display in the Belvedere palace.

The State Opera House is amongst the busiest premier opera houses in the world.

atue of the composer Johann Strauss, the 'waltz king', in Stadtpark. He composed 'The Blue Danube'.

am on the historic Ringstrasse, in front of the Burgtheater.

The Ferris Wheel is a famed symbol of Vienna, featured in *The Third Man*.

International flags flying outside the United Nations HQ, Vienna.

Vienna International Centre, including the United Nations.

At the turn of the century, the French followed the British and Germans in constructing their first ever purpose-built embassy nearby on Schwarzenbergplatz. Its art nouveau design is an homage to Vienna Jugendstil. The striking building features representations of Austria and France on the frontage facing the busy square, and '*Liberté, égalité, fraternité*' on the reverse side towards Karlsplatz. The embassy was hugely controversial in both France and Austria following its completion, with the modernist design criticised as a 'temple of poor taste', a breach of style and a provocation.[25] The Italian Embassy is also in the diplomatic quarter, located in the historic palace built in 1815 for Metternich on the Rennweg. The building interiors are amongst the grandest and most beautiful of any embassy in the city.

More recent embassies in the diplomatic quarter include the Chinese, who are located in the building immediately next to the British Embassy, and opposite the original German Embassy, which no longer stands owing to bomb damage during the Second World War.

\*

The future of the Austro-Hungarian Empire rested during this time on the young shoulders of Crown Prince Rudolf (1858–1889), the only son of Emperor Francis Joseph. While his father was largely absent with the business of state, his mother Sisi was more often than not out of the country, shying away from court life entirely. The combination was very problematic for the crown prince: 'Heir to unprecedented privilege, he had suffered through a childhood that left him psychologically damaged and emotionally abandoned. Family life offered no comfort: the distant father, absent mother, and the strained formality of the Austrian court only enhanced feelings of isolation and alienation. A haphazardly enacted education had awakened sparks of imagination within his keenly intelligent mind, yet it left him without the skills needed to analyse and reason through contradictory information. Liberal inclinations clashed with autocratic conceptions of his own position, resulting in wildly conflicting ideas for the future. And yet this was the emotionally fragile young man on whose thin shoulders rested the fate of his father's uneasy empire.'[26]

Unlike his father, Rudolf travelled widely and had broad interests, including natural science, especially ornithology, and was a keen supporter of liberal political reform. Frustrated by the constraints of the royal household and his inability to formally influence Habsburg rule, he cultivated friendships with liberal journalists like Moritz Szeps and the fellow royal dandy Britain's Prince of Wales, Albert Edward, the future King Edward VII.

Rudolf, who was known to travel incognito to better understand the conditions of ordinary Austrians, also wanted to learn from other countries. He travelled throughout Germany, Holland, Spain, Egypt and Palestine as well as Britain and Ireland. His tutor Carl Menger, the economist and founder of the Austrian School of Economics, took him on study tours, including to the industrial towns of the English Midlands and the university cities of Edinburgh and Glasgow, where he learned about the Scottish Enlightenment and saw where David Hume and Adam Smith had developed their ideas.[27]

While on his travels in Britain and Ireland he co-wrote a 48-page pamphlet anonymously with Menger: *The Austrian Nobility and its Constitutional Calling*. It is an outspoken broadside against the aristocracy's failures in supporting the state: 'There is an obvious threat to the future of our nobility in its present inglorious idleness. But at the same time, the passivity of such an important factor of our political life as the aristocracy in Austria paralyses the functions of the political organism in general, and in fact, displaces the focus of the Constitution.'

Speaking to Georges Clemenceau in December 1886, he said: 'Germany will never understand what special significance and wisdom there is in gathering Germans, Slavs, Hungarians, and Poles around the Crown. The Habsburg State already has realised Victor Hugo's dream of a "United States of Europe", if in miniature form. Austria is a block of states consisting of the most diverse nations and races under one rulership. At any rate, that is the basic idea for Austria, and it is an idea of the most tremendous importance for world civilisation. And even if, for the time being, the execution of this idea – to express myself diplomatically – is not completely harmonious, this does not mean that the idea itself is wrong. It means that such an idea in the most liberal sense would have to secure harmony and balance.'[28]

Despite all kinds of rumours swirling about the personal life of Rudolf, there were no public clues about one of the most shocking personal tragedies to befall European royalty in the entire 19th century. The last time that members of the royal family and Vienna society saw Rudolf alive was at a reception held in the German Embassy in late January 1889 to mark the 30th birthday of Kaiser Wilhelm. None of them had any idea what was about to happen to Rudolf and his young lover. The heir to the throne arrived at the party showing his public respect by dressing as Colonel-in-Chief in the uniform of the German 2nd Brandenburg Uhlan Regiment, despite privately disliking Wilhelm. He joined his father Emperor Francis Joseph, who wore the uniform of a Prussian field marshal, along with the cream of aristocratic society and the diplomatic corps, as the guest of German ambassador Heinrich VII, Prince Reuss (1825–1906). Lady Walburga Paget, wife of the British ambassador, spoke to Rudolf and described the extraordinary scenes at the reception in her diary: 'I thought the Crown Prince was changed and strange, and I could not think what was the matter with him.'[29]

While the crown prince, his wife Princess Stéphanie of Belgium (1864–1945) and the other guests mingled in the embassy ballroom, the young society beauty Baroness Mary Vetsera (1871–1889) flirted with Rudolf in plain sight. The 17-year-old daughter of an Austrian diplomat had had a crush on the dashing crown prince for some time and enjoyed demonstrating her affections for him at public events, including the opera. While it is not certain when their affair started, it was just the latest for the rakish Rudolf, who maintained a register of his conquests and gifted silver-boxes when he brought his dalliances to an end.

In an unhappy marriage with Stéphanie and barred from meaningful responsibilities by his father, Rudolf had descended into an increasingly dissolute lifestyle of sexual affairs, drink and drugs. He contracted venereal disease, infected his wife and ended hopes of having further children after their daughter was born.[30] For more than three years he had been prescribed a dangerous cocktail of opium, morphine and cocaine,[31] which he consumed in addition to 'copious amounts' of cognac and champagne.[32] Stéphanie remembered the destructive impact this was having on her husband: 'He suffered more and more from nervous unrest and from a violent temper, culminating in what was tantamount to complete mental decay.'[33] Queen Victoria, who had taken a shine to Rudolf and appointed him personally to the English Order of the Garter, confided to her granddaughter that he 'led a very bad life'.[34]

The day after leaving the German Embassy reception, Rudolf was driven through a snowstorm towards his hunting lodge at Mayerling in the Vienna woods. Collecting young Mary at a pre-arranged stop on the way, they arrived without anyone at the lodge noticing the presence of the young lover. When nobody answered from his locked bedroom on the morning of 30 January 1889, the door was forced open by Count Joseph Hoyos, the crown prince's hunting companion. He found Rudolf and young Mary dead both with gunshot wounds to the head, suggesting a murder-suicide by Rudolf. Count Hoyos raced to try to stop the Vienna-bound morning express train, so he could get to the capital quickly and tell the emperor. A telegraph to the Vienna owners of the railway line, explaining why the express had been stopped, arrived quicker than Count Hoyos, and Baron Albert Rothschild reported the shocking news to the German and British Embassies: 'Diplomatic Vienna thus learned of Rudolf's suicide before the emperor did.'[35]

German ambassador Prince Reuss immediately broke the word to embassy counsellor Count Anton Monts,[36] while at the British residence on the other side of Metternichgasse the door was 'burst open' by Baron Rothschild, in evening clothes with all his Orders on, who said: 'I have come to tell you a very sad thing, the Crown Prince is dead!'[37]

Given that Rudolf was the heir to the imperial throne, the tragedy was doubly shocking; how did it come to this and what did it mean for the future of the monarchy? It led to huge interest in the capitals of the world. 'Ambassadors in Vienna poked and pried, wrote home reams of hearsay and rumour. Queen Victoria implored her minister in Vienna, "Pray give all details you can gather, however distressing they may be." The papal nuncio, on the excuse of praying on the death scene, got admittance to the Mayerling lodge and nosed about for a morsel of truth.'[38]

Almost immediately the imperial authorities tried to order a news lockdown, heavily censoring domestic newspapers. Foreign newspapers with stories about the Mayerling deaths were confiscated but were still smuggled into the country. If you knew who to ask, you could read illicit reports kept by fiaker coach drivers or under the counter in coffee houses.

The *Chicago Tribune* on 31 January 1889 reported on its front page the official Austrian version of events that the crown prince had 'died of apoplexy of the heart',[39] but it also indicated that private telegrams from Vienna affirmed that the death was due to a gunshot wound. Within days, Reuters had reported full details of the medical bulletin: 'The Prince died of a wound doubtless inflicted on himself, and caused by a shot from revolver, which was fired quite close to the head, with the result that the skull and the fore part of the brain were shattered. The statement declares death to have been instantaneous, and in support of the assumption that the Crown Prince committed the deed in a state of mental derangement, cites a number of circumstances which medical experience has shown to be characteristic of an abnormal condition of the mind.'[40] Within days the international media reported on the involvement of Mary Vetsera, a detail that failed to get past the Austrian censors until after the fall of the empire three decades later in 1918.

The 'tragedy of Mayerling', or the 'Mayerling incident' as it became known, was the cause of feverish speculation, especially in diplomatic and royal circles. Writing to her mother Queen Victoria, the Empress Frederick of Germany reported a few weeks after the shootings: ' . . . I have heard different things about poor Rudolf which may perhaps interest you. Prince Bismarck told me that the violent scenes and altercations between the Emperor and Rudolf had been the cause of Rudolf's suicide. I replied that I had heard this much doubted, upon which he said [German Ambassador] Reuss had written it and it was so!'[41]

Queen Victoria summoned her old friend Lady Walburga Paget to her Osborne residence on the Isle of White to hear more about the tragedy. 'It's all too sad and dreadful,' said Lady Paget. 'They are most anxious to believe that it was Marie Vetsera who inveigled the Crown Prince into all this. But how silly a girl could have persuaded so clever a man as the Crown Prince of Austria to end his life in such a stupid, dirty, undignified, melodramatic way I cannot conceive. I cannot see the logic . . . It was not baffled love. The fact is that he was a maniac and she a vain unprincipled girl who wanted the world to speak of her.'[42]

Despite efforts to cover up the shocking circumstances with fictional accounts of heart failure, poisoning and a host of conspiracy theories about foreign involvement, the truth is more prosaic. Farewell letters from Mary discovered in 2015 make her suicidal intentions clear: 'Dear Mother – forgive me what I have done – I could not withstand love. In accordance with his wishes I want to be buried beside him in Alland cemetery. I am happier in death than I was in life.'[43] Rudolf wrote a number of farewell letters, although, tellingly, not to his father. To his wife, he wrote: 'Dear Stephanie, You are freed from my presence and vexation; be happy in your fashion. Be good to the poor little one, who is the only thing that remains of me.'[44]

Rudolf and Mary were destined to be buried separately, with Mary's body spirited out in the dead of night, propped up in a carriage with a walking stick to keep her upright; she was then interred in an unmarked grave in nearby Heiligenkreuz. Despite Rudolf's suicide, appeals to the Vatican for a Catholic funeral owing to his 'mental unbalance' were accepted, although papal nuncio Galimberti clearly had misgivings: 'This will probably be the first time that a

Papal Nuncio will attend the funeral of a murderer and a suicide representing the Pope.'[45]

Some 100,000 people waited to pay their respects to the crown prince as he lay in state in the Hofkapelle, the small court chapel in the Hofburg. Owing to the large throngs, only 30,000 mourners were able to view Rudolf in his open coffin before his state funeral began. Following elaborate Spanish court etiquette, his coffin was transported by carriage and accompanied by a military cortège to the imperial vault in the Church of the Capuchins.

While Rudolf never left a detailed explanation for his suicide, respected historians like Brigitte Hamann have exhaustively detailed his growing disillusion with the prospects for the Austro-Hungarian Empire, his lack of ability to influence reform and his worsening health condition, which would have claimed his life sooner rather than later, regardless of his suicide.

Since 1889 a small industry of Mayerling accounts, conspiracy theories and alternative histories have been created. Scores of books have been written and films shot, including the star-studded schmaltzy 1968 movie *Mayerling* with Catherine Deneuve, Omar Sharif, James Mason and Ava Gardner in the lead roles. Directed by Terence Young, who had just completed three of the early James Bond blockbusters, it was filmed on location at the Hofburg, Schönbrunn and Mayerling itself.

We will never know what might have happened had Rudolf survived and succeeded his father on the throne. What is clear is that he was a liberal, he favoured reforms to better include Slav ambitions within the empire, and he opposed the growing anti-Semitic politics of the time. Brigitte Hamann makes clear there was much more to him than his private life and sad demise: 'Crown Prince Rudolf is remembered by history mainly as a womaniser (which he was), as an anti-clerical free spirit (which he also was), and as a political fool (which he was not at all). For he was a politician only in secret – behind the back of his father – who jealously kept him from having any official influence . . . Unlike almost everyone else, he swam against the stream of modern political trends in the eighties. He was a philo-Semite at a time when anti-Semitism was at its worst. He thought and acted supranational at a time of embittered struggles among the nationalities of the Empire. He polemicised against the German-Austrian Alliance – at a time when not only Schönerer saw the solution to many a problem in siding with the German Empire. He also declared his tolerance in religious matters at a time when Catholicism was politically correct. Finally, he fought against the supreme rule of the aristocracy and clergy and saw in the middle class the "basis for a modern State".'[46]

\*

The year 1889 was also a fateful one in Upper Austria, west of Vienna: on 20 April a child was born to Klara and Alois Hitler in Braunau am Inn, close to the German border. Adolf Hitler grew up in one of the heartland German-speaking regions of the Habsburg Monarchy, where his father served as a customs official. While young Adolf was close to his mother, he had an antagonistic relationship with his father and had no intention of following him into the civil service. After schooling in Linz and Steyr, he left without any firm plans for further education, but, despite a lack of affinity to the multinational Austro-Hungarian state, he had a growing interest in heading for the big city lights of the imperial capital.

The large growth in Vienna's population during the second half of the 19th century – from 430,000 in 1850 to 1,674,000 in 1900 – was driven by incoming populations from the rest of the empire. These included both 'assimilated' Jews, many of whom played a significant role in the professions, business life, cultural and artistic ascendency of the city, as well as 'Ostjuden' from eastern provinces like Galicia. They were easily identifiable by their traditional clothing and often congregated in the same parts of the city, like Leopoldstadt, and were the target of growing anti-Semitism. By 1890, 118,495 Vienna residents were Jewish, constituting 8.8 per cent of the city's residents.

Anti-Jewish discrimination and sentiment had a long and sad history in Vienna. Even more enlightened and educated Viennese were prone to anti-Semitism, including the emperor, who on one occasion reportedly told a UK military attaché: 'Mark my word, the day will come when the Jews will ruin England like they have ruined my country.'[47] Many would dispute that this was representative of the emperor's views, given his tolerance and consideration towards his Jewish subjects and their faith. During his reign he allowed the creation of Jewish organisations and formally instituted equality rights. The King of Jerusalem, which was one of Francis Joseph's more fanciful titles, visited the Holy Land during a trip to attend the opening of the Suez Canal in 1869. While there he contributed financially to the completion of the Tiferet Yisrael Synagogue. In his beloved army, a hugely disproportionate 18 per cent of reserve officers were Jewish at the start of the new century.

Political anti-Semitism did, however, become a major feature of Vienna politics in the last decades of the 19th century and was weaponised as a successful campaign theme by two of the leading politicians of the age: Georg Schönerer (1842–1921) and Karl Lueger (1844–1910).

Schönerer was an early exponent of anti-Semitic, authoritarian pan-Germanism and a strong opponent of political Catholicism. He was a firebrand public speaker and powerful parliamentary orator in the Imperial Council on Vienna's Ringstrasse, where he railed against both Jews and Slavs, appealing also strongly to working-class Viennese with calls for social solidarity. The first to adopt the Führer title and *Heil* greeting, he promoted the wearing of the cornflower in lapels as a public sign of German nationalist affiliation, which was later adopted by undercover Austrian Nazis as well as the present-day Freedom Party of Austria (FPÖ).

Schönerer had strong political competition on the anti-Semitic right from Karl Lueger, who became Vienna's deputy mayor in 1895 and then served as mayor from 1897 until 1910. He was also a member of the Imperial Council and Lower Austrian state parliament, representing the Christian Social Party, which became the dominant political force of the time in Vienna. Lueger, who is still remembered for many civic improvements in the city, was so controversial in his time that Emperor Francis Joseph repeatedly refused to ratify his election as mayor, but eventually relented and sanctioned his appointment after the intervention of Pope Leo XIII. Hitler would later say that he was 'the greatest German mayor of all times . . . a statesman greater than all the so-called "diplomats" of the time . . . If Dr Karl Lueger had lived in Germany he would have been ranked among the great minds of our people.'[48]

Lueger's anti-Semitic rhetoric played a significant part in his popularity, although he was a less rabid racialist than Schönerer. Surprisingly, even some prominent Vienna Jews like the author Stefan Zweig were naively prepared to overlook his rhetoric and believed 'his city administration remained perfectly just and even typically democratic', while Jews lived with 'the same rights and esteem as heretofore'.[49]

Anti-Semitism and anti-Semitic ideology was also promoted and developed in 1890s Vienna by the author and thinker Houston Stewart Chamberlain (1855–1927). The English-born Germanophile, Anglophobe and Wagnerite, who went on to marry Eva von Bülow-Wagner, the daughter of composer Richard Wagner, lived in the Austrian capital for two decades from 1889 until 1909 before moving to Bayreuth to be amongst the Wagner family. In Vienna, he attended botanical lectures at the university on the Ringstrasse, with a view to completing his dissertation and taking up a scientific career, while also immersing himself in the city's Wagner Society.

Over time, he developed more of an interest in writing and penned the infamous *The Foundations of the Nineteenth Century* ('*Die Grundlagen des neunzehnten Jahrhunderts*'), which was commissioned by the Munich publisher Hugo Brockmann, who nearly 30 years later would publish Hitler's *Mein Kampf*. *The Foundations* was a racialist, pseudo-scientific history of civilisations and developed the Aryan race theory and anti-Semitism later adopted by the Nazis. Within ten years of its publication, the book was on its eighth edition, having sold 60,000 copies. By the time of the First World War it was on its 24th edition and had sold 100,000 copies. By the outbreak of the Second World War, more than a quarter of a million copies of the 1,200-page tome had been sold.

During his time in Vienna, Chamberlain got to know and impress the German ambassador to the Habsburg court Philipp zu Eulenburg, who was a close friend of German Emperor Wilhelm II. So enthused was Eulenburg with Chamberlain, and his writing and philosophy, that he engineered a meeting between the emperor and Chamberlain at his country estate in Liebenberg, north of Berlin. The two stayed in contact by letter thereafter, and the emperor sent him a signed portrait as a mark of his appreciation and interest. Inspired by Chamberlain's anti-Semitic theories, Wilhelm II remained an anti-Semite until his dying days in exile in the Netherlands after the First World War.

Schönerer, Lueger and Chamberlain all influenced one other particular figure living in Vienna at the time: Adolf Hitler. The future Nazi dictator wrote about all three in *Mein Kampf*. Hitler met Chamberlain in person in 1923, which was then followed by a letter from the Englishman saying: 'You are not at all, as you have been described to me, a fanatic. In fact, I would call you the complete opposite of a fanatic. The fanatic enflames the mind, you warm the heart. The fanatic wants to overwhelm people with words, you wish to convince, only to convince them, and that is why you are successful.'[50] In what was the first public endorsement by a prominent writer of national and international note, Chamberlain made a prediction of monstrously incorrect proportions: 'You have immense achievements ahead of you, but for all your strength of will I do not regard you as a violent man. You know Goethe's distinction between force and force. There is force which shapes the universe . . . It is this creative sense that I mean when I number you among the constructive men rather than those who are violent.'[51] One month later, on 8 November 1923, Hitler launched the violent Munich Beer Hall Putsch, which resulted in the deaths of 14 Nazis and four policemen. It marked the beginning of Hitler's brutish ascent to power, which culminated in the Second World War and the deaths of tens of millions of people, including 6 million Jews.

Chamberlain joined the Nazi Party shortly before his death in 1927. His funeral in Bayreuth was attended by Siegfried Wagner, the ex-King Ferdinand of Bulgaria, Prince August Wilhelm of Prussia as representative of exiled Emperor Wilhelm II, the Duke of Hohenlohe-Langenburg and Adolf Hitler.[52]

\*

The last decade of the 19th century that followed Crown Prince Rudolf's death and the first decade of the 20th century were characterised by an unparalleled flowering of cultural and creative innovation. Vienna was the world centre of cutting-edge music, art, architecture, design, literature and new thinking about the human condition.

After decades of staid society, conservative politics and constrained tastes, the particular circumstances of Vienna and Austria-Hungary turbo-charged a flowering of talents. In his Pulitzer Prize-winning work *Fin-de-siècle Vienna*, the cultural historian Carl Schorske explained the period: 'Vienna in the fin de siècle, with its acutely felt tremors of social and political disintegration, proved one of the most fertile breeding grounds of [the] century's a-historical culture. Its great intellectual innovators – in music and philosophy, in econom- ics and architecture, and of course, in psychoanalysis – all broke, more or less deliberately, their ties to the historical outlook central to the nineteenth century liberal culture in which they have been reared.'[53]

Prominent among the innovators was a group of creatives who literally declared independence from the old order by establishing the Vienna Secession, a movement and venue for new expression. Established in 1897 by the artist Gustav Klimt, the architects Josef Hoffmann and Joseph Maria Olbrich, designer Koloman Moser, painters Oskar Kokoschka and Egon Schiele and others, it soon led to the construction of the famous Secession Building, designed by Olbrich. A venue to display Secessionist art, the golden-domed gallery is one of the most recognisable buildings in Vienna with its motto 'To every age its art, to every art its freedom' above the portal. A major driver for the Secession movement was its collaboration with international artists, such as the Scottish modernists Charles

Rennie Mackintosh, his wife Margaret Macdonald, and Frances and Herbert MacNair. The 'Glasgow Four' joined other international artists Max Klinger, Eugène Grasset and Arnold Bocklin in Vienna, having been invited to display their works at the Secession.

Less than 15 minutes' walk away, the cream of the emerging writing scene was meeting at Café Griensteidl next to the Hofburg palace. The Young Vienna (Jung-Wien) society was heavily influenced by modernist thinking, including impressionism and symbolism. It included Arthur Schnitzler, Stefan Zweig, Karl Kraus, Hugo von Hofmannsthal, Hermann Bahr and Richard Beer-Hofmann, Felix Dörmann and Peter Altenberg. According to Carl Schorske, their shared agenda 'challenged the moralistic stance of nineteenth century literature in favor of sociological truth and psychological – especially sexual – openness'.[54] In a historic footnote, the group also included the diplomat and keen writer Leopold von Andrian, who worked in the Foreign Ministry in 1914 and was tasked by Foreign Minister Leopold Berchtold to draft the war aims of Austria-Hungary.[55]

In the Vienna musical scene, Gustav Mahler was the key pivot from the late romantic period to the modern era, not just as a composer but also as conductor of the Vienna Court Opera and Vienna Philharmonic Orchestra. His brother in-law and fellow composer Karl Zemlinsky was a major figure in the period, during which he was conductor at the Carltheater, then Kapellmeister of the Vienna Volksoper and the Court Opera. Zemlinsky was friends with Arnold Schoenberg, the composer who broke with musical convention as a trailblazer for chromatic expressionism, sometimes described as atonal music. Together with his pupils Alban Berg and Anton Webern, they were at the heart of the Second Viennese School, which inspired a generation of modernist composers.

One of the most important political thinkers of late 19th-century Austria-Hungary was the Jewish journalist, writer and political activist Theodore Herzl (1860–1904), who is regarded as the spiritual father of modern political Zionism and the State of Israel. Born and raised in Pest to a German-speaking family of assimilated Jews, he moved to Vienna at the age of 18 where he studied law and held surprising views in favour of total Jewish assimilation. Writing in his diary, Herzl noted: ' . . . I wanted to solve the Jewish problem, at least in Austria, with the aid of the Catholic Church. I wished to gain access to the Pope . . . and say to him: "Help us against anti-Semites and I will start a great movement for the free and honourable conversion of Jews to Christianity."'[56]

Herzl's views changed dramatically while writing for the liberal daily newspaper *Neue Freie Presse*, especially following his experiences covering the Dreyfus scandal in Paris, which saw the Jewish French army Captain Alfred Dreyfus falsely convicted of treason. The miscarriage of justice in the mid-1890s involved heavily anti-Semitic media coverage and public opinion. Herzl came to believe that combatting anti-Semitism was futile and that the answer instead was to create a Jewish state.

In 1896 he published his world-famous book *Der Judenstaat* ('The Jewish State') in which he argued: 'We have honestly endeavoured everywhere to merge ourselves in the social life of surrounding communities, and to preserve only the faith of our fathers. It has not been permitted to us. In vain we are loyal patriots, our loyalty in some places running to extremes; in vain do we make the same sacrifices of life and property as our fellow citizens; in vain do we strive to increase the fame of our native land in science and art, or by her wealth and commerce. In counties where we have lived for centuries we are still cried down as strangers, and often by those whose ancestors were not yet domiciled in the land where jews had already made experience of suffering.'[57] In his seminal work, which is little more than 100 pages, Herzl went on to conclude with great prescience: 'Therefore I believe that a wondrous generation of Jews will spring into existence. The Maccabeans will rise again. Let me repeat once more my opening words: The Jews who wish for a State will have it. We shall live at last as free men on our own soil, and die peacefully in our own homes. The world will be freed by our liberty, enriched by our wealth, magnified by our greatness. And whatever we attempt there to accomplish for our own welfare, will react powerfully and beneficially for the good of humanity.'[58]

Herzl followed the success of his book with the 1897 foundation of a weekly Zionist newspaper in Vienna, *Die Welt* ('The World') and the First Zionist Congress, which elected him president. With the help of Reverend William Hechler, the Anglican minister to the British Embassy in Vienna, Herzl made plans to meet powerful world leaders to further the case for a Jewish state, including Grand Duke of Baden Frederick I, the uncle of German Kaiser Wilhelm II, who he met as a result in Jerusalem in 1898.[59]

Herzl became an international advocate and activist for the Zionist cause but died aged only 44 of heart disease in 1904 near Reichenau an der Rax in Lower Austria. The day before his death he told Reverend Hechler: 'Greet Palestine for me. I gave my heart's blood for my people.'[60] First buried in Vienna, his remains were reinterred in Israel's national cemetery at the top of Mount Herzl in Jerusalem in 1949, which is named after him. One year earlier the Israeli Declaration of Independence was proclaimed, stating: 'In the year 5657 [1897], at the summons of the spiritual father of the Jewish State, Theodore Herzl, the First Zionist Congress convened and proclaimed the right of the Jewish people to national rebirth in its own country.'[61]

Another Austrian who made a profound international public impact during the same period as Herzl was Bertha von Suttner (1843–1914), who was the first woman to be awarded the Nobel Peace Prize. Born into the Bohemian aristocratic Kinsky family, she became a journalist before joining the peace movement. She famously ruffled many establishment feathers with her criticism: 'In the local atmosphere there is a mental ignorance of all the things that move the century. Developments, increasingly being made in social science, fall into the criminal category of "socialism" . . . If you want to change something in the world – what a crime. A world that is so beautiful, so orderly, so harmonious, so traditional and sanctified! And virtuous! Are we not brimming – we, the representatives of the status quo – are we not shining with virtues? Loyalty, piety, bravery, courage to sacrifice, patriotism: we are familiar with this . . . so leave us alone with your eternal lust for change and your accusations . . . '[62]

Suttner didn't just take aim at the older aristocrats, she also targeted the younger generation: the cavalry lieutenants, Jockey Club members, ballerina patrons and sportsmen, who 'thank god think about things that are more fun than political and social theory. They are of course also Conservative; who would not want to conserve such a privileged life?' Suttner railed against the 'ugly comedy' of the military manoeuvres so beloved by Emperor Francis Joseph and the Habsburg high command: 'Princes and generals on horseback, beneath waving plumes, adorned with golden braids, moiré sashes, tightly sown large cross decorations, with various extermination machines and machinists marching past. This is just a dress rehearsal of the piece; but it is easy to imagine how this will really turn out with flowing blood, wheezing cries of pain, skulls crushed by hoofs, swelling intestines, the parched dying in the trenches and those buried alive in the ditches.'[63]

In 1889 she published her classic pacifist novel *Lay Down Your Arms* (*'Die Waffen Nieder'*). The book was so popular it had 37 German-language editions before she received the Nobel Prize. In October 1891 Leo Tolstoy wrote to Suttner after reading it: 'I esteem your work highly, and it has occurred to me that the publication of your novel represents a good omen for the future. The abolition of slavery was preceded by a famous novel written by a woman, H. Beecher-Stowe. My God grant that the abolition of war will follow your novel . . . '[64]

Suttner received another congratulatory letter from an old acquaintance, Alfred Nobel: 'Dear Baroness and friend, I have just finished reading your admirable masterpiece, It is said that there are 2,000 languages – 1,999 too many – but there is not a single language into which your excellent work should not be translated, and then read and dwelt upon. How long did it take you to create such a marvel? You will tell me when I have the honor and good fortune to shake your hand – the hand of an amazon so bravely declaring war upon itself. It is not really right of you to declare: "Lay down your arms," because you make use of weapons yourself, and your weapons – the charm of your style and the nobility of your ideas – have a far greater range than the hellish weapons of war.'[65]

Suttner's peace activism and feminism, which in many respects was way ahead of its time, included presenting Emperor Francis Joseph in 1897 with a petition for the creation of an International Court of Justice. She also attended the first Hague Convention in 1899, which led to the first multilateral treaties on the conduct of war.[66] Suttner attended the event in The Hague as a correspondent for Theodor Herzl's Zionist newspaper *Die Welt*. She spent the rest of her life as a high-profile peace advocate and women's rights activist, speaking at conferences around Europe and the United States, where she was invited to the White House for a meeting with President Roosevelt. She died on 21 June 1914, one week before the assassination of Archduke Franz Ferdinand in Sarajevo. Her posthumous legacy includes the establishment of the League of Nations and non-violent conflict resolution.

This period also saw the emergence of Sigmund Freud (1856–1939), the founder of psychoanalysis and a range of therapeutic approaches to psychotherapy. Born in Moravia to Jewish parents from Galicia, Freud graduated from Vienna University before beginning a medical career at Vienna General Hospital, lecturing at the university on neuropathology and setting up his own private clinical practice. Writing at the same time as Freud set up his private clinical practice, the wife of a British ambassador described the impact of neurosis on general life in Vienna: 'There was an epidemic of suicides in Vienna. Servants kill themselves because they break a plate, children of seven or eight hang themselves because they cannot do a lesson, soldiers because they do not like the army, girls because they can't marry their first loves; the mania is such that I was warned not to ride in the Prater in the morning before the patrol, which takes the corpses off the trees, had gone round.'[67]

Freud became famous amongst his circle of patients at his flat in the Berggasse for using dream therapy and 'self analysis' to treat different neuroses, which he famously wrote about in his 1899 work *The Interpretation of Dreams*. His patients included the American diplomat William Bullitt, who as US ambassador to Paris later played an important role in assisting the Freud family after the Nazi takeover.

*

The last decades of the 19th century in Vienna were experienced by a group of well-placed international expatriates that lived in the city. Lady Walburga Paget (1839–1929), the diarist and writer whose opinions on the death of Crown Prince Rudolf we have already heard, is a particularly interesting Vienna observer of the period. Arriving in the city with her ambassador husband in 1884 for a diplomatic posting that lasted nine years, she described the 'beau monde' she became a part of: 'The one thing that Viennese society most heartily detests are airs of affectation; and if anybody is suspected in indulging them it is hopeless for that person to think about getting on. In this peculiarity lies the whole secret of some people.'

Lady Paget, who was born into German nobility as Countess Walburga Ehrengarde Helena von Hohenthal, gives an insight into the aristocratic mindset of the time: 'Diplomats often don't like Vienna. They have a difficult part to play, and, especially those who represent Republican Governments, are looked on with coldness and distrust. Exceptions to this rule are, however, every now and then made in favour of those endowed with good manners, distinguished appearance and a modest and retiring behaviour. In a society so closely united by the bonds of relationship, where rank is so clearly defined, every member knows its own place, and there can be no unseemly struggles or pushing, as takes place in more mixed communities. Snobbishness is also a thing unknown; for the reverence which Austrians have for good birth can hardly be designated as such. To them it is a law – nay, almost a religion – which if taken from them would make them feel as if they were landed on a quicksand.'[68]

Whether this account is entirely accurate or not, it is clear from Paget's detailed insights that Austrian aristocratic society was set in aspic. A seemingly never-ending series of balls, *soirées*, *cercles*, hunts, dinners and country-house visits, and her accounts of court life and gossip, illustrate an outdated and unreformed ruling class, completely cut off from everyday realities and developments around them.

That is also apparent from the interesting recollections of Julia Dent Grant (1876–1975), who was a young teenager when her father, Frederick, was appointed US Minister to Austria-Hungary and the family moved to Vienna for four years. The first grandchild of Ulysses S. Grant, the 18th President of the United States, she was born at the White House and was one of the few non-noble foreigners to live amongst Viennese high society, even becoming a débutante at the Court Ball. She describes a Vienna life that was soon to disappear: the Corpus Christi procession and foot-washing ceremonies, court receptions, dancing lessons with the children of other diplomats ahead of ball season and Contessen *soirées* with her friends from the grand houses of Liechtenstein, Taaffe, Hunyady, Harrach and Mensdorff-Pouilly.

Arriving at the Hofburg as a débutante, she was instructed on etiquette by her mother: 'If no-one invites you to dance, never mind, but just stand and look on. If any one does ask you, then accept and look pleased, and when the Emperor speaks to you remember to reply in whatever language he uses, and speak clearly – you don't have to be at all shy.'[69] The diplomatic corps awaited presentation standing in a semi-circle, before the emperor spoke to the chief of every mission and was introduced to new staff members of the embassies and legations. When reaching her father and mother, he said in French: 'How are you Colonel Grant? Good evening, madam! I hear your little girl is here to-night and that she is very gentille. I must meet her.' Sixteen-year-old Julia stepped forward, curtseyed low and shook the emperor's hand. Continuing in French, he said: 'I'm glad you came to my ball, Mademoiselle, and I hope you will find it pretty and will enjoy yourself. You will if you speak German; our people love those who speak their language and are at home among them. You have been here with your father – have you learned to speak?' She answered: '*Ja, Majestät* I do speak German rather better than English, and I am quite at home in Vienna. One could not dislike such a beautiful place.' The emperor laughed in amusement: 'But you speak Viennese – it is quite charming! Where did you learn our patois? I am sure you will have great success, and I shall watch it with pleasure.'[70] At the end of the *cercle*, the imperial party formed into a procession, including the diplomatic corps, and processed through the palace, past the guests in all their finery. Of particular note for Julia was the awkwardness of government ministers who were present at the Court Ball by invitation of the emperor – and not because of 16 quarterings of noble ancestry, which guaranteed automatic entry. They stood around rather helplessly and submissively, never speaking to the aristocratic elite around them. Meanwhile, Julia enjoyed an evening of dancing to the music of Strauss, conducted by the great man himself. She attended a total of 23 balls and *soirées* during the rest of the season, including the even more exclusive Ball at Court.

Growing language and nationality problems plagued the Austro-Hungarian Empire towards the end of the 19th century. In the Austrian half of the Dual Monarchy, German-speakers were only a majority population in the west of the empire, in parts of Bohemia and language islands elsewhere, while other main language groups included Czechs, Poles, Ruthenians, Slovenes, Italians and Croats. In the Hungarian half of the empire, Magyar was the mother tongue for only half the population, while other main languages included Slovakian, Croatian, Serbian, Ruthenian, Rumanian and Yiddish. Different language policies in both halves of the empire caused unhappiness and unrest.

In Hungary, the Magyar language replaced Latin as the lingua franca between nationalities as it had already been replaced as the language of public administration. The government in Budapest pursued a policy of Magyarisation, including education in Hungarian and the adoption of Hungarian surnames and place-names. Meanwhile, the Hungarian electoral system to the Budapest parliament effectively discriminated against the poorer, rural-based nationalities, which were significantly under-represented, and ensured over-representation for Magyar speakers.

In Cisleithania, the emperor's longest serving Minister-President, Count Eduard Taaffe, made a success of 'muddling through' (*Durchwursteln*), as he put it, with his 'Iron Ring' cabinet that kept all ethnic groups 'in the same well tempered dissatisfaction'. His successors were not so effective. Concerns about growing nationality problems saw Emperor Francis Joseph appoint Count Kasimir Badeni (1846–1909) as Minister-President in 1895 to reform the electoral system and language laws. In contrast to Hungarian efforts to assimilate minorities while minimising their representation, Badeni took the opposite course of action. In 1896 he widened the suffrage to include all adult men, not just higher-rate taxpayers. While this impacted only on a minority of seats in the Imperial Council, it ushered in greater numbers of Social Democrats, Christian Socialists and German Nationalists – the three main political *lagers* in Austrian politics for a century. A year later he sought to reform language laws in Bohemia, making proficiency in Czech as well as German necessary for civil-service posts, a move aimed at pleasing the Young Czech parliamentary party. This sparked a conservative reaction from German speakers in Bohemia who generally did not learn Czech, while Czechs traditionally learnt German as well.

The unrest was witnessed by the great American author Mark Twain and his family, who lived in Vienna for two years at the end of the century. Writing about 'Stirring Times in Austria' in *Harper's New Monthly Magazine* he recounted: 'Here in Vienna in these closing days of 1897 one's blood gets no chance to stagnate. The atmosphere is brimful of political electricity. All conversation is political; every man is a battery, with brushes over-worn, and gives out blue sparks when you set him going on the common topic. Everybody has an opinion, and lets you have it frank and hot, and out of this multitude of counsel you get merely confusion and despair. For no one really understands this political situation or can tell you what is going to be the outcome of it. Things have happened here recently which would set any country but Austria on fire from end to end and upset the government to a certainty; but no one feels confident that such results will follow here.'[71]

The nationality unrest caused riots in Vienna, Graz, Salzburg and Prague, where it led to the imposition of martial law. Unhappiness amongst German-speaking Austrians, who feared losing their leading position in the empire, was fanned by Georg Schönerer and his German Nationalist Party. It led to tumultuous scenes in the Imperial Council, where Twain sat in the press gallery and watched the riotous behaviour of deputies, filibuster speeches and the intervention of the police on the floor of the chamber: 'It was an odious spectacle – odious and awful. For one moment it was an unbelievable thing – a thing beyond all credibility; it must be a delusion, a dream, a nightmare. But no, it was real – pitifully real, shamefully real, hideously real.'

The same parliamentary scenes were witnessed from the diplomatic box by British ambassador Horace Rumbold (1829–1913), who watched deputies 'hurling the grossest invectives and insults . . . to a deafening accompaniment of penny trumpets, tramway whistles and hammering of desks . . . the Chamber in fact had worked itself into a frenzy bordering on lunacy'.[72] Few international observers had his length of experience – going back to his first posting in Vienna in 1856 as 'second paid attaché' – or the personal contacts with leading Austrian figures of the 19th century. Rumbold could boast a friendship with Metternich, the personal acquaintance of both the emperor and empress, and he had attended events of state ever since the funeral of Radetzky in 1858. In three volumes – *Recollections of a Diplomatist*, *The Austrian Court in the Nineteenth Century* and *An English Tribute to the Emperor Francis Joseph* – Rumbold gives an unrivalled panorama of life in the city, court, politics and international diplomacy. His vivid descriptions capture the end of an era, from his audiences with Emperor Francis Joseph to his *ricevimento* by Vienna society, the last of the 19th-century salons, the great court *chasses* (hunts), the Hofburg balls and the personalities of the age. He also describes the tragic details of the event that rocked the monarchy and created headlines around the world: the assassination of Empress Elisabeth.

For decades Sisi had been travelling across Europe and northern

Africa, trying to escape court life in Vienna and her personal sadness, especially after the suicide of her son, Rudolf. Usually she favoured the Mediterranean, where she had built a palace on Corfu, or the French or Ligurian rivieras. However, in 1898, she travelled incognito as the Countess of Hohenems to the Swiss city of Geneva. While walking along the Lake Geneva promenade towards the embarkation point for a boat trip with her lady-in-waiting, she was stabbed by an Italian anarchist. Luigi Lucheni, who had actually intended to attack another aristocratic victim, settled on the 60-year-old empress instead, mortally wounding her with a sharpened needle file. She died a few minutes later.

On hearing the news, Emperor Francis Joseph reacted to the latest tragedy to befall him and his family: 'Truly, am I spared nothing in this world.'[73] Sisi's funeral followed the long-established Habsburg traditions: a funeral procession from the Hofburg through the middle of Vienna to the Crypt of the Capuchins, where members of the dynasty were buried. Rumbold and his German colleague Philipp von Eulenberg joined French ambassador Henri-Auguste Lozé to watch the funeral procession from the French Embassy on Lobkowitz Platz.

The close of the century brought two particular further Vienna deaths that marked the end of an era. The German conductor and composer Johannes Brahms died in 1897 after spending much of his professional life in the Austrian capital. Counted as one of the great 'three Bs' of classical music, together with Bach and Beethoven, he directed the Vienna Society for the Friends of Music and the Vienna Philharmonic Orchestra. In the last year of the century, the Vienna 'Waltz King' Johann Strauss II died aged 73. He composed more than 500 works, including *The Blue Danube Waltz*, *Tales from the Vienna Woods*, *Die Fledermaus* and *Der Zigeunerbaron* ('The Gypsy Baron'). He is personally responsible for the popularity of waltz music and its association with Vienna, a reputation that endures internationally to this day.

# 9

# *Waltzing to War*

'In Berlin the situation is serious but not desperate; in Vienna, the situation is desperate but not serious.'

– Alfred Polgar[1]

The beginning of the new century saw the major powers come together to defend their international diplomatic missions, following the Boxer Rebellion in China against foreign presences in the country. Austria-Hungary was particularly focused on its position in the Balkans but wanted to maintain its Great Power status. In 1900, appeals grew for an international intervention in China, but Vienna resisted. First Section Chief Count Nikolaus Szécsen von Temerin wrote to Foreign Minister Count Agenor Gołuchowski, expressing his concern about getting involved: 'We have no direct interests in China and have no intention of creating them there.'[2]

Despite the objections, the Austro-Hungarian East Asian Squadron was dispatched to China. Commanded by Rear Admiral Count Rudolf Montecuccoli, a veteran of the historic Battle of Lissa, the squadron included four cruisers, two training ships and a company of nearly 300 marines. Amongst the deployed personnel was Lieutenant Georg Ludwig von Trapp, who would go on to command a submarine during the First World War and is more famously known for his character in the musical *The Sound of Music*.

The only forces to see significant action from the start of the intervention were detachments of marines from the SMS *Zenta* who defended the besieged diplomatic legations in Beijing, while a further detachment took part in the Seymour Expedition to relieve the siege.[3] Later in the campaign, Austrian marines joined Russian, British, Japanese, German and Italian forces in the Battle of the Taku Forts. On 14 August 1900, the siege of the legations in Beijing was ended. Atrocities on both sides were common, with the international forces guilty of widespread brutality and looting.

The early 20th century also saw diplomatic efforts by Russia and Austria-Hungary to update their arrangements in their Balkans: in the 1870s they had agreed that Bessarabia would be annexed by Russia, and Bosnia-Herzegovina by the Dual Monarchy. Vienna would also maintain a neutral position during any Russian conflict with the Ottoman Empire. What followed was the Russo-Turkish War and the Austrian occupation of Bosnia-Herzegovina, although the territory was not formally annexed.

The risk of regional instability grew following the assassination of Serbian King Alexander in 1903 and his replacement by the pro-Russian Peter I. The change in Belgrade also encouraged forces keen to extend Serbian influence into Bosnia-Herzegovina and the Sanjak of Novi Pazar, which were both occupied by Habsburg troops.

Protecting Austrian dominance in the western Balkans was seen as essential for decision-makers in Vienna keen to retain Great Power status, and finally annexing Bosnia-Herzegovina was seen as the best option. An opportunity to do this with the agreement of the Russians came with an approach by Russian Foreign Minister Alexander Izvolsky, who wrote to his opposite number in Vienna, Alois Aehrenthal, suggesting a reciprocal update to the 1878 Treaty of Berlin. Both men met on 16 September at Aehrenthal's country retreat, Buchlau Castle in Moravia, for six hours of talks, which were not minuted. While the Russians were keen to gain naval access to the Mediterranean through the Bosporus, the Austrians wanted to secure their position in the Balkans against Serbian irredentism.

On 6 October 1908 Emperor Francis Joseph I formally annexed Bosnia-Herzegovina after 30 years of occupation. The move sparked international condemnation as a unilateral breach of the Treaty of Berlin; however, as the embarrassing acquiescence of Russia was confirmed, a flurry of diplomatic activity led to the annexation being recognised as a fait accompli. Serbia and Austria-Hungary both stood down their forces and the Bosnian Crisis ended in apparent total diplomatic victory for Vienna, but ultimately it prepared the ground for the outbreak of the Great War: while Austria believed that its bold action had been a success, relations with Russia, Serbia and Italy had been badly hit.

Peace did not last long in the Balkans, with recently independent Bulgaria, Serbia, Montenegro and Greece taking on the weakening Ottoman Empire. The Balkan League nations fought the First Balkan War against the Turks from October 1912 until May 1913 and then against one other from June until August 1913. The conflict led to a large loss of Ottoman territory, a gain for Serbia, the end of the Balkan League and a reduction of Russian influence in the region except for Serbia. With Austria-Hungary concerned about the growth of Serbia, and Russia retaining only Serbia as a regional ally, the stage was set for the First World War.

\*

Dynastic diplomacy pursued by the Habsburgs was closely associated with the military of different countries, not just immediate allies. In addition to being an Austrian field marshal, Emperor Francis Joseph I had been extended the honour by Prussia and Great Britain. He was the honorary colonel of eight different German regiments, the Russian Kexholm Lifeguards, the Grenadier Guards and the British King's Dragoon Guards. To this day the regiment (now the Queen's Dragoon Guards) wears the double-headed Habsburg eagle on its cap-badge and their regimented march is the *Radetzky March*. Emperor Francis Joseph regularly received visits to the Hofburg from his Russian, British and German regiments and had special medals struck and issued to their personnel. Whenever hosting foreign royal guests, as he did for the only visit to Austria by Queen Victoria, Francis Joseph wore their national military dress, in this case a British regimental uniform, as a mark of respect.

During the late 19th and early 20th centuries, military diplomacy was a developing branch of specialist diplomatic relations, with

Vienna one of its main hubs. The work of the defence attachés from different countries was similar, reporting open-source information to their capitals about the size and organisation of the Austro-Hungarian armed forces, their size, organisation, military equipment and innovations, from munitions to new aviation capabilities. Court circulars report that major manoeuvres attended by the emperor also included the attachés of Germany, France, Britain, Italy, Spain, Switzerland, Sweden, Romania, the Ottoman Empire and the United States. Some, including the Russian attaché, was directed to collect more sensitive information, including military codes and military railway plans. Notwithstanding this, he was included in Austrian organised visits together with other attachés to military facilities such as railway communication offices, gunnery schools and factories, and cavalry and transportation training centres.

When the attachés couldn't source information directly from the host military authorities, they were happy to share information with one another. They undertook visits to sensitive parts of the country to assess defences; British attaché Colonel David Dawson travelled from Vienna to the Adriatic coast to see coastal defences, while the Russian attaché made tours of Galicia and Transylvania close to the Russian border. With rising tensions, especially between Austria and Russia, passive collection techniques were actively supplemented with the cultivation of covert sources. However, the fine line between tolerated information gathering and espionage was increasingly being exposed, especially with the growing capabilities of the Austrian military counter-intelligence Evidenzbüro, the oldest service of its kind in the world. In 1910 a Russian defence attaché became *persona non grata* after an investigation showed he was running paid agents, including Austrian army officers. Only three years later the same fate befell his successor, who was exposed for agent running, including the military cadet classmate of the son of Austrian Chief of Staff Conrad von Hötzendorf.[4]

The key military diplomatic relationship in Vienna was between Austria-Hungary and neighbouring Germany, following the formal military alliance struck in 1879. The Germans, keen to impress their hosts, largely sent aristocratic cavalry officers as military attachés to Vienna.

A detailed study of the diplomatic reporting from German military attachés in Vienna makes it plain that Berlin was clearly informed of 'serious weaknesses' in the Austrian military: 'Problems were discovered in the constructions of fortresses, strategic roads, and railways. The mobilisation plan was faulty in many respects. The government was not spending enough on the comparatively small army it had, much less did it give much thought to increasing its size. Members of some of the nationalities of the Dual Monarchy revealed a willingness to take steps that could threaten the security of the entire multinational state. The performance of the troops in manoeuvres, especially the officers, was poor.'[5]

\*

The year 1908 was important for the monarchy as it marked the 60th anniversary of the accession of Francis Joseph to the throne. Just prior to the celebrations, a young man from Upper Austria who would figure ominously in later history moved from Linz to the capital, with plans to study fine art. Adolf Hitler, who had just turned 18, arrived with his friend August Kubizek and took 'shabby' lodgings in a flat in Stumpergasse in the Mariahilf district. Writing years later, after Hitler had become dictator of Germany, Kubizek described them both seeing the emperor passing in his coach on his daily trip along the Mariahilferstrasse from the Hofburg to Schönbrunn Palace: 'We often saw the old Emperor, dressed in his gala uniform . . . Adolf did not make much ado about it neither did he refer to it later, for he was not interested in the Emperor as a person but with the state he represented: the Austro-Hungarian monarchy.'[6] In her seminal work *Hitler's Vienna – A Dictator's Apprenticeship*, the Austrian historian Brigitte Hamann charts the attitudes and experiences of Hitler in Vienna: 'There can be no doubt about Hitler's dislike for the Habsburg dynasty. Like the pan-Germans, even when he was in high school he saw no future for the German-Austrians in Habsburg's multiethnic empire but was hoping for an Anschluss to the German Reich in the near future, which first required that the multinational empire be shattered and the Habsburg dynasty removed.'[7]

236

While Kubizek succeeded in passing the musical entrance exam for the Conservatory, Hitler failed twice to get into the Academy of Fine Arts. He spent many a day studying and admiring the architecture of the Ringstrasse, especially the Court Opera and Court Theatre by Gottfried Semper. He was also a fan of the plans by Semper for Heroes Square, a place that Hitler became forever associated with after holding his speech to a packed Heldenplatz to mark the Anschluss of Austria in 1938.

In the evenings three decades earlier, Hitler would spend his time watching operas, especially Wagner, from the standing area below the imperial box in the Court Opera house. Kubizek confirmed that in the first half of 1908 he and Hitler saw every Wagner performance at the Court Opera, seeing *Lohengrin* and *Die Meistersinger von Nürnberg* at least ten times, and knew them by heart: 'When he listened to Wagner's music he was a changed man: his violence left him, he became quiet, yielding and tractable . . . as If Intoxicated by some hypnotic agent, he slipped into a state of ecstacy, and willingly let himself be carried away into that mystical universe which was more real to him than the actual workaday world.'[8]

Meanwhile, celebratory events marking the rule of Emperor Francis Joseph were gearing up towards the high point on 12 June 1908 with an anniversary parade. Some 12,000 people participated in the eight-mile-long procession, which included delegations in national and historic dress from all crown lands and regions of the empire, as well of thousands of horses, mules, carriages and cannons. For three hours, the 78-year-old emperor, wearing a field marshal's uniform with a green-plumed cocked hat, took the salute on a specially constructed tented platform and gallery. The attendance of so many participants from the economically backward eastern provinces, caused a real stir with Karl Kraus describing many as 'homely, primitive, culturally retarded', while the architect Alfred Loos wrote: 'It is a disaster for a country if its people's culture spreads over such a long time period . . . The parade included peoples who even during the migration of nations would have been considered backward. Fortunate is the country that doesn't have such stragglers and pillagers. Fortunate America!'[9]

While Hitler's recorded views on the parade were limited to complaints about Hungarian Gypsy pickpockets, there is little doubt that he abjured the multinational nature of the Habsburg Empire on show. Ironically, the style of historicist parade was one that he went on to copy in the late 1930s in Munich, with ancient 'Germanic' role-playing actors replete with omnipresent swastikas.

Within weeks, Hitler's personal circumstances worsened, having frittered his inheritance away. He was forced to move out of the apartment he shared with Kubizek, instead staying in a hostel for the next three years and trying to keep his head above water by painting postcards and working as a casual labourer. Years later, as he sat in the plush Hotel Imperial when he was annexing Austria to Nazi Germany in 1938, he recounted his bitterness at being ignored by the hotel's porter at that time and his humiliation at earning money by clearing snow outside the Imperial:

> That was the night the Habsburgs were entertaining . . . We poor devils shovelled the snow away on all sides and took our hats off every time the aristocrats arrived. They didn't even look at us, although I still smell the perfume that came to our noses. We were about as important to them, or for that matter to Vienna, as the snow that kept coming down all night, and this hotel did not even have the decency to send out a cup of hot coffee to us. We were kept there most of the night, and each time the wind blew hard it covered the red carpet with snow. Then I'd take a broom and brush it off, glancing at the same time into the brilliantly lit interior, which fascinated me. I heard the music and it made me wish to cry. It made me pretty angry, too, and feel the injustice of life. I resolved that night that someday I would come back to the Imperial Hotel and walk over the red carpet into that glittering interior where the Habsburgs danced. I didn't know how or when, but I have waited for this day and tonight I am here.[10]

The Anschluss was still 30 years off, but many of the ideas that propelled Hitler to power were already influencing him in Vienna, especially the racism and anti-Semitism of Mayor Karl Lueger and racist ideologues like Georg Ritter von Schönerer and Houston Stewart Chamberlain. In May 1913 Hitler received the final part of his father's estate and moved to Munich.

*

Vienna was rocked at the start of the century by a series of scandals that undermined the standing of the monarchy and the military. In 1906 there was much 'eagerness and curiosity' in court and diplomatic circles about the younger brother of the emperor who had been 'banished forever from the Austrian court and capital'. According to foreign media reports Archduke Ludwig Victor had been exiled 'for a mysterious escapade', and the American press went into overdrive speculating whether his vacated palace on the Ringstrasse would become the new US Embassy. The front page of the *Chicago Sunday Tribune* carried a half-page photo of 'the beautiful but empty palace of Ludwig Victor . . . formerly the home of the emperor's brother, now exiled and in disgrace',[11] while the *Indianapolis Star* headlined with 'Vienna's Palace of Mystery'.

The speculation followed an incident involving the archduke in a fracas at a popular city centre bathhouse with an 'athletic young man of the middle classes'. The transvestism and homosexuality of Archduke Ludwig Victor – at a time when there was little tolerance for either – were an open secret, with Emperor Francis Joseph even joking that he should be assigned a ballerina as an adjutant to keep him out of trouble. Although Austrian newspapers were not permitted to report on the events, the international media did, causing public humiliation for the emperor. Known affectionately from childhood as 'Luziwuzi', Ludwig Victor was very much the outsider of the inner Habsburg family circle. This was in part due to his sharp tongue and propensity to gossip. The archduke was a great art collector and lived in a magnificent Italian Renaissance palace on the Ringstrasse at Schwarzenbergplatz, designed by Heinrich von Ferstel. For Ludwig Victor its only shortcoming was a lack of a swimming pool, so he patronised the nearby public Centralbad bathhouse. Here he became involved in a spat with a young man who rejected his advances and struck him to the ground.

According to one of the great chroniclers of the court, Princess Nora Fugger: 'Reports of the scandal were made to the emperor of course, in the most lurid colours. He was terribly indignant and ordered his brother to leave Vienna at once and retire to his Castle Klesheim. The Archduke remained interned there until his death.'[12]

Old habits died hard for Archduke Ludwig Victor, whose beautiful Salzburg residence had its own swimming baths: young army officers from the local garrison were invited to use the facilities after playing tennis. Edmund Glaise-Horstenau, the last Vice-Chancellor of Austria before the 1938 Anschluss and a general in the German Wehrmacht during the Second World War, was an officer at the time. He recalled: 'They found no swimming shorts in their changing cabins so had to join their host in the pool just as God created them.'[13]

Vienna's Centralbad bathhouse, known as the Kaiserbründl, remains popular to this day as a gay bath and sauna; it proudly features a painting of Archduke Victor 'Luziwuzi' Ludwig on the wall. His palace never became the US embassy.

Scandals were never far away from other members of the imperial family, most notably Archduke Otto, who at the time was the next in line to the throne. The 'black sheep' of the Habsburgs is how the *Daily Tribune* described him, and went on to report him being 'harum scarum, hard drinking, thoughtless, brutal, who once in devilry jumped his horse back and forth over a coffin carried in a funeral procession and again tried one night to take some roisterers to the chambers of his wife, a princess of Saxony. A faithful guard would not let them in, and the archduke was placed under three months' arrest by the emperor.'[14]

Otto's most infamous high jinx also involved a drink-fuelled evening at the world-famous Hotel Sacher, where he became locked out of his private dining room wearing only his scabbard and brandishing his sword, according to reports published across the United

States. 'Here, unfortunately he came full tilt into an ambassador, who with the ambassadress and another lady of the diplomatic corps, was going into the restaurant after the opera. Naturally enough the diplomat was exceedingly angry, but at the same time he was too experienced and tactful a diplomat to make a great fuss over the incident.'[15]

While reports differ on whether the ambassador personally reported the matter to the emperor, Otto was summoned to the palace and given a stern dressing down. His misdemeanours and worsening health caused him to withdraw from court life and the further gaze of publicity. Otto's dissolute lifestyle, involving a string of affairs and illegitimate children, ended prematurely and painfully owing to syphilis. He died aged 41, ten years before his son, Charles, became the last Emperor of Austria-Hungary.

Most serious of the scandals – and a reflection of the existential crisis for Austria-Hungary emerged in 1913 with a sensational espionage and sex scandal involving the head of military counter-intelligence, who was exposed as a spy and ended up dying by suicide. Despite attempts by the military to suppress the details, newspapers splashed the story across the front pages that Colonel Alfred Redl had provided the Russians with key military secrets, rocking the military and state. In the biggest spy scandal in Austrian history, it emerged that Redl committed treason with the Russians to finance his lavish lifestyle and his male lover.

Discussing the Redl scandal in *The World of Yesterday*, the acclaimed Austrian author Stefan Zweig wrote: 'The army was shocked to the core. All knew that in case of war this one man might have been the cause of the death of hundreds of thousands, and of the monarchy being brought to the brink of the abyss; it was only then that we Austrians realised how breathtakingly near to the World War we already had been for that past year.'[16]

Alfred Redl was born in 1864 into modest family circumstances in Lemberg, the capital of the eastern crown land of Galicia. He grew up speaking German, Polish and Ruthenian, a combination that would stand him in good stead in multilingual Austria-Hungary.

During his early military career he developed an expertise in Russia and joined the Military Intelligence Service. By 1907 Redl had been promoted to the rank of colonel and appointed to head the counter-intelligence branch (Kundschaftbüro), putting him in charge of keeping tabs on foreign military espionage. He was highly thought of by colleagues and was responsible for introducing technical innovations, including the use of cameras, early recording devices and fingerprint records. But by this time he had already embarked on a dangerous course, selling highly secret military plans to the Russian General Staff: he provided the Russians with key Austro-Hungarian military plans and top secret information, including the identities of Austrian agents in the tsarist army.

Finally exposed in 1913 through suspicious money drops at a central Vienna post office, he admitted to his treasonous espionage and was forced to take his own life to minimise further damaging revelations.[17] One Hungarian newspaper noted that 'the Redl affair cannot be seen as a private matter. Redl is not an individual but a system. Whilst soldiers elsewhere are taught to love their homelands, lack of patriotism is held to be the greatest military virtue in this unfortunate monarchy. With us military education culminates in all national feeling being driven out of our soldiers . . . In the Redl affair this spirit has had its revenge. The Austrian and the Hungarian soldiers possess no fatherland; they only have a war lord.'[18]

Just over one year later, the war began between Austria-Hungary and Russia. It would bring down both empires and dynasties.

*

Vienna in the years before the First World War became a major centre for exiled Russian communists. Leon Trotsky (1879–1940) lived in the city following the 1905 Russian Revolution until 1914. Together with the wealthy Baku industrialist turned revolutionary Matvey Skobalev, he edited the bi-monthly newspaper *Pravda* ('Truth'). Beginning life in Vienna in 1908 with its famous slogan 'Workers of the World Unite', it was produced in the Austrian capital until 1912. During this time the Trotsky family was living hand to mouth, with regular trips to the pawn shop. A visiting Social Democrat described Leon Trotsky's domestic situation: 'His house in Vienna was a poor man's house, poorer than that of an ordinary American workingman earning eighteen dollars a week. Trotzky [sic] had been poor all of his life. His three rooms in a Vienna working-class suburb contained less furniture than was necessary for comfort. His clothes were too cheap to make him appear decent in the eyes of middle-class Viennese.'[19]

*Pravda's* finances were just as rocky, with subscriptions, sales and donations from émigrés in Switzerland and Austria not covering the overheads and very little money forthcoming from the Party organisations in Russia. Nevertheless, Trotsky played an influential role amongst the émigrés. Vienna 'at this time not only the Habsburg's capital, but also Trotsky's . . . Almost all of the albeit small colony of Russian Social Democratic emigrants were under Trotsky's influence . . . He had his own court . . . In his own stardom, Trotsky reigned absolute . . . They idolised him and were intimidated by him.'[20] He also spent time getting to know prominent Austrian left-wingers like Otto Bauer (1881–1938), Max Adler (1873–1937) and Karl Renner (1870–1950), the leading Austro-Marxist thinkers of the time. For Trotsky, however, they were not radical enough: 'They were well-educated people whose knowledge of various subjects was superior to mine. I listened with intense and, one might almost say, respectful interest to their conversation in the "Central" cafe. But very soon I grew puzzled. These people were not revolutionaries. Moreover, they represented the type that was farthest from that of the revolutionary.'[21] That didn't put Trotsky off spending time with the Austrian Social Democrats, including staying overnight at Karl Renner's home after missing the last streetcar to Hütteldorf: 'At that time, it never entered the head of this educated and talented Hapsburg official that the unhappy destiny of Austria-Hungary, whose historical advocate he then was, would make him, ten years later, the Chancellor of the Austrian Republic.'[22]

While Trotsky was in Vienna, the later Soviet dictator Joseph Stalin (1878–1953) arrived in the city with an assumed Greek identity of Stavros Papadopoulos, having been dispatched to learn about the nationality question in Austria-Hungary. Trotsky recalled seeing him in 1913 at the Vienna home of fellow *Pravda* editor Matvey Skobalev: 'He was a short, thin man. His greyish-brown skin was covered in pockmarks. His stare radiated little benevolence . . . He uttered a glottal sound, which, giving him the benefit of the doubt, could have been a greeting. He stepped up to the samovar and without a word made himself a cup of tea. Then, as silently as he had come, he left the room. I looked at Skobalev inquiringly. He said: "That was Dzhugashvilli [Stalin], a fellow Caucasian. He has recently become a member of the Bolshevik Central Committee. He is slowly coming to the fore amongst them."'[23] Stalin, who lived on the Schönbrunnerstrasse close to the Habsburg palace, was researching 'Marxism and the National Question', although he was less then complimentary about his own efforts in private correspondence: 'At the moment I am sitting in Vienna and scribbling all kinds of nonsense.'[24]

Much has been made of the fact that both Stalin and Hitler were in Vienna at the same time and enjoyed going for walks at the same park, but there is no reason to believe they ever met. There has been much speculation about them potentially meeting or being in the close vicinity of Gustav Mahler, Sigmund Freud or Tito and an etching even exists of an improbable chess match between Hitler and Lenin with their supposed signatures on the back.

What is undoubtedly correct is that both Hitler and Stalin were both obsessing about race and the Jews during their time in Vienna. As historian Simon Sebag Montefiore observed: 'Hitler was formulating the anti-Semitic volkische theories of racial supremacy that, as Führer, he would impose on his European empire; while Stalin researching his nationalities article was shaping a new idea for an international empire with a central authority behind an autonomous façade, the prototype of the Soviet Union. Almost thirty years later, their ideological and state structures were to clash in the most savage conflict of human history . . . The Jews did not fit into either of their visions. They repelled and titillated Hitler but irritated and confounded Stalin, who attacked their "mystical" nature. Too much of a race for Hitler, they were not enough of a nation for Stalin.'[25]

During the run-up to the First World War, Russian revolutionary leader Vladimir Ilyich Lenin never lived in Vienna, but he did find himself in exile in Austria-Hungary after being arrested in Galicia. Telegrams were sent seeking his release, including to socialist leader Victor Adler in Vienna. A Habsburg minister asked him: 'Are you sure that [Lenin] is an enemy of the Tsarist government?' to which Adler replied: 'Oh yes, a more sworn enemy than your excellency.'[26] Lenin was released, and made his way to exile in Switzerland via Vienna, which he described as 'a mighty, beautiful and vivacious city'. He thanked Adler for helping secure his release. Three years later he led the Bolshevik Revolution.

Lenin wrote to his author friend Maxim Gorky correctly predicting the impact of a war, but wrongly bet on its likelihood: 'A war between Austria and Russia would be a very useful thing for the revolution in all of Eastern Europe, but it is not likely that Franz Joseph and [Tsar] Nikolosha will give us that pleasure.'[27] Meanwhile, Victor Adler warned Foreign Minister Count Berchtold that war would provoke revolution in Russia, even if not in the Habsburg Monarchy. Berchtold replied mockingly: 'And who will lead this revolution? Perhaps Mr. Bronstein [Leon Trotsky] sitting over there at the Cafe Central?'[28] On his return to Russia, Trotsky became a leading figure in the 1917 Bolshevik Revolution and the first Soviet government, and he commanded the Red Army during the Russian Civil War.

The period before the Great War saw a further leading communist figure in Vienna: the future Yugoslav communist leader Tito, who worked in the Daimler factory in neighbouring Wiener Neustadt. Josip Broz (1892–1980) grew up in the Austro-Hungarian Kingdom of Croatia-Slavonia before moving near to Vienna. He enjoyed factory work and the cultural delights of Vienna at the weekend, but his time in and around Vienna was cut short by his call-up for military service in Croatia in 1913: 'Service in the Austro-Hungarian army did not attract me for several reasons. It was an army of oppression, which not only held my people in subjugation but served as an instrument to enslave other nations. Moreover, it was an old-fashioned and unintelligent army. It operated by rule and formula and, instead of teaching men how to fight taught them how to drill . . . individual initiative was strongly discouraged. However, I used the opportunity to learn as much about military science as I could. I was sent to the school for non-commissioned officers and became the youngest sergeant major in the regiment. I won the regimental championship in fencing and later second prize in the all-army championship in Budapest, and became a good skier. We practiced skiing on the slopes of Sljeme Mountain just outside Zagreb, where I served my term in the barrack of the Twenty-fifth Home Guards.'[29]

Like many other people in 1913, Broz enjoyed the last sunny year of peace without any sense of the impending disaster or its scale.

*

The assassination of Archduke Franz Ferdinand and his wife, Sophie, on 28 June 1914 lit the touchpaper that led to the First World War. The murder had a '9/11 effect: a terrorist event charged with historic meaning, transforming the political chemistry in Vienna'.[30] The killing of the Habsburg heir while he was in Sarajevo on a visit for troop manoeuvres, by the Bosnian Serb radical Gavrilo Princip, was a gigantic provocation. With suspicions that he and co-conspirators had received support from Belgrade, the mood in Vienna was to teach the Serbs a lesson.

The charge towards war was led by Foreign Minister Leopold Berchtold (1863–1942) and military Chief of Staff Franz Conrad von Hötzendorf (1852–1925), while Hungarian Prime Minister István Tisza (1861–1918) was opposed. Co-ordination with Germany was extremely close, with a special mission to Berlin by Count Alexander von Hoyos the chef de cabinet of Foreign Minister Berchtold. Together with Habsburg ambassador Count László Szögyény-Marich they held meetings on 5 and 6 July with the key decision-makers in Berlin, including Kaiser Wilhelm, Prime Minister Theobald Bethmann-Hollweg and Under Secretary of State Arthur Zimmerman, where they received the infamous German 'blank cheque' in firm support of military intervention. On their return, work quickened on the draft of the ultimatum to Serbia, including draconian terms designed to be unacceptable to Belgrade.

Veteran Austrian diplomat Heinrich von Lützow was so concerned about events spiralling out of control that he took the unusual step of informally warning a foreign state, with the clear intention of securing an international intervention. Lützow, who was at his summer retreat at Schloss Strelzhof in Lower Austria outside Vienna, met his friend the UK ambassador Maurice de Bunson, who had rented a nearby castle for the vacation. The conversation on 15 July was immediately relayed to British Foreign Secretary Sir Edward Gray. The diary of the ambassador's wife, Berta de Bunson, makes clear how prescient the subject was: 'M [Maurice] wired to F.O. what he had heard from L [Lützow] whose information according to after events, was quite correct and the severity of the note brought about the war as it was evidently meant to do.'[31]

The ultimatum, which was shared in advance with the German Embassy in Vienna, demanded a Serbian government crackdown on irredentist publications and groups, the removal of specified Serbian civil servants and military officials, and the presence of Austro-Hungarian officials in Serbia for the 'suppression of subversive movements'. While the Germans hoped for a speedy Invasion, the Austro-Hungarian military high command believed that the harvest needed to be collected first, so the earliest opportunity for war would be 25 July. In the knowledge that the Austrians were about to present the ultimatum, the German emperor, senior politicians and military commanders went on vacation so as not to raise suspicions about their involvement. Reports from military attachés confirmed the build-up of Austro-Hungarian army units close to Serbia and in Galicia. Austrian naval monitors moved down the Danube towards Belgrade.[32]

On 23 July the Austrian Minister to Serbia Baron Wladimir Giesl von Gieslingen officially handed over the démarche to the government in Belgrade with a 48-hour deadline for its acceptance. Were full agreement not forthcoming, the diplomat and his colleagues were ordered by the Austrian Foreign Ministry to leave the Serbian capital, as a first stage towards hostilities. Despairing Serbian leaders sought support from the Russians, who advised accepting the ultimatum, but the official reply sent on 24 July did not agree to all of the demands in full. This led directly to the acceleration of moves towards conflict. Expecting a declaration of war from Vienna, the Serbians ordered the mobilisation of their military, while Austria-Hungary formally broke off diplomatic relations. Next day, Emperor Francis Joseph ordered the mobilisation of eight army corps, in order to start operations against Serbia within days. On the same day, the Russians put their forces on alert and Germany encouraged Austria-Hungary to announce their declaration of war. With Vienna only planning to begin operations in mid-August and Britain warning that it would side with France and Russia, Germany began to get cold feet. Emperor Wilhelm called for the Austrians to take Belgrade in a limited military operation and force the Serbs to comply with the ultimatum, but senior German political and military leaders who wanted war were aghast and diplomats were ordered to disregard the suggestion. Ignoring last-minute attempts at mediation by British Foreign Secretary Grey, the die was cast and war was declared on Serbia by Austria-Hungary.

Sitting at his desk in his summer retreat in Bad Ischl, Emperor Francis Joseph signed the instrument of war, which took effect at 11 a.m. on 28 July 1914. As a result, Russia ordered a general military mobilisation on 30 July, followed by Austria-Hungary on 31 July. On 1 August Germany declared war on Russia and on 3 August against France, which was closely followed by its invasion of Belgium, which led to the declaration of war on Germany by the UK on 4 August. Two days later Austria-Hungary declared war on Russia, resulting in the UK and France declaring war on Austria-Hungary on 12 August. As British Foreign Secretary Grey noted: 'The lights are going out all over Europe; we shall not see them lit again in our life-time.'[33] Not long after the declaration of war, Emperor Francis Joseph sent a telegram to the officers' mess of the British King's Dragoon Guards, regretting that 'his regiment and his country were now at war'. As

248

honorary colonel he assured regimental personnel that if they were captured they would be 'treated as his personal guest' until the end of the conflict. It was a chivalrous gesture from another age.

The first shots of the Great War were fired by the Austrian navy on Belgrade within hours of the declaration of war. The flat-bottomed Danube monitor SMS *Bodrog* let off a shell salvo at fortifications at the Zemun–Belgrade railway bridge over the Sava river and towards the Topčider Hill overlooking the Serbian capital. The first casualties of the war were Karl Ebeling, the civilian captain of the Austrian steamer *Alkotmany*, followed not long afterwards by a 16-year-old Serbian volunteer, Dusan Djonovic.[34] In total there were 40 million further military and civilian casualties in the Great War, which also destroyed Austria-Hungary as a state and the Habsburgs as a ruling dynasty.

\*

For months prior to the outbreak of the war, senior Habsburg officials worked to explore new policies for the future: 'They wanted to protect the dynasty's existence and the Austro-Hungarian state as defined by the 1867 compromise, buttress ties with Germany, diminish the Serbian threat, forge a new alignment with Bulgaria, retain Romania in the secret alliance, protect Bosnia-Herzegovina from Serbian machinations, keep a wary eye on their erstwhile Italian ally, sustain the newly created Albanian state, and try to coax Russia into a more benevolent posture. The murders altered but did not totally overturn these foreign policy aims. Rather the decision to go to war would see them realigned and given new urgency.'[35]

At the start of the Great War, the Austro-Hungarian armed forces reflected the complicated nature of the Dual Monarchy itself. Following the compromise agreement between Austria and Hungary in 1867, there were effectively three branches of the army: the Common Army, recruited across the empire as a whole; the Imperial Austrian Landwehr, from Vienna-ruled Cisleithania; and the Royal Hungarian Honvéd. With more than 70 per cent of troops in the infantry, the core units consisted of the 102 Common Army infantry regiments, 35 Imperial Austrian Landwehr infantry regiments and 32 Royal Hungarian Honvéd infantry regiments. These were supplemented by artillery, cavalry, engineering, transportation and medical units. With 1,130 miles of nautical coastline to defend, Austria-Hungary had one of the largest navies in the world but was outsized in the Mediterranean by France and Italy. By the start of the war it had more than 20,000 personnel and 60 warships, including dreadnoughts, pre-dreadnoughts, cruisers, destroyers, torpedo craft and submarines. Main operating bases included Pula in present-day Croatia, Cattaro in Montenegro and Trieste in Italy. Air power was a relatively new development for all of the powers, especially Austria-Hungary whose aviation service was in its infancy at the outbreak of war, with less than 40 planes, 85 pilots and ten observation balloons.[36] At its peak strength, there would be 550 aircraft, which were augmented with the creation of a naval air service during the course of the war.

Before mobilisation, the size of the standing armed forces was relatively small, with only 36,000 officers, 414,000 troops and 1,200 pieces of artillery. By the end of the war, nearly 8 million men served as deployed personnel. Army make-up was as diverse as the multinational empire. Out of 1,000 enlisted troops, on average 267 were German-speakers, 223 Hungarian, 135 Czech, 85 Polish, 81 Ukrainian, 67 Croat and Serb, 64 Romanian, 38 Slovak, 26 Slovene and four Italian.[37] The officer corps, however, was very unrepresentative of the nationalities: for every 1,000 officers, 791 were German-speakers, 97 were Hungarian, 47 were Czech, 23 Polish and 22 were Croat or Serb.[38] Rules were needed to establish what constituted the most appropriate 'regimental language', so most soldiers could understand commands from their officers.

The army was as diverse religiously as well, with the officer corps amongst the few countries allowing the promotion of Jews to positions of command. Of 1,000 officers, 791 were Roman Catholics, 86 were Protestants, 84 Jews, 39 Greek Orthodox and one Uniate. More than 300,000 Jews served in the Habsburg military during the Great War, while the fez-wearing Muslim Bosnian infantry regiments were amongst the elite of the army. Christian, Jewish and Muslim chaplains were assigned to front-line units throughout the conflict.

The resources available to the military, both human and material, were significantly behind other larger countries. Conscription rates were markedly lower than Russia, France and Germany, meaning that after mobilisation the Austro-Hungarian army was significantly smaller than its rivals. This was also true when it came to the funding of the military and its equipment: 'Although the military budget had risen from 262 million crowns in 1895 to 306 million crowns in 1906, Austria was still spending proportionately less on her forces than any other European power. The Habsburg Empire was the least militarised state in Europe.'[39]

Austria-Hungary was not well prepared for war. While other powers had fought wars in recent years, like the Russians against Japan in 1905, the Habsburg military had no direct experience of modern warfare, having last deployed in any large numbers 36 years prior during the occupation of Bosnia-Herzegovina. Their last major battle was the defeat at Königgrätz 48 years previously, while still operating with muskets, field cannons and cavalry charges. In the meantime, the only competitive successes for the Austro-Hungarian military were accolades for its 170 regimental brass bands and prizes for their dashing uniforms at the 1900 Paris Exposition. In a war that would be dominated by the machine-gun and artillery fire, the Habsburg army still deployed mounted cavalry units, with Dragoons in sky-blue tunics, Hussars in red breeches and Uhlan lancers sporting a jaunty four-pointed Tschapka cap. The Germans were clear in their assessment: 'The Austrian military was adequate to wage a campaign against Serbia but inadequately prepared for any war against a major European power.'[40]

For Austria-Hungary, the war began with confusion about the extent of German support, with Vienna hoping for cover against Russia to the east as it dealt with Serbia in the south. While its early mobilisation and offensive efforts were aimed against Serbia, planners soon realised that they were exposed to a Russian offensive in Galicia. Worse than that, its pre-war planning was the first thing to fall as a casualty. The General Staff under Franz Conrad von Hötzendorf had developed a range of plans for war against different opponents: Plan I (Italy), Plan R (Russia), Plan B (Serbia), Plan R+B (Russia and Serbia). The variations underlined the challenge facing the monarchy of a war on multiple fronts. And the reality on the ground did not reflect the previously anticipated outcomes of a swift defeat of Serbia, then dealing with Russia. In fact, the Serbs handed the Austro-Hungarians a humiliating defeat, and planners who had started with Plan B (Serbia) had to dramatically change mid-deployment, and initiate Plan R+B (Russia and Serbia).

Austrian invasion plans for Serbia involved three armies crossing the Sava and Drina rivers to crush the Serbs' smaller and inferior forces. However, with one of the armies largely redirected to the Russian front, the Habsburg offensives into the Balkan kingdom proved embarrassing failures, with massive losses and little to show for them except the temporary capture of Belgrade. Austria-Hungary had hoped that the war would be localised in Serbia, although the risks were always high that this would then involve Russia and all the consequences that international alliances would bring. However, few imagined that what had become a world war would involve Habsburg forces on the other side of the world.

Although Austria had no international colonies, its German allies did, and as war raged in Europe it soon started in Africa and Asia too. Present-day Namibia was then known as German South West Africa; German East Africa included Burundi, Rwanda and Tanzania; and German West Africa included Cameroon and Togoland. All were defended by German troops. German colonial territories included part of Papua New Guinea and Pacific islands in the Micronesian, Marshall, Solomon, Caroline and Mariana groups, as well as Nauru and Samoa. Like the British in Hong Kong, the Germans had established Chinese concessions, including Tsingtao, which still celebrates its German connections today with China's most exported beer: a German colonial innovation.

Tsingtao was the base for the Far East Squadron of the German navy. At the start of hostilities in 1914 it was also hosting the warship of its Austro-Hungarian allies: the SMS *Kaiserin Elisabeth*, a coal-fired, steel-hulled protected cruiser, 98 metres in length and with a displacement of 3,967 tonnes. At the outbreak of the war she had a ship's complement of 450 officers and men including marines and a band.

Not long after the conflict started, the only First World War battle in the Far East began, with 23,000 Japanese and 1,500 British troops taking on 3,650 Germans and 324 Austro-Hungarians. Despite a Japanese blockade of the territory, the defenders held out for nearly two months. Although outnumbered by six to one, they only suc- cumbed after a sustained artillery bombardment and running out of ammunition on 6 November 1914. The German and Austro- Hungarian vessels blockaded in the port were scuttled days before the surrender.

Meanwhile, back in Europe, thousands of Habsburg troops that were destined for the Balkans had to re-routed to the east on clogged mobilisation troop trains, proceeding at walking pace and arriving too late to make a tactical difference. Speed of mobilisation had been the key advantage Conrad von Hötzendorf hoped would deliver a decisive advantage against the huge manpower of the tsarist forces. In reality, it was the Russians who took the advantage: routing four Austrian armies; overrunning Galicia, including the regional capital, Lemberg; besieging the fortress of Przemyśl, which guarded the route to Kraków; and threatening a breakthrough in the Carpathians. The losses by the end of 1914 were massive and, arguably, Austria- Hungary never recovered. One of the veterans of the offensive was the youngest sergeant major in the Habsburg military, Josip Broz, aka Tito:

> Our four regiments from Croatia, together with other divi-
> sions, raced to stop up the gap in the Austro-Hungarian
> front and to seal off the Russian advance. It was bitterly cold
> when we reached the front. A war of attrition was going on
> in the trenches. We were badly equipped and poorly armed.
> Those good uniforms and leather boots we had received

when the war broke out were replaced with boots of such poor material that they virtually melted off our feet after three days. The proportion of nettle in the army greatcoats were raised at the expense of wool and they were useless in the rain. The Russian soldiers were worse off in equipment. Moreover, their armaments were inferior to ours; there were whole Russian companies without firearms. They charged our positions repeatedly at bayonet point without any preliminary artillery barrage. It was a horrible massacre. On our own side enormous numbers of men froze to death for lack of warm clothing. I got to hate war and perceived of its senselessness. I pondered over it deeply, especially at night in the observation post.[41]

The fortress of Przemyśl, with its two rings of fortifications, was the empire's key defensive complex, an impregnable redoubt whose valiant defenders were expected to hold off the Russians. The fortified town on the San river in Galicia would go on to experience the longest siege of the war, starting on 16 September 1914 and lasting for 133 days. Defenders totalling 127,000 military personnel and 18,000 civilians were surrounded by six tsarist divisions, with only pigeon post, balloon and early airmail flights able to cross the lines. During a winter without resupply, 14,000 horses were slaughtered to provide food, but hunger and starvation became commonplace. The military command still insisted on costly engagements and suicidal break-out attempts, while the Russians shelled the fortress from 148 heavy artillery pieces that had been transported from Kronstadt, Brest-Litovsk and Kaunas.

Through the winter of 1914–1915, the Austro-Hungarians fought a terrible defensive winter war in the Carpathians to the south, in an effort to relieve Przemyśl. The heavily afforested mountain range – 1,500 kilometres long, up to 100 kilometres in breadth and with peaks up to 2,000 metres – formed a natural barrier between Russian-held Galicia and the Hungarian interior of the empire. Without any proper winter contingency plans, Habsburg forces totalling 175,000 men sought to take key mountain passes and push the Russians back, but counter-attacks and extreme weather conditions with temperatures below −20°C brought the offensive to an end.

The cost of the failed Carpathian offensive was 670,000 casualties[42] and the loss of all hope of relief for the defenders of the fortress of Przemyśl. On 22 March 1915, more than 117,000 Austro-Hungarian troops, including nine generals, 93 senior staff officers and 2,500 other officers went into Russian captivity.[43] Germany's military plenipotentiary at the Habsburg high command in Teschen reported that Austro-Hungarian forces were 'rotten and decayed'. Colonel Karl von Kageneck warned that 'this land can no longer be helped'.[44]

Atrocities against civilians on the Eastern Front were increasingly common and perpetrated by both sides. Within a month of the Russian occupation in Galicia, a pogrom took place against Jews in Lemberg. Excesses by Cossack cavalry were commonplace and the general level of suffering was extreme: 'Brutality was what really defined the Russian occupation. The Tsarist army's ideological impulse to "return" eastern Galicia to an imagined "primordial" Russian state was malevolent. The attempted cultural extermination of Ukrainians brought much suffering.'[45] Nearly half of Galicia's 400,000-strong Jewish population fled to safety, together with 300,000 other civilians, to the interior of the Dual Monarchy. Meanwhile, Habsburg military courts meted out summary executions on an immense scale against civilians suspected of supporting the enemy. It is estimated that between 11,400 and 36,000 civilians were executed in Galicia, Bukovina, occupied Serbia and Bosnia-Herzegovina. The excesses were 'arranged and planned at the highest level. They included hostage-taking and hostage-shootings, massed deportation, incarceration and forced labour – and . . . mass executions. The violent politics of the military was accompanied by further violent excesses that were in part tolerated, in part left unpunished: rape, looting, arbitrary killings and the destruction of houses.'[46]

With the Austro-Hungarian military campaigns failing on all fronts, Conrad von Hötzendorf pleaded for German support and by April 1915 a separate peace was being threatened if help wasn't forthcoming.[47] Not for the last time the Germans came to the rescue, creating a 9th Army to help on the Eastern Front. The upshot was a plan for a joint offensive, under German command, for what became known as the Gorlice–Tarnów Offensive. It ran from May to October 1915 and was a success, with the Russian lines collapsing totally and tsarist forces withdrawing hundreds of miles. The fortress of Przemyśl was retaken, as was Lemberg. To the north, the Germans advanced far into Russian Poland taking Warsaw. It was to be a false dawn on the Eastern Front.

Elsewhere during 1915, a new front had opened up when the Italians broke their undertaking to remain neutral in the hope of gaining territory like South Tyrol and Trieste. The Italian war-aim was to break through towards Slovenia and Carinthia, but they were successfully blocked along an Alpine front from Tyrol to the Adriatic. The Italian front was particularly extreme, as both sides faced one another on mountain peaks, ridges and high plateaus. At the start of hostilities, the Austro-Hungarians secured defensive positions in strategic heights from the Dolomites to the Julian Alps and Karst Plateau and were able to fend off early offensives by much larger Italian forces. Trenches, gun emplacements, tunnels, accommodation and stores were dug into the stone of the mountains, where many remain to this day. Winter conditions on the heights were appalling for both sides, with avalanches causing tens of thousands of deaths. Casualties were also particularly high because shellfire sent deadly rock splinters flying in all directions. As on the Western Front, efforts were made to excavate tunnels under enemy lines and set off huge explosive mines.

While the war raged in Europe, Austria-Hungary's Ottoman allies targeted the Russians in the Caucasus and faced British and French forces in the Middle East. In a gesture of solidarity, an expeditionary force of 3,000 Austro-Hungarians was deployed to the Holy Land, where they spent the rest of the war. A sixth of the troops lost their lives, including one Jewish officer who was buried in the Mount of Olives cemetery in Jerusalem with military honours performed by Muslim Turkish forces.[48]

Back on the Eastern Front in June 1916, it was the Russians who gained the advantage with the Brusilov Offensive, the greatest feat of arms by the Tsarist Empire during the First World War, and amongst the most lethal offensives in military history. It caused the worst crisis in the entire conflict for Austria-Hungary and the other Central Powers states.[49] Named after the Russian commander General Aleksei Brusilov, it involved a limited but accurate artillery barrage, before his 40 infantry divisions and 15 cavalry divisions focused on Austrian weak points along a 300-mile front in present-day western Ukraine. It managed what the Triple Entente powers had failed to achieve on the Western Front: a massive breakthrough.

In full retreat, the Austrians had to transfer troops from the Italian front, and the Germans from the Western Front, to slow the Russian advance. The offensive caused massive losses: one million casualties to both sides, effectively breaking the back of the Austro-Hungarian army but also inflicting such grievous damage to the Russian army that it prepared the ground for its eventual collapse a year later.

\*

In Vienna itself, it didn't take long for the impact of the war to be felt on the home front, with tens of thousands of refugees streaming into the city from Galicia, while hospitals overflowed with military casualties. At the same time, food shortages began to impact on civilians and inflation skyrocketed. War bonds were issued to pay for the conflict and 90,000 gold wedding rings were exchanged for iron in a fundraising drive.

Eyewitness accounts of Vienna during the First World War include those of Frederick Courtland Penfield (1855–1922), the last US ambassador to the Habsburg court. For most of the war the US was neutral, so while diplomats from the Triple Entente states had left Vienna, Penfield and his small embassy staff remained. One particular problem for the ambassador was that his locally employed staff had been called up to the army. Having already seen seven staff go, the mobilisation of his gardener caused Penfield to write to Foreign Minister Berchtold in December 1914: 'I can't very well live in Vienna as an Ambassador unless allowed some servants.' He tried to put in a good word for them, suggesting reasons why they were not suitable for military service: one was 'too tall and fragile to make a soldier', another 'so nearly stone deaf that I'm sure he would make a poor warrior. He is, however, a good worker in my glasshouses, and I wish the War Ministry would send him back.'[50] Berchtold supported his intervention, and both members of staff were exempted from military service.

Penfield had a difficult time in Vienna, having to navigate around the issues of neutrality, including protesting about the Austrian U-boat sinking of the Italian flagged *Ancona*, which had American passengers aboard. Diplomatic relations were also stretched by a scandal involving the Austro-Hungarian ambassador in Washington Konstantin Dumba, who supported efforts to hamper US munitions production, which led to his recall.[51]

Meanwhile, having taken on consular responsibilities in Vienna for the interests of a number of belligerent countries, Penfield and embassy colleagues toured internment and prisoner-of-war camps to inspect conditions, including French and British civilians and Italian POWs. In his view, 'this Monarchy is taking good care of its prisoners', and he returned from visits 'without finding many things to ask for change or improvement in'. In his estimation, Austria-Hungary was having to provide for a million prisoners, of which 80 per cent were Russian.[52]

During his wartime posting, Penfield sent back regular detailed reports to the State Department about developments and conditions in Vienna and across the monarchy, including the closure of parliament and the stock exchange and reports about public opinion. In his view there was war tiredness: although Vienna supported the emperor, Budapest was unhappy with the military campaign, there were pro-Italian protests in Fiume and Trieste, while in Prague people were unhappy with the way Vienna appeared to be playing to the tune of Berlin. Embassy staff were having to stress their nationality so as not to be confused for Britons. Reports include admonishments from an Austrian officer for French being spoken in public, a colleague being spat at in the street after asking a passer-by for directions, and American nationals being attacked as 'swine' on Vienna trams. Meanwhile, the embassy received news from elsewhere in the empire from four military observers, who at different times were on the southern front in Serbia, eastern front in Galicia and on the Adriatic at Pula.

On the deteriorating conditions in Vienna, by February 1915 the city was still 'the most normal, yet tensest of all the war capitals',[53] but was teeming with 50,000 injured troops, 150,000 refugees from Galicia and 1,000 Russian POWs. Penfield lamented the lack of a social life in the capital, although the character of coffee-house culture was continuing. Theatres were open but mostly showing 'war drama'.[54]

In 1916, Penfield heard the news of the death of Emperor Francis Joseph I, who passed away on 21 November at Schönbrunn Palace. He was 86. After a 67-year reign, most of his subjects could only remember him on the throne, and his death was a sign for many that the monarchy itself was coming to an end. News of the emperor's death spread quickly across the country and around the world. In his report back to the US, Penfield noted that he had received a picture from the monarch with an 'affectionate inscription' before he passed away.

After the formal intimation of the death of the emperor, Penfield was sent the following instruction by the US Secretary of State Robert Lansing: 'The President, desiring to show the high respect due to the memory of the late Emperor and King, has invested you with the rank and character of a Special Ambassador to represent him and the people of the United States at funeral obsequies. So notify Foreign Office. Send appropriate wreath in the President's name.'

The funeral was captured on newsreel showing the pomp of Habsburg tradition, with the emperor's coffin carried down the Ambassadors Steps of the Hofburg onto the black funeral carriage, pulled by black horses with black plumes and followed by a riderless horse. Imperial Lifeguards led the cortège from the Hofburg onto the Ringstrasse, thronged by thousands of silent mourners, with a huge military guard of honour despite continuing hostilities on various fronts. The procession made its way to St Stephen's Cathedral and then on to the Crypt of the Capuchins with new Emperor-King Charles I and Empress-Queen Zita processing on foot holding the hand of young Crown Prince Otto. They were followed by Habsburg archdukes in military uniform and archduchesses dressed in ghostly black from head to toe. The *New York Times* reported on the 'strict observance of Spanish ceremonial', and the other attendees included King Ferdinand of Bulgaria, King Ludwig of Bavaria, Crown Prince Wilhelm of Germany, the King of Saxony and the Crown Prince of Turkey. According to the correspondent 'over half a million Viennese turned out to see the funeral procession'.[55] Members of the diplomatic corps were also present and 'neutral royal visitors', including the Crown Prince of Sweden and Prince Waldemar of Denmark.

Only a few months later, in April 1917, the US broke diplomatic relations with Austria-Hungary. Penfield left Vienna, but a number of US diplomats remained in Vienna, based at the Spanish Embassy, which took over formal consular responsibility for the US. The Americans' furnishings were emptied and stored in the Japanese Embassy depot and the front door was locked. The United States and Austria-Hungary were now at war.

*

By this stage of the war, the common view in Germany was that the country was 'shackled to a corpse'. Austria-Hungary was incapable of independent offensive military operations and the Germans increasingly took direct military control over their allies. Late successes included the defeat of Romania and victory in the 12th Battle of Izonso (Caporetto) against Italy. In the valley of the Soča river, at Kobarid in present-day Slovenia, the Austro-Hungarians and Germans began their offensive against the Italians on 24 October 1917 with a poison gas attack. Hugely successful infantry infiltration engagements broke through the Italians lines, forcing them back 19 kilometres to the Tagliamento river on the first day of the offensive.

The successful shock-troop tactics were described in *Infantry Attacks*, by a young German lieutenant colonel who would become famous in the Second World War: Erwin Rommel. The book is still considered a classic military manual and taught in defence colleges around the world. In a conflict with largely static front lines, the joint Austro-Hungarian/German victory at Caporetto is one of the few breakthrough battles of the First World War. With more than one and a half million casualties over the 12 battles of Isonzo, it is the bloodiest mountain conflict in human history.

By the time young Charles succeeded his aged great-uncle Francis Joseph as emperor at the end of 1916, the writing was on the wall for Austria-Hungary. Unless peace could be secured, the situation both on the battlefields and home front looked dire, so he began with a change the old guard, appointing Count Ottokar Czernin as Austro-Hungarian Minister of Foreign Affairs, dismissing Chief of Staff Franz Conrad von Hötzendorf, taking personal control over the armed forces and forcing the resignation of anti-reformist Hungarian Prime Minister Count István Tisza.

In early 1917 he launched a secret diplomatic initiative to secure a separate peace with the Triple Entente powers. The Sixtus Affair, as it became known, was named after the intermediary, who happened to be the emperor's brother-in-law, Prince Sixtus of Bourbon-Parma, who was an officer in the Belgian army. Meetings and communications ran via dynastic and aristocratic channels in Switzerland, but also involved Sixtus being spirited over the border to a secret rendezvous at Laxenburg Castle outside Vienna. With fears of the Germans finding out about the secret discussions, knowledge of the discussions was kept largely within the ruling family. Not even Foreign Minister Czernin was fully aware, a mistake that would later lead to terrible consequences.

French conditions for peace included the return of Alsace-Lorraine by Germany, the independence of Belgium as well as Serbia, and control over Constantinople by Russia. Emperor Charles signalled his agreement to the first three points in a letter to the French president. However, the attempt at dynastic diplomacy failed, with the

Germans refusing to negotiate about Alsace-Lorraine amid signs that Russia was about to collapse. Things got even worse after a public speech from Czernin claiming the peace efforts were initiated by the French. Emperor Charles denied any involvement, but French Prime Minister Georges Clemenceau then published the letters signed by him. It was a domestic and international disaster for the dynasty: 'The Sixtus Affair ended with the worst possible result, the opposite of its intended outcome: no peace, and certainly not an "honourable" outcome; the Emperor seen as a stammering, crazy, liar; the Empress branded a "traitor"; with respect for both from their main ally fatally undermined. Every hope from the Triple Entente that Austria-Hungary could free itself from German hegemony and play a welcome counterweight after the exit of Russia had evaporated . . . domestically the loss of trust hit the standing of the monarchy as an institution and the monarch was damaged, even amongst the middle-class and rural population and rocked the Empire.'[56]

Meanwhile, conditions for ordinary people across the empire were becoming perilous, with shortages of food and supplies. Vienna residents had a daily food allocation amounting to just 830 calories, while in reality people often endured significantly less than their ration allowance. A medical study at the end of the war concluded that 91 per cent of Viennese children of school age were mildly to severely undernourished.[57] Symbolic of the injustice meted out on the civilian public was news that unpopular Prime Minister Karl Stürghk was assassinated in the upmarket Meissel und Schaden restaurant during a slap-up lunch. While initial media reports concentrated on the fact that his assassin Fritz Adler was the son of socialist party leader Viktor Adler, the focus quickly shifted to the fact that Stürghk had been eating mushroom soup, boiled beef with mashed turnips, and a pudding accompanied by a wine spritzer. Not many ordinary Viennese could dream of such a meal, and consequently there was little public sympathy following his demise.

By the end of 1917, the options for the future of Austria-Hungary were being openly discussed by the international leaders who would play a key role determining its fate. On 4 December, in his Fifth

Annual Message to Congress, President Woodrow Wilson (1865–1924) said: 'Austria-Hungary is for the time being not her own mistress but simply the vassal of the German Government. We must face the facts as they are and act upon them without sentiment in this stern business. The government of Austria-Hungary is not acting upon its own initiative or in response to the wishes and feelings of its own peoples but as the instrument of another nation. We must meet its force with our own and regard the Central Powers as but one.'[58]

These comments were soon followed up by British Prime Minister David Lloyd George, who outlined British war aims to a Trades Union conference on January 1918 in London's Caxton Hall: 'The settlement of the new Europe must be based on such grounds of reason and justice as will give some promise of stability . . . though we agree with President Wilson that the break-up of Austria-Hungary is no part of our war aims, we feel that unless genuine self-government on true democratic principles is granted to those Austro-Hungarian nationalities who have long desired it, it is impossible to hope for the removal of those causes of unrest in that part of Europe which have so long threatened its general peace.'[59]

The growing international momentum recognising the right of self-determination for the nationalities of the Austro-Hungarian Empire gained even greater prominence within days when Wilson outlined the principles he believed should be applied at the end of the Great War. In an address to Congress on 8 January 1918, he outlined 'Fourteen Points' that should guide the negotiations with the aim of securing long-term peace. Point Ten was: 'The people of Austria-Hungary, whose place among the nations we wish to see safeguarded and assured, should be accorded the freest opportunity to autonomous development.'[60]

Despite the end of the war on the Eastern Front following the Russian Revolution and Treaty of Brest-Litovsk on 3 March 1918, Austria-Hungary was still militarily and economically exhausted. Promised grain supplies from Ukraine did not materialise in the scale necessary to make up for the dramatic domestic deterioration in agricultural production. Declining yields, reduced livestock numbers and failing food distribution was having a huge impact on the home front, especially in Vienna. In April 1918, Emperor Charles reappointed Baron Stephan Burián von Rajecz to the post of Imperial Foreign Minister as part of efforts to secure a negotiated end of the war.

In Serbia, where the war had started in 1914, the Austro-Hungarians and Germans came under major pressure from Entente powers attacking north from Greece. A combined force of French, British, Serbian and Greek troops under the command of French General Franchet d'Espèrey caused a major retreat by Bulgarian troops, the seeking of an armistice and the abdication of Tsar Ferdinand I of Bulgaria. Allied advances continued northward, liberating Albania, Montenegro and into Serbia. Austro-Hungarian Field Marshal Hermann Kövess von Kövessháza ordered a strategic retreat behind the Danube, Sava and Drina rivers,[61] the last line of defence before the Hungarian hinterland.

As the Habsburg collapse in the Balkans was underway, calls were made by Vienna for diplomatic negotiations to end the war, even though the Entente powers were demanding unconditional surrender, which Germany would still not yet accept. Unsurprisingly, the US Secretary of State Robert Lansing stressed that the US would 'entertain no proposal for a conference upon a matter concerning which it has made its position and purpose so plain'.[62] A follow-up peace note was again communicated to President Wilson proposing an armistice on the basis of the Fourteen Points, while Emperor Charles made a last attempt to hold the restless nationalities together. He invited parliamentarians of different ethnic communities to discuss the formation of a 'ministry of all the peoples', but Czech and southern Slav representatives turned down the invitation.

By mid-October 1918 Foreign Minister Burián formally requested an armistice from the Entente, and Emperor Charles issued the proclamation of a Peoples' Manifesto, which had precious little chance of success:

To My faithful Austrian peoples!

Since I ascended the throne, I have constantly endeavoured to achieve for all my peoples the peace they long for and to show to the peoples of Austria the paths along which they may, unhindered by obstacles and conflict, bring their powerful national identities to richly beneficial fruition. The terrible struggle of the world war has hitherto impeded the work of peace. [ . . . ] In accordance with the will of its peoples, Austria is to become a federal state in which each nationality shall form its own polity on the territory on which it lives. [ . . . ] This reshaping, which shall in no way affect the integrity of the lands of the holy Hungarian crown, is intended to give each individual national state its independence.[63]

It took only days for the initiative to hit the skids with a reply from US Secretary of State Lansing that the proposals for mere autonomy were not sufficient. On 14 October the self-declared Czechoslovak provisional government joined the Allies, and events were moving fast in the Hungarian half of the Dual Monarchy. Foreign Minister Burián travelled to Budapest to meet with Hungarian politicians who were considering a bill on reducing the Austro-Hungarian state to a personal union, including the creation of their own foreign ministry and direct representation in peace negotiations. He arrived a day after tumultuous scenes in the Magyar parliament on the banks of the Danube, including the resignation of the Hungarian cabinet. 'The situation, as I found it at Budapest on 24 October, clearly proved to me the untenability of my position. I submitted my resignation and it was accepted.'[64]

Also on 24 October, the Italians began the Battle of Vittorio Veneto, which led to the complete military collapse of Austria-Hungary on the Italian front. It was the backdrop to the ultimate dissolution of the empire, with various constituent nations declaring independence from Vienna and Budapest. Just prior to the Italian offensive, the government in Budapest announced the recall of Hungarian regiments from the Italian front, causing chaos to the chain of command and the accelerating problem of troops refusing to follow orders. In the face of advances by the Italians and with the Austro-Hungarian state coming apart at home, the Habsburg high command ordered a general retreat and then agreed to an armistice.

The armistice of Villa Giusti, signed on 3 November 1918, ended the war between Italy and Austria-Hungary, with a ceasefire, the withdrawal of Central Powers forces and free transit to the borders of Germany. Within days, more than 20,000 Italian troops had occupied northern Tyrol, including the regional capital of Innsbruck.

Italian army Chief of Staff General Armando Diaz reported the famous *Bollettino della Vittoria* ('Victory Bulletin') from Supreme Headquarters on 4 November 1918, declaring Austro-Hungarian army 'annihilated': 'The remains of what was one of the most powerful armies in the world are going back, in disorder and hopeless, up the valleys they descended with proud surety.'[65]

In addition to the chaotic withdrawal of remaining Habsburg forces, who began the long walk home, the Italians captured 350,000 Austro-Hungarian troops and more than 5,000 field artillery pieces. It marked the effective end of the Austro-Hungarian Empire. Emperor Charles sent a telegram to German Emperor Wilhelm II ending their alliance.

On 28 October, only days before the armistice, Czech political leaders took over the reigns in Prague. On 29 October, a declaration of independence followed for the Slovenes, Croats and Serbs. On 31 October, pro-independence Hungarian revolutionaries led by Count Mihály Károlyi took over Budapest in a coup, leading to the cancellation of the 1867 Austro-Hungarian compromise. The state had effectively ceased to exist.

In Vienna, members of the Austrian Imperial Council representing German-speaking areas met at the Lower Austrian Provincial Diet on Herrengasse near the Hofburg and proclaimed themselves to be the Provisional National Assembly for German-Austria. They agreed that 'the German people in Austria are resolved to determine their own future political organisation to form an independent

German-Austrian state, and to regulate their relations with other nations through free agreements with them'.[66] Within days, early steps were taken towards union with Germany, with the adoption of a resolution declaring: 'German-Austria is a constituent part of the German Republic. Special laws shall regulate the participation of German-Austria in the law-making and administration of the German Republic, as well as the extension of the sphere of validity of the laws and institutions of the German Republic to German-Austria.'[67]

Emperor Charles, who had been staying at his Hungarian residence at Gödöllő, returned to Vienna after ministers were appointed for the new state of German-Austria without his involvement. At Schönbrunn Palace it became evident that the monarchy was being deserted, with the Lifeguards disappearing from their posts and only young cadets taking their place. Charles was insistent that despite the hopeless situation he would not abdicate, but he was persuaded by leaders of the now powerless imperial 'government of liquidation' that he should renounce his continuing role in the affairs of state. On 11 November 1918 Charles signed his declaration in the Blue Chinese Salon of Schönbrunn Palace:

Since my accession I have incessantly tried to rescue my peoples from this tremendous war.

I have not delayed the re-establishment of constitutional rights or the opening of a way for the people to substantial national development. Filled with an unalterable love for my peoples I will not, with my person, be a hindrance to their free development.

I acknowledge the decision taken by German Austria to form a separate State. The people has by its deputies taken charge of the Government. I relinquish every participation in the administration of the State. Likewise I have released the members of the Austrian Government from their offices.

May the German Austrian people realise harmony from the new adjustment. The happiness of my peoples was my aim from the beginning. My warmest wishes are that an internal peace will be able to heal the wounds of this war.

[Signed] CHARLES[68]

In an attempt to keep a low profile, Charles and Zita left the palace in a convoy of cars through a side gate and travelled to the Habsburg hunting lodge of Eckartsau Castle in Lower Austria. Fearing for their safety, Zita's brother Prince Sixtus spoke with King George V to ask for assistance. British army officers were sent to Vienna with orders to arrange safe passage for the emperor and get his family out of the country. The last official journey of the imperial court train took them to exile, first in Switzerland. Later they moved on to Madeira, where they lived for a number of years. Two attempts to regain the Hungarian throne followed soon after the First World War, but both failed, as did the health of former Emperor Charles, who died of pneumonia in 1922, aged just 34. Zita wore black mourning dress for 67 years until her death in 1989. She was buried in Vienna in the Crypt of the Capuchins, according to Habsburg custom. In 2004 Emperor Charles was beatified by Pope John Paul II as the 'Blessed Karl of Austria' for his efforts to secure peace.

The end of the Dual Monarchy and collapse of the Austro-Hungarian state in 1918 was a direct result of the First World War and the huge toll it exerted on its people and economy. It is estimated that 1.2 million troops lost their lives, in addition to 450,000 soldiers that died while being held as prisoners of war, and 300,000 troops who remained listed as 'missing'. Some 465,000 civilians died as a result of famine, cold and epidemics before September 1918 and a further 260,000 died of Spanish flu between September and October 1918.[69]

On 12 November 1918 the Austrian Republic was officially proclaimed in Vienna.

# 10

# *The First Republic to the Third Reich*

'The rest is Austria'

– attributed to Georges Clemenceau

The First Austrian Republic literally emerged from the wreckage of the Austro-Hungarian Empire, with its founding democratic representatives all elected before the war in 1911 from German-speaking areas to the then Imperial Council. Without time to organise fresh elections in the new state, parliamentarians took up their seats in the Provisional National Assembly that met in the Lower Austrian provincial assembly building on Herrengasse. The 208 all-male deputies included representatives from Bohemia, Moravia, Carnolia, Silesia and Bukovina, regions of newly declared independent neighbouring states.

Social Democrat Karl Renner (1870–1950) became the first chancellor of the new state and is remembered as 'Father of the Republic' not just because of his role after the First World War, but also for restoring the republic after the Second World War. Renner, who hailed from a poor family of wine growers in Moravia, studied law at Vienna University before his election to the Imperial Council in 1907 for the Social Democratic Workers' Party of Austria (SDAP).

One of the first acts of the new Provisional National Assembly was an appeal made directly to President Wilson for the Entente powers to agree to a union of Austria and Germany: 'We hope that you, Mr. President, in accordance with the principles which you have so often expressed, will support the endeavour of the German people in Austria. You have fought that Poles, Italians, and South Slavs, formerly members of the Austrian State, should have the right to unite their national states outside of Austria; we are convinced that you will recognise the same right also for the German people in Austria.'[1] Immediately after the war there was cross-party consensus that the much-reduced German-Austria wasn't a viable political or economic entity and that union with Germany was the only way forward. That, however, was not in the minds of Allied negotiators, who did not want to 'reward' Germany with a significant territorial gain.

Allied representatives gathered in early 1919 to hammer out a joint negotiating position at the French Foreign Ministry on the Quai d'Orsay in Paris. The main focus was on the peace terms in relation to Germany, but work also progressed with regard to both Austria and Hungary as the successor states of the Dual Monarchy.

Chancellor Renner and an Austrian delegation arrived at Château de Saint Germain in May 1919 but were excluded from the deliberations. Negotiations only involved the victorious powers, especially the 'big four': the US, UK, France and Italy, with their delegations led by US Under Secretary of State Frank Polk, UK Secretary of State for Foreign Affairs Arthur Balfour, French Prime Minister Georges Clemenceau and Italian Minister of Foreign Affairs Tommaso Tittoni. The Treaty of Saint-Germain-en-Laye highlighted that the Great War was started by Austria-Hungary declaring war on Serbia in July 1914, and that the Habsburg Monarchy had since ceased to exist and was replaced in Austria by a new republican government.

Austria had to accept responsibility for 'the aggression of Austria-Hungary and her Allies', and the loss and damage caused to the victorious Entente nations and their nationals. Under the provisions of the treaty, Austria had to recognise the independence of the new Czech-Slovak state, Poland, the Serb-Croat-Slovene state and territorial losses to Italy, Poland and Romania. The treaty detailed the dismemberment of the Austrian half of the empire: more than 60 per cent of former Cisleithanian territory was assigned to largely new independent neighbouring states. Clemenceau is widely attributed with saying: *'Le reste c'est l'Autriche'* ('The rest is Austria'). In the north and east, the crown lands of Bohemia and Moravia became the western half of Czechoslovakia, the Austrian Duchy of Silesia was split between Poland and Czechoslovakia, the Kingdom of Galicia and Lodomeria became part of Poland, and Bukovina was assigned to Romania. In the west, the regions of South Tyrol and Trentino became part of Italy as did further territories including Gorizia, Gradisca, Trieste and Istria. In the south, the crown land of Dalmatia, Duchy of Carnolia, Lower Styria as well as Bosnia-Herzegovina became parts of the Yugoslav Kingdom of Serbs, Croats and Slovenes. A referendum was to be held in southern Carinthia, which was significantly Slovene speaking, and also in Ödenburg/Sopron in 'German West Hungary' (Burgenland) which had a significant German-speaking population. Both areas largely decided to become part of the Austrian republic following local plebiscites.

During the First World War, the Allies had increasingly spoken up for the right of self-determination for minorities in the Austro-Hungarian Empire. As ethnolinguistic maps of the Dual Monarchy illustrate, this was a near impossible task without creating substantial minorities in the newly created successor states. According to the 1910 census, 37 per cent of people in Bohemia, 27 per cent in Moravia and 44 per cent in Austrian Silesia spoke German; 38 per cent of people in Bukovina spoke Ruthenian and 21 per cent German; in Galicia 40 per cent spoke Ruthenian, and German was overwhelmingly spoken in South Tyrol. The German-speaking minorities in regions coterminous with the new Austrian republic presented a particularly vexing question, particularly in the Sudetenland and South Tyrol where people were not allowed to take part in the February 1919 general election by the Czechoslovak and Italian authorities.

As for the new Austrian republic itself, it was to be denied the right of self-determination and the choice to become part of Germany. Article 88 of the treaty made clear that an Anschluss with Germany would not to be permitted by the international community.[2] The terms of the treaty were non-negotiable and not subject to amendment. The new republican government in Germany had already been informed that refusal to sign would lead to a military invasion. Chancellor Renner and the Austrian delegation had no option but to bow to the inevitable and signed the treaty on 10 September 1919.

A separate peace agreement was reached between the Allies for Hungary in 1920. The Treaty of Trianon cut Hungary's pre-war size and population by two thirds and left it landlocked. Only 7.6 million people would remain in Hungary out of a previous total of 21 million. Slovakia and Carpathian Ruthenia became part of Czechoslovakia, Transylvania transferred to Romania, the Kingdom of Croatia-Slavonia and neighbouring regions formed part of the new southern Slav state, while German West Hungary largely transferred to Austria. The areas assigned to newly independent neighbouring states were predominantly populated by the ethnicity of the new country, although considerable Hungarian minorities were included as well. Transylvania had more than one and a half million Hungarians and half a million German speakers. In Slovakia, more than a fifth of the population was Hungarian-speaking, while in Vojvodina it was more than a quarter. In total, 3.3 million Hungarians found themselves in neighbouring countries.

Border conflict between Hungary and Romania during the treaty negotiations led to a communist takeover and violent crackdown, known as the Red Terror. A counter-revolutionary offensive was launched with support from the Entente powers and retook Budapest with war hero Admiral Miklós Horthy at its head. Horthy (1868–1957), who had been the last Commander-in-Chief of the Austro-Hungarian navy and a past aide-de-camp to Emperor Francis Joseph, went on to become Regent of Hungary and rule until 1944. The Hungarian government signed the Treaty of Trianon at Versailles on 4 June 1920.

The peace treaties ending the First World War had a significant impact in the decades to come. Far from resolving conflict, in many ways they prepared the ground for its resumption, as described by Zara Steiner, the leading historian of European international relations between the First and Second world wars.[3] In her classic work *The Lights that Failed – European International History 1919–1933*, she concluded that 'the treaties with Austria [and] Hungary . . . were far harsher and more vindictive than the one with Germany. The Austrian and Hungarian settlements were punitive in the extreme:

the former was left in a perilous economic state, and the latter, if economically viable, was so stripped of territory and people as to guarantee its revisionist status.'[4]

Other major decisions in 1919 also chartered the future course of Austria, including the first democratic elections in the new state in February 1919, which enfranchised women for the first time. Laws were passed marking a formal break with the Habsburgs and the nobility that had supported the monarchy over centuries. The Habsburg Law formalised the removal of the former ruling house of Habsburg-Lorraine from state business and confiscated their properties. It also banned the return of members of the Habsburg family to Austria. Meanwhile the Law on the Abolition of Nobility abolished the aristocracy and the use of noble titles and privileges. It also meant the end of associated nobiliary particles, such as 'von' and 'zu'. The Austrian love of titles, however, has continued in academic and professional life, including the rank of Hofrat (Court Councillor), which remains more than a century after the end of the court. Little controversy remains about the outlawing of the nobility or the position of the Habsburgs, although the family head at the time of writing, Karl Habsburg, has been outspoken on the issue: 'The Habsburg law is absurd, there's nothing else to be said about it. All our rights were taken away from us, we were dispossessed and sent into exile. Our assets were put into a fund and should have been returned to us after that fund was dissolved. But that never happened.' He also highlighted the unfairness of being banned from the country: 'I grew up with the grotesque situation that I as a child had an Austrian passport, issued in Munich, in which it said that I could travel to every country in the world apart from Austria. That rule was only changed at the end of the 60s.'[5] Parts of the law have subsequently been found to violate the human rights of members of the Habsburg family and have been repealed, including their past prohibition from running for the country's presidency.

The early months and years of the new Austrian state were hugely challenging for most of its citizens, who struggled with the economic and social dislocation caused by the war and the end of the empire. Austrian identity, which had previously been associated with the multinational empire and its monarchy, did not immediately transfer to the new republic. Ödön von Horváth, who authored the famous play *Tales from the Vienna Woods*, explained: 'If you ask me what is my native country, I answer: I was born in Fiume, grew up in Belgrade, Budapest, Pressburg, Vienna and Munich, and I have a Hungarian passport, but I have no fatherland. I am a very typical mix of old Austria-Hungary: at once Magyar, Croatian, German and Czech; my country is Hungary; my mother tongue is German.'[6]

In Vienna, one group in particular was trying to find its place in the city: the 'Eastern Jews' that arrived as refugees during and at the end of the Great War. The great Austrian author Joseph Roth (1894–1939), who was Jewish and hailed from Galicia, wrote masterfully about the end-of-empire period in *Radetzky March*, Jewish life in *Job* and the movement of Jews from Eastern to Western Europe in *The Wandering Jews*. In particular, he captured the extreme poverty faced by the new arrivals living in the Leopoldstadt district, and the success of many of the second generation in the 1920s and early 1930s: 'The sons and daughters of Eastern Jews are productive. Their parents may be takers and paddlers, but among the younger generation are many of the most gifted lawyers, doctors, bankers, journalists and actors. The Leopoldstadt is a poor district. There are tiny apartments that house families of six. There are tiny hostels where fifty or sixty bed down on the floors.'[7]

In early post-war Vienna, the arrivals from the east were not made welcome. Efforts were made to deny them citizenship rights and seek their expulsion. A review of early debates of the new republic's parliament by historian Margaret Grandner shows that there was cross-party support for the assertion that 'provisions would have to be made that would make citizenship impossible for Jewish refugees in German-Austria'.[8] The Lower Austrian regional authority, which included Vienna, passed an order on 9 September 1919 compelling people without legal domicile to leave within less than two weeks: 'The exceedingly difficult overall economic condition of German-Austria makes it absolutely necessary to remove those persons from the territory who do not have domicile. The foodstuffs available to German-Austria for provisioning its own population are completely inadequate. One-time subjects of the Austro-Hungarian Monarchy who do not have domicile in a municipality within German-Austria, who have not been in permanent residence since before August 1, 1914, or have not since acquired German-Austrian citizenship are required to leave German-Austrian territory by September 1919. Persons who have not left voluntarily by this date will be summarily . . . deported.'[9] Although deportations did take place, the Jewish community in Vienna remained significant. Having numbered 175,294 before the war, it rose to 201,513 afterwards, which constituted 10.8 per cent of the population in the 1923 census.

Before the outbreak of the Great War, Vienna and its 2.1 million inhabitants had been the capital of an empire of 52 million people. At the end of the conflict it was a city of 1.8 million in a shrunken state of 6.4 million. Population churn saw demobilised troops, prisoners of war, some civilians and refugees return to other parts of the former Dual Monarchy. Meanwhile, many former Habsburg administrators and senior military personnel preferred to settle in Vienna rather than remain in newly independent nations of the former empire. Significant numbers of displaced people remained, often squatting in shanty conditions on the edge of the city. In common parlance, Vienna had become Austria's *Wasserkopf* – the oversized hydrocephalus in an undersized, economically unsustainable rump.

Within a short period, however, the capital earned an international reputation for groundbreaking housing and social policies, which transformed the city. This began with the municipal elections on 4 May 1919, where the Social Democrats won an absolute majority with 54 per cent support, securing 100 of 165 seats. The Christian Social Party, which had governed the city for nearly three decades, was in second with 27 per cent, followed by the Czechoslovak Socialist and Democratic Party in third with 8 per cent. Vienna became the first city of its size in Europe to be run by a social democratic administration, and they intended to hit the ground running with an unparalleled programme of public housing construction and 'a vast new infrastructure of social services and cultural institutions'.[10]

Number one priority for the new administration of 'Red Vienna' was to solve the city's housing crisis, with a vast building programme. Between 1919 and 1934 there were 63,924 new dwellings constructed, accommodating 200,000 Viennese residents in newly built *Gemeindebauten* – municipal housing buildings and estates.[11] The construction programme was funded by an annual wealth-related housing tax on householders and an additional luxury tax on conspicuous consumption, including households maintaining domestic service.

The scale of the reforms was unprecedented and earned Vienna the epithet of a 'world city of global conscience', with the aim being much more than improving what was amongst the worst working-class city housing stock in Europe. Eve Blau, author of *The Architecture of Red Vienna*, describes the scale of the ambition: 'For the Social Democrats the building programme was the centrepiece of a wide-ranging programme of municipal reforms designed to reshape the traditional *Volkskultur* (popular or folk culture) of the Viennese working class into a new *Arbeiterkultur* (socialised working-class culture) through a broad set of social and cultural institutions concerned with education, housing, health, and child care. Through these organisations, which drew male and female workers into an extensive network of communal activities (from athletic competitions to travel clubs and music societies), the Social Democrats set about to transform the Viennese proletariat into "a new socialised humanity". The *Gemeindebauten*, which were distributed throughout Vienna (most within two to three miles of the city centre) were to be the principal sites for the development of this new socialised urban culture. Incorporating worker housing with the new cultural and social institutions, they were part dwellings, part public buildings.'[12]

Amongst the municipal housing projects were a series of mammoth complexes, including Karl-Marx-Hof, which at over one kilometre in length is one of the longest residential constructions in the world. Built between 1927 and 1930 in the north of the city at Heiligenstadt, it housed over 5,000 people in 1,382 apartments with shared amenities for residents, including a laundry, nursery, doctor's surgery, library and public baths. Other large-scale super-block *Gemeindebauten* included George-Washington-Hof in the southern working-class district of Favoriten, the Reumannhof on the Margaretengürtel, Rabenhof in the Landstrasse district and Karl-Seitz-Hof in Floridsdorf. Any journey through present-day Vienna is likely to pass municipal housing with large-scale signage proudly commemorating its construction. The city remains the largest public landlord in Europe, and a majority of residents live in property owned by the municipality or housing associations.

*

After the Great War, Vienna was no longer the capital of a large empire but it was still the best place to follow developments in what had become a volatile region. Throughout the 1920s and 1930s it was the centre for international journalism in Mitteleuropa, including the most celebrated, high-profile and controversial correspondents of the age.

Foremost amongst them was Dorothy Thompson (1893–1961), from Lancaster, New York, who would go on to become lauded as the 'First Lady of American Journalism'. A trailblazing female correspondent, she reported from Vienna during the 1920s for the *Philadelphia Public Ledger* and then from Berlin in the 1930s, during which time she interviewed Hitler. Before becoming the first US journalist to be expelled by the Nazis, she described Hitler as follows: 'He is formless, almost faceless, a man whose countenance is a caricature, a man whose framework seems cartilaginous, without bones. He is inconsequent and voluble, ill poised and insecure. He is the very prototype of the little man.'[13] Thompson featured on a 1939 front cover of *Time* magazine, pictured speaking into a radio microphone. 'She and Eleanor Roosevelt are undoubtedly the most influential women in the US,' is how she was described by *Time*.[14]

Thompson was in Vienna at the same time as Marcel Fodor (1890–1977), who grew up in Budapest and was the Vienna correspondent of the *Manchester Guardian* and contributor to *The Nation*, *The New Republic* and the *American Mercury*. Fodor and US colleague Robert Best established the tradition of foreign correspondents in Vienna meeting at the Café Louvre, on the corner of Wipplingerstrasse and Renngasse in the first district and close to the telegraph office and the headquarters of Radio Austria. The regulars' table (*Stammtisch*) of the international journalists was the place to go to find out what was happening in Vienna and neighbouring countries, with Fodor the doyen of the correspondents. Robert Best (1896–1952), from South Carolina, used a Pulitzer travelling scholarship to begin work as a foreign correspondent for the United Press in Vienna in 1923. He went on to file reports for the *New York Times*, *Chicago Daily News*, *Time* and *Newsweek*. Best surprised his international colleagues by becoming a Nazi broadcaster from Berlin during the war. He was jailed for treason in the United States afterwards and died in prison.

Fodor and Best were founders of the Anglo-American Press Association in Vienna, along with John Gunther and G.E.R. Gedye, in 1930.[15] The German-American John Gunther (1901–1970), from Chicago, came from a family that anglicised their surname Guenther during the First World War. Gunther was Vienna bureau chief for the *Chicago Daily News* and authored *Inside Europe,* the first of the popular *Inside* series of books. Although not a regular attendee at the Café Louvre, G.E.R. (George) Gedye (1890–1970) spent two decades in central Europe reporting for the London *Times*, the *Daily Express*, the *Daily Telegraph* and the *New York Times*. One of the first correspondents to warn about the rise of Nazism, his reports were so influential that Winston Churchill would call the night desk at the *Daily Telegraph* to ask 'what Gedye has written'.

The other leading international journalist in Vienna during the late 1930s was William Shirer (1904–1993), the only American broadcaster in the city on 15 March 1938, when Hitler triumphantly arrived in the Austrian capital. The first of the 'Murrow Boys', hired by Edward Murrow of CBS, his broadcasts from Nazi Germany and the early stages of the war in Poland and France were hugely influential in the US. Married to the Viennese painter Theresa 'Tess' Stiberitz, he later wrote the seminal work *The Rise and Fall of the Third Reich*.

All of these star international journalists, with the exception of George Gedye who preferred to work alone, spent a great deal of time together in Café Louvre, including John Gunther of the *Chicago Daily News*: 'The coffee house is, of course, the inner soul of Vienna, the essential embodiment of the spirit of the town. It is, as everyone knows, much more than just a place to drink coffee in. Coffee you may have, in literally forty different varieties, but you have also literature, conversation, and peace of soul and mind. And in the Café Imperial, in the morning, and in the more modest Café Louvre, in the afternoon, you get journalism, Viennese-brand.'[16]

The Café Louvre no longer exists, having been closed by the Nazis in 1940 and its building hit by a bomb during the Second World War. It was, however, described by John Gunther's biographer, Ken Cuthbertson: 'The interior was typical. It was spacious, with about forty marble-topped tables and violin-backed chairs in the center of the high-ceilinged room. Along one wall were booths, finished in dark brocades. Along another was a buffet of snacks and pastries and some rattan racks holding the day's newspapers . . .'[17]

Visiting young American student J. William Fulbright arrived in Vienna ahead of a fact-finding tour of the region with Fodor in 1929. He described the scene at their favourite meeting place: 'The correspondents would sit around there in the Cafe Louvre, 10 and 11 o'clock at night and old Fodor would tell them what had happened that day. They'd talk to Fodor for over an hour, and they'd all write it down and then send it off to the telegraph office across the street. I remember people would come in there from *The New York Times* and other papers, big papers in the U.S. and have a long conversation with Fodor. About two weeks later I'd read it all in *The New York Times Magazine*.'[18] Fulbright went on to serve as the US Senator for Arkansas for three decades, was the longest-serving chairman in the history of the Senate Foreign Relations Committee and created the international exchange scheme that bears his name: the Fulbright Program.

In 1921, when Dorothy Thompson arrived in Vienna, the city and the country was in an appalling economic state. Paid $50 a week and a tiny expense account, she was expected to cover Austria, Hungary, Yugoslavia, Czechoslovakia, Rumania, Bulgaria, Albania, Turkey and Greece. Originally hoping to enjoy a capital of 'Strauss waltzes, Spanish Baroque, damask interiors . . . a sumptuous court', in contrast she discovered 'a city of dread', with famine conditions and 'teeming with refugees soldiers, welfare commissioners, freebooters, profiteers, displaced peasants and an assortment of gentlefolk starving gracefully in Biedermeier salons'.[19] Not long after her arrival, social tensions boiled over when Austria failed to get financial backing from the newly founded League of Nations to help shore up the economy. Marchers headed from the parliament to the Opernring and began rioting and looting upmarket shops and hotels, including the Hotel Sacher. Despite looking 'exceedingly prosperous' in a wildcat fur, Thompson was taken aside by one of the rioters: 'Miss, I think you should take that coat off. We don't want to hurt you, and it might excite somebody.' From then on she would advise: 'Never wear a fur coat when you go to a revolution.'[20]

Social and political tensions were never far from the surface in 1920s Austria, where 'Red Vienna' found itself in a country governed by the conservative Catholic right, led by the prelate Ignaz Seipel (1876–1932). Serving two terms as Federal Chancellor for the Christian Social Party established by Vienna mayor Karl Lueger, he sought to steady the weak economy and combat hyperinflation. Seipel secured financial support through the League of Nations in 1922 with the Protocol for the Reconstruction of Austria, which promised 650 million gold crowns for stabilisation measures, including the introduction of the new schilling currency. A series of painful austerity measures followed, including cuts to public spending, a reduction in public-sector employment and monetary controls. The measures, which led to a growth in unemployment, were opposed by the Social Democrats and hugely unpopular amongst the labour organisations, which were strongly represented in Vienna. Chancellor Seipel survived an assassination attempt by an unhappy worker in 1924.

While in Vienna at this time, Thompson wrote a series of Sunday supplement feature pieces for the *Public Ledger*. The articles were full of local colour, describing the black economy that thrived in Vienna, especially at the Café Atlantis on the Ringstrasse, opposite the Hotel Imperial: 'It [was] a great gaudy, showy place, the last place you would look for anything illegal. Yet here for the flick of an eyelid toward the waiter, you could be put in touch with someone – at a neighbouring table – who would sell you anything you liked, or buy from you anything to sell, from old clothes, to Gobelins.'[21] Different parts of the café were taken up by people offering different services: the currency speculators sat in heavy red leather armchairs, the black-marketeers were positioned in the middle, female prostitutes to the right of the main door, male prostitutes to the left, and 'every revolutionary in the Balkans' in all corners, by day and by night.[22] While she was in Vienna, she covered political events, including the attempt by former ruler Karl Habsburg to regain the throne in neighbouring Hungary. Dressed as a Red Cross nurse, she managed to inveigle herself into Tata Castle, where he and fellow plotters were assembled after the failed coup.

After a series of enforced moves, owing to the post-war housing shortage, Thompson finally moved into an apartment on the Prinz-Eugen-Strasse overlooking the Belvedere Palace. During her time in Vienna, she befriended Eugenie Schwarzwald, a pioneer of girls' education and one of the first women in Europe to hold a doctorate. Her school produced a generation of hugely influential women, including the authors Hilde Spiel, Alice Herden-Zuckmayer and Vicki Baum; the actresses Helene Weigel (Bertold Brecht's wife) and Elisabeth Neumann-Viertel; the painter Ruth Karplus' and the psychoanalysts Anna Freud and Elsa Pappenheim. The eclectic social circle around 'Genia' Schwarzwald soon became part of Thompson's Vienna life, and it included the literary, intellectual and cultural greats of the time: the composer Arnold Schönberg; the artist Oskar

'Koko' Kokoschka; the architect Adolf Loos; the Danish writer Karin Michaelis, who lived in Vienna; and the Prussian student Helmuth von Moltke, of the famous von Moltke family of military commanders, who went on to set up the anti-Hitler Kreisau Circle and was executed by the Nazis.

Not long after Thompson left for Berlin in 1925, political tensions in Vienna worsened considerably. Both the right and left had uniformed militias: the Home Guard (Heimwehr), the Great War veterans' associations and the socialist Republican Protection League (Republikanische Schutzbund). A 1927 shooting incident between both sides in rural Schattendorf, outside Vienna, led to large-scale disturbances in the capital after the right-wing culprits were found not guilty. The July Revolt involved hundreds of protesters rioting and setting fire to the Palace of Justice. Ensuing heavy-handed policing caused the deaths of 89 protesters and five police officers, which in turn led to a general strike. Although violence receded after the riot and the strike was broken, the polarised politics of the country continued and was exacerbated by the impact of the Great Depression.

In *Fallen Bastions – The Central European Tragedy*, the Vienna-based *Daily Telegraph* correspondent G.E.R. Gedye recorded the slide towards dictatorship: 'The impartial historian, while recording and condemning the many mistakes of the Austrian Social-Democratic leaders, will not forget that from 1927 to 1934 they doggedly fought a losing battle with one hand tied behind their backs by successive chancellors who robbed them step by step of the chances of defending Parliament, democracy and the impressive reforms of the Vienna Socialist municipality against the gathering hordes of their enemies.'[23]

\*

In the late 1920s and early 1930s, at the same time as Hitler's Nazis were making progress in German elections and his brown-shirted stormtroopers were targeting social democrats and communists, the ideological divide was widening in Austria as well. The right-wing

Home Guard committed itself to a patriotically Austrian conservative platform, which distinguished it from the pan-German ideology of the Nazis, while rejecting liberal democracy, parliamentarianism and Marxism. This formalised a major divide with the Nazis, who were becoming increasingly popular in Austria at the same time as they were in Germany.

In the midst of another crisis for the conservative Austrian government in 1932, the young Engelbert Dollfuss (1892–1934) became Chancellor and Foreign Minister. The 39-year-old led a coalition including the parliamentary wing of the Home Guard, with a single-vote majority over the socialist-led opposition. After only one year of office, he used the pretext of a voting irregularity in parliament to suspend democracy and rule with absolute power by emergency decree. His authoritarian rule was aimed at consolidating power against the strength of the social democratic movement on the left and the growing popularity of the Nazis on the right. Modelling itself on Italian fascism, Dollfuss sought improved relations and protection from Benito Mussolini, who extended a guarantee of Austrian independence. Austro-fascism under Dollfuss involved the formation of the Fatherland Front, which included parties from the ruling right-wing coalition, but banned other parties such as the Social Democrats, Communists and Nazis. The Front, which claimed to be non-partisan, was aligned to the Catholic Church and established an authoritarian corporate state, known as the *Ständestaat*. While the Front adopted the aesthetic of fascist parties – including a cross symbol, uniforms, parades and the greeting *Front Heil* – it was not avowedly anti-Semitic or racist, incorporating the League of Jewish Front Soldiers in its membership.

Dollfuss escalated his two-front campaign firstly against the left in February 1934, with a crackdown on the Republican Protection League (the Social Democrats' paramilitary wing), which still existed despite being outlawed. The Austrian Civil War lasted for just four days, with fighting in towns and cities across the country involving socialist activists defending positions in municipal housing estates against the Home Guard, police and Austrian army. What began as skirmishes involving small arms escalated when the army started shelling socialist strongholds like Karl-Marx-Hof in Vienna. With hundreds killed on both sides and thousands injured, desperate efforts were made to get casualties out of the country to safety, as recalled by Vienna *Daily Telegraph* correspondent G.E.R. Gedye: 'One day a young Englishman whom I knew slightly came in to my flat and demanded a suit of clothes to enable a wounded Socialist to get out of the country. I opened my wardrobe to select something. When he saw several suits hanging there he cried: "Good God, man – one suit – and you have seven! I must have five – I have six wounded friends in the sewers in danger of the gallows." What could I say? He took the suits.'[24] The young man in question was Kim Philby, a young revolutionary volunteer helping refugees from Nazi Germany. Recruited the same year by the Soviets, he went on to be one of the most notorious double agents in the history of British intelligence. A member of the 'Cambridge Five' spy ring, he provided MI6 secrets to the USSR for 23 years before being exposed and fleeing to Moscow.

After the victory of government forces in the Austrian Civil War, the authorities cracked down on the socialist opposition. More than 1,500 people were arrested, nine leaders were executed and many sought safety in exile, including leaders like Otto Bauer. The Vienna correspondent of the *Chicago Daily News*, John Gunther, described the sentences handed out as 'mercilessly severe'.[25] By suppressing and ostracising Austrian Social Democrats, the seeds were being sown for the success of the much larger threat: National Socialism.

Despite only polling 779 votes in the 1927 Austrian general election and 3.6 per cent in the 1930 general election, the Nazis in Austria began to grow in popularity at the same time as Hitler came to power in Germany in 1933. After the party was banned in Austria, its members went underground or into exile, where they set up military-style camps to train and prepare for their return and takeover. With financial and logistical support from the German Nazis, they pursued a campaign of terrorism in Austria, which killed scores and injured hundreds of people.

On 25 July 1934, Nazi terrorism moved onto a new level with an attempted coup d'état, involving SS men dressed as Austrian soldiers and police storming the Federal Chancellery on the Ballhausplatz and the headquarters of Austrian Radio. Chancellor Dollfuss was fatally shot twice by a putschist, but many government ministers managed to escape. The evolving putsch attempt was witnessed by John Gunther, who described it as 'the entrance of gangsterism into European politics on an international basis',[26] and G.E.R. Gedye of the *Daily Telegraph*: 'I found steel-helmeted storm detachments of police taking cover and opening rapid fire with carbines and machine-guns on the RAVAG, the building of the Austrian broadcasting company . . . In Vienna the Nazi Putsch was a complete failure. I saw hundreds of young Nazis in their white stockings standing on the Ringstrasse while their leaders were besieged in the chancellery, doing nothing.'[27] Italy deployed tens of thousands of troops to the Brenner Pass on the Austrian border in a move to deter German intervention. While fighting continued in different parts of Austria for a number of days, the Nazi coup d'état was quashed. In total, it is estimated that 223 people lost their lives: 111 Nazis, 101 on the Austrian government side and 11 civilians.[28] Some 4,000 Nazi sympathisers were detained and 13 were executed for their part in the July putsch.

Dollfuss was replaced as chancellor by Education Minister Kurt Schuschnigg (1897–1977), who spent most of the next four years resisting a Nazi takeover; however, developments in both Germany and Italy were undermining Austria's position. Hitler had steadily consolidated his domestic position since taking power in 1933, begun massive rearmament and flexed his muscles internationally with the remilitarisation of the Rhineland in 1936; meanwhile, Mussolini was warming to Hitler after he supported the Second Italo-Abyssinian War (1935–1937). In 1936, Schuschnigg signed an agreement with Germany aimed at improving relations with Berlin, the price of which included the release of jailed Nazis involved in the 1934 putsch attempt. Despite the appointment of two new cabinet ministers who would act as liaisons with German Nazi authorities, Schuschnigg insisted: 'There is no question of ever accepting Nazi representatives in the Austrian cabinet. An absolute abyss separates Austria from Nazism. We do not like arbitrary power, we want law to rule our freedom. We reject uniformity and centralisation . . . Christendom is anchored in our very soil, and we know but one God: and that is not the State, or the Nation, or that elusive thing, Race. Our children are God's children, not to be abused by the State. We abhor terror; Austria has always been a humanitarian state. As a people, we are tolerant by predisposition. Any change now, in our "status quo", could only be for the worse.'[29]

However, the power of the Nazis in Austria was growing from day to day. This included a massive public diplomacy campaign run by the German Embassy and German tourism office on the Ringstrasse. This was fronted by the former German Chancellor Franz von Papen, who Hitler dispatched as his new ambassador to Vienna after the failed putsch. Years later, following the Second World War, the prosecutor at the Nuremberg war crimes trial Robert H. Jackson was outspoken about the role he played: 'Von Papen, pious agent of an infidel regime, held the stirrup while Hitler vaulted into the saddle, lubricated the Austrian annexation and devoted his diplomatic cunning to the service of Nazi objectives abroad.'[30]

The acceleration towards Anschluss came during 1936 and 1937 when both Hitler and Hermann Göring concluded that Germany needed control of Austria and Czechoslovakia's natural resources. Göring had responsibility at the time for the Nazi four-year economic plan and wanted to keep German rearmament on track by using Austrian iron and steel. At a top-level internal leadership conference in November 1937, Hitler confirmed his plans to adopt an aggressive and expansionist foreign policy, and the future of Austria was sealed.[31] In 1938, a police raid on the Nazi liaison headquarters in Vienna uncovered weapons and the plans for another takeover attempt. With tensions rising, German ambassador von Papen suggested mendaciously to Chancellor Schuschnigg: 'Go to Berchtesgaden, Herr Bundeskanzler, and you will talk to our Führer and Reichskanzler as one brother to another.'[32] Hitler's Alpine retreat close to Salzburg at Berchtesgaden was within sight of Austria, which is where Schuschnigg travelled in trepidation on Saturday 12 February 1938. What followed was amongst the most grotesque diplomatic dressing downs ever recounted, as Hitler threatened, insulted and pressured the Austrian leader: 'How have you dared all these years to oppress and torture *my* people – *my* German people in Austria? Now your hour has come. God has made me Führer and ruler of every man and woman of German blood, in every country on earth. You shall bow to my will as all the rest of the world shall bow, or I will break you. I demand obedience from you and shall enforce it, if necessary with my armies. You have played your last card Herr Schuschnigg, and you will accept and sign here at once before you leave this house the terms I have prepared for you, or I give the order to march into Austria immediately.'[33]

Hitler presented him a set of demands, before introducing a German general who was to give a presentation of military occupation plans for Austria, if the ultimatum was not signed. Schuschnigg sought to buy time by agreeing to include a number of Nazis in the cabinet but insisted that some of the demands were only within the competence of Austrian President Wilhelm Miklas. Hitler pledged that he would publicly give reassurances about Austrian sovereignty in a forthcoming major speech in return. Fulfilling his part of the bargain, Schuschnigg appointed the Nazi Arthur Seyss-Inquart, who as Minister of Public Security would have full control of the police. In his speech to the German Reichstag on 20 February, Hitler broke his word by not giving any assurances, instead ratcheting up the pressure by saying: 'The German Reich is no longer willing to tolerate the suppression of ten million Germans across its borders.'

In an attempt to regain the initiative, Schuschnigg announced on 9 March that a referendum would be held to affirm public support for Austrian independence. To improve the chances of a positive outcome, he lifted the ban on the Social Democrats and trades unions. In response, Hitler raised the stakes on 11 March with an ultimatum threatening to invade the country if Schuschnigg didn't resign and Seyss-Inquart replace him. No major power came to the aid of Austria in its hour of need. Sir Walford Selby, who had been

British ambassador in Vienna until the previous year, confirmed that he had, over four and a half years, communicated to Austria 'explicit assurances from H.M. Government that they would be supported in their struggle with Hitler'.[34] He rued the 'betrayal of Austria . . . as criminal as it was stupid. The final blunder which made the war inevitable.'[35]

Without any international support or realistic prospect of resisting the Nazi threats, Schuschnigg made a radio address to the nation the same evening:

> This day has placed us in a tragic and decisive situation. I have to give my Austrian fellow countrymen the details of the events today.
>
> The German Government today handed to President Miklas an ultimatum, with a time limit, ordering him to nominate as chancellor a person designated by the German Government and to appoint members of a cabinet on the orders of the German Government; otherwise German troops would invade Austria.
>
> I declare before the world that the reports launched in Germany concerning disorders by the workers, the shedding of streams of blood, and creation of a situation beyond the control of the Austrian government are lies from A to Z. President Miklas has asked me to tell the people of Austria that we have yielded to force since we are not prepared even in this terrible situation to shed blood. We have decided to order the troops to offer no resistance.
>
> So I take leave of the Austrian people with a German word of farewell uttered from the depth of my heart: God protect Austria.[36]

The address was followed by the playing of the old national anthem, Haydn's *Kaiserhymne*, the same melody as the German national anthem but played to the original slower speed. It was the end. As Sigmund Freud noted in his diary: *Finis Austriae!*[37]

As the Nazi takeover of Vienna neared, CBS reporter William Shirer headed for the Café Louvre to pick up the latest news, which he described in his diary as a mixture of rumours, tears and fears, with some colleagues planning to head over the border to safety in Bratislava. His former assistant Emil Maass, half-American and half-Austrian, and who previously made himself out to be anti-Nazi, arrived saying: 'Well, *meine Damen and Herren*, it is about time,' before turning over his coat lapel to unpin a hidden Nazi badge and ostentatiously placing it in his buttonhole for all to see. The horrified reactions included cries of 'shame', while the monarchist campaigner Major Goldschmidt, whose father was Jewish, got up and said: 'Thank you for your friendship, even if you didn't like what I was up to.' Taking his leave from the group of international journalists, he shook everyone's hands. 'You will please excuse me,' he said. 'I shall go home now and get my revolver.' He shot and killed himself later that evening.[38]

Denied access to the studios of Radio Austria to broadcast the news of the Nazi takeover, Shirer flew from Vienna to London via Berlin. En route he picked up German newspapers featuring mendacious reports that the German invasion of Austria was to restore order and protect the country from armed socialists and communists. In a groundbreaking half-hour CBS radio report anchored from BBC Broadcasting House in London, Shirer brought together correspondents from different European capitals to report on the Anschluss and its consequences. It was the start of a broadcasting format used to this day on radio and television the world over.

On 15 March 1938 the German 8th Army crossed into Austria, followed by Hitler and his motorcade. He first went to his birthplace at Braunau am Inn and then on to Leonding, where he visited his parents' grave, before driving to Linz. Fears that the Austrians would oppose an Anschluss were quickly dispelled as Hitler was greeted by large, wildly enthusiastic crowds on his way to Vienna. The new Nazi puppet leader, Seyss-Inquart, repudiated the provisions of the Treaty of Saint-Germain that banned the unification of Austria and Germany. Hitler arrived in Vienna on 15 March and triumphantly addressed a crowd estimated at 200,000 in Heroes Square by the Hofburg. Speaking from the heights of the palace balcony overlooking the throngs of adoring supporters shouting *Sieg Heil* and *Ein Volk, Ein Reich, Ein Führer*, he announced the Anschluss of Austria: 'The oldest eastern province of the German people shall be, from this point on, the new bastion of the German Reich. As leader and chancellor of the German nation and Reich, I announce to German history now the entry of my homeland into the German Reich.'

Vienna was bedecked with red swastika flags, and units of the German army paraded around the Ringstrasse and Luftwaffe formations overflew the city. Newsreel reports of the day show public spaces teeming with joyous Austrian Nazi supporters.

Hitler insisted on staying in the grand Hotel Imperial on the Ringstrasse, the pavement of which he cleared of snow in his youth as an impoverished itinerant: 'I shall have this hotel listed as our party hotel and I shall come here each time I am in Vienna. I shall have it renovated and modernised, but the name shall remain the same. And a red carpet shall be on the sidewalk every time I come so that I can walk over it into the hotel the same as those aristocrats did back in the days when I shovelled snow. I have never forgotten the resolution I made. Providence fulfilled my wish.'[39] Within a month, the Nazis organised a plebiscite which excluded the 18 per cent of the electorate in Vienna who were Jewish, had supported Schuschnigg or were in some other way 'undesirable'. With an unprecedented one-sided national campaign and endorsements from public figures including Karl Renner, the former chancellor and socialist leader, a 99 per cent vote was recorded as being in favour of the Anschluss. Austria no longer officially existed, only the Ostmark region of Greater Nazi Germany.

Hitler's relationship to Austria in general, and Vienna in particular, was tied into his repudiation of the multinational monarchy and its cosmopolitan capital, which had rejected him. Writing his autobiography *Mein Kampf* in 1923 during his imprisonment at Landsberg jail, he railed against the Danube Monarchy and Vienna, which he described as the 'personification of incest' due to the mix of races.[40]

In later years, however, Hitler waxed lyrically about the city: 'One thing of course, one cannot create artificially and that is the unusually intense intoxication which Vienna offered in past centuries, just as it does today.'[41] By the time Hitler was in power, he also seemed to talk positively about the Habsburg Empire: 'When I encounter the leaders of the other tribes in the Germanic realm, I am in a wonderful position by virtue of where I'm from: I can point out that through five centuries my homeland was a large, powerful empire with an imperial city.'[42] For Hitler, that imperial city was in many respects a more impressive capital than Berlin, and one of the Third Reich's tasks was to transform Berlin so that 'even someone from Vienna would be overwhelmed'.[43]

Despite having described Vienna at the time of the Anschluss as 'a pearl', Hitler had no intention of maintaining its importance or investing in it significantly: 'Otherwise Vienna's cultural attraction will be too great. That would lead to an increase in political attraction, and that simply cannot be. History has taught me that.'[44] In contrast, Hitler had major plans for the Austrian city of his adolescence: Linz. Not only should it become one of the five 'Führer Cities' – together with Berlin, Hamburg, Nuremberg and Munich – it would be the cultural capital of the Third Reich. Linz was to become home of the Führermuseum, a massive art gallery that would house artworks being bought, borrowed and stolen from across occupied Europe. The city was to feature gargantuan neo-classical party headquarters and public buildings along a new urban axis, as well as a large bridge across the Danube and waterfront development to rival Budapest. Hitler intended to retire to Linz, where he would eventually be buried in a crypt beneath the large hall and tower of a special Nazi Party building.

As Hitler's propaganda minister Joseph Goebbels made clear in his diary: 'The Führer doesn't have any particularly great plans for Vienna . . . On the contrary, Vienna has too much and it might lose something than gain anything.'[45] Hitler's aversion to Vienna came up again and again in Goebbels' diary: 'The Führer stressed that even though Vienna is a city with over a million people, its role has to be reduced to one of a provincial city . . . Besides, he said, Vienna used to always treat the Austrian provinces so badly that for that reason alone it shouldn't be given a leading role in the Reich not even in Austria.'[46]

\*

The humiliating mistreatment of Vienna's Jews began immediately after the Nazi takeover, with Brownshirts forcing Jewish men and women to clean the streets on their hands and knees. Hundreds of Jews died by suicide. The worsening crackdown was reported in the London *Times*:

> In Vienna and Austria, no vestige of decency or human-
> ity has checked the will to destroy, and there has been an
> unbroken orgy of jew-baiting such as Europe has not seen
> since the darkest days of the Middle Ages . . . what was once
> a community outstanding in intellect and culture is being
> turned into a community of beggars.
> . . . Tens of thousands of Jews have been thrown out of
> employment. All important Jewish businesses have been
> confiscated directly or placed under an 'Aryan' commissar
> . . . if anyone holds out, he is arrested on any charge – or
> no charge – and held until he signs away all his property
> and gives a declaration that he 'willingly' leave the country
> within two weeks or a month.
> . . . There can be no Jewish family in the country which
> has not one or more of its members under arrest . . . Not a
> day still passes without its toll of arrests and suicides . . . The
> Jew is a helpless scapegoat and an outlet for the stored-up
> hatred of the Austrian Nazis which is not yet satisfied . . .
> Thousands stand outside the Consulates, waiting through
> the night so that they may register their names.[47]

Amongst the 70,000 apartments and businesses that were 'Aryanised' were the two grandest hotels, the Bristol and the Imperial, whose part-owner Samuel Schallinger died in the Theresienstadt concentration camp in 1942. Amongst the many coffee houses to be Aryanised was Café Bräunerhof, known before the Anschluss as the Sans Souci, and the famous restaurant Zu Den Drei Husaren. The famous Vienna landmark Ferris wheel in the Prater park was Aryanised, and its Jewish owner Eduard Steiner was murdered in Auschwitz. The famous Adolf Loos building on Michaelerplatz was taken over by the Opel car company.[48]

At the time of the Anschluss, Vienna was still a capital with a significant diplomatic presence. According to the 1938 *Austrian Gazette* ('Amtskalender') there were 30 missions with more than 150 career diplomats in total. Most European countries were represented, with the Germans having the most diplomats (13), followed by the UK (ten), Hungary (ten) France (nine), Italy (nine), Romania (nine) and Czechoslovakia (seven). Countries from further afield included the US with ten diplomats, Japan (four), China (four) and the Soviet Union (four).

Almost immediately after the Anschluss, most diplomatic staff were recalled to their home capitals or redirected to another posting. Many countries closed or disposed of their embassy buildings, including the British residence, which became the Vienna headquarters of the National Socialist Flying Corps.[49] The Soviet Embassy was used by the Hitler Youth and later as the Japanese Consulate-General,

Most states previously represented in sovereign Austria maintained a consular presence in what was now the provincial capital of the German Ostmark. This was of particular consequence for those seeking or having to secure visas to flee the new Nazi authorities and their Brownshirt thugs and supporters. While most consular staff sadly did not make any efforts to help Jewish Austrians flee the Nazis, a small number did, in particular the Chinese Consul General Ho Feng-Shan (1901–1997). Thousands of Jews are believed to have been saved because of visas he issued to Shanghai, against the orders of his embassy seniors in Berlin. Unlike Oskar Schindler or Raoul Wallenberg, his efforts have only recently been recognised and in 2000 he was posthumously awarded the title 'Righteous Among the

Nations' by Yad Vashem in Israel. 'Nowadays most people believe that he saved more than 5,000 lives at the time,' said Xu Xin, a professor and a leading expert on Jewish studies at Nanjing University. 'More importantly, Ho was probably the first diplomat to really take action to save the Jews.'[50]

One of those who owes their life to Ho is Lilith-Sylvia Doron, who met him by chance when both watched Hitler entering Vienna on 15 March 1938, just as Jews were being targeted and physically attacked by Nazis on the streets of the city and elsewhere in Austria. 'Ho, who knew my family, accompanied me home,' said Doron, who eventually managed to emigrate to Israel. 'He claimed that, thanks to his diplomatic status, the [Nazis] would not dare harm us as long as he remained in our home. Ho continued to visit our home on a permanent basis to protect us from the Nazis.'[51]

Eric Goldstaub, who went on to emigrate to Canada, recalled that in July 1938, he secured Chinese visas for his entire family after spending 'days, weeks, and months visiting one foreign consulate or embassy after the other trying to obtain visas for [himself, his] parents and [their] near relatives, numbering some 20 people'.[52]

At one stage the Nazi authorities forced the Chinese Consulate out of its premises as they confiscated the Jewish-owned property. Ho continued his lifesaving efforts by opening the consulate at a new address at his own personal expense.

A plaque now stands outside the former Chinese Consulate on Beethovenplatz, with the following text in Chinese, German and English:

From this building in 1938 and 1939 Dr Feng Shan Ho, China's Consul General to Vienna, saved thousands of lives after the Anschluss and the Kristallnacht Pogrom. Defying direct orders, he issued visas to Shanghai to help Jews escape certain death at the hands of the Nazis. For acting with humanitarian courage at a time when others would not, he was posthumously designated a RIGHTEOUS AMONG THE NATIONS by the state of Israel in 2000.

Ho died in 1997 with only a single sentence in his obituary as a clue to his actions in Austria, having never discussed his deeds with his wife, children or friends.

At the same time as Ho helped Jews escape, major efforts to protect Vienna Jews were also being undertaken at the Anglican Church opposite the British Embassy. More than 1,800 Jewish Austrians were baptised at Christ Church by the Reverends Hugh Grimes and Fred Collard; 229 of them on one day in July 1938.[53] Baptismal certificates greatly helped in securing transit papers and visas. Most of them would survive the Holocaust.

At the British Embassy, the passport control officer Captain Thomas Kendrick, who was in fact the MI6 station chief, issued visas to an estimated 10,000 Jews. Betrayed because of his activities, he was arrested and interrogated by the Gestapo at their feared Hotel Metropole headquarters on Morzinplatz, and expelled from the country. After 13 years in Vienna, during which time he crossed paths with Soviet spies Kim Philby and Edith Tudor-Hart and dealt with Adolf Eichmann, who was organising the expulsion of Jews from Vienna, Kendrick was expelled from Austria and the whole MI6 network in Vienna was closed down. Kendrick went on to run the secret operations in Britain bugging senior German prisoners of war, and he eavesdropped on Deputy Führer Rudolf Hess after his flight to Scotland in 1941.[54]

As foreign embassies were being downgraded in Vienna, the embassies of Austria around the world were being wound up, closed or being turned over to the Nazi German Foreign Ministry. On 14 March 1938 orders were sent to embassies directing them to report to their host governments about the Anschluss and transfer their embassy 'offices, archives, files, seals, accounts etc to the nearest representative authority of the German Reich'. For one week the flag of Austria and Nazi Germany flew from Austrian diplomatic buildings and then, together with embassy signage, were taken down by 20 March 1938. Austria had ceased to exist as an independent country with its own diplomatic representation. Back in Vienna the Austrian Foreign Ministry had been downgraded to a satellite office of the German Foreign Ministry in Berlin. By August 1938 it too was closed down. Vienna was no longer a diplomatic capital.

The fate of most Austrian diplomats, especially the senior grades, was not a good one. Before the Anschluss, the Austrian Foreign Service totalled 379 members of staff: 115 in the Federal Chancellery; 203 staffed 21 diplomatic legations; a further 61 in 9 consulate-generals and consulates, and 6 honorary postings.[55] It was clear to many in the service that they faced arrest and detention by the Gestapo or in a concentration camp, which is why a high number decided not to return, including the envoys to the US, the UK, Italy, the Netherlands, Czechoslovakia, Turkey and Brazil. Many of those who did return were pensioned off, while some faced a worse fate: Austria's representative to France, Alois Vollgruber, was arrested by the Gestapo then sacked; the envoy to Poland, Heinrich Schmidt, was forced to divorce his wife of 17 years for 'racial reasons' and was then not taken up in the German foreign service; while the envoy to Hungary, Eduard Baar-Baarenfels, was arrested and then detained in concentration camps before being sent into internal exile. The fate of Austrian diplomatic buildings was also mixed: in Berlin the residence became the office of Admiral Wilhelm Canaris, head of the Abwehr military intelligence, while the historic London residence on Belgrave Square became a consular visa office for the German Embassy before being shut during the war years, when it was damaged by two bombs dropped by the Luftwaffe.

Meanwhile, the Nazi crackdown against their political opponents and Austria's Jews and other minorities was brutal. The Nazi Nuremberg Race Laws and other anti-Semitic decrees were applied in Austria, forcing Jews out of their schools, universities and jobs, and compelling them to wear a yellow star. When the anti-Jewish pogroms reached their zenith on Reichkristallnacht in November 1938, all of Vienna's synagogues were destroyed, with the exception of the Stadttempel, which was spared because of its location in the heart of a residential area of the first district.

The Nazis established a Central Office for Jewish Emigration in Vienna in 1938, under Adolf Eichmann of the SS, who after the war faced trial and execution in Israel for his horrific crimes as one of the main architects of the Final Solution. His efforts in 1938 were focused on forcing Jews to leave their homes and the country, while making them pay for their emigration and forfeit their savings and possessions. During 1938, more than 130,000 people emigrated from Austria, including Sigmund Freud and his family. His former Vienna patient William Bullitt, who had become US ambassador to France, alerted President Roosevelt to the worsening situation facing the Freuds. This led to regular monitoring of their apartment at Bergasse 19 by the US consul general, who also intervened with the Gestapo during their interrogation of Anna Freud before they finally left the country.

The Freuds were joined in exile by some of the finest minds in world, like Karl Popper and Erwin Schrödinger, the composer Arnold Schönberg, the film-makers Fritz Lang and Billy Wilder, the authors Robert Musil and Stefan Zweig, the poet Erich Fried, the 1936 Nobel laureate in medicine Otto Loewi and Austrian nuclear scientist Lise Meitner. Political exiles included Bruno Kreisky, who like his fellow Social Democrat exile Willy Brandt from Germany, went on to become a post-war chancellor

During the war, German policy towards the Jewish community in Vienna and elsewhere shifted from forced emigration and expropriation to forced deportation to ghettos and concentration camps in the occupied east, followed by industrialised extermination. In Austria, a large-scale concentration camp system was established at Mauthausen and Gusen in Upper Austria, with 100 sub-camps located around the country. Prisoners faced extermination through labour at quarries and plants manufacturing armaments and fighter planes.

Resistance to the Nazis was evident in Austria from shortly after the Anschluss, when the first signs of unhappiness about the new Nazi regime manifested themselves. In what became the biggest demonstration of the Nazi period, more than 8,000 young Catholics attended a rosary mass on 8 October 1938 at St Stephen's Cathedral, where Cardinal Theodore Innitzer declared that 'we must confess our faith in our Führer, for there is just one Führer: Jesus Christ'. Innitzer, who had supported the Anschluss – to the delight of the Nazis, who used it as an endorsement – was now making his unease clear. Amongst the youngsters in the cathedral was 15-year-old Wilfried Daim who recalled the cardinal saying that 'a bishop can make mistakes'. The worshippers started to roar enthusiastically in appreciation and then gathered outside the cathedral to continue their act of civil disobedience. Fritz Molden was only 14 at the time: 'First of all we sang Catholic songs but then became cheeky, chanting Nazi slogans of the time with the word Führer changed to Bishop: "Dear bishop, be so kind as to show yourself at the window," and "We don't want to go home, we want to see our bishop."'[56]

The next day, Nazi protesters stormed the archbishop's palace by the cathedral, ransacked the building and desecrated religious symbols. A painting of Jesus Christ still hangs in the residence to this day, bearing knife slashes and stabs to the canvas made by members of the Hitler Youth. Both Molden and Daim went on to become leading members of the Austrian Catholic resistance.

The Gestapo was very keen to monitor the public mood in Austria, especially in Vienna with its strong social democratic tradition, and even football could provide an indication. In June 1939 the final of the German championship saw Berlin team Schalke 04 outclass Admira Vienna 9–0, a humiliation for Austrian football supporters who believed their players to be superior. The disappointment was heightened by the German weekly newsreel featuring the 100,000-strong crowd celebrating at the Berlin Olympic Stadium. The Gestapo highlighted that Vienna was 'very tense', with a situation report on 3 July 1939 suggesting that 'the activities of all opposition circles has increased, especially Marxist opposition groups who operate with unimaginable cheek ... according to word of mouth propaganda the differences between Germans "the Prussians" and the Austrians is being emphasised to create unhappiness ... in conclusion, the atmosphere in Austria is tense and most pronounced in Vienna.' One year later Rapid Vienna won the German championship and a 'reconciliation game' between Schalke 04 and

Admira Vienna ended in a draw after the referee from Saxony disallowed two goals by the Austrian team, which led to a pitch invasion from the 50,000-strong crowd. The referee and German club bus was attacked and the tyres slashed on Vienna Nazi Gauleiter Baldur von Schirach's car.

*

The main lesson for Hitler from the Austrian Anschluss was that the international community had no stomach to stand up to his aggressive expansionist ambitions. Within weeks he turned his attentions to Czechoslovakia, using the pretext of the 3 million German-speaking minority in the Czech Sudetenland to ramp up the pressure on the government of Edvard Beneš. As a result of the appeasement policy of British Prime Minister Neville Chamberlain and French counterpart Édouard Daladier, Hitler secured the Munich Agreement on 29 September 1938, which directed the Czechoslovak government to hand over the Sudetenland to Germany and within days the Wehrmacht rolled over the border. The dismemberment of the Czechoslovak state continued a month later with the First Vienna Diktat, which was signed at the Belvedere Palace on 2 November 1938, when Nazi Germany and Fascist Italy 'awarded' largely Magyar-speaking parts of Slovakia to Hungary.

After successfully incorporating Austria and the Sudetenland, Hitler cynically claimed in a speech in the Berlin Sportpalast this was 'the last territorial demand I have to make in Europe'.[57] In less than a year Germany invaded Poland, beginning the Second World War, its military forces swollen by former Austrian army personnel amounting to the equivalent of eight divisions. They took part in all subsequent campaigns, from the invasions of France and the Low Countries to the Soviet Union. Austrian over-representation amongst the mountain light-infantry (*Gebirgsjäger*) was promoted for propaganda purposes early in the war, with their participation in the Narvik operations and occupation of Norway.[58]

Over 1.2 million Austrians volunteered or were conscripted into the German military during the war and a quarter of a million never returned. Over 10,000 exiled Austrians fought in the uniforms of Allied countries against the Nazis.

Apart from the octogenarian former Habsburg field marshal Eduard von Böhm-Ermolli, who was granted the same rank in the Wehrmacht as an honorific title, the most senior Austrians served as colonel general (*Generaloberst*): Erhard Raus and Lothar Rendulic with the Wehrmacht, and Alexander Löhr with the Luftwaffe, who faced a firing squad after the war for war crimes. Other senior military officers included General Edmund Glaise-Horstenau, whom we last encountered as a junior Habsburg officer swimming naked in the pool of Archduke Ludwig 'Luziwuzi' Viktor. He served in Croatia as a military diplomat, where he highlighted concerns about atrocities by local Ustaše fascist forces, before being removed from his post.

While Austrians made a proportionate personnel contribution to the Wehrmacht, they were heavily over-represented in the SS machinery of the Holocaust, including Obersturmbannführer Adolf Eichmann (1906–1962) and his staff who organised the mass deportation and extermination of millions of Jews. Although born in the Rhineland, Eichmann grew up in Linz, attending the same high school as Hitler 17 years before him. An early Nazi activist in Austria, he joined the feared SD Security Service of the SS and after the 1938 Anschluss headed the Central Agency for Jewish Emigration in Vienna. He went on to become responsible for the forced deportation of Jews in occupied Europe and a leading participant in the Wannsee Conference in 1942, where plans for the extermination of European Jewry were debated. After the war he fled to Argentina, before being spectacularly kidnapped by Israeli Mossad agents and put on trial in Jerusalem. He was executed in 1962.

Other prominent Austrians in the Holocaust included Arthur Seyss-Inquart (1892–1946), who grew up in Vienna and, after his key role in the Anschluss, became a leading administrator of Nazi-occupied Poland and was then put in charge of German-occupied Netherlands from 1940 until 1945. Convicted at Nuremberg for the harsh suppression of Nazi opponents and atrocities against Jews during his postings, he was hanged together with Hermann Göring and other leading Nazis.

In Vienna itself during the war, Odilo Globočnik (1904–1945) was Nazi gauleiter before becoming a senior SS commander responsible for some of the worst crimes in the Second World War, at the heart of decision-making about the killing machine in Poland and elsewhere in Eastern Europe. After commanding the 'liquidation' of the Warsaw ghetto and its 500,000 Jewish inhabitants in 1944, he was described as 'the vilest individual in the vilest organisation ever known'.[59] His colleague Ernst Kaltenbrunner (1903–1946), who grew up in Ried im Innkreis, Upper Austria, was Vienna Police President at the beginning of the war and in charge of an intelligence network across Austria, which brought him to the attention of SS Chief Heinrich Himmler. Appointed head of the Reich Main Security Office (RSHA) after the assassination of Reinhard Heydrich in 1942, Kaltenbrunner was in charge of the feared SD Security Service and the Gestapo. Serving at the highest levels of the Nazi killing machine, the rabid anti-Semite accompanied Adolf Eichmann to Hungary ahead of the rounding up and deportation of Hungary's 750,000 Jews to extermination camps in 1944. The highest ranked member of the SS to face trial at Nuremberg after the war, he was found guilty of war crimes and crimes against humanity at the International Military Tribunal and hanged in 1946.

Men of service age were conscripted in Vienna as elsewhere in the Nazi Reich and fought on all fronts. Units with a particularly high proportion of personnel from the city took part in the siege of Stalingrad, including the 44th Infantry Division, later named Hoch- und Deutschmeister after one of the most famous Habsburg regiments. Stalingrad is generally regarded to be not only the biggest battle of the Second World War but the biggest battle in human history. Initial military progress by the Germans into the industrial city in the autumn of 1942 turned into brutal house-to-house close combat, with dogged Soviet resistance. The Red Army launched a pincer attack into the badly defended Axis flanks in November 1942, cutting off the 6th Army in the city and leaving it dependent on airdrops. More than 270,000 German and Axis troops were trapped in the Stalingrad cauldron, and over the winter months continued to fight on in ever more desperate and hopeless military conditions. By February 1943 the Germans had run out of food and ammunition and, after a battle that lasted five months, one week and three days, they surrendered. Casualties totalled between 1.8 and 2 million killed, wounded or captured. Of the 44th Infantry Division from Vienna that went into captivity amongst 91,000 Axis prisoners, only about 100 returned from Russia after the war.[60]

As the war moved into its last years, Soviet forces advanced from the east and Allied forces landed in southern Italy in 1943 and Normandy in 1944. As the front moved closer, American and British bombers were in range of Vienna for the first time and began aerial attacks on industrial and oil refinery targets. Six massive flak towers were constructed in the city to site searchlights and anti-aircraft guns, as well as air-raid shelters. The nine-storey concrete colossuses stand to this day. As Soviet forces encircled Budapest with more than a million men in late 1944, the tempo of aerial bombing raids on Vienna increased, causing growing numbers of civilian deaths and destruction to the city, including direct hits to the State Opera House, the Albertina Museum and the Federal Chancellery. More than 300 civilians were buried and never recovered beneath the Phillip-Hof, the home to the high-society Jockey Club opposite the Albertina. Today it is the site of the Memorial against War and Fascism featuring sculptures by Alfred Hrdlicka.

At the beginning of 1945 the Red Army defeated German and Hungarian forces in Budapest, in what was the largest major operation in the southern front. It opened up the way towards Vienna, with only a glorified defensive ditch in the way. With little more than the 6th SS Panzer Army under Sepp Dietrich holding the line, the Soviets made steady north-westerly progress on both sides of the Danube. The decisive Soviet breakthrough came on the southern approaches to Vienna, with the 3rd Ukrainian Front capturing Wiener Neustadt and Eisenstadt. To the north, the 2nd Ukrainian Front took Bratislava. As the Vienna offensive was about to enter the city, 77 Soviet divisions numbering more than 1.1 million men faced bedraggled defenders less than one quarter in number. While the Soviets had more than 5,000 field guns at their disposal, the Germans had little over 400. From 2 until 13 April, the Soviet forces advanced into the city, facing stiff resistance in places like the Danube Canal, the Gürtel ring-road and Simmering district.[61] Members of the Austrian resistance, O5 ('O' plus the fifth letter of the alphabet: *Oe* for Österreich), planned Operation Radetzky to assist the Soviet advance, but they were betrayed and executed.

As the Russians came ever closer to capturing both Vienna and Berlin, Hitler fled from reality, reviewing his plans for his favourite city, Linz. On 9 February 1945 his chief architect for the Linz project, Hermann Giesler, brought a large-scale model of the plans to the Reich Chancellery, which Hitler had demanded. 'Bent over the model, he viewed it from all angles, and in different kinds of lighting. He asked for a seat. He checked the proportions of the different buildings. He asked about the details of the bridges. He studied the model for a long time, apparently lost in thought. While Geisler stayed in Berlin, Hitler accompanied him twice daily to view the model, in the afternoon and again during the night. Others in his entourage were taken down to have his building plans explained to them as they pored over the model. Looking down on the model of a city which, he knew, would never be built, Hitler could fall in reverie, revisiting the fantasies of his youth, when he would dream with his friend Kubizek about rebuilding Linz.'[62]

Meanwhile, Soviet shells were landing in Vienna. The former Austrian diplomat Joseph Schöner kept a diary, noting on Monday 9 April: 'Slept well overnight, but woken by stronger artillery fire. The explosions come in an increasing tempo, partly in the vicinity, so I dared not leave the house despite not having any news and wanting to know what was going on . . . An armoured personnel carrier stands in Sigmundgasse, outside number 15 a pair of SS men from the "Grossdeutschland" division are lying in a bomb crater with a light machine-gun and are observing the road crossing . . . Every hour Russian planes fly overhead in small formations of 3–6 aircraft without dropping anything. They are shot at from all streets with light flak and machine gun fire.'[63]

One day later Soviet forces had advanced close enough to take the streets around Schöner's home: 'On the seventh anniversary of the so-called referendum after the Anschluss Russian troops are moving into the heart of Vienna . . . Just after 8am I was woken by excited voices in the courtyard shouting to me "The Russians are here."'[64] Not long afterwards, when Russian forces had captured the first district, Schöner ventured into the city centre to see the damage to Vienna's historic heart:

The view at Stephansplatz is terrible – everything is completely burnt . . . with naked blackened facades and empty window recesses. The front of the Cathedral has many visible pockmarks in the darkened stone from shell fragments and shrapnel. Beautiful epitaphs and gravestones are badly damaged. Soldiers with machine-guns are guarding civilians who are removing rubble. I make a big detour around the group to avoid being press-ganged with a shovel.

The view from Graben is harrowing: the steep cathedral roof with its inlaid eagle [crest] has disappeared, the uncompleted left hand tower is burnt out. The blackened gables and pinnacles stand out against the sky. Alone the main tower remains standing the emblem of my beloved city. People stand with tears in their eyes and something forces me to take off my hat. The Nazis fired directly at it. I can't make it out, but people say the roof of the nave has collapsed. After 500 years and the storms of the Turkish times it has been the Nazi pigs who have destroyed this treasure . . . God is already punishing them.[65]

Some 500 kilometres to the north in his Berlin bunker, Hitler was cursing the Viennese. Nazi propaganda chief Joseph Goebbels noted in his diary on 9 April 1945: 'The Führer certainly has figured out the Viennese correctly. They are a repulsive bunch, consisting a mix between Poles, Czechs, Jews and Germans.' It was necessary to 'keep a tighter rein on them'.[66]

Next day, heavily outnumbered and out-gunned, the German commander in Vienna, Infantry General Rudolf von Bünau, ordered mobile units to pull back to the northern banks of the Danube, leaving the largest part of Vienna to the Soviets. The city had been a German 'bastion' for seven years in a Nazi Third Reich that was supposed to last a thousand years.

# 11

# *Occupation, Intrigue and Espionage*

'I never knew the old Vienna.'
– Graham Greene, *The Third Man*

Restored government in Austria began to be re-established even before the Soviets had retaken Vienna. Karl Renner, who had lived under Nazi house arrest during the war, took up contact with advancing Red Army forces and within weeks was asked to form a provisional government by the Soviets. Renner, who had led the First Republic as a socialist chancellor immediately after the Great War, formed a cabinet including communist ministers and declared Austria independent from Nazi Germany and began to re-establish a democratic state. This all occurred without the involvement of the Western Allies, who were suspicious of Soviet political influence and were still fighting German forces further west.

Like Germany, the liberation of Austria occurred with the Allied forces advancing from both east and west. The Soviets had faced the stiffest resistance in and around Vienna, suffering more than 17,000 casualties. US forces had crossed into Upper Austria on 26 April 1945, the French advanced into Vorarlberg on 29 April, and the British arrived in Carinthia on 8 May.

Vienna was a city that had suffered considerable damage in the final stages of the war. While not comparable to the destruction in Berlin, 41 per cent of buildings in Vienna were damaged and nearly 87,000 homes were uninhabitable. Serious damage included the destruction of many bridges over the River Danube and Danube Canal, which were blown up by retreating Nazi troops. Landmarks like St Stephen's Cathedral, the State Opera, the Albertina Museum and the Federal Chancellery had all suffered serious bomb damage. Water, sewage and power supplies were severely affected, and the inhabitants of the city were destitute, with food supplies little to non-existent.

Josef Schöner (1904–1978) was eyewitness to the fall of Vienna and, in the 491 pages of his *Vienna Diary 1944–1945*, he described the difficult daily existence for civilians during the battle for Vienna and the Soviet takeover, and the chaos in the city as it gradually made its way towards a new existence. As a patriotic young diplomat before the war, Schöner had been pensioned off by the Nazis as politically unreliable after the Anschluss, while he was only in his mid-30s. But in 1945 he played an important role behind the scenes in the early moves to establish a national government and as preparations were made to re-establish Austrian international relations.

Schöner witnessed the last days of fighting in the city centre, the graves dug on the roadside verges and parks, the detritus of war on the Ringstrasse and the destruction of beautiful historic buildings. Soviet heavy artillery was positioned on the streets in case of a German counter-offensive and trains were manoeuvred to block streets. At first, Soviet units repeatedly searched houses for German soldiers, Nazis, weapons, food and alcohol, watches and women. Civilians took to flying white flags outside their houses and wore red or red-white-red armbands to show their socialist or Austrian patriotic allegiances, while men wore workers' clothing or traditional Austrian Styrian hats to set themselves visibly apart from the Soviet impression of how Nazis looked.

Even as house-to-house fighting continued in Vienna, the Austrian resistance opened formal headquarters on the Kärntner Ring and Palais Auersperg to begin an administrative transition from the Nazi authorities. Schöner heard some surprising early news about the communists and accurately predicted the tensions that would soon manifest themselves: 'The KPÖ have apparently received the order from Moscow to work with all Austrian forces, even conservatives . . . Domestic political battles will however not be small – between the emigres and those who stayed, between victorious communists and people with other political orientations, those who were locked up and those who were not, the genuinely idealistic and those hunting for positions.'[1]

While fighting continued in the rest of the country, Schöner and other former staff at the Federal Chancellery were called for their first meeting at the Ballhausplatz on 16 April. The historic building that had been home to Metternich had suffered bad bomb damage on its easterly side, while its abandoned and wrecked offices used until only days before by the Nazi administration were a scene of destruction. Schöner and colleagues started a clean-up, locating typewriters, paper and trusted former members of the typing pool, but no real power was yet being exercised in the building. Schöner noted ruefully on 18 April: 'Nothing to do in the Foreign Ministry, we only receive visitors!' However, 'the signs of orderly administration are beginning to grow'.

Within days, a potential government under the 75-year-old Renner was being actively discussed in the Federal Chancellery, as were the potential members of the cabinet, the reintroduction of the schilling as Austrian currency, and that Vienna might become a seat for the successor organisation of the League of Nations. The new Austrian government was formally constituted on 27 April, with the three leading anti-fascist parties pledging themselves to the restoration of the democratic republic 'in the spirit of the Constitution of 1920'. The Social Democrats, now called the Socialist Party of Austria (Sozialistische Partei Österreichs – SPÖ), the Christian Socialists, now named the Austrian People's Party (Österreichische Volkspartei – ÖVP), and the Communist Party of Austria (Kommunistische Partei Österreichs – KPÖ) formed the first post-war government, with a cabinet and government responsibilities that were balanced between left and right.

Shortly after, Karl Renner arrived at the war-damaged chancellery to speak to the 50 or so volunteer staff: 'Despite his age he looked sprightly and healthy . . . His white goatee and stoutness gave him a fatherly, trustworthy appearance . . . [He] gave a half hour speech in unsentimental, cordial and jovial tones.'[2] Renner said that ordinary Nazi supporters and party members should expect mild treatment and could stay in government jobs, just so long as they proved themselves to be loyal and decent Austrian civil servants. Just as he didn't expect an immediate change of mind from the monarchists in 1918, he also didn't from those who weren't yet anti-fascist. Renner recounted speaking to the Habsburg civil servants in the Ballhausplatz in 1918, saying: 'Work with me for a year and you will come to love the republic.' He was convinced that even those whose hearts lay elsewhere would soon come to value the democratic freedom of the new Austria.

Schöner and his colleagues were appalled at Renner's misapprehension that they had been staff of the Nazi administration. He was similarly shocked by Renner's defence of the Anschluss idea, which he acknowledged was now dead and buried because of the Nazi crimes and outcome of the war. Schöner's conclusion about the ageing statesman was that 'apparently nobody really gets away from the sins of their youth or earlier resentments'.[3] His insights from Renner's speech neatly captured the trap many Austrians fell into after the war: failing to face up to significant culpability for the Anschluss and its consequences; and believing the mantra that because Austria was the first victim of Hitlerite aggression, this somehow absolved the country from responsibility for dealing with Nazi crimes. Austria's role in Nazi Germany was only really faced after the election of Kurt Waldheim as Austrian president 30 years later, when a huge domestic and international scandal erupted about his wartime military service.

Schöner went on become one of Austria's greatest post-war diplomats, serving as part of the negotiating team for the Austrian State Treaty, and reaching the pinnacle of the diplomatic service as General Secretary of the Foreign Ministry just as Austria regained its sovereignty. In the years that followed he became ambassador to West Germany and then the UK. Schöner died in 1978.

While Schöner was describing Vienna in the weeks and months after the hostilities, so was the likes of Paul Sweet of the Office of

Strategic Services, the wartime US intelligence agency and forerunner of the CIA. The Americans arrived after the worst of the war's immediate aftermath in Vienna, which included the rape of tens of thousands of women by Soviet troops, mass-scale looting and lawlessness. Sweet reported there had been some improvements but that the city was still in a calamitous situation: 'The looting and raping in Vienna itself has ceased completely, according to (my anonymous) informant. Punishment for looting and raping is death, and while there was no enforcement up to recently, a number of Russian soldiers and even officers have been shot for these crimes.' Lack of supplies was a particular problem for the civilian population: 'The food shortage in Vienna is serious and acute . . . The bread situation is getting worse. There is no gas or coal in the city, and to get the existing wood from the Wienerwald, the city lacks the necessary vehicles . . . ' Just as after the First World War, people were prepared to buy, sell or swap anything to survive: 'The black market is flourishing, although every attempt is now being made to eliminate it. Thus the trading on the Karlsplatz in the Resselpark is subject to frequent joint raids by Russian MPs and the Austrian police (who are armed). A watch brings about 4 to 6 pounds of fat . . . the Austrians are anxiously awaiting the Americans . . .'[4]

Another of the first Americans to get to Vienna was the young Major Martin F. Herz, who served as political officer of the US legation, arriving in the lead jeep of the US army headquarters company. Herz had been educated in the city during the 1920s and 1930s and was a fluent German speaker. In more than 160 reports to the US administration, he provided insights into the political and social situation in Vienna, including the grinding poverty for many of its inhabitants. In one account he described visiting a family of three in the Russian zone: a mother and two children under five, who were trying to get by without the father who had been missing in action since January 1945. Their accommodation consisted of a single room with a solitary lightbulb and where all windowpanes were broken. Without anything to trade on the black market, their rations were extremely limited and the mother had lost 20 kilograms since April, while the health of the children was 'good, except that children frequently get diarrhea'.[5] It would take some time until social conditions improved and government structures got to grips with the massive challenges.

*

Prior to the end of the war, the future of Austria had already been discussed and agreed in principle by the Allies, who issued a declaration at a Moscow conference during October and November 1943 stating that:

> The governments of the United Kingdom, the Soviet Union and the United States of America are agreed that Austria, the first free country to fall a victim to Hitlerite aggression, shall be liberated from German domination.
>
> They regard the annexation imposed upon Austria by Germany on March 15, 1938, as null and void. They consider themselves as in no way bound by any changes effected in Austria since that date. They declare that they wish to see re-established a free and independent Austria and thereby to open the way for the Austrian people themselves, as well as those neighbouring states which will be faced with similar problems, to find that political and economic security which is the only basis for lasting peace.
>
> Austria is reminded, however that she has a responsibility, which she cannot evade, for participation in the war on the side of Hitlerite Germany, and that in the final settlement account will inevitably be taken of her own contribution to her liberation.[6]

The declaration echoed the commitment made earlier during the war by Churchill when he highlighted the Alpine republic first amongst 'all the countries with whom and for whom we have drawn the sword – Austria, Czechoslovakia, Poland, Norway, Holland, Belgium; greatest of all, France; latest of all, Greece. For all these we will toil and strive, and our victory will supply the liberation of them all.'[7] A commitment for the re-establishment of a free and independent Austria was also declared by the French Committee of National Liberation, the provisional government of a free France.

In the initial post-war period, power was exercised by the Allied Commission for Austria, based at the grand Haus der Industrie on Schwarzenbergplatz, and headed by the military commanders of the occupying powers. The Soviet Union was represented by Marshall Ivan Konev (1897–1973), who, as a Red Army commander, retook much of occupied Europe from the Nazis and helped in the capture of Berlin. He later went on to command Soviet ground forces, as well as becoming commander-in-chief of the armed forces of the Warsaw Pact as a whole, a role in which he put down the Hungarian uprising of 1956.

General Mark W. Clark (1896–1984) was the youngest four-star general in the US army during the Second World War, commanding the US 5th Army in the Italian campaign, including the capture of Rome in June 1944. When he took up his Vienna posting, he was extremely sympathetic to the view that Austria was not a militaristic nation and that it should not be treated the same as Germany: 'Austria was drawn into the war after the Nazi invasion. Our task is to create a democratic and independent government capable of running the country on its own. It must remain separated from Germany and free of Nazi influence. Austria must be treated better than Germany.'[8]

Britain was represented by General Sir Richard Loudon McCreery (1898–1967), who led one of the last cavalry charges in the First World War, and during the Second World War fought his way from Africa, up Italy and to Austria, where he took command of British occupation forces. A senior staff officer at the Battle of El Alamein, he commanded the victorious British 8th Army in Italy before it was redesignated as British Forces in Austria.

General Antoine Béthouart (1889–1982) was the first chief of French occupation forces in Austria and High Commissioner for France from 1946 until 1950. Under his command, the 1st Army

Corps of Free French forces became the first Allied unit to reach the Danube and enter Austria in the west. Béthouart is warmly remembered in the formerly French-occupied Vorarlberg and Tyrol, where he installed border signs stating *Autriche, pays ami* and laid a wreath at the Andreas Hofer memorial, commemorating the Tyrolean freedom fighter who resisted Napoleonic French rule.

In early September 1946, the US dispatched a career foreign service officer, John Erhardt, who presented his credentials as Envoy Extraordinary and Minister Plenipotentiary in Vienna and took up his post with the US legation in the former Consular Academy in the Bolzmanngasse. US troops first commandeered the building, which had previously been used as a Wehrmacht military hospital during the war; it was purchased shortly thereafter by the US following the recommendation of Eleanor Lansing Dulles (1895–1996), the US financial attaché at the legation. Dulles was one of the most interesting and intellectually brilliant female pioneers in the US State Department. With a background as a college professor in economics, she played a key role in US post-war economic planning, including international financial cooperation. Dulles took part in the 1944 Bretton Woods Conference, which established the International Monetary Fund and the International Bank for Reconstruction and Development. She came from a family that produced a host of leading public servants, including her grandfather John Watson Dulles, who was Secretary of State under President Benjamin Harrison, and her oldest brother, John Foster Dulles, who was Secretary of State under President Dwight D. Eisenhower (and after whom Washington DC's Dulles Airport is named). Another brother, Allen Dulles, was director of the CIA.

Arriving in September 1945 and remaining until 1948, Eleanor Dulles worked under Erhardt and General Clark, but chose to follow a less than strictly formal approach: 'Since I had early decided that time spent with the Austrians was more productive than the cultivation of the generals and colonels, even though the military officers seemed to hold the power and had obvious prestige, my friendships with the Austrians led to several constructive plans. I felt a tremendous sense of accomplishment as tires were produced and trucks rolled, as cotton went to the textile mills and coal to the steel mills. I had never before had a chance to exert a comparable influence. The Austrians thought I had a rank – which I had not. What I had was the will to manoeuvre and to manipulate the power that others had. It was a serious, exacting, yet rewarding game.'[9]

Her social and professional circle in Vienna included a 'Who's Who' of re-emergent Austria: 'the doughty Leopold Figl [Chancellor and leader of the People's Party]; urbane and well-balanced Adolf Schärf [Deputy Chancellor, leader of the Social Democrats and future Austrian President]; energetic Andreas Korp [State Secretary for Food]; handsome Karl Gruber, Foreign Minister; Peter Krauland, Minister of Reconstruction; the stolid Julius Raab, future Chancellor ... There were many others, glad to relax in the warm and friendly atmosphere in my panelled study. We discussed Europe's future – and the possible release of Austria from communist pressures.'[10]

Dulles looked back on her time in Vienna as having a particularly positive impact on the reconstruction of the country: 'The fact that Austria gained steadily from the first days of work there, in spite of the large removals of capitulant equipment by the Russians from the Soviet zone, is proof of the constructive nature of the Western powers' decisions. More and more factories opened. And even before the Marshall plan began to pump resources into the economy in 1948, the signs of recovery and the hard work of the Austrians convinced the outside world that the country would be able to stand on its own feet after outside help was terminated.'[11]

The Marshall Plan – or European Recovery Program, as it was officially known – involved more than US$12 billion (almost US$100 billion in today's terms) investment by the Americans to help reconstruction efforts across Europe. While funding was rejected by Eastern European countries occupied by the Soviets, for fear of US influence, it was accepted in Austria, which received the highest level of per capita support. It is estimated that 14 per cent of national income was from the Marshall Plan aid, the highest amongst participating countries.[12] Meanwhile, Austria was paying the highest levels of reparations amongst former Axis countries, including the profits of businesses in the Soviet zone and the removal of machinery and material.[13]

The regaining of Austria's sovereignty in 1955 was also something that Dulles had been involved with in the early diplomatic stages. Her Secretary of State brother, Foster, gifted her a beautifully inlaid Austrian box for her birthday in 1955, with the dedication *To Eleanor with love for June 1, 1955, and in memory of another happy day May 15, 1955, Vienna – a day you helped bring about. Foster.* Her role was recognised by the Austrian government, which invited her to attend commemorations over the next three decades in Vienna.

From 1945 to 1955, when the occupation of Austria ended, Vienna was on the front line of the situation that Churchill famously described in his 'Iron Curtain' speech of 1946: 'From Stettin in the Baltic to Trieste in the Adriatic an iron curtain has descended across the continent. Behind that line lie all the capitals of the ancient states of Central and Eastern Europe: Warsaw, Berlin, Prague, Vienna, Belgrade, Bucharest, and Sofia. All of these famous cities and the populations lie in what I must call the Soviet sphere . . .' and Vienna was the easternmost capital with Western influence. As in other central and Eastern European capitals, the Soviets were seeking to promote and install their communist allies. However, the Austrian Communist Party (KPÖ) significantly underperformed in the 1945 national elections, securing a little over 5 per cent of the vote, instead of the 30 per cent hoped for. The first post-war regional elections in Vienna and the Soviet-occupied provinces of Lower Austria, Burgenland and part of Upper Austria also confirmed the weakness of the communists, especially when measured against the moderate Social Democrats (SPÖ). According to the former Swedish ambassador to Austria Sven Allard, a Soviet diplomat confided in him years later that 'only now do we understand that we had already conclusively lost Austria by the election of November 1945'.[14]

Austria had been divided between the occupying powers, with the French in control in Vorarlberg and Tyrol in the west, the Americans in Salzburg and Upper Austria, the British in east Tyrol, Carinthia and Styria, and the Soviets controlling the north and east of the country as well as a quarter of Vienna. Unlike Berlin, which was divided into a Soviet east and a Western west, Vienna's central first district was shared by all four as an international zone. The Soviets were responsible for everything to the north of the Danube Canal as well as the outer southern and western districts. In between were the British, who had responsibility for the 3rd and 11th districts in the south as well as the 5th, 12th and 13th in the south-west. The French sector was in the west with the 6th, 14th, 15th and 16th districts, and the Americans in the north-west with the 7th, 8th, 9th, 17th, 18th and 19th districts. All four powers had separate headquarters, with the Soviets in Palais Epstein on the Ringstrasse next to the parliament, the Americans in the Austrian National Bank building on Otto Wagner Platz, the British at Schönbrunn Palace, and the French at Hotel Kummer (now Hotel Motto) on Mariahilferstrasse. In central Vienna, responsibility rotated between the occupying powers on the last day of the month with a ceremony at the Inter-Allied command at the Justice Palace, with detachments of troops and military bands. The four powers also took joint responsibility for patrolling the city, with one serviceman from of each of the four armies sharing the jeep.

At the height of the occupation more than a quarter of a million Allied troops were stationed in Austria, with the Soviets making up the bulk with more than 150,000, the British with 55,000, the Americans with 40,000 and the French with 15,000. The costs for the occupation were to be fully born by the Austrian government but were later capped at 35 per cent of state spending. It didn't just help offset the Allies' military and administrative overheads but also their ever-burgeoning espionage operations . . .

\*

Immediately after the Second World War, Vienna became the international capital of espionage. More than any other city it was the Cold War centre for spying, a reputation cemented on the global consciousness by one of the greatest spy films of all time, *The Third*

316

*Man*, written by the great novelist Graham Greene (1904–1991), who also worked for MI6. In researching the story in Vienna, he was guided through the city by the *Times* newspaper correspondent Peter Smollett, who had headed the Russian section of the British Ministry of Information during the war. Smollett's deep understanding of Vienna owed much to the fact that he was actually from the city, having been born and raised there as Hans-Peter Smolka. In a bizarre example of life imitating art, Smollett/Smolka was himself a Soviet spy having been recruited by the NKVD, the forerunner of the KGB, when he moved to Britain. Before leaving Austria for London, he was a left-wing activist, who together with the later Soviet spy Kim Philby and his wife, Alice 'Litzi' Friedmann, smuggled injured socialists and communists out of Vienna during the civil war through the city's sewers.

According to one account of how the draft script was developed at the Café Mozart and Sacher Hotel: 'Peter Smolka offered Greene his best ideas and came up with most of the plot outline for *The Third Man*. The penicillin racket, around which the entire film hangs, was his. So too was the classic chase through the sewers at the end, based on his derring-do in spiriting comrades to safety in the civil war . . . What is undeniable, though, is that Harry Lime – the movie's charismatic, morally squalid central character, played memorably by Orson Welles – was partly based on the British double agent but also at least partly on the sinister Smolka.'[15]

The atmospheric black-and-white movie was filmed on location in Vienna in 1948, directed by Carol Reed and starred Joseph Cotten, Alida Valli, Orson Welles and Trevor Howard. Set at the beginning of the Cold War in the exhausted and war-damaged city and featuring the division of the capital into Allied occupation zones, it followed the search for Harry Lime and his suspected involvement in black-market racketeering. The film is particularly remembered for its soundtrack and memorable Vienna locations. Set to the now-immortalised zither melody by Anton Karas, which became an international hit in the 1950s, the film's scenes involved the iconic Ferris wheel in the Prater park, the Vienna sewers below Karlsplatz, the doorway to Palais Pallavicini on the Josefsplatz opposite the Hofburg palace, and Schreyvogelgasse on the Mölkerbastei, close to the residences of Beethoven and Prince de Ligne. Visitors to present-day Vienna can watch the movie at the Burgkino, visit the Third Man Museum and go on numerous walking tours of the film locations.

Vienna has also repeatedly featured in leading international spy novels, most notably written by David Cornwell, better known by his pen name John le Carré, who was himself a British intelligence officer in Austria in the early 1950s. His characters included Magnus Pym, the MI6 Head of Station and 'Counsellor for Certain Unmentionable Matters' at the British Embassy in Vienna, in his bestseller *A Perfect Spy*. The Scots-American author Helen MacInnes, who was also associated with MI6, wrote a series of international espionage bestsellers, including a number that were set in Austria. The queen of spy writers sold more than 25 million copies in the US alone and has been translated into more than 20 languages. *Prelude to Terror* is set in Vienna, while *The Salzburg Connection* was also made into a movie of the same name starring Joan Crawford.

These and a wider range of post-war spy novels built on the Vienna reputation for espionage, which had been cemented by the Alfred Redl spy scandal just prior to the First World War (see Chapter 9). The story of the Habsburg spymaster turned traitor, who sold military secrets to tsarist Russia, has been a national and international inspiration for movie-makers and writers. It has featured in scores of books and five films, including the 1985 period movie drama, *Oberst Redl*, starring Klaus Maria Brandauer and directed by István Szabó. It won the Jury Prize at the Cannes Film Festival and was nominated for an Academy Award for best Foreign Language Film. The story of Redl was the inspiration for the John Osborne play *A Patriot for Me*, the book *The Panther's Feast* by the historian Robert Asprey and features in *The World of Yesterday* Stefan Zweig.

While the high point for espionage in Vienna was immediately after the Second World War, there were significant cases before its outbreak that would have an impact over the decades to come. The communist intelligence orbit that left-wing English activist Kim

Philby came into while in Vienna during the 1934 civil war included Gábor Péter, the later head of the Hungarian ÁVH State Protection Authority. He was at the time romantically involved with the young Jewish Austrian communist Alice Friedmann, who would go on to marry Philby. When the newlyweds returned to London, Alice arranged for Philby to meet with another Austrian, Arnold Deutsch, codenamed 'Otto', who formally recruited him for the NKVD during a meeting in Regent's Park. At about the same time, Deutsch recruited Donald Maclean and Guy Burgess and became the controller of the infamous 'Cambridge Five' spy ring. His replacement as handler was another Austrian, Theodore Maley, who spent 20 years working across Europe for Soviet intelligence as an illegal recruiter and controller.[16]

The Cambridge Five also included Anthony Blunt, whose value to the Soviets was particularly important during the war when he passed on intercepted German military communications that had been decoded at Bletchley Park. After the war, the respected art historian worked closely with the British royal family as Surveyor of the Queen's Pictures. Blunt was formally recruited by another Austrian exile, Edith Tudor-Hart (née Suschitzky), the daughter of a wealthy Viennese publisher and friend of Alice Friedmann.[17]

A further Vienna espionage connection of the time involved the brilliant young scientist Engelbert 'Bertie' Broda, who left for the UK in 1938 and worked as a nuclear researcher at the Cavendish Laboratory at Cambridge University. According to KGB records, he provided thousands of documents on the British and America nuclear programmes, but, despite the suspicions of MI5, he was never unmasked. Codenamed 'Eric', the brother of a later Austrian justice minister, Broda was the 'main source' of atomic intelligence, including the blueprint for the nuclear reactor used in the US Manhattan Project.[18] He returned to Austria after the war where he taught at Vienna University from 1955 until 1980 as Professor of Physical Chemistry. He was a leading supporter of the Pugwash movement of international scientists seeking a nuclear-free world. Broda, who died in 1983 aged 73, is buried amongst Austria's scientific elite in the Vienna Central Cemetery. The espionage author Ben Macintyre, who described him as 'Bertie the spy who started the Cold War', also suggested that his epitaph should read: 'The spy who got away.'[19]

The real-life espionage conducted in post-war Vienna largely involved the occupying powers: the US, UK and Soviet Union. With widespread anticipation that war might erupt imminently between East and West, huge efforts were undertaken to better understand the capability and plans of the other side. The Soviets were first to establish an intelligence presence, including four regiments of NKVD troops to 'mop up' Vienna and seal the border with Czechoslovakia.[20] Shortly thereafter, the Americans deployed the army's Counter Intelligence Corps (CIC) and personnel from the Office of Strategic Services (OSS), which was the forerunner of the CIA. For the British, most of the groundwork was conducted by the Field Security Sections of the Army Intelligence Corps, which reported to MI6 in the UK Embassy and Schönbrunn barracks.

In a leading study of Cold War spying activities in Austria, it is clear why the country and its capital played such a major role: 'Austria emerged as an operational territory and front line in the game of espionage played out against the backdrop of the Cold War, pitting the intelligence agencies of the two superpowers and their allies against those of the other side. Austria was less the aim than the setting for the two blocs' military intelligence operations. The Western intelligence services increasingly shifted their focus from the security-political field and denazification at the end of the 1940s to the Soviet occupation forces and the combat strength of the Soviet and East European militaries.'[21]

In the intense Vienna espionage environment, the assignments tasked and tradecraft deployed by the Western intelligence operatives included the use of dead-letter drops, where information could be stashed and collected; maintaining safe houses for the recruiting and running of agents; developing connections with the many émigré groups; as well as debriefing people who had crossed frontiers from neighbouring Eastern European countries. As a British intelligence officer, John Le Carré recruited people from this group and from Austrians 'who had connections with Eastern Europe and were prepared to go back. We were certainly not averse to former Nazis; they were not seen as a security risk. The ex-Nazis were obedient, and were "our type of chaps".'[22] Significant effort was expended in developing 'stay-behind' networks and providing weapons dumps, munitions and radios for them to use. Often, however, the espionage work was more mundane, including observing military transports for bi-annual military manoeuvres and keeping tabs on the NKVD footsloggers who were doing the same in reverse.

Another focus of the espionage effort was running ratlines and infiltrating other routes that people of intelligence interest were using to get to safety and a new life. These included Soviet troops drawn to the West and who might have information to impart; former Nazis and their allies from Croatia and elsewhere who were trying to find sanctuary; and the thousands of displaced people and refugees, including many Jews who had escaped Nazi concentration camps and were trying to travel to Palestine. This group was assisted by the underground Jewish organisations Mossad LeAliyah Bet and Bricha, which in Austria was headed by the Vienna-born Asher Ben-Natan (1921–2014), who grew up in the capital before the Anschluss. Working undercover as a journalist and using the pseudonym of Arthur Pier, a shortened version of his birth-surname Piernikarz, he played a major role in facilitating the transit and travel of many of the 250,000 Eastern European Jews who made it to Palestine. The American authorities turned a blind eye to the thousands of Holocaust survivors crossing the border from their occupation zone into Italy; but the UK, which controlled Mandate Palestine, sought to stop the flow. British agents went so far as to sabotage transport ships for Jewish refugees with limpet mines. The ironically named Operation Embarrass ultimately failed in its mission to stop the humanitarian flotillas getting to Palestine. Ben-Natan, who did so much to help the refugees to safety, went on to lead the hunt for the Nazi war criminal Adolf Eichmann and became the state of Israel's first ambassador to West Germany and then France.

Meanwhile, in the Soviet-controlled zone in Vienna, Burgenland,

Lower Austria and part of Upper Austria, there was a constant risk of abduction. Between 1947 and 1955, more than 2,000 Austrians were kidnapped by the Soviet occupation authorities, with around half the victims given long jail sentences in the Soviet gulag system. More than 160 of 500 convictions for spying ended with execution.[23] According to contemporary analysis, 'most of the abductions involved persons suspected of espionage or of associations with the United States or other Western intelligence activities. Such kidnappings were the result of Soviet counterintelligence activity, primarily out of considerations of military security. Former German intelligence personnel were added to Western agents on the Soviet wanted lists . . . A special objective of the kidnappings was to destroy networks of Austrian informants employed by the CIC. The Russians were relentless in the abductions of their own informants who were believed to have doubled as agents for the West.'[24]

With Vienna being the front line for espionage activity, it is no surprise that it became a prime location for talented intelligence operatives from all of the powers. They included George K. Young, who was SIS Head of Station and later became Deputy Director of MI6. Immediately after the war, success was limited, partly because he only had about 20 officers and admin staff, the majority of whom were known to the Russians.[25] His dashing successor, Peter Lunn, who was a talented skier and competed at the 1936 Olympics at Garmisch-Partenkirchen, masterminded one of the most audacious spy operations of the entire Cold War. Operation Silver involved the major interception of Soviet military communications by building a tunnel and tapping their telephone and telegraph communication from their HQ at the Hotel Imperial. British intelligence became aware that the Soviets were using the normal trunk lines that ran through the UK control sector in Vienna's third district to the Soviet military airport and from there on to Moscow and other Eastern European capitals. Under the cover of a tweed clothing store on Aspangstrasse, the tunnel – nearly 20 metres long and two metres below the road surface – was dug by Royal Engineers. After the installation of listening equipment, a team of 13 Intelligence Corps personnel worked on rolling shifts to record the calls onto wax cylinders. Amongst the young eavesdroppers, who were aged mostly 18 or 19, was the teenage private Rodric Braithwaite, who later became the British ambassador to Moscow and Chairman of the UK Joint Intelligence Committee (JIC). According to the excellent account of espionage in Vienna by security correspondent Gordon Correra, so much recorded material was collected that a new Section Y of MI6 was established on Calton Gardens in the heart of London to translate and transcribe the communications. In his groundbreaking book, *MI6 – Life and Death in the British Secret Service*, he recounts how the Vienna tunnel and the later larger Berlin tunnel it inspired were betrayed by the double agent George Blake. Despite this, other tunnels remained in operation in Vienna until 1955, beneath a 'jewellery shop' and in the house of a British official.[26]

At the same time as the British were successfully collecting important communication intelligence, the Americans upped their efforts to secure higher grade human intelligence. To that end, Richard Helms, who oversaw CIA stations in Germany and Austria, and later became the CIA's director, assigned greater resources to Vienna. This included the young Tennent Bagley, who would go on to serve 22 years in the CIA as a handler of spies and defectors before becoming chief of Soviet bloc counterintelligence: 'Vienna at the beginning of the 1950s was a prime first assignment. Then and for decades afterwards it was aptly described as a "turntable for espionage" . . . Life for many was reduced to getting along as best as they could, at or beyond the edge of legality and with little room for morality. It was a climate made for adventurers, black marketers, information pedlars and fabricators, soldiers without an army, refugees from the East without prospects of going further, and former intelligence operatives with a cunning sense of what the increasingly hostile occupiers would want to know about each other.' Bagley, who was only 25 when he got to Vienna, also found that 'the city offered extraordinary access to Soviet officials, the only potential human sources of critical military-political intelligence the White House was desperately demanding of us in the CIA'.[27]

One of those sources was NKVD's Major Peter Deriabin who took up the post of Chief of Soviet Counterintelligence at the Soviet Embassy in Vienna and was head of the Communist Party for the whole of the Austro-German section. His motives for defecting are not entirely clear: whether through political disillusionment or falling out of favour and jumping before he was pushed. However, Deriabin had cause to be careful, as the case of his pre-war Soviet military intelligence colleague in Vienna proved: after Walter Krivitsky defected to France with information about the Molotov-Ribbentrop pact between Nazi Germany and the USSR, he was found shot dead in a Washington DC hotel room. The value of Deriabin became apparent soon after he left his office in the Hotel Imperial and walked into US military police headquarters in the Stiftskaserne barracks and asked for asylum. As the most senior of 71 state security officials in Vienna, his job was to keep an eye on the Soviet diplomats, from the ambassador down, and his defection sparked a huge Soviet operation to try and find him. Within 24 hours, however, he had been spirited out of Vienna by the Americans – on a train, in a wooden crate – to the safety of the US occupation zone. The defection caused such a sensation when it became public, it made the front cover of *Life* magazine, headlined: 'Secrets of Secret Police – The Most Valuable Soviet Agent to Escape and Talk.'[28] He worked for the CIA for nearly 30 years after his defection and co-authored a series of books about Soviet intelligence.

In contrast to Deriabin, who defected and brought his secrets with him, the Americans had another significant human intelligence coup when Lieutenant Colonel Pyotr Popov became the first Soviet military intelligence officer to start working as a mole after making contact by throwing a note into the car of an American diplomat: 'I am a Russian officer attached to the Soviet Group of Forces Headquarters in Baden bei Wien. If you are interested in buying a copy of the new table of organisation for a Soviet armoured division, meet me on the corner of Dorotheerstrasse and Stallburggasse at 8.30 p.m., November 12. If you are not there I will return at the same time on November 13. The price is 3,000 schillings.'[29]

Popov, who was recruited by the Americans and given the codename 'ATTIC', provided voluminous information to the US during his time in Vienna and then East Berlin, including details on Soviet nuclear submarines and guided missiles. Popov was forced to become a double agent after incriminating evidence was discovered, but he was subsequently arrested and executed in 1960.[30] Although Vienna had become a hotbed of Cold War espionage, the occupation could not continue indefinitely, and the reasons for its ending go right back to its start.

*

Within a year of the occupation beginning, the penny was already dropping with the Soviet authorities that there was better economic than ideological potential in Austria.[31] In signing the second Allied Control agreement with the US, UK and France in June 1946, the USSR was refocusing its efforts on economic priorities rather than cementing its political influence in the way it was in Eastern European countries. Almost immediately after signing the agreement, the Soviet authorities established the Administration of Soviet Properties in Austria (USIA), which took control of 450 formerly German-owned businesses in their occupation zone. With the country then being the third-largest European oil producer (after Russia and Romania) and extraction facilities lying largely in the Soviet zone, this had the potential to be extremely lucrative. At its height, the USIA's nationalised industries accounted for 30 per cent of industrial output in the zone and controlled 10 per cent of the Austrian workforce.[32] Even as early as 1946, Russian diplomats were quoted as saying: 'Moscow has nothing against Austria and nothing against its government. Very much in contrast to Hungary, it is not considering keeping Austria occupied. When Russian economic needs are satisfied, the Red Army will leave the country.'[33] However, it did not take long for the Soviets to conclude that their economic expectations were not going to be realised in Austria. Without significant investment, many of the nationalised firms began to struggle and underperform. By 1953 their value began to drop significantly in contrast to their competitors in other occupation zones, and it became obvious that the economic imperative to maintain the Soviet foothold in Austria was a mirage. By 1955 most of the nationalised firms were nearing bankruptcy or were significantly indebted to the Soviet military bank.

At the same time as the economic rationale reduced for the Soviets, their ideological allies in the Austrian Communist Party (KPÖ) were becoming even more of a political irrelevance. Despite their miserable performance in the 1945 general election with only 5 per cent of the vote, at least they held important cabinet posts in the government of national unity, including the Interior and Education portfolios. In 1947 they decided to turn their backs on the government but failed to improve their poor electoral support in the subsequent elections in 1949 and 1953. As they lost political relevance, they appealed for their Soviet masters to effectively take over from the Austrian government in their zone. In contrast to backing communist takeovers in neighbouring Czechoslovakia, the Moscow authorities made clear to the KPÖ leadership in Vienna that 'the separation of Austria was against Soviet interests and therefore to be avoided; such a small territory in eastern Austria would prove to be a liability rather than an asset, economically and strategically'.[34]

Meanwhile, mainstream Austrian politics continued to be dominated by the conservative Austrian Peoples Party (ÖVP) and the Austrian Social Democrats (SPÖ), who governed in a grand coalition from 1949 under Nazi concentration camp survivor Chancellor Leopold Figl (1902–1965) of the ÖVP and Vice-Chancellor Adolf Schärf (1890–1965) of the SPÖ. Together with Foreign Minister Karl Gruber and later Chancellor Julius Raab, they drove the efforts to restore Austrian independence and an end to the occupation. Negotiations began to make headway following the death of Stalin in 1953, when his successor, Nikita Khruschev (1894–1971), sought to signal willingness for 'peaceful coexistence' between East and West.

According to legend, the Austrian negotiators made major progress with the Soviets during wine-soaked visits to Vienna's Heuriger taverns, which specialise in the sweet immature wines from the

vineyards skirting the edge of the city. Different versions of the diplomatic urban myth include the singing of the Heuriger drinking
song *Die Reblaus* ('The Vine Louse'), with Foreign Minister Leopold
Figl whispering in the ear of the zither-playing Chancellor Raab:
'Raab – now let's play the *Reblaus* and then they will agree.' This version of events owes more to a political cartoon illustrating 'Viennese
Charm in Moscow'; however, Raab's zither was rediscovered in 2011
with accompanying musical score sheets with Russian handwriting
on it, so maybe there was something to the story, after all. What is
beyond dispute is that the Austrians managed to have a partial war-
guilt clause expunged from the text of the eventual treaty. According
to the Austrian-born journalist, *Kindertransport* survivor and historian Hella Pick: 'Figl argued that it would be unfair to burden
Austria with guilt about past behaviour at the very moment of its
relaunch as an independent nation. Austria's internal and external
development would be handicapped by such a moral slur.' She went
on to highlight this as a reason why the issue of war-guilt and taking
responsibility was delayed in Austria for decades, and that it was also
the responsibility of the occupying powers: 'When the international
community finally began to question Austria's failure to face up to its
past, the four Great Power signatories might have acknowledged that
they bore a large share of responsibility for creating and sustaining
a misleading image of Austria. But they preferred to remain silent,
and let Austria take all the blame for the long-lasting cover-up of the
country's moral failings.'[35]

The Austrian breakthrough came in 1955, when the division of
Germany became formalised with the Federal Republic of Germany
joining the North Atlantic Treaty Organisation (NATO) and the
German Democratic Republic becoming a founder member of the
Warsaw Pact. With skilled negotiations by the Austrians, agreeing
to the neutrality of Austria as a safeguard for the Soviets, it broke
the earlier deadlock and secured agreement for the end of the occupation. The USSR ensured that Austria wouldn't join NATO, no
Western military forces would be based there and guarantees were
received against another Anschluss; however, the country would be

within the Western sphere of influence and a liberal democratic state. The UK ambassador to Vienna Sir Geoffrey Wallinger reported to the Foreign Office that the agreement 'was far too good to be true, to be honest'.[36]

On 15 May 1955 the Austrian State Treaty was signed at the Upper Belvedere Palace in Vienna by the Allied foreign ministers – Vyacheslav Molotov of the USSR, John Foster Dulles of the US, Harold Macmillan of the UK and Antoine Pinay of France – and by Leopold Figl on behalf of Austria. The representatives sat at a long table in the beautiful Marble Hall, with its reddish-brown marble walls, rich gilding, large ceiling fresco and chandeliers. After the signing ceremony, Figl famously declared that 'Austria is free', which has gone down as one of the most iconic moments in Austrian national history. He was then photographed on the Belvedere balcony with the other signatories, showing off the document to the thousands of jubilant people in the crowd below.

The Austrian State Treaty marks the only major example of Russian voluntarily giving up territory it gained in the Second World War without leaving Soviet authorities in charge.[37] In July 1955 the last train carrying Austrian prisoners of war held in the USSR since the end of the Second World War arrived in Vienna. Three months later, the last of the occupation forces left and on 26 October 1955 the Austrian parliament passed a constitutional act declaring the country to be permanently neutral. On 14 December 1955 Austria became a member of the United Nations. Austria was free and a member of the global community, while Vienna was again capital of a sovereign nation and seeking to re-establish itself both domestically and internationally.

# 12

# *Diplomatic Capital*

'Our great aim in Austria is to be a bridge-builder.'

– Chancellor Sebastian Kurz[1]

Austria had been fully sovereign for less than a year before the Hungarian Revolution of 1956, which led to a massive wave of refugees streaming into Austria and raised the prospect of wider regional instability. What began as student protests on 23 October 1956 quickly escalated to a level of civil disorder that threatened communist rule and Soviet political and military influence in Hungary. A new reformist government under Imre Nagy announced plans for Hungary to hold free elections and withdraw from the Warsaw Pact, following the path that Austria had taken with the State Treaty in 1955: 'Mr Nagy had in his writings referred to the possibility of Hungary adopting a neutral status on the Austrian pattern and that he had informed the Hungarian Workers's Party and the Soviet leaders of his views in this respect.'[2]

In what was an outspoken appeal from newly sovereign and neutral Austria, Chancellor Julius Raab called for the USSR to respect Hungary's human rights: 'The Austrian federal government observes with sorrowful sympathy the bloody and casualty-fraught events in neighbouring Hungary. The government requests the government of the USSR to cooperate in putting an end to the fighting in order to stop the bloodshed. Based on the freedom and independence of Austria, ensured by her neutrality, the Austrian federal government advocates a normalisation of conditions in Hungary with the aim that by the restoration of freedom in the spirit of human rights, the peace of Europe be strengthened and assured.'[3]

The call for restraint fell on deaf ears: 17 divisions of the Red Army surrounded Budapest and targeted other areas of resistance, with the express aim to crush the revolution and restore a biddable communist government. Fighting claimed the lives of more than 2,500 Hungarians and 700 Soviet troops, while about 200,000 Hungarians fled the country, mostly across the 374-kilometre border with Austria. Amongst the many who remained in exile was the Hungarian journalist and foreign policy expert Paul Lendvai, who went on to become the ubiquitous Austrian media commentator on Eastern Europe: 'The Austrians, both the government and the people, behaved in an exemplary manner in 1956. In spite of warnings and broadsides from the Eastern Bloc media, the question never arose, not even in the form of the slightest hint, that Austria would consider closing her borders to the Hungarians or to conduct a selection of the refugees.'[4]

The American author James Michener spent six weeks at the border documenting the scene and the experiences of the refugees: 'Then came the floods! Hundreds upon hundreds of refugees came across the frail footbridge. They would come down the canal bank in an excess of joy, having found rescue when all seemed lost. They would hear the Austrian students cry, "This is Austria!" and they would literally collapse with gladness.' The footbridge gave him the name of his bestselling book *Bridge at Andau*.

The Pulitzer Prize-winning author described the desperate lengths the refugees went to, including one man who waded back and forth across an icy canal, carrying each member of his family to freedom: 'Not one of his family got even so much as a foot wet, and if this man lives today – it seemed doubtful when I last saw his totally blue body – he is a walking monument to the meaning of the word love.'[5]

Michener was also struck by the warm welcome offered by the Austrian people: 'Austria is a small nation, with only seven million people and no great resources to share. Had Austrians been niggardly, they could understandably have refused charity to the revolutionists on the grounds that they had few spare goods to share. Instead, they shared them in abundance.' On 21 November 1956 the Soviet army blew up the bridge at Andau after 70,000 refugees had used it to cross to freedom. Michener suggested that some day a memorial bridge would be constructed: 'It need not be much, as bridges go: not wide enough for a car nor sturdy enough to bear a motorcycle. It need only be firm enough to recall the love with which Austrians helped so many Hungarians across the old bridge to freedom, only wide enough to permit the soul of a free nation to pass.'[6] In 1996, on the 40th anniversary of the Hungarian Revolution, the bridge was jointly rebuilt by the Austrian and Hungarian armies, as a symbol of tolerance.

In December 1956 US Vice-President Richard Nixon made a high-profile fact-finding mission to Austria to learn about the refugee situation, as did future President Gerald Ford, who visited Andau. The US went on to become the most popular location for Hungarian refugees.

*

Austria's international relations after the Hungarian Revolution are synonymous with the role of the Social Democrat politician Bruno Kreisky (1911–1990) who served as Foreign Minister from 1959 until 1966 and then as Chancellor from 1970 until 1983. Pursuing an ambitious foreign policy agenda to develop Austria as a bridge-builder between East and West, and Vienna as the pre-eminent location for international organisations, his impact is still felt today.

Kreisky was born into a non-observant Jewish family in Vienna's Margareten district and he became a young socialist activist aged 15 in reaction to the extreme poverty in the capital. He continued his political activities during his law studies at Vienna University and as an underground member when the Socialist Party was banned by the Dollfuss regime in 1934. Following his arrest and conviction for high treason under the Austro-fascist dictatorship and the Nazi Anschluss, he sought refuge in Sweden, where he lived throughout the war with other social democratic exiles, including the future German Chancellor, Willy Brandt.

Kreisky began working for the Austrian diplomatic service after the war, was an adviser to President Theodor Körner and in 1956 was appointed as undersecretary of state in the foreign affairs department of the Federal Chancellery. He was part of the negotiating team for the 1955 State Treaty and, on becoming Foreign Minister in 1959, started involving himself in international mediation efforts during the Berlin Crisis of 1961, when the Russians demanded the withdrawal of armed forces from the city. While his efforts did not bear immediate fruits, they did raise his profile in national capitals and with significant world leaders dealing with East–West relations.[7]

Vienna's growing standing in multilateral international relations received a boost not long afterwards with the United Nations Conference on Diplomatic Intercourse and Immunities, hosted at the Neue Hofburg. Nearly one and half centuries after the Congress of Vienna first agreed general regulations on diplomacy, the 1961 Vienna Convention on Diplomatic Relations codified the updated rules that steer diplomatic relations between states to this day. Its 53 articles clarified the rules on the inviolability of diplomatic missions and diplomatic residences, free communications between missions and their home country, and the freedom of diplomats from arrest, detention or civil prosecution (and the same protections for their family members). The agreement was followed by the Vienna Convention on Consular Relations (1963), the Vienna Convention on the Law of Treaties (1969), the Vienna Convention on Succession of States in respect of Treaties (1978), and the Vienna Convention on the Law of Treaties between States and International Organisations or Between International Organizations (1986).

Only a few months after the 1961 UN conference, Vienna hosted a summit between US President John F. Kennedy and Soviet Premier Nikita Khrushchev on 3 and 4 June 1961 to reduce Cold War tensions over issues including Germany, Laos and Cuba. The two superpower leaders agreed to come together in the neutral capital after a suggestion by Foreign Minister Bruno Kreisky that it would be the best location. On his arrival at Vienna's Schwechat Airport with his wife Jackie, President Kennedy said he was pleased to be back in Austria, having spent a month in the south of the country some decades before. Soviet premier Khrushchev arrived by train at the Südbahnhof, where he was met by President Schärf. Both leaders stayed at the Hotel Imperial, received a formal presidential reception at the Hofburg and a gala dinner at Schönbrunn Palace followed by the chamber ensemble of the Vienna Philharmonic playing Mozart, and the dance company of the Vienna State Opera performing *The Blue Danube Waltz.*

More than a thousand journalists covered the summit, which involved formal discussions at the residence of the US ambassador and at the Soviet Embassy; however, the talks were not generally seen as a great success. 'Kennedy was very upset,' recalled his press secretary Dean Rusk, according to the Cold War specialist Michael Beschloss. 'He wasn't prepared for the brutality of Khruschev's presentation . . . Khrushchev was trying to act like a bully to their young President of the United States.'[8] The Soviet leader, on the other hand, was much happier: 'I was generally pleased with our meeting in Vienna. Even though we came to no concrete agreement, I could tell that [Kennedy] was interested in finding a peaceful solution to world problems and avoiding conflict with the Soviet Union.'[9] He did, however, acknowledge that Kennedy was not pleased, recalling that he 'looked not only anxious, but deeply upset . . . I hadn't meant to upset him. I would have liked very much for us to part in a different mood. But there was nothing I could do to help him . . . Politics is a merciless business.'[10] After the discussions, Kennedy famously conceded that Khrushchev 'just beat the hell out of me . . . it was the worst thing in my life. He savaged me.'[11] However, the discussions were not entirely a failure: the leaders did reach a consensus about the neutral future of Laos, inspired by the Austrian solution. Before leaving Vienna, Kennedy and the First Lady attended mass at St Stephen's Cathedral and heard the Vienna Boys' Choir. Khrushchev laid wreaths at the memorial for the Austrian Resistance and at the Red Army Heroes' Monument.

Despite the underwhelming diplomatic outcomes of the summit, the Austrian capital had successfully held an international event of the highest order and underlined its ideal neutral location between West and East. Bruno Kreisky had reinforced his mediating credentials, contacts and 'active neutrality' policy for Austria. He summed this up in a discussion with the later British Prime Minister Edward Heath as 'the creation of as much confidence as possible in the West and as little distrust as possible'.[12] During the 1962 Cuban Missile Crisis, Kreisky passed on a message to the Americans that the Soviets had been in touch to raise the potential of another Vienna summit, which was overtaken by the secret missile exchange deal that ended the stand-off. In 1963, one month before his assassination, President Kennedy invited Kreisky for a one-to-one meeting at the White House while he was on a visit to the US to discuss East–West relations.

Back in Austria, the 1960s saw efforts to improve relations with eastern neighbours. This included the first-ever live East–West television discussion programme, which saw Austrian public broadcaster ORF link-up with Czechoslovak television. Charismatic presenter Helmut Zilk, who later became mayor of Vienna, hosted the studio audience programme where the questions had not been vetted or scripted by the authorities.

In 1966, Austria confronted its own past by allowing the heir to the throne, Otto Habsburg, to visit the country for the first time since he departed in 1918 as a child. His day trip to Tyrol was accompanied by strike action involving 250,000 workers opposed to his presence, even though he had renounced all claims to the throne.[13] Habsburg visited Vienna in 1967, just before the country was catapulted back into the middle of another East–West international crisis with the Prague Spring.

On 5 January 1968 the Czechoslovak communist party elected the reformist Alexander Dubček (1921–1992) as its First Secretary and began a period of liberalisation and democratisation. After he published an 'Action Programme' of reformist measures and declared the aim was to deliver 'socialism with a human face', the Soviet leadership began to fear a weakening of the Warsaw Pact. On 20–21 August troops from the Soviet Union, Bulgaria, Poland and Hungary invaded Czechoslovakia with 200,000 soldiers and 2,000 tanks. There was not the same level of violence as during the

Hungarian Revolution in 1956, but the invasion did trigger a similar exodus of refugees: 'Thousands of people were heading to the West. They found their first shelter in Austria thanks to the Austrian Embassy in Prague, which granted hundreds of visas every day. It was due to the devoted effort of the ambassador [and later Austrian president] Rudolf Kirchschläger, who ordered to issue the visas despite of reverse instructions coming from the Austrian Ministry of Foreign Affairs headed by [later Austrian president] Kurt Waldheim. Within the first months after the invasion almost 162,000 refugees came to the country.'[14]

Both the Hungarian Revolution and Prague Spring ensured that Vienna continued to be an espionage hotspot, even after the end of four-power occupation in 1955. The city remained the premier springboard for Western intelligence services into neighbouring communist states, and vice versa from Eastern bloc spies. While CIA Chief of Station in Vienna Peer de Silva was monitoring the Hungarian situation in 1956, the Warsaw Pact espionage services in Vienna were assessing the threat of Western intervention.[15] The Czechoslovak State Security Service had always been particularly active in Vienna, and Austria more generally, because of Czechoslovak political and Sudeten German exiles. Around the time of the Prague Spring, three well-placed Austrian spies working for the Czechs were arrested: Alois Euler, the press secretary of Interior Minister Franz Soronics; Johann Ableitinger, a State Police veteran; and Josef Adamek of the Federal Press Service of the Chancellery, who provided information to Warsaw Pact espionage services, including information on Czechoslovak refugees. In 1971 another staff member of the Federal Press Service, Karl Erwin Lichtenecker, was arrested after passing on information from the Chancellery using a dead-drop in public toilets on the Hoher Markt.

Czechoslovak spies in Vienna were run by Major Ladislav Bittman, the former deputy head of Department 'D' for 'active measures', the secret service department in Prague dealing with black propaganda and disinformation. He operated as a resident agent in Vienna with cover as the press attaché at the Czechoslovak Embassy, where an unusually high 80 per cent of the legation staff were secret service personnel.[16] Bittman boasted that their deep penetration of Austria meant that there were few matters dealing with counterintelligence or foreign trade that the Czechs didn't know before Austrian cabinet ministers. When it came to trade negotiations, Czechoslovak officials would be fully briefed about the bargaining tactics of the Austrian side in advance. 'There were no secrets in Austria,' according to Bittman, but none of the agents were politically motivated: 'They were either bought, blackmailed, or doing it for adventure.'[17]

Two weeks after the Soviet tanks invaded Czechoslovakia to depose the Dubček government, Bittman decided to defect, but he didn't have the confidence to do that in Vienna. 'The Austrian police and counterintelligence service were largely penetrated by Eastern European agents. Even at the highest level of the Austrian security forces was a Czech intelligence agent called Mr. Seven by my colleagues. I did not want to be captured by him. Should I ask a Western embassy for political asylum? The side effects, mainly the subsequent press coverage, also did not appeal to me. There was no other choice than wait for the right moment to leave the country on my own. I had no idea where I would go, but I did know I had to leave.'[18] Bittmann evaded a Soviet snatch squad and drove to West Germany, where he sought asylum and defected to the US.

The most controversial of alleged Czech agents in Austria was the high-profile broadcaster and later Vienna mayor Helmut Zilk. Despite denying reports that he was the agent codenamed 'Holec', his role was beyond doubt according to Austria's leading espionage expert Siegfried Beer, who described him as being 'transparently a spy'.[19] For others, like Czech former Foreign Minister Karel Schwarzenberg, Zilk was probably also working for the US. 'Vienna was of course an interesting center for the exchange of information for the Eastern bloc countries. Helmut Zilk was a double agent, providing information to the Czech secret service, and later the Americans. He lived in a flat in Naglergasse 2 where it is known that the US Embassy also rented apartments for agents.'[20]

Vienna was also an important location for Stasi operatives of the

East German Ministry for State Security, which ran the 'Vienna Residency', a spy ring feeding information to the DDR's high technology programme.[21] As an increasingly wealthy neutral country, Austria was prepared to trade with the Eastern bloc, but the US Department of Defense warned about technology transfer to Warsaw Pact countries: 'Each year Moscow received thousands of pieces of Western equipment and many tens of thousands of unclassified, classified, and proprietary documents as part of this campaign. Virtually every Soviet military project – well over 4,000 each year in the late 1970s and well over 5,000 in the early 1980s, benefits from these technical documents and hardware. The assimilation of Western technology is so broad that the United States and other Western nation are thus subsidising the Soviet military buildup.'[22] Particular fears were raised about 'technobandits' in Vienna, who damaged Western interests by leaking embargoed technology, information and know-how to Eastern intelligence services.[23]

Vienna has also been an important location for the North Korean regime, with the city hosting the only European branch of a North Korean financial institution. The Golden Star Bank exchanged foreign currencies and kept accounts for North Korean citizens and companies. It opened in 1982 and was forced to close in 2004, following suspicions of money laundering and financing the illegal weapons trade. Lots of money was required in Vienna to supply late dictator Kim Il-sung and his son Kim Jong-il with luxury goods. Working out of the North Korean Embassy and on special shopping missions, the later defector Kim Jong-ryul bought expensive cars, planes, gold-plated handguns and exotic food for the ruling family.[24] 'He only ate foreign food,' the North Korean colonel said. 'In Vienna, there was a special attaché, a friend of mine, who only procured special foreign food for the dictator.' Kim Il-sung's culinary demands led to a delegation of chefs being sent to Austria to visit renowned cookery schools and top restaurants to collect recipes. '"Learn everything!" – that's what they were told,' the defector said. 'The crazy dictators heard rumours that Austrian cuisine was world famous and that's why they wanted [the cooks] to come here.'[25]

More recently, Vienna was used for the largest spy-swap since the end of the Cold War. In 2010, ten Russian spies were exchanged for four American spies at Vienna's Schwechat Airport. The Austrian domestic security agency BVT recently reported that Austria is 'a preferred operation area for foreign intelligence services' because of 'the favourable geographical position of the country, its scientific and economic activities particularly in the fields of technology and the energy industry, its membership in the European Union and the fact that a number of international organisations, such as the United Nations, have their headquarters in Austria'. The BVT also noted that foreign intelligence services 'showed an increased interest in foreign opposition members and groups in Austria'.[26]

*

The goal of attracting international organisations to Vienna has been a high priority for Austrian governments since the end of the occupation in 1955. Initially viewed as an insurance policy against aggression from the east, the growing concentration of multilateral bodies has helped redefine Vienna's international importance. The first major organisation to be based in the city was the International Atomic Energy Agency (IAEA), created in 1957 in response to the hopes and fears following breakthrough discoveries about nuclear technology. The agency was set up as the world's 'Atoms for Peace' organisation, as part of the UN. From its inception, its mandate has been to work with UN member states and international partner organisations on the safe, secure and peaceful applications of nuclear technologies. The agency's dual mission is outlined in Article II of the IAEA Statute: 'The Agency shall seek to accelerate and enlarge the contribution of atomic energy to peace, health and prosperity throughout the world. It shall ensure, so far as it is able, that assistance provided by it or at its request or under its supervision or control is not used in such a way as to further any military purpose.'[27] At the first IAEA general conference in 1957, delegates decided that the organisation should be headquartered in Vienna, initially at the Grand Hotel close to the Vienna Opera House.

Less than a decade later, in 1966, Vienna secured its second major headquarters with the newly created United Nations Industrial Development Organisation (UNIDO). Although ten different UN member states offered a home for the new organisation, the UN General Assembly chose Vienna, where office buildings were provided in the Felderhaus next to the Rathaus and nearby at Weghuberpark. The main aim of UNIDO was, and continues to be, the promotion of industrial development and to encourage the mobilisation of national and international resources to boost the industrialisation of developing countries, with a strong focus on the manufacturing sector.

In the next initiative to underline Austria's bridge-builder status, Bruno Kreisky helped to secure the headquarters of the only East–West think tank, the International Institute for Applied Systems Analysis (IIASA). In unprecedented cooperation during the Cold War, 12 national member organisations from Canada, Czechoslovakia, Bulgaria, East Germany, France, Italy, Japan, Poland, the Soviet Union, the UK, the US and West Germany signed the founding charter. They were subsequently joined by Austria, Hungary, Sweden, Finland, the Netherlands and Norway.

Originally destined to be headquartered in the UK or France, IIASA decision-makers accepted instead the offer of the renovated 18th-century Habsburg palace of Schloss Laxenburg on the edge of Vienna. The Austrian offer to entice the organisation also included 'income-tax-free status for the Institute and its non-Austrian staff [Austrians received the same privilege later], full restoration of the Schloss buildings, a nominal rent of one Austrian schilling per year, and half a million schillings in annual structural repairs'.[28] In recalling the international diplomatic efforts to secure the prestigious organisation, the IIASA's first director, Howard Raiffa, concluded that the right decision had been made: 'Austria was clearly the right choice. Symbolically, it was fantastically appropriate. The reception that we got from Austrian President Rudolf Kirchschläger and Chancellor Bruno Kreisky and the facilities were absolutely right. Even the French agreed, years afterwards, that we made the right choice.'[29] In having secured the world's main north–south development institution with UNIDO, Vienna was with IIASA also home to the only East–West scientific research organisation.

IIASA continues to flourish with its aims largely unchanged: 'policy-oriented research into issues that are too large or complex to be solved by a single country or academic discipline. This includes pressing concerns that affect the future of all of humanity, such as climate change, energy security, population ageing, and sustainable development.'[30] Approximately 200 researchers from over 35 countries research at the institute every year. Ten IIASA scientists were among the authors of the international report on global warming that received the joint award of the 2007 Nobel Peace Prize.

As well as securing the presence of international institutions in Vienna, Bruno Kreisky also re-established a domestic institution with international pedigree: the Diplomatic Academy of Vienna. Following in the traditions of the pre-existing Consular Academy and Oriental Academy, its lineage goes back to the time of Empress Maria Theresa in the 18th century, which makes it the oldest school of international relations in the world. Reopened in the consular wing of the Theresian Academy in 1964 by Kreisky, it represented his ambition for Austria to punch above its weight, with a well-trained next generation of young diplomats. Kreisky believed that being internationally relevant was of domestic advantage. It was, in his words, 'national politics in the best sense of the word . . . Austria can have a confident foreign policy in sensible relation to its possibilities, that adds to its reputation but goes beyond its economic and political strengths.'[31]

Kreisky came to personify that confident foreign policy. Henry Kissinger described him as Austria's 'shrewd and perceptive Chancellor, who had parlayed his country's formal neutrality into a perception of influence beyond its strength, often by interpreting the motives of competing countries to each other. That he could bring off this balancing act was a tribute to his tact, intelligence and his instincts for the scope – and the limits – of indiscretion. He was much travelled; his comments on trends and personalities were invariably illuminating. He had a great sense of humour and far more geographical insight than many leaders from more powerful countries . . . On the asymmetries of history is the lack of correspondence between the abilities of some leaders and the powers of their country . . . Nixon remarked later that he wished Kreisky could change places with some of the Socialist leaders in larger European countries whose insight and sturdiness he rated less highly.'[32]

The big prize for Kreisky was to secure for Vienna the status as third headquarters of the United Nations, so he and Finance Minister Hannes Androsch flew to Washington to meet and lobby President Gerald Ford on 12 November 1974. At a meeting in the Oval Office of the White House, things began well when Henry Kissinger, then Secretary of State, fondly recalled: 'I lectured at the Diplomatic Academy in Vienna when the Chancellor was there. It is hard there; they put whipped cream into everything.' Ford went on to talk affectionately about a vacation in Austria with his wife, when they stayed in Burgenland and Vienna and went to the opera. Kreisky invited them back, but then cut to the chase with the top agenda item: Vienna as a UN centre. As the declassified minutes of the discussion make clear, Kreisky pushed the geographic proximity to the Iron Curtain as a key consideration: 'It would be only 40 kilometres from the Communist borders. It would give us additional security . . . we already have two international organisations in Vienna: UNIDO and [the IAEA]. I would be grateful for your support.' President Ford committed to discuss the issue more with Kissinger, who confirmed: 'We are basically favourable. There are a lot of technical details – such as taxation . . . most of our objections are bureaucratic, not in principle.' Kreisky then reiterated his priority: 'We need to preserve Vienna as one of Europe's great capitals.'[33]

President Ford did take up the invitation to visit Austria the next year when he met with Chancellor Kreisky and Egyptian President Anwar Sadat. After discussions on the Middle East, Kreisky pressed Ford on the airport tarmac as he was leaving: 'So we will go ahead with the UN plans for Vienna?' Drowned out by the aircraft noise, Ford took his hand, smiled and nodded, but his words weren't recorded for posterity. Legend has it that Kreisky smiled back, took the reply as affirmation and welcomed the positive news immediately.

In the same year, Kreisky, who had himself been a refugee after the Nazi Anschluss, received the Freedom Award of the International Rescue Committee for Austria's humanitarian support for refugees. At the awards dinner, President Ford said: 'Austria's central location in Europe has made a natural resting point for uprooted peoples on their way to new lands. But geography alone does not determine policy. Our respect for Austria's exceptional record of aid for refugees stems from that country's wholehearted acceptance as first haven.' Ford's fulsome praise reflected on the impact of Austria's foreign policy: 'Modern Austria has proved again and again in recent years that a small country can make a big contribution to peace and world understanding.'[34] In his acceptance speech, Kreisky drew attention to Austria's welcome for people from the rest of the former Dual Monarchy, for Hungarian and Czechoslovak refugees after the 1956 and 1968 revolutions, for displaced Indian Ugandans and Chileans as well as transit for nearly 200,000 Eastern European Jews.

Kreisky became a significant figure in Middle East politics during the 1970s and he used his position as a Jewish social democratic head of government in a neutral European state to significant effect. Austria had a locus in the region, as the country was the main transit point for Russian Jews emigrating to Israel. This became the focus of Arab terrorists, who sought to close the main Schönau transit facility outside Vienna, where Israel had significant influence. Kreisky used the opportunity to open a new camp at Wollersdorf, which was fully under Austrian control and where émigrés had the opportunity to go to different locations, not just Israel. During a visit to Austria, Israeli Prime Minister Golda Meir was scathing: 'In Vienna for the first time a government has come to an understanding with terrorists. A basic principle of any freedom of movement of peoples has been put under question, at any rate for Jews, and this is a great victory for terrorism and terrorists.'[35] Leaving immediately after the fraught discussions and refusing to take part in a scheduled joint press conference with Kreisky, she returned straight to Israel, where she claimed her reception in Vienna was so bad she wasn't even offered a glass of water. Kreisky famously said afterwards that he was 'the only politician in Europe Golda Meir can't blackmail'. The number of Eastern European and Soviet Jews that transited through Austria between 1968 and 1986 reached 270,199, more than half of them after the closure of the Schönau transit camp.

Kreisky developed close relations with political leaders across the Arab world and sought to pursue a mediation role, especially in seeking the recognition of the Palestine Liberation Organization (PLO) as the legitimate representative of the Palestinians. His closest partnership and friendship was with Egyptian President Sadat, who had learnt German from a fellow prisoner while he was in jail, and whom Kreisky influenced to make a highly symbolic visit to Jerusalem.[36] 'There are two Jews who really impress me,' Sadat wrote to one of his intimates. 'One is Henry Kissinger; the other is Bruno Kreisky,' before adding: 'If there are Jews like Kissinger and Kreisky, then there is a chance that Israel can produce a government with a less intransigent posture than Golda Meir's.'[37] In 1974, Kreisky led the first of three Socialist International delegations to the Middle East, with stops in Egypt, Syria and Israel, during which he first met PLO leader Yasser Arafat in Cairo. Arafat was viewed at the time by most of the international community as a terrorist, so the meeting was risky for Kreisky. However, he was effectively the trailblazer for Arafat and the PLO becoming internationally recognised and a partner of Israel in peace discussions.

The early Middle East mediation efforts in the 1970s were hugely complicated by international terrorist attacks, including high-profile incidents in Austria. In 1975, the Vienna headquarters of OPEC was targeted by Palestinian-supporting terrorists. The oil cartel had been based in Vienna since 1965 after the organisation was extended diplomatic privileges, but it was the first time that Arab countries had been targeted by this kind of terrorist operation. The siege, led by the Venezuelan terrorist Ramírez 'Carlos the Jackal' Sánchez involved 96 people being taken hostage, amongst them a number of OPEC ministers, and three people were killed, including an Austrian police officer. The fundraising plan of the six-strong terrorist unit was to ransom the ministers as part of efforts by the self-styled 'Arm of the Arab Revolution' to liberate Palestine. The Austrians provided a plane for the attackers and their hostages, and the embarrassing image went around the world of Interior Minister Otto Rösch shaking the hand of Carlos the Jackal at the bottom of the aircraft steps before he flew to safety in north Africa.

For Hella Pick, the Vienna-born foreign affairs editor of the *Guardian*, Kreisky's record was mixed, but on balance positive: 'Kreisky's involvement in the Middle East is a tangled story; certainly not one that always reflects to his credit: he antagonised Israel, made compromises with terrorists, provoked critics into branding him an antisemitic Jew, sought to reduce America's key role in the Middle East peace process by relying more on the UN, and overestimated the extent to which Europe could influence the search for a settlement. And yet . . . [he made] a significant contribution to the initiatives that led to the Camp David Accord and paved the way for the acceptance of the PLO as a legitimate partner in Middle East peace negotiations. Kreisky's role in facilitating the exodus of Jews from the Soviet Union will also come to be better appreciated, as will secret diplomacy that helped free Israeli prisoners in Syrian hands.'[38]

At the start of the 1970s Kreisky became Austrian Chancellor for the first time and ruled initially with a minority Social Democratic administration, with the acquiescence of the right-wing Austrian Freedom Party, led by former SS Obersturmführer Friedrich Peter. His willingness to deal with Peter became the focus of a huge falling-out with legendary Vienna-based Nazi hunter Simon Wiesenthal. Wiesenthal (1908–2005) was an Austrian Holocaust survivor originally from Galicia in the east of the Habsburg Empire. After the war he dedicated the rest of his life to tracking down Nazi war criminals so they could be brought to justice. Pointing out that Kreisky had four former Nazis in his 1970 cabinet irritated the chancellor considerably, but it was Wiesenthal's assertion that Peter had served in an SS unit that participated in the mass killing of Jewish civilians that had the potential to cause a major political scandal. As it turned out, Kreisky won the next three general elections and didn't have to rely on the Freedom Party for support; however, the feud with Wiesenthal continued: 'Kreisky attacked me and hurt me as no other individual had done since the Nazi period. He accused me of using the methods of the "political mafia". Even though he knew it was hard to survive [during the Holocaust], he had information that my relationship with the Gestapo was different and that I lived in freedom etc. Naturally the journalists built this up. In the end, he retracted.'[39]

The *Guardian's* Hella Pick knew both Kreisky and Wiesenthal well: 'The story is Byzantine in its twists and turns and ramifications. It involves two men representing fundamentally different strands of Jewishness, who were totally unable and unwilling to understand each other, and eventually fell into a deep trough of mutual hatred.' According to Pick: 'Wiesenthal saw Kreisky as a man who betrayed both his heritage and also the Holocaust.' Kreisky, on the other hand, wanted to 'prove that his Jewishness would never stand in the way of loyalty to Austria' and saw Wiesenthal 'as a meddler and a hypocrite'.[40]

In 1971 Kreisky won an absolute majority, the first ever such socialist victory in Austrian history. His 13 years as chancellor included a wide range of progressive social, economic and polit-ical reforms, similar to the Scandinavian social democratic model. Kreisky pursued an 'Austro-Keynsian' approach towards full employ-ment, invested heavily in the country's health and education systems, expanded rights and benefits for employees, cut the working week to 40 hours, and passed legislation providing for equality for women. Austria became one of the wealthiest countries in Europe, but it is his groundbreaking 'bridge-building' efforts that are best remem-bered internationally. Most notably this included the success of East–West détente through the 'Helsinki process', as well as strategic arms limitation by the US and USSR with the SALT-II agreement signed in Vienna.

The Helsinki process aimed to reduce tensions between the Soviet and Western blocs with East–West discussions on human rights and fundamental freedoms, as well as encouraging economic, scientific and humanitarian cooperation. It led to the Conference on Security and Co-operation in Europe (CSCE) and signing of the Helsinki Accords in 1975. Because the initiative had come from Moscow, there had been a great deal of scepticism in the West, which Kreisky sought to assuage, becoming one of the key figures behind the eventual agreement. Now known as the Organization for Security and Co-operation in Europe, the OSCE is headquartered in Vienna's Hofburg palace and is the world's largest intergovernmental security organisation, with 57 member states from Europe, Asia and North America. The OSCE mandate includes arms control, the promotion of human rights, freedom of the press and fair elections. Its work also includes conflict early warning, conflict prevention, crisis management and post-conflict rehabilitation.

The Cold War arms race meant that both the US and Soviet Union developed large nuclear arsenals during the 1960s, with the capacity to destroy the world several times over. Strategic arms limitation talks led to the SALT-I agreement in 1972, which limited the number of intercontinental ballistic missiles (ICBMs) and submarine-launched ballistic missiles (SLBMs). Discussions between the US and USSR continued afterwards in the neutral capitals of Helsinki and Vienna, with a view to reducing their nuclear stockpiles, and led to the SALT-II agreement, signed in Austria.

The year 1979 was the unsurpassed high point for Austria's 'active neutrality' and the personal success of Kreisky's international diplomacy. In mid-June US President Jimmy Carter and Soviet premier Leonid Brezhnev arrived in Vienna with large delegations to finalise the SALT-II agreement and were hosted at the Hofburg by Austrian President Rudolf Kirchschläger and Chancellor Kreisky. With no Vienna summit seeming complete without the involvement of the State Opera, a special performance of Mozart's *Die Entführung aus dem Serail* was performed. The *Washington Post* reported that 'the audience in this city of opera lovers clapped politely when Carter and Brezhnev arrived, but reserved stormy applause for 84-year-old conductor Karl Böhm, one of Europe's most famous maestros, who was making a special guest appearance'.[41] The signing ceremony for the agreement on 18 June saw the youthful Jimmy Carter and the frail Leonid Brezhnev sitting at a long, formal table at the end of the gilded Redoutensaal in the Hofburg. In front of a massed bank of TV cameras and lights, photographers, and journalists, the two leaders exchanged handshakes and kissed one another on the cheeks.

On 9 July Kreisky became the first Western-oriented head of government to host PLO Chairman Yasser Arafat, bringing him together with German SPD leader Willy Brandt, who was in Vienna to chair a meeting of the North–South Commission (Brandt Commission). Later that year Kreisky made a speech at the UN General Assembly calling for the international recognition of the PLO: 'It seems to me that it is high time to be absolutely clear on this issue. Since all Arab peoples, including Egypt, recognise the Palestinian Liberation Organization as the legitimate representative of the Palestinians, since the group of non-aligned countries has clearly demonstrated similar recognition and since the representative of the PLO has his place here in this Assembly with the consent of practically all of us, the time must soon come when all states in this great community of nations will recognise that the PLO today is simply the representative of the Palestinian people. For its part, the Austrian Federal government will take this fact fully into account and will advocate this position with all due clarity in its relations with other states.'[42] Kreisky was way ahead of other Western countries, and prepared the ground for others to follow. It took another decade for an open dialogue to begin between the US and the PLO.

Still in 1979, Vienna officially became a global headquarters of the UN. On 23 August the Austrian government officially handed over the complex of buildings it constructed for the UN as its third headquarters, after New York and Geneva. Austria first offered to host the UN with a purpose-built complex in 1967 on a prime 180,000-square-metre plot next to the Danube. Designed by the Austrian architect Johann Staber, the Vienna International Centre (VIC) was constructed over seven years at a cost of over 8.8 billion schillings. Construction involved 80,000 tonnes of cement, 40,000 tonnes of steel, 200,000 cubic metres of concrete and the excavation of half a million cubic metres of earth.[43] The six Y-form buildings are between 48 and 120 metres high and contain over 4,500 individual offices, which are all outer facing. The UN pays a symbolic one schilling (0.07 euro) in annual rent for the 99-year lease of the 'UNO City'. The facility, which is extraterritorial to Austria and guarded by UN security officers, includes a built-in station connecting it to the Vienna underground network. More than 5,000 staff from over 125 countries work at the VIC, which also incorporates the Austria Center Vienna, the country's largest conference centre. The huge facility contains 24 halls, 180 meeting rooms, 26,000 square metres of exhibition space over five floors with capacity for more than 22,800 people. It is the only conference centre in the world that is co-located with a UN headquarters, and it hosted the first World Conference on Human Rights after the fall of the Iron Curtain, with 171 attending states, 800 NGOs and 7,000 participants. It led to the establishment of the Office of the UN High Commissioner for Human Rights. Part of the package to attract the UN to Vienna included the establishment of the English-language Blue Danube Radio by the Austrian Broadcasting Corporation (ORF), with news and content aimed at the diplomatic community.

Bruno Kreisky served as Chancellor of Austria until 1983, with international relations at the forefront of his efforts. When he died in 1990 at the age of 79, his state funeral was attended by the prime ministers or foreign ministers of ten European countries and Yasser Arafat. While Kreisky did much to improve the international standing of Austria, he did so without resolving the country's relationship with its wartime past and responsibility. That would soon come to the forefront of national and international attention with the Waldheim affair.

\*

Kurt Waldheim (1918–2007) was the Austrian diplomat and former foreign minister who reached the highest office in international diplomacy in 1972, when he became Secretary-General of the UN.

348

Over the course of ten years and two terms in the top UN job, he was viewed as competent, capable and unremarkable, just as he had been in Austrian diplomacy and politics. It was during his later attempt to become Austrian president in 1986 that an international and domestic scandal about his wartime service with the German Wehrmacht unwittingly catapulted him to global consciousness and caused Austria to profoundly reflect on its role in the war for the first time.

Waldheim, who grew up in a rural village close to the capital, graduated from the Vienna Consular Academy (now Diplomatic Academy) in 1939 and began his diplomatic career after the war in 1945. His first overseas posting was as First Secretary in Paris in 1948, then a stint at the Foreign Ministry in the run-up to the 1955 State Treaty. Waldheim's association with the UN went back to Austria's admission as its 70th member state in December 1955. There is still a photograph on the UN website of him sitting behind the Austria nameplate before a plenary meeting at the General Assembly Hall at UN Headquarters in New York the day after Austria's admission. Waldheim became the Permanent Representative of Austria to the UN in 1964.

After taking two years out from New York to serve as Austrian Foreign Minister, he returned as Permanent Representative in 1970 before he ran for election to become Secretary-General of the UN aged 53. Despite the opposition of China, the US and UK, a mix-up between them about the use of the veto as permanent members of the Security Council, and their subsequent abstention, meant that Waldheim was surprisingly elected. During his tenure as Secretary-General, he convened a series of UN-hosted international conferences, was involved in Middle East diplomacy and sought to find a resolution to the Iran hostage crisis in 1980. Brian Urquhart, a senior UN contemporary, felt that Waldheim 'had qualities that did not readily present themselves to casual acquaintance or to the public. He was conscientious, hardworking, and had a great physical stamina. Once he accepted an idea, he was prepared to follow it up, and he was never too tired to undertake an awkward journey, have an unpleasant interview, or make a difficult telephone call.'[44]

After failing to secure a third term as Secretary-General, he returned to Austria where he pursued a candidacy for Federal President on behalf of the Austrian People's Party (ÖVP). In the run-up to the 1986 election, the Vienna-based current affairs magazine *Profil* published an investigation into Waldheim's war record, which, according to his biography, ended with his medical discharge in 1942 after being wounded on the Eastern Front. This signalled the start of the Waldheim affair, 'the most sensational of post-war Nazi scandals' and a metaphor for the wider amnesia about Austrian wartime participation. Further journalistic research, aided by the World Jewish Congress (WJC), confirmed that Waldheim had been a member of the mounted corps of the Nazi SA Brownshirts and that he had been a junior intelligence officer in the Balkans from 1942 until 1944, when the Wehrmacht conducted reprisal killings of civilians and where he was at one stage close to a notorious concentration camp. In March 1986 the WJC alleged that, according to the UN War Crimes Commission, Waldheim had been implicated in mass murder and should face justice. Rather than acknowledge the emerging facts of his wartime service, Waldheim called the allegations against him 'pure lies and malicious acts'. In an interview with the Vienna correspondent of *Time* magazine, Austria's Jewish ex-Chancellor Bruno Kreisky said that the war crime allegations were 'an extraordinary infamy!' and that Austrian voters 'won't allow the Jews abroad to order us about and tell us who should be our President'.[45] Despite Kreisky's huge differences with veteran Austrian Nazi-hunter Simon Wiesenthal, they both agreed that Waldheim was not proven to be responsible for war crimes. In reaction to what had become an international cause célèbre, Waldheim's election campaign adopted the slogan 'Now more than ever', and he went on to win with 54 per cent of the vote in the second round.

As a consequence of the international scandal, the Austrian government established a committee of historians who analysed Waldheim's record from the 1938 Anschluss to the end of the war in 1945. It concluded that he did not commit war crimes, but that it was not credible that he was unaware of them, especially since he initialled military reports that detailed them. In a contrast that could not be more marked, Waldheim's German presidential contemporary, Richard von Weizsäcker, who also had been a junior intelligence officer, took full responsibility and apologised for his service with the Nazis.

Senior UN colleagues like Brian Urquhart, who were once outspoken supporters of Waldheim, began to see things in a different light. Urquhart, who served as UN Under-Secretary-General for Special Political Affairs, had once said of Waldheim that 'in terms of usefulness, not glamor, he's actually been the best Secretary-General'. Once the scandal erupted, however, he 'felt betrayed and angry' saying: 'It is hard to understand why he should have lied . . . United States intelligence had interrogated him extensively about the Balkans in 1945, so the US had always had the true story of his military career in its files, as had other governments, but they had failed to recall this at the time of his election as Secretary-General. When the story of his misrepresentations came out in 1986 when Waldheim was President of Austria, it was regarded . . . as a highly damaging reflection on the United Nations.'[46]

The consequence of the Waldheim affair included him being put on the US 'watchlist' barring him entry to the United States and becoming an international pariah more widely. It also forced a national debate about Austria's war guilt, which was reported internationally by the likes of the *Financial Times*: 'The agonising reappraisal of its recent history has been forced on a reluctant people by the wide publicity given to President Waldheim's role in the German Wehrmacht which coincided with the commemoration of the Anschluss. The conjunction of these two events has undermined not only the traditional consensus between the two grand coalition partners, but has split the Austrian people right down the middle. For the first time in 40 years, the public and the body politic have found themselves passionately involved in a nationwide debate on an issue of major national and international importance.'[47]

Waldheim did not seek re-election at the end of his term in 1992. He died in 2007 at the age of 88 leaving a public letter where he acknowledged: 'Yes, I also made mistakes – and luckily I have had a long time to reflect on them. These were certainly not those of a follower let alone an accomplice of a criminal regime.'[48]

*

While Austria was agonising over the Waldheim affair in the late 1980s, few people predicted that far bigger events were about to unfold with crumbling communist rule in neighbouring nations and the end to the border of barbed wire and watchtowers between East and West.

The first physical sign that the Iron Curtain was coming down occurred on 27 June 1989 when Austrian Foreign Minister Alois Mock and his Hungarian counterpart, Gyula Horn, took part in a highly symbolic fence-cutting ceremony near Sopron, 70 kilometres south-east of Vienna. Early freedom of movement for Hungarians to Austria was soon embraced by East Germans, who were allowed to holiday in Hungary but not yet travel freely to the West. On 19 August 1989 a peace demonstration was held at the Austro-Hungarian border and became the opportunity for more than 600 East German refugees to cross into Austria without being stopped by Hungarian border guards. Under the patronage of Otto Habsburg MEP, whose father reigned over both sides of the border until 1918, and Hungarian opposition groups, the 'Pan-European picnic' was promoted as an event of solidarity and friendship.[49] While the organisers did not expect hundreds of East Germans to attend the picnic event or for the border to be opened, the West German Embassy organised buses to transport the refugees to Vienna, where they issued them with passports and onward travel. Within weeks the border was crossed by tens of thousands of East Germans.

In the midst of these historic events, Austria submitted its formal application to the European Communities. Foreign Minister Mock handed over the accession document in Brussels and signalled Austria's changing role: from being a neutral state between East and West, to becoming a uniquely placed nation at the heart of Europe as the continent began to come together. For Mock's biographer

and former Austrian ambassador to London Martin Eichtinger, the timing was hugely significant: 'It is all too often forgotten that Austria was the only neutral country that submitted its application for membership before the fall of the Berlin Wall: a very courageous step given the skepticism of the Soviet leadership!'[50]

Vienna played an important role with the emerging democratising nations in central and Eastern Europe, but Austria was also an immediate neighbour to Yugoslavia, which began to break up in 1991. Austria had historic connections, especially with Slovenia and Croatia, which had been part of the Habsburg Empire, and Foreign Minister Mock was one of the key international figures to press for the formal recognition of Slovenian and Croatian independence from Belgrade, which Austria and the European Communities member states did in January 1992. Dimitrij Rupel, Slovenia's first foreign minister after independence, described Mock as 'the fairy godmother of Slovenian foreign relations. Alois Mock performed immeasurable service for Slovenia, for our diplomacy and statehood.'[51]

As Serb aggression threatened to overwhelm Bosnia-Herzegovina it was Mock who led a delegation of European foreign ministers to the White House for talks with President George H. Bush, warning that the Balkan nation 'will be the first country of the free world since World War II to fall victim to aggression and will disappear' unless the 'Greater Serbia' campaign is halted. He left the discussions convinced that 'the United States will use all political means to get a coalition, particularly with Western European countries', to enforce UN Security Council resolutions, including a no-fly zone over Bosnia-Herzegovina.[52] Mock also initiated the international adoption of 'safe havens', which initially helped protect Bosnian Muslim civilians, but, without adequate UN protection, tragically failed completely. In the eastern Bosnian town of Srebrenica, Serb forces captured the haven and then murdered more than 8,000 people, in the worst genocide event since the Second World War.

As with the Hungarian Revolution of 1956 and Prague Spring in 1968, Austria again became the place of safety for tens of thousands of refugees fleeing fighting across the former Yugoslavia. The

Austrian Broadcasting Corporation launched a huge fundraising appeal, 'Neighbour in Need', collecting more than €221 million. After brutal ethnic cleansing, many of the refugees never returned and preferred to build a new life in Austria. One such was Alma Zadic who fled her homeland as a ten-year-old; in 2020 the Bosnian refugee became Austrian Justice Minister.

Throughout the early 1990s the European accession negotiations proceeded with Austria, Sweden, Finland and Norway. For Austria, the most politically sensitive issues related to the agricultural sector, where it was feared there would be a negative impact on Alpine farming, and on the potential for uncontrolled, environmentally damaging north–south road traffic between Germany and Italy across the Alpine region of Tyrol. In a foretaste of what was to come later in other countries, Austria's populist Freedom Party and its charismatic leader, Jörg Haider (1950–2008), used the European issue and growing numbers of migrants and refugees to assail the 'old parties' of the political establishment. Haider also made repeated comments that were seen as flirtations with the extreme right. At one stage he described Hitler's employment policies as 'orderly', and he spoke at a meeting of Second World War veterans, including former SS members, describing them as 'decent individuals with character who stick to their beliefs despite strong opposition and remain true to them today as well'.[53]

Austria's accession to the European Union followed an 80-hour mammoth negotiating session in Brussels, after which Alois Mock emotionally announced to the TV cameras that 'Austria's way to Europe is now free', in an homage to the famous declaration about the 1955 State Treaty that 'Austria is free'.[54] In the referendum that followed on 12 June 1994, Austrians voted by 66.6 per cent to join the EU and formally joined on 1 January 1995, together with Sweden and Finland. Mock, who earned the nickname 'Mr Europe', managed the feat of negotiating Austria's accession and the referendum campaign with visibly worsening symptoms of Parkinson's disease, which didn't deter him from delivering his lifetime political ambition.[55] He died in 2017 with European leaders and figures across the Austrian political spectrum praising his achievements, which, in addition to Austria's EU accession, included a resolution to the long-running dispute with Italy over the majority German-speaking region of South Tyrol. Since joining the EU, Austria's gross domestic product has increased by 9.7 per cent, 13,000 additional jobs have been created annually, foreign direct investment has tripled and Austria's exports have more than doubled.[56]

In 1998, Austria took on the rotating presidency of the EU for the first time. Decision-makers in Vienna were again directing developments for the whole continent, with the symbolism that 'the Chancellor and his ministers sketched their ambitions in the white and gold chamber where Metternich chaired the Congress of Vienna in 1815'.[57]

Austria's EU membership has only suffered one serious setback since, which followed the 1999 general election and the formation of a federal coalition government between the moderate Austrian People's Party and populist Freedom Party of Jörg Haider. Despite Haider not personally taking a seat in government, the new government faced a wave of international political condemnation. California Governor and *Terminator* film star Arnold Schwarzenegger said: 'As an immigrant myself, I am offended by anyone who makes anti-immigrant statements, and it is my opinion that someone who makes statements like Haider's has no place in government. I have never supported him in the past and do not now. I am hopeful that Austria will find a way through this. As an Austrian-born, I am so saddened that, with all the progress we have made working for an open and tolerant society, one man's statements can taint world opinion of an entire country. I know that there are many tolerant people in Austria. It is my hope that their voices can and will be heard.'[58]

In reaction to the inclusion of the Freedom Party in the new government, the 14 other EU member states imposed sanctions against Austria, which were only lifted after specific guarantees about the acceptance of European norms on the observation of human rights. All of Austria's chancellors since the 1990s – Franz Vranitzky, Victor Klima, Wolfgang Schüssel, Alfred Gusenbauer, Werner Faymann,

Christian Kern, Sebastian Kurz and Brigitte Bierlein – and presidents – Thomas Klestil, Heinz Fischer and Alexander van der Bellen – have been outspoken about the country's culpability for its wartime role and communicated the need to show contrition, take responsibility, and deliver on reparations and restitution.

\*

Since the end of the Cold War, the international status of Vienna has arguably become more important to Austria, now that the rationale of the capital of a neutral state at the meeting point of East and West has changed forever. Vienna has established itself over decades as a significant 'bridge-builder' between states and also as the optimal location for international organisations. It is also of huge economic importance, as the scale of diplomatic representation and multilateral organisations dwarfs that in other comparatively sized countries.

The significant financial and economic benefits to Vienna's status as a leading international capital have been calculated to have an annual gross value-added effect amounting to €1.3 billion and supporting 18,100 employees.[59] Despite widespread tax exemptions, this still brings in €483 million in tax revenue. Although there is significant public expenditure in support of international organisations and diplomatic representations in Vienna, it is estimated that this hardly exceeds one fifth of the fiscal returns.

At present, more than 40 international organisations and quasi-international organisations are headquartered in Vienna, and they employ 6,422 people. Diplomatic representation in Vienna amounts to 120 bilateral missions and 197 multilateral missions, including 143 permanent representations, observers and liaison offices to the international organisations and 54 permanent representations and delegations to the OSCE. Some 3,300 people are accredited as diplomats in these missions, but locally employed staff double the total workforce. The economic benefit from the diplomatic presence in Vienna amounts to an annual total of €585 million in staff costs, mission overheads and accommodation, all of which is a net transfer from abroad.

The concentration and scale of international organisations and diplomatic representation also creates a huge demand for meetings, conferences and summits. In 2017 this amounted to 9,400 conference days involving more than 142,000 participants, with UN-associated events alone totalling 47,000 people and an estimated economic value of €538 million. In 2018 the Austrian presidency of the EU brought an additional 300 international meetings, all of which together has contributed to Vienna becoming one the largest and best-rated general conference venues in the world, with 611,000 participants, supporting 21,000 jobs and generating more than €1.1 billion a year.[60]

Further benefits of Vienna's international status includes education, where seven schools teach towards the International Baccalaureate (IB), including the Vienna International School, Lycée Français and American International School. Many of the city's junior and secondary public schools are part of the Vienna Bilingual Schooling initiative, teaching in English as well as German.

Even after the end of the Cold War, Vienna has shown itself to be best placed to host global diplomatic events. Following years of confrontation about the Iranian nuclear programme, in 2015 the international community sought to reach an agreement that would ensure Tehran could not develop nuclear weapons. Final negotiations in Vienna led to the Joint Comprehensive Plan of Action (JCPOA), an agreement between Iran, the P5 five permanent members of the United Nations (the US, Russia, China, UK and France) plus Germany and the EU.

The Austrian government provided the stunning Palais Coburg as the location for the talks and bore the costs for the different delegations and the hosting of hundreds of international journalists in tented media facilities adjacent to the neoclassical palace. The colonnaded, white-stuccoed Palais Coburg sits atop one of the last remaining sections of the Vienna city wall and is now a five-star boutique hotel with 33 suites. Despite the 18 days of talks becoming fraught at times and threatening to stall, the Iranian Foreign Minister Mohammad Javad Zarif and US Secretary of State John Kerry managed to secure the breakthrough. The Vienna-headquartered IAEA was the arbiter of the deal, which made headlines around the world, including in the *Guardian*: 'The 18 days in Vienna proved to be one of the most epic diplomatic marathons in modern times. At the end of it, the ministers and diplomats stumbled out into the daylight . . . some of them for the first time in a week. They left behind substantial bills for the Austrian government. But, as diplomats often like to point out, while peaceful negotiations are often costly, they are much cheaper then the alternatives.'[61]

As with famous previous diplomatic summits over the centuries, Vienna showed itself to be the optimal location for discussions, as reported by international media like the *Financial Times*: 'Vienna has put itself at the centre of the diplomatic world map with the signing of a landmark nuclear accord. Neutrality and excitement make for uncommon bedfellows. The global centres of diplomacy do not tend to be places where you would want to spend a great deal of time. Vienna, though, with its cafés, its culture and its size, is a possible exception. At the very least, it has two things going for it: it is not Geneva. And it is certainly not Lausanne, that other Swiss negotiating hub. This year, Austria's capital beat both to put itself again at the centre of the diplomatic world map.'[62]

Austria has also managed to maintain annual events that bring participants from around the world, like the European 'Festival of Ideas', the Alpbach Forum. Established after the war by the Austrian resistance founder Otto Molden, the Vienna-headquartered forum has been dubbed the 'Davos of ideas' and meets in the Tyrolean community of Alpbach every summer. Nobel Prize winners and world leaders who have attended include German Chancellor Helmut Kohl, Indian Prime Minister Indira Ghandi, UN Secretary-General Ban Ki-Moon, Austrian-born philosopher Karl Popper and economist Friedrich von Hayek, Israeli Prime Minister Yitzhak Rabin, Irish President and UN High Commissioner for Human Rights Mary Robinson and many, many more. Thousands of young people from around the world receive scholarships every year to attend the forum.

More recently established annual international events include the environmental Austrian World Summit hosted by the climate-change campaigner, film star and former California Governor Arnold Schwarzenegger. Over a thousand delegates and international organisations take part in the discussions in Vienna's Hofburg palace, with key speakers including high-profile activists like Greta Thunberg and world leaders headed by UN Secretary-General António Guterres.

Both the Austrian government and Vienna city authorities place a high priority on the protection and promotion of Vienna's international status. Specialist departments in the Foreign Ministry and City Hall support relations with the international organisations, the management of diplomatic events and promotion of Vienna as a global centre. The diplomat Wolfgang Angerholzer, who served as Director for International Organisations at the Austrian Foreign Ministry, hopes that 'more NGOs could establish offices in Vienna, particularly those whose work is overlapping with the UN', and is acutely aware that Vienna's status as third UN headquarters might remain merely 'a symbol for peace in the world'.[63] However, with Vienna's repeated rating as the city with the best quality of life in the world, it will continue to be a major draw for international organisations, global NGOs, diplomats and visitors from around the world.

Vienna has consistently been crowned first in the Mercer global rankings for quality of life. When rated against 450 other cities with living conditions analysed according to 39 factors in ten categories, Vienna has come out top again and again. In a comprehensive analysis covering the political and social environment, economic environment, socio-cultural environment, medical and health considerations, schools and education, public services and transportation, recreation, consumer goods, housing and natural environment, it is Vienna that is rated as the best international capital. This is supported with a number-one world ranking by the *Economist* Intelligence Unit's Global Liveability Index, a number-one world ranking in the Smart City Index and a number-two global ranking by the International Congress and Convention Association. Vienna is also extremely well connected, with 600 daily flights linking the

Austrian capital to 195 cities worldwide. All European routes are within three hours' flying time and it only takes 30 minutes to get from the airport to the centre of town.

The cultural status of Vienna as one of the great world capitals remains a huge draw with the Vienna State Opera, Vienna Philharmonic (including the New Year's concert broadcast to a worldwide audience from the Musikverein), Burgtheater and the Vienna Festival. The Kunsthistorisches Museum, Albertina, Belvedere and many other galleries attract substantial visitor numbers, as do the main tourist attractions: Schönbrunn Palace, the Hofburg palace, St Stephen's Cathedral and a myriad of coffee houses.

While the Habsburgs have left the Austrian stage as a ruling house, family members continue to make a contribution to national life and international relations. Karl, the family head at the time of writing, was an Austrian member of the European Parliament, is Honorary President of the Paneuropean Movement and President of the Blue Shield international organisation to protect the world's cultural heritage from threats such as armed conflict and natural disasters. His brother, Georg Habsburg, is Hungarian ambassador to France, cousin Eduard is the Hungarian ambassador to the Holy See, and Gabriela Habsburg was ambassador of Georgia to Germany.

*

For centuries, Vienna has been a product of different cultures from the different nationalities and faith groups in the Habsburg Empire. In recent decades, people from the former Yugoslavia, Turkey and other EU member states have helped make up just under half of the city's population. Although the most popular surnames in Vienna include traditional Austrian names, like Wagner, Weber, Bauer, Müller and Wolf, they have been joined by many Czech and Slovak names, like Böhm, Swoboda, Horvath, Nowak and Sobotka. Surnames originally from the former Yugoslavia have become more common, including Jovanovic, Vasic, Nikolic, Petrovic and Markovic, while Turkish surnames include Yilmaz, Öztürk, Yildirim, Yildiz and Özdemir. The most successful Viennese sports personality in recent years has been David Alaba, the black Austrian footballer of Nigerian and Philippino heritage, who has excelled for Bayern Munich and the national team. Vienna is, literally, an international capital.

Over the centuries, Vienna established itself as the seat of the Habsburgs, the most powerful dynasty in Europe. The Habsburg Monarchy straddled the heart of Europe, heading both the Holy Roman Empire and ruling territories across central and Eastern Europe. Vienna was the capital of a multinational empire that became the bulwark of European Christendom against the advance of the Muslim Ottoman Empire and was also the greatest musical and cultural capital in the world. After Europe was rocked by the Napoleonic Wars, it was the greatest ever diplomatic gathering at the Congress of Vienna that re-established stability on the continent.

British historian Simon Sebag Montefiore superbly encapsulated the evolution of the city from the 1815 congress onwards: 'Vienna was back and bigger than ever: more imperial, more majestic. A city of composers, conquerors and courtesans, palaces and coffee-houses. But it was about to evolve into something much more.' As the 20th century began, 'the city created the modern age while the Habsburgs headed for extinction and the imperial city became the capital of ideas and the battlefield of extremes. Monarchy versus revolution, fascism versus communism, wild decadence versus Catholic piety. It all happened here in Vienna, the world city.'[64]

Vienna has reinvented itself as a multilateral world city since 1945: the bridge-builder between East and West; a global meeting place for international relations; a neutral place in the heart of Europe. Modern diplomacy began in Vienna, its rules were agreed in Vienna and world leaders regularly attend summits, negotiations and high-level meetings in the Austrian capital. It is the home of more multilateral organisations than any other city in the world. Vienna is the international capital.

# *Epilogue*

> 'We need to preserve Vienna as one of Europe's great capitals.'
>
> – Chancellor Bruno Kreisky

Arriving in the city's gleaming Haupbahnhof, the journey through Vienna's amazing history and international pre-eminence starts immediately outside the main train station. This journey, by foot and U1 underground line, is one that I have regularly made over the decades, never tiring of revisiting and can't recommend more highly. Whether your Interests are history, architecture, art, culture or music, there are few places on Earth with so many first-class locations that allow you to follow in the footsteps of some of the most significant people in history.

The first place to start is at the military history museum next to the station, which marks the centuries of Austria as one of Europe's great powers. Situated in the city's Arsenal complex, its halls showcase the international importance of the Habsburg dynasty and their resident capital. On display is the rich booty left by the Ottoman besiegers of Vienna, and themed collections include the Thirty Years' War to the time of Prince Eugene, followed by the War of the Spanish Succession and Maria Theresa, the Hall of Revolutions, the era of Field Marshal Radetzky and then the Francis Joseph Hall and Sarajevo. Here, the Gräf & Stift automobile that drove Archduke Franz Ferdinand and his wife is on display, complete with bullet holes, next to the glass display case with his blood-stained uniform and the pistol that was used to assassinate the heir to the throne as he was driven through the Bosnian capital, causing the outbreak of the First World War.

Opposite the Arsenal is the beautiful baroque Belvedere Palace, the residence of Franz Ferdinand, and built two centuries previously for the military commander Prince Eugene. It was here that the post-Second World War occupation ended in 1955 and the declaration made from its balcony that 'Austria is free'. Today, the Belvedere houses a world-class art collection, including the best-known works of Gustav Klimt, Egon Schiele, Oskar Kokoschka, Elena Luksch-Makowsky, Helene Funke and Rueland Frueauf the Elder.

The next station on the northbound U1 is Taubstummengasse, my workplace stop for nearly ten years at the Austrian Broadcasting Corporation, which overlooked the Diplomatic Academy in the old Favorita Palace. Adjacent is the embassy district and the Soviet war memorial commemorating the 17,000 Red Army troops that died freeing the city from the Nazis in April 1945.

Next U1 stop is Karlsplatz, the large square with its art nouveau station entrance designed by Otto Wagner, the Secession Building, as well as adjoining architectural masterpieces including Karlskirche and the Musikverein, home of the Vienna Philharmonic Orchestra. From here, a two-minute walk takes you past the Academy of Fine Arts, which twice rejected Adolf Hitler as a student, to the world-famous State Opera House and the Albertina Museum with its 1 million old master prints. Crossing the square with its 'Memorial against War and Fascism', one reaches the Church of the Capuchins and the biggest dynastic crypt anywhere in Europe, where the remains of 145 Habsburgs, including 12 emperors and 18 empresses, lie. They include Otto Habsburg, who died in 2011 aged 97. As son of the Emperor Charles, he was the last crown prince of the dynasty and last living link to Emperor Francis Joseph, with whom he was photographed as a child.

A stone's throw from the crypt is the Hofburg palace: the centre of Habsburg power and main venue for activities at the Congress of Vienna and more recent diplomacy, including the Kennedy–Khruschev summit. Today, the largest palace in Europe is the residence of both the Austrian president and the OSCE, the treasury holding the Crown Jewels of the Holy Roman and Austrian Empires, the

Spanish Riding School and Habsburg state rooms. Immediately next to the palace is the historic Heroes Square and Ringstrasse boulevard, built on the site of the old city walls. Here, the grandest buildings include Vienna City Hall, the Austrian Parliament, Burgtheater, the Art and Natural History Museums and behind them the Museums Quartier, one of the largest extended centres for contemporary art and culture in the world.

Walking towards the city centre through the oversized St Michael's Gate you come to the Roman architectural remains in the middle of the square featured at the beginning of this book, reminding visitors and residents alike of 2,000 years of city history from Vindobona to present-day Vienna. A stroll down the historic thoroughfares of Kohlmarkt and Graben lead to St Stephen's Cathedral and its surrounding narrow streets, which have been home to a legion of historic figures including Wolfgang Amadeus Mozart.

A short walk further north is Schwedenplatz, where the town centre meets the Danube Canal and the oldest church in the city, St Rupert's, which stands close to the main synagogue. From here, the U1 underground takes you further north to Nestroyplatz at the heart of Vienna's Jewish community in the Leopoldstadt district. Here, as in the rest of the city, small brass pavement plates outside houses mark the names of their Jewish residents who were murdered during the Holocaust. Many of Vienna's Jews or their ancestors arrived in the city during Habsburg times at the next U1 stop, Praterstern, which was the terminus for trains from the rest of the empire. Not far from the station stands the Ferris wheel in the Prater park, made famous in the classic movie *The Third Man*.

Staying on the U1, one soon crosses the River Danube, which flows eastwards on its 2,850-kilometre course, passing ten countries, to the Black Sea. The next stop is the Vienna International Centre, the extraterritorial complex that is the third global headquarters of the UN and includes the IAEA. UN staff on higher floors look down onto the site of the Battle of Aspern-Esslingen, where Austria defeated Napoleon, onto the site of the Battle of Wagram, where Austria lost to Napoleon, and towards the Slovakian capital Bratislava and the former Iron Curtain, only 55 kilometres away.

In the space of a 14-minute underground journey, one has travelled across Vienna from the scenes of its great imperial, military and cultural past to its vibrant cosmopolitan, artistic and international present. Vienna has been a key European and global crossroads for centuries and successfully reinvented itself as times changed, while retaining its essential charm and flair. When I first arrived to live and work in Vienna, I looked far and wide for a dedicated account of the city as an international capital and couldn't find one in either German or English. Having spent the subsequent three decades delving into Vienna's past and present, I decided to write it myself.

# Notes

## Introduction

1 Wandruszka, Adam, *The House of Habsburg*, pp. 183–184
2 Taylor, A.J.P., *The Habsburg Monarchy 1809–1918*, p. 12
3 Ingrao, Charles, *The Habsburg Monarchy 1618–1815*, p. 237
4 Churchill, Winston, *The Second World War – The Gathering Storm*, Vol. I, pp. 9–10

## Chapter 1
### From Vindobona to Vienna

1 Tacitus, *Annals*, XII.29.2
2 Aurelius, Marcus, *Meditations*, p. 25
3 *Gladiator*, directed by Ridley Scott, Dreamworks Pictures and Universal Pictures, 2000
4 Brandstätter, Christian, *Stadt Chronik Wien*, p. 61
5 Hinterschweiger, Hubert, *Wien im Mittelalter*, p. 19
6 Eugippius, *The Life of St. Severinus*, p. 52
7 Thompson, E.A., *Romans and Barbarians: The Decline of the Western Empire*, p. 122
8 Eugippius, Ibid., p. 69
9 Ibid., p. 79
10 Pohl, Walter, *Die Welt der Babenberger*
11 Wilson, Peter H., *The Holy Roman Empire*
12 Lechner, Karl, *Die Babenberger – Markgrafen und Herzöge von Österreich 976–1246*
13 Clauss, Martin, *The Oxford Encyclopedia of Medieval Warfare and Military Technology*, Vol. I, p. 552

14 Whitman, Sidney, *Austria – The Story of Nations*, p. 79

15 Montagu, Lady Mary Wortley, *Letters and Works*

16 Kühnel, Harry, *Die Hofburg zu Wien*

17 'Enea Silvio Piccolomini', www.gedaechtnisdeslandes.at

18 Ilgen, Theodore, *Die Geschichte Kaiser Friedrich III von Aeneas Silvius*

19 Wheatcroft, Andrew, *The Enemy at the Gate – Habsburgs, Ottomans and the Battle for Europe*

20 Nagel, Ulrich, *Zwischen Dynastie und Staatsräson – Die habsburgischen Botschafter in Wien und Madrid am Beginn des Dreißigjährigen Krieges*

21 Fetus, Andreas, *Die Reise des kaiserlichen Gesandten David Ungnad nach Konstantinopel im Jahre 1572*

22 Forster, E.S., *The Turkish Letters of Ogier Ghislean de Busbecq*, pp. 91–99

23 Berridge, G.R., *Notes on the Origins of the Diplomatic Corps – Constantinople in the 1620s*, p. 6

24 Pursell, Brennan, *The Winter King – Frederick V of the Palatinare and the Coming of the Thirty Years' War*, pp. 112–113

25 Bellen, E.A., *The Thirty Years War*, Vol. IV, p. 353

26 *Diarium Volmar, 1643–1647*

27 Croxton, D., Tischer, A., *The Peace of Westphalia – A Historical Dictionary*, p. 315

28 *Diarium Lamberg, 1645–1649*

29 Kissinger, Henry, *World Order – Reflections on the Character of Nations and the Course of History*

## Chapter 2
## The Imperial Habsburg Capital

1 Voltaire, *Essai sur l'histoire générale et sur les mœurs et l'esprit des nations*, chapter 70

2 Eder, Franz, and Vocelka, Karl, 'The World of the Habsburgs', www.habsburger.net

3 Trost, Ernst, *Das blieb vom Doppeladler*, p. 360

4 Wilson, Peter, *The Holy Roman Empire*, p. 283

5   Ibid., p. 284

6   *Kayserlicher Und Königlicher Wie auch Ertz-Hertzoglicher Und Dero*, Residentz-Stadt Wien Staats- und Stands- Calender, 1702

7   *Hof- und Staats-Schematismus des österreichischen Kaiserthums*, 1807, p. 177

8   Gschliesser, Oswald von, *Der Reichshofrat – Bedeutung und Verfassung, Schicksal und Besetzung einer obersten Reichsbehörde von 1559 bis 1806*

9   Gross, Lothar, *Die Geschichte der Deutschen Reichhofkanzlei von 1559 bis 1806*, p. 36

10  'Reichskanzleitrakt', See www.geschichtewiki.wien.gv.at

11  Lorenz, Helmut, and Mader-Kratky, Anna, *Die Wiener Hofburg 1705–1835 – Die Kaiserliche Residenz vom Barock bis zum Klassizismus*, pp. 582–590

12  Tietze, Hans, *Berichte und Mitteilungen des Altertums-Vereines zu Wien*, Vol. 50, pp. 23–57

13  Crowne, William, *A true relation of all the remarkable places and passages observed in the travels of the right honourable Thomas Lord Hovvard, Earle of Arundell and Surrey, Primer Earle, and Earle Marshall of England, ambassadour extraordinary to his sacred Majesty Ferdinando the second, emperour of Germanie, anno Domini 1636*, p. 23

14  Keller, K., Scheutz, M., and Tersch, H., *Einmal Weimar – Wien und retour. Johann Sebastian Müller und sein Wienbericht aus dem Jahr 1660*, p. 67

15  Kreutel, Richard Franz, *Im Reiche des goldenen Apfels*, p. 190

16  Lewis, Bernard, *The Muslim Discovery of Europe*, p. 112

17  Evliyâ, *Seyahatnâme*, Vol. 7, 61a

18  Ibid.

19  See Lewis, Ibid., p.113

20  Ibid.

21  Schreiner, Stefan, *Die Osmanen in Europa – Erinnerungen und Berichte türkischer Geschichtsschreiber*, p. 196

22  Macartney, C.A., (ed.), *The Habsburg and Hohenzollern Dynasties in the Seventeenth and Eighteenth Centuries*, p. 58

23 Ibid.

24 Ibid., p. 62

25 Henderson, Nicholas, *Prince Eugen of Savoy*, p. ix

26 Ibid., p. 267

27 Rousseau, J.B., *Lettres de Rousseau*, pp. 98–99

28 Melman, Billie, *Women's Orients – English Women and the Middle East 1718–1918*

29 Montagu, Lady Mary Wortley, *Letters and Works*, Vol. I, pp. 235–236

30 Ibid.

31 Ibid., p. 238

32 Kuefstein, Karl Graf, *Studien zur Familiengeschichte*, Vol. IV, p. 150

33 Montagu, Ibid., p. 240

34 Ibid., p. 241

35 Ibid., p. 242

36 Ibid., p. 244

37 Ibid., p. 246

38 See Möckl, Karl, *Hof und Hofgesellschaft in den deutschen Staaten im 19. und beginnenden 20. Jahrhundert*, pp. 24–25

39 Blum, Stella, *Fashions of the Hapsburg Era – Austria-Hungary*

40 Mutschlechner, Martin, 'Eine Frage der Ehre – die Botschafter-audienz'

41 Levetus, Amelia Sarah, *Imperial Vienna – An Account of Its History, Traditions and Arts*, p. 154

## Chapter 3
### The Empire Strikes Back

1 Crankshaw, Edward, *Maria Theresa*, p. 21

2 Kleisner, Tomáš, *Coins and medals of the emperor Francis Stephen of Lorraine*, p. 76

3 Macartney, C.A. (ed.), *The Habsburg and Hohenzollern Dynasties in the Seventeenth and Eighteenth Centuries*, p. 97

4 Browning, Reed, *The War of Austrian Succession*, p. 44

5 Coxe, William, *The House of Austria*, Vol. III, p. 259

6   Mahan, J. Alexander, *Maria Theresa of Austria*, p. 230

7   Macartney, Ibid., p. 118

8   Worthington, David, *Scots in Hapsburg Service, 1618–1648*, pp. 153–288

9   Burke, Edmund (ed.), *Annual Register, for 1766*, p. 80

10  General O'Kelly, Field Marshal Conal Count O'Donel, Lieutenant-General Philip Georg von Browne, Feldzeugmeister Johann Sigismund Count Macquire von Inniskillin, General McElligott and Major General Thomas von Plunkett

11  Burke, Ibid, p. 80

12  *The Wild Geese in Austria – Irish Soldiers and Civilians in the Habsburg Service 1618–1918*

13  Crankshaw, Ibid., p. 271

14  Duffy, Christopher, *The Wild Goose and the Eagle – A Life of Marshal von Browne 1705–1757*, p. 87

15  Mutschlechner, Martin, 'Maria Theresa in the eyes of her contemporaries', www.habsburger.net

16  McGuigan, Dorothy Gies, *The Habsburgs*, p. 248

17  Crankshaw, Ibid., p. 252

18  Eisen, Cliff, and Keefe, Simon P. (eds), *The Cambridge Mozart Encyclopedia*, p. 268, letter dated 12 December 1771

19  Coxe, Ibid., p. 363

20  Carlyle, Thomas, *History of Friedrich II of Prussia*, Vol. V, p. 252

21  Ibid., p. 258

22  Mutschlechner, Martin, 'Old times, new times – The coronation of Joseph II in Frankfurt', www.habsburger.net

23  Goethe, Johann Wolfgang, *Truth and Poetry From my Own Life – The Autobiography of Goethe*, Vol. I, p. 169

24  Ibid., p. 172

25  Mutschlechner, Martin, 'Joseph II: The long-awaited son. World of the Habsburgs', www.habsburger.net

26  Beales, Derek, *Joseph II – Against the World, 1780–1790*

27  Vehse, Karl Eduard, *Memoires of the Court and Aristocracy of Austria*, Vol. II, p. 314

28  Padover, Saul, *The Revolutionary Emperor Joseph the Second*, p. 120

29  Wraxall, Nathanial, *Memoirs of the Courts of Berlin, Dresden, Warsaw and Vienna*, pp. 457–458

30  Reiners, Ludwig, *Frederick the Great: A Biography*, pp. 247–248

31  Ibid., p. 453

32  Rady, Martyn, *The Habsburgs – The Rise and Fall of a World Power*, p. 185

33  Beales, Derek, *Joseph II – In the Shadow of Maria Theresa 1741–1780*, Vol. I, p. 154

34  Burney, Charles, *The present state of music in Germany, the Netherlands, and United Provinces*, Vol. I, pp. 204–205

35  Ibid., p. 364

36  Duffy, Christopher, *The Army of Maria Theresa – The Armed Forces of Imperial Austria 1740–1780*, p. 13

37  Ibid., p. 25

38  Ligne, Prince de, *Mélanges militaires, littéraires et sentimentales*, Vol. I, p. 156

39  Swinburne, Henry, *The Courts of Europe at the Close of the Last Century*, Vol. I, pp. 354–355

40  Ibid., p. 345

41  *Dictionary of National Biography, 1885–1900*, Vol. 55, p. 239

42  Keith to Stormont, 29 November 1780, PRO SP 80/223

43  Dell'Orto, U., *La nunziatura a Vienna di Giuseppe Garampi (1776–1785)*, pp. 244–245

44  Beales, Derek, *Enlightenment and Reform in Eighteenth Century Europe*, p. 258

45  Arneth, A. Ritter von, *Joseph II und Leopold II von Toscana – Ihr Briefwechsel von 1781 bis 1790*, Vol. I, p. 82 (quote translated by Beales)

46  Keith, Sir Robert, *The Romance of Diplomacy*, pp. 152–153

47  Ibid., p. 154

48  Beales, Derek, *Joseph II – Against the World, 1780–1790*, pp. 229–231

49  Ibid., p. 238

50  Ibid., p. 341

51  Ibid., p. 447

52  Ibid., p. 521
53  Smith, Gillespie, *Memoirs and correspondence of Sir Robert Murray Keith, K.B., envoy extraordinary and minister plenipotentiary at the courts of Dresden, Copenhagen, and Vienna, from 1769–1792*, p. 209
54  Ibid., p. 217
55  Abert, Hermann, *W.A. Mozart*
56  From correspondence by Joseph von Sonnenfels quoted in Radlecker, Kurt, *Gottfried von Swieten – Eine Biographie*, p. 9
57  Burrows, Donald, *Händel-Jb*, 47, p. 192
58  Braunbehrens, Volkmar, *Mozart in Vienna 1781–1791*, p. 318
59  Volek, Tomislav, *Mozart Studien*, Vol. 25, p. 203
60  Anderson, Emily, *The Letters of Mozart and His Family*, p. 800
61  Griesinger, Georg August, *Biographische Notizen über Joseph Haydn*, p. 67
62  Jahn, Otto, *Life of Mozart*, Vol. 2, p. 291
63  Ibid., p. 287, footnote 51
64  Süleyman, İzzî: *Tarih-i İzzi*, p. 190
65  Gutman, Robert, *Mozart – A Cultural Biography*
66  Rosen, Charles, *The Classical Style*, p. 370
67  Schindler, Anton, *Beethoven As I Knew Him*, p. 49
68  See McLean, George F., Magliola, Robert R., Fox, William (eds), *Democracy: In the Throes of Liberalism and Totalitarianism*, p. 71

## Chapter 4
### Revolting French and Napoleon

1  McGuigan, Dorothy Gies, *The Habsburgs*, p. 273
2  Stewart, John Hall, *A Documentary Survey of the French Revolution*, pp. 221–223
3  Saint-Amand, Imbert de, *Marie Antoinette and the Downfall of Royalty*, p. 26
4  Schroeder, Paul, *The Transformation of European Politics, 1763–1848*, p. 64
5  Saint-Amand, Ibid., p. 127
6  Mansel, Philip, *Prince of Europe – The Life of Charles-Joseph de Ligne*, p. 204

7    Minto, Countess Emma Elliot-Murray-Kynynmound, *Life and Letters of Sir Gilbert Elliot – First Earl of Minto from 1751–1806*, Vol. III, p. 120

8    Robbins, Landon, *H.C. Haydn: Missa in angustiis (Nelson Mass)*, CD notes p. 7

9    Richter, Joseph, *Der wiederaufgelebte Eipeldauer: mit Noten von einem Wiener*, p. 13

10   Minto, Ibid., p. 147

11   Pichler, Karoline, *Denkwürdigkeiten aus meinem Leben 1769–1843*, Vol. I, p. 276

12   Ibid., pp. 277–278

13   *Cobbett's Political Register*, Vol. IX, No. 5, 1 February 1806, p. 156

14   Wilson, Peter, *The Holy Roman Empire – A Thousand Years of Europe's History*, p. 654

15   Ries, Ferdinand, *Biographische Notizen über Ludwig van Beethoven*, p. 121

16   Alison, Archibald, *History of Europe During the French Revolution*, Vol. VII, p. 304

17   Bassett, Richard, *For God and Kaiser – The Imperial Austrian Army*, p. 256

18   Marbot, Jean-Baptiste-Antoine-Marcelin, Baron de, *The memoirs of Baron de Marbot, late lieutenant-general in the French army*, p. 343

19   Rothenberg, G.E., *Military Affairs*, Vol. 37, p. 3

20   Castle, Ian, *Aspern and Wagram 1809 – Mighty Clash of Empires*, p. 88

21   Marbot, Ibid., p. 400

22   Seidl, Jakob, *Monatsblatt des Vereines für Geschichte der Stadt Wien*, Vol. XVII (52), p. 49

23   *The Gentleman's Magazine*, November 1809, Vol. 79, Part 2, p. 1065

24   Saint-Amand, Imbert de, *The Happy Days of Empress Marie Louise*, p. 86

25   Ibid.

26 Herold, Stephen, 'The Austrian Auxiliary Corps in Russia in 1812', http://www.antiquesatoz.com/habsburg/1812/

## Chapter 5
### The Glorious Moment: The Congress of Vienna

1 Ehrlich, Anna, and Bauer, Christa, *Der Wiener Kongress – Diplomaten, Irrigen und Skandale*, p. 136

2 King, David, *Vienna 1814 – How the Conquerers of Napoleon Made Love, War and Peace at the Congress of Vienna*, p. 2

3 La Garde-Chambonas, Count Auguste, *Anecdotal Recollections of the Congress of Vienna*, p. 137

4 Morritt, John, *The Letters of John Morritt of Rokeby*, p. 35

5 Bew, John, *Castlereagh – A Life*, p. 374

6 Schneider, K., Werner, E.M., Mazohl, B., *Europa in Wien – Who is Who beim Wiener Kongress 1814/15*, p. 49

7 Erickson, Raymond, *Schubert's Vienna*, p. 244

8 Stevenson, Struan, *The Course of History*, p. 77

9 Thürheim, Ludovika Gräfin von, *Mein Leben – Erinnerungen aus Österreichs grosser Welt*, p. 107

10 Schönfeld, Friedrich von, *Traditionen zur Charakteristik Oesterreichs, seines Staats- und Volkslebens unter Franz dem Ersten: Band 2*, p. 114

11 HHStA, OMeA 1814, Nr. 451

12 La Garde-Chambonas, Count Auguste, *Anecdotal Recollections of the Congress of Vienna*, p. 209

13 Ibid., p. 68

14 *Hof- und Staats- Schematismus des österreichischen Kaiserthums*, p. 227

15 Fournier, August, *Die Geheimpolizei auf dem Wiener Kongress*, p. 261

16 Günzel, Klaus, *Der Wiener Kongress – Geschichte und Geschichten eines Welttheaters*, p. 116

17 Dallas, Gregor, *1815 – The Roads to Waterloo*, p. 205

18 Pichler, Caroline, *Denkwürdigkeiten aus meinem Leben*, Vol. II, p. 31

19  *Der glorreiche Augenblick*, Op. 136. Text: Aloys Weissenbach (1766–1821). English translation: Keith Anderson

20  Goldschmidt, Harry, *Beethoven, Werkeinführungen*, p. 49

21  Ehrlich and Bauer, Ibid., p. 170

22  See Jackson, Sir George, *The Bath Archives: A further selection from The Diaries and Letters of Sir George Jackson from 1806–1816*, Vol. II, p. 467

23  Eynard, Jean Gabriel, *Au Congrès de Vienna*, p. 45

24  Musulin, Stella, *Vienna in the Age of Metternich – From Napoleon to Revolution 1805–1848*, p. 56

25  See http://www.wiener-kongress.info/files/wiener_kongress_delegierte.pdf

26  McGuigan, Dorothy Gies, *Metternich and the Duchess*, cover notes

27  Gentz, Friedrich von, *Tagebücher*, p. 352

28  Adams, John Quincy, *Writings*, Vol. II, p. 463

29  Ehrlich and Bauer, Ibid., p. 86

30  Andrew Roberts reviews *Talleyrand: Betrayer and Saviour of France*, by Robin Harris, *Daily Telegraph*, 25 February 2007

31  Klinkowström, Carl, *Memoirs of Prince Metternich*, Vol. II, No. 125, p. 285

32  Stevenson, Ibid.

33  Oberzaucher-Schüller, Gunhild, *Emilia Bigottini – die Etoile des Wiener Kongresses*, www.tanz.at

34  Memoir of the Prince de Ligne, p. 284

35  Tweddell, John, *Correspondence*, p. 77

36  Jackson, Ibid., p. 27

37  La Garde-Chambonas, Ibid., p. 205

38  Fournier, August, *Die Geheimpolizei auf dem Wiener Kongress – Eine Auswahl aus ihren Papieren*, p. 469

39  Feurzeig, Lisa, and Sienicki, John (eds), *Quodlibets of the Viennese Theater*, p. xv

40  La Garde-Chambonas, Ibid., p. 151

41  Ibid., p. 342

42  Zamoyski, Adam, *Rites of Peace – The Fall of Napoleon and the Congress of Vienna*, p. 482

43  Spiel, Hilde, *The Congress of Vienna*, p. 244

44  Berthuch, Carl, *Bertuchs Tagebuch vom Wiener Kongress*, p. 245

45  Spiel, Hilde, *Fanny von Arnstein – A Daughter of the Enlightenment 1758–1818*, p. 292

46  Sebag Montefiore, Simon, *Romanovs*, footnote 106

47  King, Ibid., p. 32

48  Nostitz, Carl von, *Leben und Briefwechsel*, p. 144

49  Christopher, Andrew, *The Secret World – A History of Intelligence*

50  Fournier, Ibid., p. 242

51  Gentz, Friedrich von, *Tagebücher*, p. 351

52  Mce, Charles, *Seven fateful moments when great men met to change the world*

53  Corti, Egon, *Metternich und die Frauen*, Vol. I, p. 471, 19 September 1814

54  Jackson, Ibid., p. 45

55  Kissinger, Henry, *A World Restored: Metternich, Castlereagh and the Problems of Peace 1812–1822*, p. 149

56  Nicolson, Harry, *The Congress of Vienna – A Study of Allied Unity 1812–1822*, p. 158

57  Gill, A.A., *The Sunday Times*, 14 February 2010. Quoted in Bew, John, *Castlereagh – A Life*, p. XII

58  *Hansard*, Vol. 32, 1 February to 6 March 1816, pp. 71–72

59  Zamoyski, Ibid., p. 550

60  Napoleon, *Lettres Inédites de Napoleon Ier*, Vol. II, p. 60–61

61  Sunders, Edith, *The Hundred Days*, p. 52

62  Cornwall, Bernhard, *Waterloo – The History of Four Days, Three Armies and Three Battles*

63  Creevey, Thomas, *The Creevey Papers*, p. 236

64  King, Ibid., pp. 322–323

## Chapter 6
### The Concert of Europe: The Age of Metternich

1  Musulin, Stella, *Vienna in the Age of Metternich – From Napoleon to Revolution 1805–1848*

2   Sealsfield, Charles, *Austria as it is; or, Sketches of continental courts, by an Eyewitness*, p. 150

3   Wellesley, F.A., *The Diary and Correspondence of Henry Wellesley, First Lord Cowley 1790–1846*, diary entry on 27 August 1822, p. 101

4   Sealsfield, Ibid., p. 153

5   Wellesley, Ibid., undated note on Metternich, p. 195

6   Günzel, Klaus, *Der Wiener Kongress*, p. 124

7   Sealsfield, Ibid., pp. 194–195

8   Lansdale, Marie Hornor, *Vienna and the Viennese*, p. 2

9   Stiles, William Henry, *Austria in 1848–49*, pp. 87–88

10  Wilmot, Martha, *More Letters from Martha Wilmot – Impressions of Vienna 1821–1829*, letter of 8 December 1819, p. 38

11  Stratton, Stephen Samuel, *Nicolo Paganini – His Life and Work*, p. 23

12  'Berlioz in Germany and Central Europe – Vienna', www.hberlioz.com/Germany/vienna.htm

13  Ibid.

14  Wilmot, Ibid.

15  Ibid., letter of 23 May 1820, p. 65

16  Ibid., letter of 4 May 1820, p. 61

17  Ibid., letter of 26 September 1825, p. 223

18  'Characters in the Grand Fancy Dress Ball given by the British Ambassador Sir Henry Wellesley at Vienna at the conclusion of the Carnival 1826; in thirteen highly coloured Plates, with a Description of the Entertainment on that Occasion', London, 1827

19  Wertheimer, Eduard von, *The Duke of Reichstadt (Napoleon II) : a biography compiled from new sources of information*

20  Napoleon, *Correspondance de Napoleon*, Vol. XXVII, letter to his brother Joseph, 8 February 1814, p. 133

21  Aubry, Octave, *Napoleon II, The King of Rome, 'L'Aiglon'*, p. 205

22  Castelot, André, *King of Rome – A Biography of Napoleon's Tragic Son*, p. 357

23  Kaiser, Gloria, 'Leopoldine (1797–1826)', www.habsburger.net

24  Ibid., 'A Masterpiece of Diplomacy'

25  Andlaw, Franz Freiherrn von, *Mein Tagebuch – Auszüge aus Aufzeichnungen der Jahre 1811 bis 1861*, p. 138

26  Vehse, Karl Eduard, *Memoirs of the Court, Aristocracy and Diplomacy of Austria*, Vol. II, p. 470

27  Ibid., p. 471

28  Mutschlechner, Martin, 'The "good emperor Franz" and his hatchet man', www.habsburger.net

29  Trollope, Frances Milton, *Vienna and the Austrians*, Vol. II, p. 9

30  Ibid., Vol. I, p. 372

31  Ibid., Vol. II, pp. 162–165.

32  Scarisbrick, Diana, *Margaret de Flahaut (1788–1867) – A Scotswoman at the French Court*

33  Bernady, Françoise de, *Son of Talleyrand – The Life of Comte Charles de Flahaut 1785–1870*, p. 227

34  Ibid., p. 234

35  Usedom, Karl Ludwig Guido von, *Politische Briefe und Charakteristiken aus der deutschen Gegenwart*, p. 69.

36  Bérenger, Jean, *The Habsburg Empire 1700–1918*, p. 166

37  Bideleux, Robert, *A History of Eastern Europe – Crisis and Change*, p. 215

38  Stiles, Ibid.

39  Garrity, Patrick, 'Austria in 1848–9 by William H. Stiles', *Classics of Strategy and Diplomacy*

40  Smith IV, Miles, *American Nineteenth Century History*, Vol. 14, No. 1, pp. 27–51

41  Department of State Reports: Austria, NA, Vol. 2, No. 21, 17 January 1848

42  Ibid., No. 13, 13 March 1848

43  Rath, John, *The Southwestern Social Science Quarterly*, Vol. 34, No. 2, pp. 3–20

44  Stiles, William Henry, *Austria in 1848–9*, Vol. II, p. 404

45  Ibid., p. 405

46  Politisches Archiv, XXXII, Vereinigte Staaten Karton 11, Haus-, Hof- und Staatsarchiv, Vienna

47  Sked, Alan, *Radetzky – Imperial Victor and Military Genius*, p. 217

48  Stiles, Ibid., p. 406

49  61st Congress, 2nd Session, Senate Documents No. 279, Affairs of Hungary, 1849–50

50  Roberts, Ian, *Nicholas I and the Russian Intervention in Hungary*, p. 139

51  Szilassy, Sándor, *The Slavonic and East European Review*, Vol. 44, No. 102, p. 187

52  *Hansard*, 3rd Series, CVII, 808–815, 21 July 1848

## Chapter 7
### The Longest Reign

1   Schubert, Peter, *Beruf Kaiser. Geschichte der Familie Habsburg für junge Leser*

2   Palmer, Alan, *Twilight of the Habsburgs*, p. 54

3   Schroeder, Paul, *Austria, Great Britain, and the Crimean War: The Destruction of the European Concert*

4   Schroeder, Paul, *The Journal of Modern History*, Vol. 40, No. 2, 1968, pp. 193–217

5   Scharding, Carlo, *Das Schicksal der Kaiserin Elisabeth*

6   Meyendorff, Peter von, *Ein russischer Diplomat an den Höfen von Berlin und Wien. Briefwechsel 1826–1863*, Vol. III, p. 145

7   *The Times*, 26 April 1854, p. 9

8   Tschudy von Glarus, Johann Jakob, *Illustriertes Gedenkbuch*, p. 28

9   Scharding, Ibid.

10  Hamann, Brigitte, *Elisabeth – Kaiserin wider Willen*, p. 65

11  Taylor, A.J.P., *The Habsburg Monarchy 1809–1918*, p. 99–100

12  Schroeder, Ibid., p. 425

13  See Hall, Thomas, *Planning Europe's Capital Cities – Aspects of Nineteenth Century Urban Development*, pp. 172–173

14  Mutschlechner, Martin, 'The Italians and the Habsburg Monarchy', www.habsburger.net

15  Hübner, Joseph Alexander, *Neun Jahre der Erinnerungen eines*

österreichischen Botschafters in Paris unter dem zweiten Kaiserreich 1851–1859, p. 150

16 Dunant, Henry, *The Origin of the Red Cross – 'Un souvenir de Solferino'*, pp. 7–8

17 Palmer, Alan, *Twilight of the Habsburgs*, p. 110

18 Haslip, Joan, *The Lonely Empress – Elizabeth of Austria*, p. 151

19 Weiss, David, and Schilddorfer, Gerd, *Die Novara – Österreichs Traum von der Weltmacht*

20 *Te ao Hou The New World*, Issue 24, October 1958

21 *Frank Leslie's Illustrated Newspaper*, 31 March 1860

22 *Te ao Hou The New World*, Ibid.

23 *Te ao Hou The New World*, Issue 25, December 1958

24 Biddle, Donna-Lee, 'Postmaster, sailor, freedom fighter – The man behind Waikato's first newspaper', www.stuff.co.nz

25 Palmer, Alan, *Twilight of the Habsburgs – The Life and Times of Emperor Francis Joseph*, p. 131

26 Murphy, William Walton, *Report of US Consul General to Frankfurt to Secretary of State Seward*, No. 83, 21 August 1863

27 Rowland, Buford, and Easton, J.C., *The Journal of Modern History*, Vol. 14, No. 4, pp. 480–499

28 Redlich, Joseph, *Emperor Francis Joseph of Austria – A Biography*, p. 321

29 Kiste, John van der, *Windsor and Habsburg – The British and Austrian Reigning Houses 1848–1922*, p. 54

30 La Marmora, Alfonso, *Un Po' Più Di Luce Sugli Eventi Politici E Militari Dell' Anno 1866*, p. 30

31 Rothfels, Hans, *Bismarck-Briefe*, p. 320

32 Wawro, Geoffrey, *The Austro-Prussian War – Austria's War with Prussia and Italy in 1866*, p.73

33 Petersdorff, Hermann von, *Otto von Bismarck, Reden 1847–1869*, pp. 139–140

34 Moltke, Helmut von, 'Memorandum on the Possible War between Prussia and Austria (1866)', http://ghdi.ghi-dc.org

35 Rothenberg, Gunther, *The Army of Francis Joseph*, p. 70

36 Craig, Gordon A., *The Battle of Königgrätz*, p. 166

37  Stoffel, Oberst Baron von, *Militärische Berichte erstattet aus Berlin 1866–1870*, p. 2

38  Wawro, Ibid., p. 296

39  Gillespie-Addison, A.D., *The Strategy of the Seven Weeks War*, p. 37

40  Motley, John Lothrop: *The Correspondence of John Lothrop Motley*, Vol. II, p. 160

41  Ibid., pp. 166–167

42  Ibid., p. 237

43  Ibid., p. 341

44  Owens, Karen, *Franz Joseph and Elisabeth – The Last Great Monarchs of Austria-Hungary*, p. 121

45  *The Times*, 12 June 1867, p. 9

46  Palmer, Alan, *Twilight of the Habsburgs*, p. 159

47  Haslip, Joan: *Imperial Adventurer – Emperor Maximilian of Mexico*, p. 498

48  Ibid., pp. 506–507

## Chapter 8
### Nervous Splendour: Fin de Siècle

1  Johnson, Julie, 'Museums and Material Culture in Vienna – A Comment', p. 89

2  Chushichi and Young, *Japan Rising – The Iwakura Embassy to the USA and Europe 1871–73*, p. xxviii

3  Ibid.

4  Ibid., pp. 417–418

5  Ibid., p. 422

6  Ibid., p. 432

7  Allwood, John, *The Great Exhibitions*, p. 50

8  Findling, John, *Historical Dictionary of World's Fairs and Expositions 1851–1988*, p. 53

9  Allwood, Ibid., p. 50

10  *Internationale Austellungs Zeitung* – A supplement of the *Neue Frei Presse* that was published daily from 2 May until 1 November 1873

11  Reports on the Universal Exhibition of 1873. See appendix by H.C. Sweny

12  Albertini, Luigi, *The Origins of the War of 1914*, Vol. I, p. 4

13  'The Three Emperors' League, 18 June 1881', www.wwi.lib.byn. edu.

14  Taylor, A.J.P., *The Struggle for the Mastery of Europe 1848–1918*, p. 221

15  Rupp, George Hoover, *A Wavering Friendship: Russia and Austria 1876–1878*, p. 39

16  Baker, Susan, *The Shadow*, p. 10

17  Treaty between Great Britain, Austria-Hungary, France, Germany, Italy, Russia and Turkey, 13 July 1878, https://www.dipublico. org/100517/treaty-between-great-britain-austria-hungary france-germany-italy-russia-and-turkey-berlin-july-13-1878

18  Flotow, Ludwig, Freiherr von, *November 1918 auf dem Ballhausplatz*, p. 213

19  Albertini, Luigi, *The Origins of the War of 1914: European relations from the Congress of Berlin to the eve of the Sarajevo murder*, pp. 33–34

20  Pribram, Alfred, *Austro-Hungarian Monarchy – The Secret Treaties of Austria–Hungary 1879–1914*, pp. 50–52

21  Hort, Jakob, *Architektur der Diplomatie*, p. 382

22  Rumbold, Sir Horace, *Final Recollections of a Diplomatist*, p. 266

23  Paget, Ibid., Vol. II, p. 359

24  Schweinitz to Bismarck, 10 June 1875

25  Lewin, André, *Die Französische Botschaft in Wien*

26  King, Greg, and Wilson, Penny, *Twilight of Empire – The Tragedy at Mayerling and the End of the Habsburgs*, p. 37

27  Dekker, Erwin, *The Viennese Students of Civilisation*, p. 54

28  Szeps-Zuckerkandl, Berta, *I Lived Fifty Years of World History*, pp. 135–138

29  Paget, Lady Walburga, *Embassies Other Days*, Vol. II, p. 46

30  King and Wilson, Ibid., p. 51

31  Salvendy, John, *Royal Rebel – A Psychological Portrait of Crown Prince Rudolph of Austria Hungary*, p. 89

32  Ibid., p. 151

33  Stephanie, Princess of Belgium, Archduchess of Austria-Hungary, *I Was to Be Empress*, p. 256

34  Hough, Richard (ed.), *Advice to my Granddaughter – Letters from Queen Victoria to Princess Victoria of Battenberg*, pp. 87–99

35  King and Wilson, Ibid., p. 128

36  Monts, Graf Anton von, *Erinnerungen und Gedanken des Botschafters Anton Graf Monts*, p. 105

37  King and Wilson, Ibid.

38  McGuigan, Doris Gies, *The Habsburgs*, p. 368

39  *Chicago Tribune*, 31 January 1889, p. 1

40  *Glasgow Herald*, 2 February 1889, p. 9

41  Ponsonby, Frederick (ed.), *Letters of the Empress Frederick*, p. 370

42  Paget, Ibid., Vol. II, p. 470

43  See https://web.archive.org/web/20150731165412/http://www.onb.ac.at/services/presse_23385.htm

44  Hamann, Brigitte, *Rudolf – Kronprinz und Rebell*, p. 458

45  See Hantsch, Hugo, and Novotny, Alexander (eds.), *Festschrift für Heinrich Benedikt*, p. 140

46  Hamann, Brigitte, *Crown Prince and Rebel*, p. xvi

47  Dawson, Brigadier-General Sir Douglas, *A Soldier-Diplomat*, p. 131

48  Hitler, Adolf, *Mein Kampf*, p. 55

49  Zweig, Stefan, *Die Welt von Gestern*, p. 58

50  Field, Geoffrey G., *Evangelist of Race – The Germanic Vision of Houston Stewart Chamberlain*, p. 436

51  Ibid., p. 437

52  Bermbach, Udo, *Houston Stewart Chamberlain – Wagners Schwiegersohn – Hitlers Vordenker*, p. 509

53  Schorske, Carl, *Fin-De-Siècle Vienna: Politics and Culture*, p. xviii

54  Ibid., p. 212

55  Rauchensteiner, Manfried, *Der Tod des Doppeladlers – Österreich-Ungarn und der Erste Weltkrieg*, p. 199

56  Herzl, Theodor, *The Complete Diaries of Theodor Herzl*, Vol. 1, p. 7

57  Herzl, Theodor, *A State of the Jews*, p. 5

58  Ibid., p. 102

59  Klinger, Jerry, 'Reverend William Hechler – The Christian minister who legitimised Theodor Herzl'

60  Elon, Amos, *Herzl*, pp. 400–401

61  The Declaration of the Establishment of the State of Israel. See www.mfa.gov.il

62  Suttner, Bertha von, *High Life: Gesammelte Schriften*, Vol. 1, Heinrichs, 1886, p. 210

63  Suttner, Ibid, p. 121

64  Kempf, Beatrix, *Suffragette for Peace – The Life of Bertha Von Suttner*, p. 27

65  Ibid., pp. 26–27

66  Hamann, Brigitte, *Bertha von Suttner – Ein Leben für den Frieden*

67  Paget, Ibid., Vol. II, p. 455

68  Paget, Lady Walpurga, *Scenes and Memories*, p. 228

69  Grant, Julia Dent, *My Life Here and There*, p. 124

70  Ibid., pp. 128–129

71  Twain, Mark, *Harper's New Monthly Magazine*, Vol. 96, pp. 530–540

72  Rumbold, Sir Horace, *Final Recollections of a Diplomatist*, p. 317

73  Owens, Karen, *Franz Joseph and Elisabeth: The Last Great Monarchs of Austria-Hungary*, p.153

## Chapter 9
## Waltzing to War

1  https://www.kraus.wienbibliothek.at/content/die-lage-ist-hoff nungslos-aber-nicht-ernst

2  Private Correspondence between Szécsen and Gołuchowski, Haus-, Hof- und Staatsarchiv Wien, PA XXIX, Karton 18, 6 July 1900, p. 163

3  Sondhaus, Lawrence, *The Naval Policy of Austria-Hungary, 1867–1918 – Navalism, Industrial Development, and the Politics of Dualism*, p. 140

4  Kronenbitter, Günther, *Krieg im Frieden – Die Führung der k.*

*u. k. Armee und die Grossmachtpolitik Österreich-Ungarns 1906–1914*, p. 236

5 Hadley, Tim, *Military Diplomacy in the Dual Alliance – German Military Attaché Reporting from Vienna, 1879–1914*, p. 209

6 Kubizek, August, *The Young Hitler I Knew*, p. 162

7 Hamann, Brigitte, *Hitler's Vienna – A Dictator's Apprenticeship*, p. 107

8 Kubizek, Ibid., p. 189

9 Loos, Adolf, 'Sämtliche Schriften', Vol. I

10 Huss, Pierre J., *Heil! And Farewell*, pp. 19–20

11 *Chicago Sunday Tribune*, 4 March 1906

12 Fugger, Nora Fürstin, *Im Glanz der Kaiserzeit*

13 Broucek, Peter (ed.), *Ein General im Zwielicht – Die Erinnerungen Edmund Glaises von Horstenau*, p. 160

14 *The Daily Tribune*, 7 January 1903

15 *Los Angeles Times*, 4 March 1906

16 Zweig, Stefan, *Die Welt von Gestern – Erinnerung eines Europäers*, p. 241

17 Moritz, Verena, and Leidinger, Hannes, *Oberst Redl – Der Spionagefall, der Skandal, die Fakten*

18 Budanovic, Nikola, *Colonel Redl: The Spy Who Destroyed the Austro-Hungarian Empire*, War History Online

19 Olgin. M., 'Biographical Notes' in Trotsky, L.D., *Our Revolution*, pp.18–19

20 Garvi, Petr, *Vospominaniia – Peterburg*, p. 6

21 Trotsky, Leon, *My Life*, p. 161

22 Ibid., p. 162

23 Kun, Miklós, *Stalin – An Unknown Portrait*, p. 156

24 Ibid., p. 157

25 Sebag Montefiore, Simon, *Young Stalin*

26 Service, Robert, *Lenin – A Biography*, p. 224

27 Letter from Vladimir Lenin to Maxim Gorky, *Lenin Collected Works*, Vol. 35, p. 77

28 Evans, Richard J., *The Pursuit of Power*

29 Dedijer, Vladimir, *Tito*, pp. 30–31

30 Clark, Christopher, *Month of Madness*, BBC Radio 4, 25 June 2014

31 Bunsen, Bertha de: 'The Vienna Diary of Bertha de Bunsen 28 June–17 August 1914', *Bulletin of the Institute of Historical Research*, Volume LI, entry 15 July 1914

32 Gooch and Temperley, *British Documents on the Origins of the War, 1898–1914*, HMSO 1926–1938, telegrams from Bunsen to Grey 26–29 July 1914

33 Grey, Viscount of Falloden, *Twenty Five Years 1892–1916*, p. 20

34 1914/2014 'Erste Kriegsopfer waren zwei österreichische Zivilisten', Austria Presse Agentur APA, 24 January 2014

35 See Afflerbach, Holger, and Stevenson, David (eds), *An Improbable War: The Outbreak of World War I and European Political Culture Before 1914*, p. 7

36 O'Connor, Martin, *Air Aces of the Austro-Hungarian Empire, 1914–1918*, p. 258

37 Rothenberg, Gunther, *The Army of Francis Joseph*, p. 128

38 Deák, István, *Der k.(u.)k. Offizier 1848–1914*, pp. 219–221

39 Bassett, Richard, *For God and Kaiser – The Imperial Austrian Army*, p. 459

40 Cramon, August von, *Unser Oestereichisch-Ungarische Bundesgenosse im Weltkrieg*, p. 20

41 Dedijer, Vladimir, *Tito*, p. 33

42 Watson, Alexander, *The Fortress – The Great Siege of Przemyśl*, p. 428

43 Rothenberg, Gunther, Ibid., p. 185

44 See Herwig, Holger, *The First World War – Germany and Austria-Hungary*, pp. 143–144

45 Watson, Alexander, Ibid., p. 117

46 Holzer, Anton, *Das Lächeln der Henker – Der unbekannte Krieg gegen die Zivilbevölkerung 1914–1918*, p. 12

47 Foley, Robert T., *German strategy and the path to Verdun – Erich von Falkenhayn and the development of attrition, 1870–1916*, p. 129

48 Zohar, Gil Stern, 'Been there: A forgotten time', *Jerusalem Post*, 27 August 2010

49 Tunstall, Graydon, *The Historian*, 70 (1), p. 52

50 Bednar, Kurt, *Der Papier Krieg zwischen Washington und Wien 1917/18*

51 Lansing, Robert, *War Memoirs of Robert Lansing*, pp. 66–67

52 Bednar, Ibid., p. 45

53 House Papers, Box 178, Folder 1–4, Yale University, New Haven

54 Bednar, Ibid., p. 41

55 'St Stephen scene of splendor at Franz Joseph's funeral', *New York Times*, 1 December 1916

56 Haider, Edgard, *Wien 1918 – Agonie der Kaiserstadt*, pp. 80–81

57 Healy, Maureen, *Vienna and the Fall of the Habsburg Empire*, p. 31

58 See www.presidency.ucsb.edu

59 David Lloyd George's address before the Trade Union Conference at London, 5 January 1918. See https://history.state.gov/historical documents/frus1918Supp01v01/d4

60 Address of the President of the United States, delivered at a joint session of the two houses of Congress, 8 January 1918, House Doc. 765, 65th Cong., 2d sess.

61 Herwig, Holger, Ibid., p. 421

62 Lansing, Robert: US Secretary of State to the Swedish Minister (Ekengren) on 17 September 1918

63 Mutschlechner, Martin, 'The End of the War', www.habsburger.net

64 Burián, Count Stephan, *Austria in Dissolution*, p. 418

65 Horne, Charles (ed.), *Source Records of the Great War*, Vol. VI, p. 374

66 Ball, Mary Margaret, *Post-war German-Austrian Relations – The Anschluss Movement, 1918–1936*, p. 8

67 Provisorische Nationalversammlung für Deutschösterreich, 1918–19, 2 Sitzung, den 30 Oktober 1918, I. Band, Beilagen, No. 8. Translation in Ball.

68 Horne, Ibid., p. 385

69 Schmied-Kowarzik, Antol, 'War Losses (Austria-Hungary)', *International Encyclopaedia of the First World War*

## Chapter 10
## The First Republic to the Third Reich

1 *Neue Freie Presse*, 16 November 1918. Translation in Palmer, Mary Jessie, *The Anschluss Movement, 1918 and 1919*, unpublished MA thesis, Library of Stanford University, p. 46

2 Treaty of St Germain, Signed Article 88

3 Zara Steiner obituary, *The Guardian*, 23 February 2020

4 Steiner, Zara, *The Lights that Failed – European International History 1919–1933*, p. 99

5 Kahlweit, Cathrin, 'Archduke Franz Ferdinand descendant: "Don't blame us for first world war"', *The Guardian*, 15 January 2014

6 Rupnik, Jacques, *Central Europe or Mitteleuropa*, p. 251

7 Roth, Joseph, *The Wandering Jews*, pp. 55–56

8 See Heiss und Rathkolb, *Asylland Wider Willen – Flüchtlingen in Österreich im europäischen Kontext sit 1914*, p. 63

9 'Sever Erlass' cited in Grandner, p. 72

10 Blau, Eve, *The Architecture of Red Vienna 1919–34*, p. 1

11 Bauböck, Reiner, *Wohnungspolitik im sozialdemokratischen Wien 1919–1934*, p. 152

12 Blau, Ibid.

13 Thompson, Dorothy, 'Goodbye to Germany', *Harper's Magazine*, December 1934

14 *Time* magazine, 12 June 1939, Vol. XXXIII, No. 24,

15 Scheu, Friedrich, *Der Weg im Ungewisse: Österreichs Schicksalskurve 1929–1938*, p. 23

16 Gunther, John, 'Dateline Vienna', *Harpers Magazine*, July 1935, p. 201

17 Cuthbertson, Ken, *Inside – The Biography of John Gunther*, p. 108

18 Johnson, Haynes, and Gwertzman, Bernard, *Fulbright: The Dissenter*, pp. 30–31

19  Kurth, Peter, *American Cassandra – The Life of Dorothy Thompson*, p. 61

20  Ibid., p. 74

21  Ibid., p. 63

22  Ibid.

23  Gedye, G.E.R., *Fallen Bastions – The Central European Tragedy*, p. 50

24  Gedye, Ibid., p. 114

25  Gunther, John, *Inside Europe*, p. 416

26  Ibid., p. 397

27  Gedye, Ibid., p. 127 and p. 132

28  Bauer, Kurt, *Elementar-Ereignis – Die Österreichischen Nationalsozialisten und der Juliputsch 1934*, p. 325

29  Thompson, Dorothy, *Let the Record Speak*, p. 135

30  Jackson, Robert, 'Summation for the Prosecution by Justice Robert Jackson, Nuremberg Trial, 26 July 1946', https://famous-trials.com/nuremberg/1933-jacksonsummation

31  Messerschmidt, Manfred, 'Foreign Policy and Preparation for War', *Germany and the Second World War*, Vol. I, pp. 636–637

32  Gedye, Ibid., p. 223

33  Ibid., p. 227

34  Selby, Sir Walford, *Diplomatic Twilight 1930–1940*, p. 96

35  Letter by Walford Selby. Possession of the author.

36  Sheridan, R.K., *Kurt von Schuschnigg – A Tribute*, p. 288

37  Diary of Sigmund Freud, March 1938, US Library of Congress

38  Shirer, William, *Berlin Diary – The Journal of a Foreign Correspondent 1934–41*, p. 86

39  Huss, Ibid., p. 20

40  Hitler, Ibid., pp. 160–161

41  Picker, *Hitler's Tischgespräche*, p. 339

42  Hitler, Adolf, *Monologe in Führerhauptquartier 1941–44*

43  Picker, Ibid., p. 339

44  Hitler, *Monologe*, p. 404

45  Goebbels, Joseph, *Tagebücher*, Part 2, Vol. 7, p. 608

46  Ibid., Part 2, Vol. 8, p. 540

47  Report in *The Times* quoted in Gedye, *Fallen Bastions*, p. 356

48 Walzer, Tina, and Templ, Stephan, *Unser Wien – 'Arisierung' auf österreichisch*

49 Catalogue of British embassy and consulate buildings, 1800–2010 (Vienna) https://roomfordiplomacy.com/ausria-vienna/

50 'Ho Feng Shan – The "Chinese Schindler" who saved thousands of Jews', CNN, https://edition.cnn.com/2015/07/19/asia/china-jews-schindler-ho-feng-shan/index.html

51 'Chinese Visas in Vienna', http://www.yadvashem.org/righteous/stories/ho.html

52 Ibid.

53 Dowley, Tim, *Defying the Holocaust: Ten Courageous Christians Who Supported Jews*

54 Fry, Helen, *Spymaster: The Secret Life of Kendrick*

55 Agstner, Rudolf, *Handbuch der Österreichischen Auswärtige Dienst*, p. 55

56 Daim and Molden interviews on 'Österreich – Der Krieg'. Austrian broadcasting Corporation (ORF)

57 Domarus, Max, *Hitler: speeches and proclamations, 1932–1945 – The chronicle of a dictatorship*

58 Scheuch, Manfred, *Österreich im 20. Jahrhundert*, p. 120

59 Miller, Michael, *Leaders of the SS and German Police*, Vol. I, p. 401

60 Dettmer F., Jaus, O., Tolkmitt, H., *Die 44. Infanterie-Division – Reichs-Grenadier-Division Hoch- und Deutschmeister 1938–1945*

61 Gosztony, Peter, *Endkampf an der Donau 1944/45*

62 Kershaw, Ian, *Hitler: 1936–45: Nemesis*, pp. 777–778

63 Schöner, Joseph, *Wienertagebuch 1944–45*, p. 135

64 Ibid., pp. 134–135

65 Ibid., p. 160

66 Goebbels, Joseph, *Tagebücher*, Part 2, Vol. 15, p. 692

### Chapter 11
### Occupation, Intrigue and Espionage

1 Schöner, Ibid., p. 141

2 Ibid., p. 201

3 Ibid., p. 203

4  Rathkolb, Oliver, *Gesellschaft und Politik am Beginn der Zweiten Republik: vertrauliche Berichte der US-Militäradministration aus Österreich 1945*, pp. 281–283

5  Wagnleitner, Reinhold, *Understanding Austria: The political reports and analyses of Martin F. Herz, Political Officer of the US Legation in Vienna 1945–48*, p. 42

6  Declaration on Austria, Moscow Conference, 1943

7  Winston Churchill speech at Mansion House, London, 9 November 1940

8  Mark Clarke in *The Times*, 25 July 1945

9  Dulles, Eleanor Lansing, *Chances of a Lifetime*, p. 210

10  Dulles, Ibid., p. 208

11  Dulles, Ibid., p. 222

12  Berg, Matthew Paul, 'Caught between Iwan and the Weinachtsmann – Occupation and Austrian Identity', in *The Marshall Plan in Austria*, p. 169

13  Bischof, Günter, et al., *The Marshall Plan in Austria*, p. 85

14  Allard, Sven, *Russia and the Austrian State Treaty – A Case Study of Soviet Policy in Europe*, p. 99

15  Foges, Peter, 'My Spy – The story of H.P. Smolka, Soviet Spy and inspiration for the *Third Man*', *Laphams's Quarterly*, January 2016

16  Christopher, Andrew, *The Defence of the Realm – The Authorized History of MI5*, pp. 180–181

17  West, Nigel, *The Crown Jewels – The British Secrets Exposed by the KGB Archives*, p. 274

18  Haynes, J., Klehr, H., Vassiliev, A., *Spies – The Rise and Fall of the KGB in America*, p. 68

19  MacIntyre, Ben, 'Revealed – Bertie the Spy who started the Cold War', *Irish Independent*, 10 June 2009

20  See Bischof, Günter, et al., *New Perspectives on Austrians and World War II*, pp. 252–255

21  See *Journal of Cold War Studies*, October 2012, pp. 174–175

22  Pick, Hella, *Guilty Victim – Austria from the Holocaust to Haider*, p. 47

23  See Karner, Stefan, and Stelzl-Marx, Barbara (eds), *Die Rote Armee in Österreich: Sowjetische Besatzung 1945–1955*, pp. 275–322

24  Sayer, Ian, and Botting, Douglas, *America's Secret Army – The Untold Story of the Counter Intelligence Corps*, p. 358

25  Jeffrey, Keith, *MI6 – The History of the Secret Intelligence Service 1909–1949*, pp. 669–671

26  Corera, Gordon, *MI6 – Life and Death in the British Secret Service*, pp. 45–48

27  Bagley, Tennant, *Spy Wars – Moles, Mysteries and Deadly Games*, p. 33

28  *Life Magazine*, 23 March 1959

29  Richelson, Jeffrey, *A Century of Spies: Intelligence in the Twentieth Century*, p. 258

30  Hart, John, 'Pyotr Semyonovich Popov: The tribulations of faith', *Intelligence and National Security*, Vol. 12, Issue 4

31  Hillhouse, Raelynn, 'A Reevaluation of Soviet Policy in Central Europe – The Soviet Union and the Occupation of Austria', *Eastern European Politics and Societies*, 3 (1), 1989, pp. 83–104

32  Beer, Siegfried, *The Soviet Occupation of Austria 1945–55 – Recent Research and Perspectives*

33  Rauchensteiner, Manfried, *Der Sonderfall – Die Besatzungszeit in Österreich 1945–1955*, p. 11

34  Müller, Wolfgang, 'Die Teilung Österreichs als politische Option für KPÖ und UDSSR 1948', *Zeitgeschichte*, 32 (1), pp. 47–54

35  Pick, Ibid., p. 31

36  Steininger, Rolf, *Austria, Germany, and the Cold War: From the Anschluss to the State Treaty 1938–1955*, p. 128

37  The other example is the Finnish peninsula of Porkkala, which the Soviets withdrew from in 1956 after Finland undertook to become neutral.

## Chapter 12
### Diplomatic Capital

1  'Kurz welcomes Orban to Vienna, claiming to act as '"bridge builder"', *The Local*, AFP, 31 January 2018

2   United Nations Report of the Special Committee on the Problem of Hungary, UN General Assembly, 1957, para. 339, p. 105

3   Rauchensteiner, Manfried, *Spätherbst 1956 – Die neutralität auf dem Prüfstand*, p. 101

4   Lendvai, Paul, *One Day That Shook the Communist World: The 1956 Hungarian Uprising and its Legacy*, p. 204

5   Michener, James, *The Bridge at Andau: The Compelling True Story of a Brave, Embattled People*

6   Ibid.

7   Kofler, Martin, 'Kreisky – Brandt – Austrian Mediation during the Berlin Crisis, 1958–1963', *Contemporary Austrian Studies*, Vol. 14, pp. 170–185

8   Beschloss, Michael, *The Crisis Years: Kennedy and Khrushchev*

9   Khrushchev, Nikita, *Khrushchev Remembers*, p. 458

10  Kempe, Frederick, *Berlin 1961*, pp. 225–257

11  Ibid., p. 257

12  Bruno Kreisky in discussion with UK Prime Minister Sir Edward Heath, 14 July 1961, FCO 371, 160815/CU 1052/4, National Archives, Kew

13  Brook-Shepherd, Gordon: *Uncrowned Emperor – The Life and Times of Otto von Habsburg*, p. 181

14  Haváč, Ondrey, 'Czech Refugees in Austria 1968–1985', Prague Papers on the History of International Relations, *Central European Journal of Social Sciences and Humanities*, Issue 1, p. 87

15  De Silva, Peer, *Sub Rosa – The CIA and the Uses of Intelligence*

16  Bittmann, Lasdislav, *The KGB and Soviet Disinformation*, p. 26

17  Souherland, Daniel, 'France the height of international intrigue; Paris copes with a new kind of spy', *Christian Science Monitor*, 24 September 1980

18  Bittmann, Ladislav, *The Deception Game – Czechoslovak Intelligence in Soviet Political Warfare*, p. 22

19  Beer, Siegfried, 'Helmut Zilk war glasklar ein Spion', *Die Presse*, 27 March 2009

20 Bobi, Emil, *Die Schattenstadt – Was 7.000 Agenten über Wien aussagen*, p. 100

21 Ziegler, Thomas, 'Die "Wiener Resident" der Stasi – Mythos und Wirklichkeit', *Journal for Intelligence, Propaganda and Security Studies*, Vol. 7, No. 2, 2013, pp. 89–113

22 'Soviet Acquisition of Militarily Significant Western Technology', http://insidethecoldwar.org

23 Melvern, Linda, et al., *Technobandits – How the Soviets are Stealing America's High-Tech Future*, pp. 142–157

24 Steiner-Gashi, Ingrid, *Im Dienst des Diktators: Leben und Flucht eines nordkoreanischen Agenten*

25 'Personal Shopper for North Korea Dictator Speaks Out', Associated Press, 4 March 2010

26 See https://www.bvt.gv.at/bmi_documents/2202.pdf, p. 78

27 See www.iaea.org

28 *A Brief History of IIASA and Laxenburg*, p. 1

29 Raiffa, Howard, 'IIASA Founding of the Institute', talk given to IIASA on 23 September 1992, www.iiasa.ac.at

30 'IIASA Overview', www.iiasa.ac.at

31 Rathkolb, Oliver, *Festschrift 250 Jahre – Von der Orientalischen zur Diplomatischen Akademie in Wien*, p. 201

32 Kissinger, Henry, *White House Years*, p. 1204

33 Memorandum of conversation between President Gerald Ford and Chancellor Kreisky, The White House, 12 November 1974. Available online via Ford Library Museum.

34 *Austrian Information Service*, Vol. 28, No. 3, May 1975

35 Meir, Golda, *My Life*, p. 351

36 Kreisky, Bruno, *The Struggle for Democratic Austria*, p. 406

37 Pick, Hella, *Guilty Victim*, p. 127

38 Ibid., p. 118

39 Schnelting, Karl, *Jüdische Lebenswege*, p. 107

40 Pick, Hella, *Simon Wiesenthal – A Life in Search of Justice*, p. 246

41 'Carter Meets Brezhnev', *Washington Post*, 16 June 1979

42 Kreisky, Bruno, *The Struggle for a Democratic Austria – Bruno Kreisky on Peace and Social Justice*, p. 465

43 'Vienna International Centre', Wien Geschichte Wiki

44 Urquhart, Brian, 'Character Sketches – Kurt Waldheim', www.news.un.org

45 'Sequels Running Out of Answers', *Time Magazine*, 7 April 1986

46 Urquhart, Ibid.

47 *Financial Times*, 11 April 1988

48 Waldheim, Kurt, 'Scheide mit Dankbarkeit. Das Vermächtnis im Wortlaut', ORF Online, July 2007

49 Lahodynsky, Otmar, 'Paneuropäisches Picknick: Die Generalprobe für den Mauerfall', *Profil*, 9 August 2014

50 Eichtinger, Martin, 'Obituary for Alois Mock – A visionary politician who shaped Austria's history', *Österreichisches Jahrbuch für Politik Kohl*, 2017

51 'Mock-Ableben – Slowenien und Kroatien trauern um "großen Freund"', *Tiroler Tageszeitung*, 1 June 2017

52 Kramer, Gene, 'Bosnia-Herzegovina Threatened With Extinction, Bush Warned', Associated Press, 23 December 1992

53 Wodak, Ruth, and Pelinka, Anton, *The Haider Phenomenon in Austria*, p. 8

54 Iber, Walter, and Teibenbacher, Peter, *Österreich, Europa und die Welt: Internationale Beziehungen im 20. und 21. Jahrhundert*, Vol. I, p. 87

55 Eichtinger, Martin, and Wohnout, Helmut, *Mock – Ein Politiker schreibt Geschichte*

56 'Austria in the EU – Invest in Austria Statistics: Economic Situation and Outlook', Federal Chamber of the Economy (WKO), December 2019

57 *The Times*, 2 July 1998

58 Schwarzenegger, Arnold, 'Arnold "offended" by Austria's Haider', *Variety*, 16 February 2000

59 Kluge, Jan, et al., *Die ökonomische Effekte internationale Organisationen in Österreich*, IHS/BMEIA, 7 December 2017

60 '2017 Wiener Tagung-Bilanz bricht erneut Rekorde', www.wien.gv.at

61  Borger, Julian L., 'Eighteen Days in Vienna – How the nuclear deal was done', *The Guardian*, 14 July 2015

62  Jones, Sam, 'A heady mix of diplomatic dining, spies and torte in Vienna', *Financial Times*, 20 November 2015

63  Liechtenstein, Stephanie, 'Celebrating 40 Years of the UN in Vienna', *Metropole Magazine*, 30 May 2019

64  Sebag Montefiore, Simon, *Vienna*, BBC TV Series, Episode 2

# Bibliography

Abert, Hermann, *W.A. Mozart*, Yale University Press, 2007

Adams, John Quincy, *Writings*, Macmillan, 1913

Afflerbach, Holger, and Stevenson, David (eds), *An Improbable War: The Outbreak of World War I and European Political Culture Before 1914*, Berghahn Books, 2007

Agstner, Rudolf, *Handbuch der Österreichischen Auswärtige Dienst*, Lit Verlag, 2015

Albertini, Luigi, *The Origins of the War of 1914*, Vol. I, Oxford University Press, 2005

Alison, Archibald, *History of Europe During the French Revolution*, William Blackwood and Sons, 1839

Allard, Sven, *Russia and the Austrian State Treaty – A Case Study of Soviet Policy in Europe*, Pennsylvania State University Press, 1970

Allwood, John, *The Great Exhibitions*, Studio Vista, 1977

Anderson, Emily, *The Letters of Mozart and His Family*, Palgrave Macmillan, 1985

Anderson, M.S., *The Rise of Modern Diplomacy 1450–1919*, Routledge, 2013

Andlaw, Franz Freiherrn von, *Mein Tagebuch. Auszüge aus Aufzeichnungen der Jahre 1811 bis 1861*, Sauerländer, 1862

Angermüller, Rudolf, *Florilegium Pratense: Mozart, seine Zeit, seine Nachwelt*, Königshausen & Neumann, 2005

Arneth, Alfred Ritter von, *Joseph II und Leopold II von Toscana – Ihr Briefwechsel von 1781 bis 1790*, Braumüller, 1872

Aubry, Octave, *Napoleon II, The King of Rome, 'L'Aiglon'*, Routledge, 1933

399

Aurelius, Marcus, *Meditations*, Jeremy Collier (trans.), Walter Scott, 1887

Autengruber, Peter, *Lexicon der Wiener Straßennamen*, Pichler Verlag, 2012

Bagley, Tennant, *Spy Wars – Moles, Mysteries and Deadly Games*, Yale University Press, 2008

Baker, Susan, *The Shadow. Intermarium*, Columbia University, Vol. 4, No.3, 2000–01

Ball, Mary Margaret, *Post-war German-Austrian Relations – The Anschluss Movement, 1918–1936*, Stanford University Press, 1937

Barth-Scalmani, Gunda (ed.), *Politische Kommunikation zwischen Imperien – Der diplomatische Aktionsraum Südost- und Osteuropa*, Studienverlag, 2013

Bassett, Richard, *For God and Kaiser – The Imperial Austrian Army*, Yale University Press, 2016

Bauböck, Reiner, *Wohnungspolitik im sozialdemokratischen Wien 1919–1934*, Neugebauer, 1979

Bauer, Kurt, *Elementar-Ereignis – Die Österreichischen Nationalsozialisten und der Juliputsch 1934*, Czernin Verlag, 2003

Beales, Derek *Enlightenment and Reform in Eighteenth Century Europe*, Bloomsbury, 2005

Beales, Derek, *Joseph II – In the Shadow of Maria Theresa 1741–1780*, Cambridge University Press, 2008

Beales, Derek, *Joseph II – Against the World, 1780–1790*, Cambridge University Press, 2009

Bednar, Kurt, *Der Papier Krieg zwischen Washington und Wien 1917/18*, Studien Verlag, 2017

Beer, Siegfried, 'The Soviet Occupation of Austria 1945–55 – Recent Research and Perspectives', https://www.eurozine.com, 2007

Bein, Alex, *Theodore Herzl – A Biography*, The Jewish Publication Society of America, 1942

Bellen. E.A., *The Thirty Years War*, New Cambridge Modern History, 1970

Bérenger, Jean, *The Habsburg Empire 1700–1918*, Routledge, 1997

# Bibliography

Berg, Matthew Paul, 'Caught between Iwan and the Weinachtsmann – Occupation and Austrian Identity', *The Marshall Plan in Austria*, Transaction Publishers, 2000

Bermbach, Udo, *Houston Stewart Chamberlain – Wagners Schwiegersohn – Hitlers Vordenker*, Metzler Verlag, 2015

Bernady, Françoise de, *Son of Talleyrand – The Life of Comte Charles de Flahaut 1785–1870*, Lucy Norton (trans.), Collins, 1956

Berridge, G.R., *Notes on the Origins of the Diplomatic Corps – Constantinople in the 1620s*, Netherlands Institute of International Relations 'Clingendael', 2004

Berthuch, Carl, *Bertuchs Tagebuch vom Wiener Kongress*, Hermann Freiherr von Egloffstein (ed.), Gebrüder Paetell, 1916

Beschloss, Michael, *The Crisis Years: Kennedy and Khrushchev*, Harper Collins, 1991

Bew, John, *Castlereagh – A Life*, Riverrun, 2012

Bideleux, Robert, *A History of Eastern Europe – Crisis and Change*, Routledge, 2007

Bischof, Günter, et al., *New Perspectives on Austrians and World War II*, Transaction Publishers, 2009

Bischof, Günter, et al., *The Marshall Plan in Austria*, Transaction Publishers, 2000

Bittman, Ladislav, *The Deception Game – Czechoslovak Intelligence in Soviet Political Warfare*, Syracuse University Research Corporation, 1972

Bittmann, Lasdislav, *The KGB and Soviet Disinformation*, Pergamon Press, 1995

Blau, Eve, *The Architecture of Red Vienna 1919–34*, MIT Press, 1999

Blum, Stella, *Fashions of the Hapsburg Era – Austria-Hungary*, Costume Institute of Metropolitan Museum, 1979

Bobi, Emil, *Die Schattenstadt – Was 7.000 Agenten über Wien aussagen*, Benevento Publishing, 2014

Brandstätter, Christian, *Stadt Chronik Wien*, Verlag Christian Brandstätter, 1986

Braunbehrens, Volkmar, *Mozart in Vienna 1781–1791*, André Deutsch, 1990

Bright, Richard, *Travels from Vienna though lower Hungary – With some remarks on the state of Vienna during the Congress in the year 1814*, Archibald Constable & Co., 1818

Brook-Shepherd, Gordon, *The Austrians*, Harper Collins Publishers, 1997

Brook-Shepherd, Gordon, *Uncrowned Emperor – The Life and Times of Otto von Habsburg*, Hambledon Continuum, 2003

Broucek, Peter (ed.), *Ein General im Zwielicht – Die Erinnerungen Edmund Glaises von Horstenau*, Böhlau Verlag, 1980

Browning, Reed, *The War of Austrian Succession*, Griffin, 1995

Buchmann, Bertrand Michael, *Militär, Diplomatie, Politik: Österreich und Europa von 1815–1835*, Lang, 1991

Budanovic, Nikola, *Colonel Redl: The Spy Who Destroyed the Austro-Hungarian Empire*, War History Online, 2016

Bullock, Alan, *Hitler and Stalin – Parallel Lives*, Fontana Press, 1993

Bunsen, Bertha de, 'The Vienna Diary of Bertha de Bunsen 28 June– 17 August 1914', *Bulletin of the Institute of Historical Research*, Vol. LI, University of London IHR, 1978

Burián, Count Stephan, *Austria in Dissolution*, Ernest Benn, 1925

Burke, Edmund, *Annual Register, for 1766*, Dodsley, 1767

Burney, Charles, *The present state of music in Germany, the Netherlands, and United Provinces*, Becket and Co., 1773

Burrows, Donald, 'Gottfried van Swieten and London Publication of Handel's Music', *Händel-Jahrbuch*, Vol. 47, Georg-Friedrich-Händel-Gesellschaft, 2002

Calinger, Ronald, 'Reform absolutism of Joseph II in the Austrian monarchy in 1781', in George F. McLean, Robert R. Magliola, William Fox (eds), *Democracy: In the Throes of Liberalism and Totalitarianism*, CVRP, 2004

Cantacuzène, Countess Spéransky, Princess née Dent, *My Life Here and There*, Charles Scribner's Sons, 1921

Carlyle, Thomas, *History of Friedrich II of Prussia*, Chapman and Hall, 1865

Castelot, André, *King of Rome – A Biography of Napoleon's Tragic Son*, Harper and Brothers, 1960

Castle, Ian, *Aspern and Wagram 1809 – Mighty Clash of Empires*, Osprey, 1994

Christopher, Andrew, *The Defence of the Realm – The Authorized History of MI5*, Penguin, 2009

Christopher, Andrew, *The Secret World – A History of Intelligence*, Allen Lane, 2018

Churchill, Winston, *The Second World War – The Gathering Storm* (Vol. I), Cassell and Co., 1949

Chushichi and Young, *Japan Rising – The Iwakura Embassy to the USA and Europe 1871–73*, Cambridge University Press, 2009

Cooper, A., Heine, J., and Thakur, R. (eds), *The Oxford Handbook of Modern Diplomacy*, Oxford University Press, 2013

Corera, Gordon, *MI6 – Life and Death in the British Secret Service*, Weidenfeld & Nicholson, 2011

Cormons, Ernest, *Schicksale und Schatten – Eine Österreichische Autobiographie*, Otto Müller Verlag, 1951

Cornwall, Bernhard, *Waterloo – The History of Four Days, Three Armies and Three Battles*, William Collins, 2014

Corti, Egon, *Metternich und die Frauen*, Europa Verlag, 1948

Coxe, William, *The House of Austria*, H.G. Bohn, 1864

Craig, Gordon A., *The Battle of Königgrätz*, University of Pennsylvania Press, 1964

Cramon, August von, *Unser Oestereichisch-Ungarische Bundesgenosse im Weltkrieg*, Mittler und Sohn, 1922

Crankshaw, Edward, *Maria Theresa*, Longmans, Green and Co., 1969

Crankshaw, Edward, *The Fall of the House of Habsburg*, Papermac Pan Macmillan, 1981

Creevey, Thomas, *The Creevey Papers*, John Murray, 1903

Crowne, William, *A true relation of all the remarkable places and passages observed in the travels of the right honourable Thomas Lord Hovvard, Earle of Arundell and Surrey, Primer Earle, and Earle Marshall of England, ambassadour extraordinary to his sacred Majesty Ferdinando the second, emperour of Germanie, anno Domini 1636*

Croxton, D., Tischer, A., *The Peace of Westphalia – A Historical Dictionary*, Greenwood, 2001

Cuthbertson, Ken, *Inside – The Biography of John Gunther*, Bonus Books, 1992

Dallas, Gregor, *1815 – The Roads to Waterloo*, Pimlico, 2001

Dankoff, Robert, and Kim, Sooyong (eds), *An Ottoman Traveller – Selections from the Book of Travels of Evliya Çelebi*, Eland Publishing Ltd., 2011

Dawson, Brigadier-General Sir Douglas, *A Soldier-Diplomat*, John Murray, 1927

Deák, István, *Der k.(u.)k. Offizier 1848–1914*, Böhlau Verlag, 1991

Dedijer, Vladimir, *Tito*, Simon & Schuster, 1953

Dekker, Erwin, *The Viennese Students of Civilisation*, Cambridge University Press, 2016

Dell'Orto, U., *La nunziatura a Vienna di Giuseppe Garampi (1776–1785)*, Vatican City Archive, 1995

de Silva, Peer, *Sub Rosa – The CIA and the Uses of Intelligence*, Times Books, 1978

Dettmer, F., Jaus, O., Tolkmitt, H., *Die 44. Infanterie-Division. Reichs-Grenadier-Division Hoch- und Deutschmeister 1938–1945*, Nebel-Verlag, 2004

*Diarium Lamberg, 1645–1649. Acta Pacis Westphalicae, Serie III Abt. C Band 4*, Aschendorffsche Verlagsbuchhandlung, 1986

*Diarium Volmar, 1643–1647. Acta Pacis Westphalicae, Serie III Abt. C Band 2*, Aschendorffsche Verlagsbuchhandlung, 1984

Dickinger, Christian, *Habsburgs schwarze Schafe*, Piper Verlag, 2005

Domarus, Max, *Hitler: speeches and proclamations, 1932–1945 – The chronicle of a dictatorship*, Tauris, 1990

Dowley, Tim, *Defying the Holocaust: Ten courageous Christians Who Supported Jews*, Intervarsity Press, 2020

Duffy, Christopher, *The Army of Maria Theresa – The Armed Forces of Imperial Austria 1740–1780*, David and Charles, 1977

Duffy, Christopher, *The Wild Goose and the Eagle – A Life of Marshal von Browne 1705–1757*, Chatto Windus, 1964

Duindam, Jeroen, *Vienna and Versailles – The Courts of Europe's Dynastic Rivals, 1550–1780*, Cambridge University Press, 2008

Dulles, Eleanor Lansing, *Chances of a Lifetime*, Prentice Hall, 1980

Dunant, Henry, *The Origin of the Red Cross – 'Un souvenir de Solferino'*, John Winston Co., 1911

Ehrlich, Anna, and Bauer, Christa, *Der Wiener Kongress – Diplomaten, Irrigen und Skandale*, Almathea Verlag, 2014

Eichtinger, Martin, and Wohnout, Helmut, *Mock – Ein Politiker schreibt Geschichte*, Styria Verlag, 2008

Eichtinger, Martin, 'Obituary for Alois Mock – A visionary politician who shaped Austria's history', *Österreichisches Jahrbuch für Politik Kohl*, Böhlau, 2017

Eisen, Cliff, and Keefe, Simon P. (eds), *The Cambridge Mozart Encyclopedia*, Cambridge University Press, 2006

Egerton, George, *Political Memoir – Essays on the Politics of Memory*, Routledge, 1994

Elon, Amos, *Herzl*, Holt, Rinehart and Winston, 1975

Erickson, Raymond, *Schubert's Vienna*, Yale University Press, 1997

Erzlstorfer, Hannes, *Der Wiener Kongress – Redouten, Larousses & Köllnerwasser*, Verlag Kremayr & Scheriau, 2014

Eugippius, *The Life of St. Severinus*, George Robinson (trans.), Harvard University Press, 1914

Evans, Richard J., *The Pursuit of Power – Europe 1815–1914*, Penguin, 2016

Evliyâ, *Seyahatnâme*, Vol. 7, pp. 398–399. Translation in Lewis, Bernard, *The Muslim Discovery of Europe*, W.W. Norton, 2001

Eynard, Jean Gabriel, *Au Congrés de Vienna – Journal de Jean Gabriel Eynard*, Plon Nourrit, 1914

Fetus, Andreas, *Die Reise des kaiserlichen Gesandten David Ungnad nach Konstantinopel im Jahre 1572*, dissertation, University of Vienna, 2007

Feurzeig, Lisa, and Sienicki, John (eds), *Quodlibets of the Viennese Theater*, Middleton, 2008

Field, Geoffrey G., *Evangelist of Race – The Germanic Vision of Houston Stewart Chamberlain*, Columbia University Press, 1981

Findling, John, *Historical Dictionary of World's Fairs and Expositions 1851–1988*, Greenwood Press, 1990

Flotow, Ludwig Freiherr von, *November 1918 auf dem Ballhausplatz – Erinnerungen Ludwigs Freiherrn von Flotow, des letzten Chefs des Österreichisch-Ungarischen Auswärtigen Dienstes 1895–1920*, Böhlau, 1982

Foley, Robert T., *German strategy and the path to Verdun – Erich von Falkenhayn and the development of attrition, 1870–1916*, Cambridge University Press, 2005

Forster, E.S., *The Turkish Letters of Ogier Ghislean de Busbecq*, Clarendon Press, 1927

Fournier, August, *Die Geheimpolizei auf dem Wiener Kongress Eine Auswahl aus ihren Papieren*, Vero Verlag GmbH & Co., 1914

Franckenstein, Georg von, *Zwischen Wien und London: Erinnerungen eines Österreichischen Diplomaten*, Stocker, 2005

Friedjung, Heinrich, *Geschichte in Gesprächen: 1904–1919*, Böhlau Verlag, 1997

Fry, Helen, *Spymaster: The Secret Life of Kendrick*, CreateSpace, 2014

Fugger, Nora Fürstin, *Im Glanz der Kaiserzeit*, Amalthea Verlag, 1980

Garvi, Petr A., *Vospominaniia Sotsial-Demokrata – Peterburg*, Fond po izd. literaturnogo nasledstva P.A. Garvi, 1946

Garrity, Patrick, 'Austria in 1848–9 by William H. Stiles', *Classics of Strategy and Diplomacy*, 2010

Gedye, G.E.R., *Fallen Bastions – The Central European Tragedy*, Faber Finds, 2009

Gentz, Friedrich von, *Tagebücher*, Brockhaus, 1861

Gerber, Pietro, *Formen und Stile der Diplomatie*, Rowohlt Taschenbuch Verlag, 1964

Gilbert, Oscar Paul, *The Prince de Ligne*, Fisher Unwin Ltd., 1923

Gillespie-Addison, A.D., *The Strategy of the Seven Weeks War*, Scheineman, 1902

Godsey, William D., *Aristocratic redoubt. The Austro-Hungarian – Foreign Office on the Eve of the First World War*, Purdue University Press, 1999

Goebbels, Joseph, *Tagebücher 1923–45*, K.G. Saur Verlag, 1993–2006

# Bibliography

Goethe, Johann Wolfgang, *Truth and Poetry from My Own Life – The Autobiography of Goethe*, George Bell and Sons, 1881

Goldschmidt, Harry, *Beethoven, Werkeinführungen*, Reclam, 1975

Gooch and Temperley, *British Documents on the Origins of the War, 1898–1914*, HMSO, 1926–1938

Gosztony, Peter, *Endkampf an der Donau 1944/45*, Molden Taschenbuch Verlag, 1978

Grafenberg, Schloss (Hgb), *Das Zeitalter Kaiser Franz Josephs 2. Teil 1880–1916*, Amt der NÖ Landesregierung, 1987

Grant, Julia Dent, *My Life Here and There*, Charles Scribner and Sons, 1921

Grey, Viscount of Falloden, *Twenty Five Years 1892–1916*, Frederick Stokes, 1925

Griesinger, Georg August, *Biographische Notizen über Joseph Haydn*, Leipzig, Breitkopf & Härtel, 1810

Gross, Lothar, *Die Geschichte der Deutschen Reichhofkanzlei von 1559 bis 1806*, Selbstverlag des Haus-, Hof-, und Staatsarchivs, Wien, 1933

Gschliesser, Oswald von, *Der Reichshofrat – Bedeutung und Verfassung, Schicksal und Besetzung einer obersten Reichsbehörde von 1559 bis 1806*, Holzhausen, 1942

Gunther, John, *Inside Europe*, Harper and Brothers, 1940

Günzel, Klaus, *Der Wiener Kongress – Geschichte und Geschichten eines Welttheaters*, Koehler & Amelang, 1995

Gutman, Robert, *Mozart – A Cultural Biography*, Harcourt Brace International, 2000

Hadley, Tim, *Military Diplomacy in the Dual Alliance – German Military Attaché Reporting from Vienna, 1879–1914*, Lexington Books, 2016

Haider, Edgard, *Wien 1918 – Agonie der Kaiserstadt*, Böhlau Verlag, 2018

Hall, Thomas, *Planning Europe's Capital Cities – Aspects of Nineteenth Century Urban Development*, Routledge, 2009

Hamann, Brigitte, *Bertha von Suttner – Ein Leben für den Frieden*, Piper Verlag, 2002

Hamann, Brigitte, *Hitler's Vienna – A Dictator's Apprenticeship*, Oxford University Press, 1999

Hamann, Brigitte, *Elisabeth – Kaiserin wider Willen*, Piper Verlag, 2010

Hamann, Brigitte, *Kronprinz Rudolf – Ein Leben*, Piper Verlag, 2006

Hamann, Brigitte, *Hitlers Wien – Lehrjahre eines Diktators*, Piper Verlag, 1996

Hamann, Brigitte, *Rudolf – Kronprinz und Rebell*, Piper Verlag, 2004

Hantsch, Hugo, and Novotny, Alexander (eds), *Festschrift für Heinrich Benedikt*. Verlag Notring der wissenschaftlichen Verbände Österreichs, 1955

Haslip, Joan, *The Lonely Empress – Elizabeth of Austria*, Phoenix Press, 2001

Haslip, Joan, *Imperial Adventurer – Emperor Maximilian of Mexico*, Weidenfeld and Nicolson, 1971

Haynes, J., Klehr, H., Vassiliev, A., *Spies – The Rise and Fall of the KGB in America*, Yale University Press, 2010

Healy, Maureen, *Vienna and the Fall of the Habsburg Empire*, Cambridge University Press, 2004

Heiss, Gernot und Rathkolb, Oliver: 'Asylland Wider Willen – Flüchtlingen in Österreich im europäischen Kontext seit 1914', Ludwig Bolzmann Institut, 1995

Henderson, Nicholas, *Prince Eugen of Savoy*, Frederick Praeger Publishers, 1964

Herre, Franz, *Maria Theresia – Die grosse Hamburgerin*, Piper Verlag, 2004

Herwig, Holger, *The First World War – Germany and Austria-Hungary*, Bloomsbury, 2014

Herzl, Theodor, *A State of the Jews*, The Maccabaean Publishing Company, 1904

Herzl, Theodor, *The Complete Diaries of Theodor Herzl*, Raphael Patai (ed.), Herzl Press, 1960

Hinterschweiger, Hubert, *Wien im Mittelalter*, Pichler Verlag, 2014

Hitler, Adolf, *Mein Kampf* (English translation), Houghton Mifflin Company, 1971

# Bibliography

Hitler, Adolf, *Monologe in Führerhauptquartier 1941–44*, Werner Jochmann (ed.), Albrecht Klaus Verlag, 1980

*Hof und Staats-Schematismus des österreichischen Kaiserthums,* Wien Aus der Kais. Kön. Hof- und Staats-Druckerey, 1807

Hollaender, Albert, 'Streiflichter auf den Kronprinzentragödie von Mayerling' in Hantsch, Hugo, and Novotny, Alexander (eds), *Festschrift für Heinrich Benedikt*, Verlag Notring der Wissenschaftlichen Verbände Österreichs, 1957

Holmes, Oliver Wendell, *John Lothrop Motley – A memoir*, Houghton, Osgood and Company, 1879

Holzer, Anton, *Das Lächeln der Henker – Der unbekannte Krieg gegen die Zivilbevölkerung 1914–1918*, Primus Verlag, 2008

Horne, Charles, *Source Records of the Great War*, Vol. VI, National Alumni, 1923

Hort, Jakob, *Architektur der Diplomatie: Repräsentation in europäischen Botschaftsbauten, 1800–1920. Konstantinopel – Rom – Wien – St. Petersburg*, Vandenhoeck & Ruprecht, 2014

Hough, Richard (ed.), *Advice to my Granddaughter – Letters from Queen Victoria to Princess Victoria of Battenberg*, Simon & Schuster, 1975

Hübner, Joseph Alexander, *Neun Jahre der Erinnerungen eines Österreichischen Botschafters in Paris unter dem zweiten Kaiserreich 1851–1859*, Gebrüder Paetel, 1904

Hughes-Wilson, John, *On Intelligence – The History of Espionage and the Secret World*, Constable, 2016

Huss, Pierre J., *Heil! And Farewell*, Herbert Jenkins Ltd., 1943

Iber, Walter, and Teibenbacher, Peter, *Österreich, Europa und die Welt: Internationale Beziehungen im 20. und 21. Jahrhundert. Wissenschaft kompakt: Wirtschaft, Gesellschaft, Politik*, Vol. I, LIT Verlag Münster, 2019

Ilgen, Theodore, *Die Geschichte Kaiser Friedrich III von Aeneas Silvius*, Dyk, 1889

Illies, Florian, *1913 – Der Sommer des Jahrhunderts*, S. Fischer Verlag, 2012

Ingrao, Charles, *The Habsburg Monarchy 1618–1815*, Cambridge University Press, 1994/2000

Jackson, Sir George, *The Bath Archives: A further selection from The Diaries and Letters of Sir George Jackson from 1806–1816*, Vol. II, Richard Bentley and Son, 1873

Jahn, Otto, *Life of Mozart*, Novello, Ewer & Company, 1882

Jeffrey, Keith, *MI6 – The History of the Secret Intelligence Service 1909–1949*, Bloomsbury, 2010

Jelavich, Barbara, *Modern Austria – Empire and Republic 1815–1986*, Cambridge University Press, 1987

Johnson, Haynes, and Gwertzman, Bernard, *Fulbright: The Dissenter*, Doubleday & Co., 1968

Johnson, Julie, 'Museums and Material Culture in Vienna – A Comment', *Austrian History Yearbook*, Center for Austrian Studies, Vol. 46, 2015

Johnston, William, *The Austrian Mind – An Intellectual and Social History 1848–1938*, University of California Press, 1972

Judson, Peter, *The Habsburg Empire – A New History*, Belknap Press of Harvard University Press, 2016

Karner, Stefan, and Stelzl-Marx, Barbara (eds), *Die Rote Armee in Österreich: Sowjetische Besatzung 1945–1955*, Oldenburg Verlag, 2005

Kastner, Richard, *Glanz und Glorie – Die Wiener Hofburg unter Kaiser Franz Joseph*, Amalthea Verlag, 2004

Kauz, Ralph (ed.), *Diplomatisches Zeremoniell in Europa und im Mittleren Osten in der frühen Neuzeit*, Verlag der Österreichischen Akademie der Wissenschaften, 2009

Keith, Sir Robert, *The Romance of Diplomacy*, James Hogg and Sons, 1861

Keller, Katrin, Scheutz, Martin & Hersch, Harald, *Einmal Weimar-Wien und retour. Johann Sebastian Müller und sein Wienbericht aus dem Jahr 1660*, Boehlau Verlag, 2005

Kempe, Frederick, *Berlin 1961*, Penguin Group, 2001

Kempf, Beatrix, *Suffragette for Peace – The Life of Bertha Von Suttner*, Oswald Wolff, 1972

Kennedy, Paul, *The Rise and Fall of the Great Powers*, William Collins, 2017

## Bibliography

Kershaw, Ian, *Hitler: 1936–45: Nemesis*, Norton, 2000

Khrushchev, Nikita, *Khrushchev Remembers*, Little, Brown and Company, 1970

King, Greg, and Wilson, Penny, *Twilight of Empire – The Tragedy at Mayerling and the End of the Habsburgs*, St Martin's Press, 2017

King, David, *Vienna 1814 – How the Conquerors of Napoleon Made Love, War, and Peace at the Congress of Vienna*, Broadway Paperbacks, 2008

Kissinger, Henry, *Diplomacy*, Simon & Schuster Paperbacks, 1994

Kissinger, Henry, *World Order – Reflections on the Character of Nations and the Course of History*, Penguin, 2015

Kissinger, Henry, *A World Restored – Metternich, Castlereagh and the Problems of Peace 1812–1822*, Echo Point Books & Media, 2013

Kissinger, Henry, *White House Years*, Simon & Schuster, 1979

Kiste, John van der, *Emperor Francis Joseph – Life, Death and the Fall of the Habsburg Empire*, Sutton Publishing, 2005

Kiste, John van der, *Queen Victoria and the European Empires*, Fonthill Media Ltd., 2016

Kiste, John van der, *Windsor and Habsburg – The British and Austrian Reigning Houses 1848–1922*, Alan Sutton Publishing, 1987

Kleisner, Tomáš, *Coins and medals of the emperor Francis Stephen of Lorraine*, Czech National Museum, 2011

Klinger, Jerry, 'Reverend William Hechler – The Christian minister who legitimised Theodor Herzl', July 2010

Klinkowström, Carl, *Memoirs of Prince Metternich*, Richard Bentley & Son, 1880

Kramer, Konra, and Stuiber, Petra, *Die schrulligen Habsburger – Marotten und Allüren eines Kaiserhauses*, Piper Verlag, 2005

Krauske, Otto, *Die entwickelung der ständigen diplomatie vom fünfzehnten jahrhundert bis zu den beschlüssen von 1815 und 1818*, Duncker & Humbolt, 1885

Kreisky, Bruno, *The Struggle for Democratic Austria*, Berghahn Books, 2000

Kreutel, Richard Franz, *Im Reiche des goldenen Apfels*, Styria Verlag, 1957

Kronenbitter, Günther, *Krieg im Frieden – Die Führung der k. u. k. Armee und die Großmachtpolitik Österreich-Ungarns 1906–1914*, Oldenburg Verlag, 2003

Kubizek, August, *The Young Hitler I Knew*, Frontline Books, 2011

Kuefstein, Karl Graf, *Studien zur Familiengeschichte*, Wilhelm Braumüller, 1928

Kühnel, Harry, *Die Hofburg zu Wien*, Böhlau Verlag, 1971

Kun, Miklós, *Stalin – An Unknown Portrait*, Central European University, 2003

Kurth, Peter, *American Cassandra – The Life of Dorothy Thompson*, Little, Brown and Company, 1990

La Garde-Chambonas, Count Auguste, *Anecdotal Recollections of the Congress of Vienna*, Chapman & Hall Ltd, 1902

La Marmora, Alfonso, *Un Po' Più Di Luce Sugli Eventi Politici e Militari Dell' Anno 1866*, Barbera, 1873

Lansdale, Marie Hornor, *Vienna and the Viennese*, Coates & Co., 1902

Lansing, Robert, *War Memoirs of Robert Lansing*, Rich and Cowan, 1935

Lechner, Karl, *Die Babenberger – Markgrafen und Herzöge von Österreich 976–1246*, Böhlau Verlag, 1976

Leidinger, Hannes, and Moritz, Verena, *Russisches Wien – Begegnungen aus vier Jahrhunderten*, Böhlau, 2004

Lendvai, Paul, *One Day That Shook the Communist World: The 1956 Hungarian Uprising and its Legacy*, Princeton Press, 2008

Lenin, Vladimir, 'Letter to Maxim Gorky', *Lenin Collected Works*, Progress Publishers, 1976

Leonard, Lewis Alexander, *Life of Alphonso Taft*, Hawke Publishing Company, 1920

Levetus, Amelia Sarah, *Imperial Vienna – An Account of Its History, Traditions and Arts*, J. Lane, 1905

Lewin, André, *Die Französische Botschaft in Wien*, Verein für Geschichte der Stadt Wien, 1995

Lewis, Bernard, *The Muslim Discovery of Europe*, Phoenix Press, 2000

Ligne, Prince de, *Mélanges militaires, littéraires et sentimentales*, 1795

Loos, Adolf, 'Sämtliche Schriften', *Ornament und verbrechen*, 1963

Lorenz, Helmut, and Mader-Kratky, Anna, *Die Wiener Hofburg 1705–1835 – Die Kaiserliche Residenz vom Barock bis zum Klassizismus*, Verlag der Österreichischen Akademie der Wissenschaften, Anhang Quartierpläne, 2016

Lowe, John, *The Concert of Europe – International Relations 1814–70*, Hodder & Stoughton, 1990

Lutz, Heinrich, *Zwischen Habsburg und Preußen – Deutschland 1815–1866*, Siedler Taschenbücher Goldmann Verlag, 1998

Macartney, C.A. (ed.), *The Habsburg and Hohenzollern Dynasties in the Seventeenth and Eighteenth Centuries*, Walker and Company, 1970

Macek, Bernhard, and Holzschuh-Hofer, Renate, *Die Wiener Hofburg – Die unbekannten Seiten der Kaiserresidenz*, Sutton Verlag, 2014

Mahan, J. Alexander, *Maria Theresa of Austria*, Thomas Y. Crowell Company, 1933

Mansel, Philip, *Prince of Europe – The Life of Charles-Joseph de Ligne*, Phoenix, 2003

Marbot, Jean-Baptiste-Antoine-Marcelin, Baron de, *The memoirs of Baron de Marbot, late lieutenant-general in the French army*, Longmans, 1903

Mason, John W., *The Dissolution of the Austro-Hungarian Empire 1867–1918*, Longman Group Limited, 1985

Matsch, Erwin, *Der Auswärtige Dienst von Österreich (-Ungarn) 1720–1920*, Böhlau Verlag, 1986

Matsch, Erwin, *Flotow Erinnerungen – November 1918 auf dem Ballhausplatz*, Böhlau Verlag, 1982

Matzke, Manfred, *Die Staatskanzlei – 300 Jahre Macht und Intrige am Ballhausplatz*, Brandstätter Verlag, 2017

McGuigan, Dorothy Gies, *The Habsburgs*, Doubleday & Co., 1966

McGuigan, Dorothy Gies, *Metternich and the Duchess*, Doubleday, 1975

McLean, George F., Magliola, Robert R., and Fox, William, *Democracy: In the Throes of Liberalism and Totalitarianism*, CVRP, 2004

Mee, Charles, *Seven Fateful Moments When Great Men Met to Change the World*, New World City, 2015

Meir, Golda, *My Life*, Weidenfeld and Nicolson, 1975

Melman, Billie, *Women's Orients – English Women and the Middle East 1718–1918*, University of Michigan Press, 1992

Melvern, Linda, et al., *Technobandits – How the Soviets are Stealing America's High-Tech Future*, Houghton Mifflin, 1984

Menzel, Ulrich, *Die Ordnung der Welt, Imperium und Hegemonie in der Hierarchie der Staatenwelt*, Suhrkamp Verlag, 2015

Messerschmidt, Manfred, 'Foreign Policy and Preparation for War', *Germany and the Second World War*, Clarendon Press, 1990

Metzig, Gregor, *Kommunikation und Konfrontation: Diplomatie und Gesandtschaftswesen Kaiser Maximilians I (1486–1519)*, De Gruyter, 2016

Meyendorff, Peter von, *Ein russischer Diplomat an den Höfen von Berlin und Wien – Politischer und privater Briefwechsel 1826–1863*, De Gruyter, 1923

Michener, James, *The Bridge at Andau: The Compelling True Story of a Brave, Embattled People*, Random House, 2014

Miller, Michael, *Leaders of the SS and German Police*, Vol. I, James Bender Publishing, 2006

Minto, Countess Emma Elliot-Murray-Kynynmound, *Life and Letters of Sir Gilbert Elliot – First Earl of Minto from 1751–1806*, Vol. III, Longmans, Green and Co., 1874

Möckl, Karl, *Hof und Hofgesellschaft in den deutschen Staaten im 19. und beginnenden 20. Jahrhundert*, Oldenburg Wissenschaft, 1990

Montagu, Lady Mary Wortley, *Letters and Works*, Henry G. Bohn, 1861

Monts, Graf Anton von, *Erinnerungen und Gedanken des Botschafters Anton Graf Monts*, Verlag für Kulturpolitik, 1932

Moritz, Verena, and Leidinger, Hannes, *Oberst Redl – Der Spionagefall, der Skandal, die Fakten*, Residenz Verlag, 2012

Morritt, John, *The Letters of John Morritt of Rokeby*, John Murray Publishing, 1914

Morton, Frederic, *A Nervous Splendour – Vienna 1888/1889*, Penguin Books, 1979

Motley, John Lothrop, *The Correspondence of John Lothrop Motley*, Harper & Brothers, 1889

Müller, Johann Sebastian, 'Reisse-Diarium – §55 Juden-Stadt – 14 April 1660', in Keller, K., Scheutz, M., and Tersch, H., *Einmal Weimar – Wien und retour. Johann Sebastian Müller und sein Wienbericht aus dem Jahr 1660*, Oldenburg Verlag, 2005

Musulin, Stella, *Vienna in the Age of Metternich – From Napoleon to Revolution 1805–1848*, Faber and Faber, 1975

Mutschlechner, Martin, *Eine Frage der Ehre – die Botschafteraudienz*, https://www.habsburger.net/de/kapitel/eine-frage-der-ehre-die-botschafteraudienz

Nagel, Ulrich, *Zwischen Dynastie und Staatsräson – Die habsburgischen Botschafter in Wien und Madrid am Beginn des Dreißigjährigen Krieges*, Vandenhoeck & Ruprecht, 2018

Napoleon, *Lettres Inédites de Napoleon Ier*, 1897

Nickles, David Paul, *Under the Wire – How the Telegraph Changed Diplomacy*, Harvard University Press, 2003

Nicolson, Harry, *The Congress of Vienna – A Study of Allied Unity 1812–1822*, Constable and Co., 1946

Niederkorn, Jan Paul, *Die berichte der päpstliche Nuntien und der Gesandten Spaniens und Venedigs am kaiserlichen Hof aus dem 16. und 17. Jahrhundert – Quellenbuch der Habsburgermonarchie (16.-18. Jahrhundert) – Ein exemplarisches Handbuch*, R. Oldenburg Verlag, 2004

Nostitz, Carl von, *Leben und Briefwechsel*, Arnoldische Buchhandlung, 1848

Oberzaucher-Schüller, Gunhild, *Emilia Bigottini – die Etoile des Wiener Kongresses*, Wiener Tanzgeschichten, 2015

O'Connor, Martin, *Air Aces of the Austro-Hungarian Empire, 1914–1918*, Flying Machines Press, 1986

Owens, Karen, *Franz Joseph and Elisabeth – The Last Great Monarchs of Austria-Hungary*, McFarland and Co., 2014

Padover, Saul, *The Revolutionary Emperor Joseph the Second*, Ballou, 1934

Paget, Lady Walburga, *Scenes and Memories*, Charles Scribner's Sons, 1912

Paget, Lady Walburga, *Embassies of Other Days and Further Recollections*, Hutchinson, 1923

Paget, Lady Walburga, *In my Tower*, Hutchison and Co., 1924

Palmer, Alan, *Metternich – Councillor of Europe*, History Book Club, 1972

Palmer, Alan, *The Chancelleries of Europe – Hidden Diplomacy 1815–1918*, Faber and Faber, 2011

Palmer, Alan, *Twilight of the Habsburgs – Life and Times of Emperor Francis Joseph*, Atlantic Monthly Press, 1994

Palmer, Alan, *Twilight of the Habsburgs*, Weidenfeld and Nicholson, 1994

Petersdorff, Hermann von (ed.), *Otto von Bismarck, Reden 1847–1869*, Otto Stolberg, 1924–35

Picard, Bertold, *Das Gesandschaftswesen Ostmitteleuropas in der frühen Neuzeit*, Böhlau, 1967

Pichler, Karoline, *Denkwürdigkeiten aus meinem Leben 1769–1843*, Emil Karl Blümel, 1914

Pick, Hella, *Guilty Victim – Austria from the Holocaust to Haider*, Tauris, 2000

Pick, Hella, *Simon Wiesenthal – A Life in Search of Justice*, Orion, 1996

Picker, Henry, *Hitler's Tischgespräche*, Ullstein Verlag, 1993

Pieper, Dietmar, and Saltzwedel, Johannes, *Die Welt der Habsburger – Glanz und Tragik eines europäischen Herrscherhauses*, Goldmann Verlag, 2011

Podewils, Otto Christoph Graf von, *Friedrich der Grosse und Maria Theresia: Diplomatische Berichte*, 1937

Pohl, Walter, *Die Welt der Babenberger*, Styria Verlag, 1995

Ponsonby, Frederick (ed.), *Letters of the Empress Frederick*, Macmillan and Co., 1928

Pribram, Alfred, *Austro-Hungarian Monarchy – The Secret Treaties of Austria–Hungary 1879–1914*, Harvard University Press, 1920

Pursell, Brennan, *The Winter King – Frederick V of the Palatinare and the Coming of the Thirty Years' War*, Ashgate, 2003

Radlecker, Kurt, *Gottfried von Swieten – Eine Biographie*, Universität Wien, 1950

Rady, Martyn, *The Habsburgs – The Rise and Fall of a World Power*, Allan Lane, 2020

Rath, John, 'The Failure of an Ideal: The Viennese Revolution of 1848', *The Southwestern Social Science Quarterly*, Vol. 34, No. 2, September 1953

Rathkolb, Oliver (ed.), *Festschrift 250 Jahre – Von der Orientalischen zur Diplomatischen Akademie in Wien*, Studien Verlag, 2004

Rathkolb, Oliver, *Gesellschaft und Politik am Beginn der Zweiten Republik: vertrauliche Berichte der US-Militäradministration aus Österreich 1945*, Böhlau, 1985

Rauchensteiner, Manfried, *Der Erste Weltkrieg und das ende der Habsburger Monarchie*, Böhlau Verlag, 2013

Rauchensteiner, Manfried, *Der Sonderfall – Die Besatzungszeit in Österreich 1945–1955*, Styria Verlag, 1979

Rauchensteiner, Manfried, *Der Tod des Doppeladlers – Österreich-Ungarn und der Erste Weltkrieg*, Böhlau Verlag, 1993

Rauchensteiner, Manfried, *Spätherbst 1956 – Die neutralität auf dem Prüfstand*, Österreichischer Bundesverlag, 1981

Rauscher, Walter, *Die fragile Grossmacht – Die Donaumonarchie und die europäische Staatenwelt 1866–1914*, P.I.E. – Peter Lang, 2014

Redlich, Joseph, *Emperor Francis Joseph of Austria – A Biography*, Macmillan, 1929

Reiners, Ludwig, *Frederick the Great: A Biography*, Putnam, 1960

Richelson, Jeffrey, *A Century of Spies: Intelligence in the Twentieth Century*, Oxford University Press, 1997

Richter, Joseph, *Der wiederaufgelebte Eipeldauer: mit Noten von einem Wiener*, Heft 20, 1800

Ries, Ferdinand, *Biographische Notizen über Ludwig van Beethoven*, Rädeker, 1838

Robbins, Landon, H.C. *Haydn: Missa in angustiis (Nelson Mass)* CD, Notes, p. 7, Decca, 2000

Roberts, Ian, *Nicholas I and the Russian Intervention in Hungary*, Macmillan, 1991

Rogers, Clifford, *The Oxford Encyclopedia of Medieval Warfare and Military Technology*, Vol I, Oxford University Press, 2010

Röhr, John, *The Kaiser and His Court*, Cambridge University Press, 1994

Rosen, Charles, *The Classical Style*, Norton, 1971

Roth, Joseph, *The Wandering Jews*, Granta Books, 2001

Roth, Joseph, *Emperor's Tomb*, Granta Books, 2013

Rothenberg, Gunther, *The Army of Francis Joseph*, Purdue University Press, 1998

Rothenberg, G.E., 'The Habsburg Army in the Napoleonic Wars', *Military Affairs*, Vol. 37, 1973

Rothfels, Hans, *Bismarck-Briefe*, Verlag Vandenhoeck & Ruprecht, 1979

Rousseau. J.B., *Lettres de Rousseau*, 1750

Rumbold, Sir Horace, *Final Recollections of a Diplomatist*, Vol. I, Edward Arnold Publishers, 1902

Rumbold, Sir Horace, *Final Recollections of a Diplomatist*, Edward Arnold Publishers, 1905

Rumbold, Sir Horace, *The Austrian Court in the Nineteenth Century*, Methuen, 1909

Rupnik, Jacques, *Central Europe or Mitteleuropa*, Daedalus, 1990

Rupp, George Hoover, *A Wavering Friendship: Russia and Austria 1876–1878*, Harvard University Press, 1941

Saint-Amand, Imbert de, *The Happy Days of the Empress Marie Louise*, Scribner and Sons, 1901

Saint-Amand, Imbert de, *Marie Antoinette and the Downfall of Royalty*, Charles Scribner's Sons, 1899

Salvendy, John, *Royal Rebel – A Psychological Portrait of Crown Prince Rudolph of Austria Hungary*, University Press of America, 1988

Satow, Ernest Mason, *A Guide to Diplomatic Practice*, 1917

Satow, Ernest Mason, *An Austrian Diplomatist in the Fifties*, Cambridge, 1908

Sayer, Ian, and Botting, Douglas, *America's Secret Army – The Untold Story of the Counter Intelligence Corps*, Franklin Watts, 1989

Scarisbrick, Diana, *Margaret de Flahaut (1788–1867) – A Scotswoman at the French Court*, John Adamson, 2019

Scharding, Carlo, *Das Schicksal der Kaiserin Elisabeth*, 1960

Scheu, Friedrich, *Der Weg im Ungewisse: Österreichs Schicksalskurve 1929–1938*, Fritz Molden Verlag, 1972

Scheuch, Manfred, *Österreich im 20. Jahrhundert*, Christian Brandstätter Verlag, 2000

Schindler, Anton, *Beethoven As I Knew Him*, 3rd edition, Constance S. Jolly (trans.), Courier Dover Publications, 1860/1996

Schmied-Kowarzik, Antol, 'War Losses (Austria-Hungary)', *International Encyclopaedia of the First World War*, 2016

Schneider, K., Werner, E.M., Mazohl, B., *Europa in Wien – Who is Who beim Wiener Kongress 1814/15*, Böhlau Verlag, 2015

Schnelting, Karl, *Jüdische Lebenswege*, Fischer Verlag, 1992

Schöner, Joseph, *Wienertagebuch 1944–45*, Böhlau, 1992

Schönfeld, Friedrich von, *Traditionen zur Charakteristik Oesterreichs, seines Staats- und Volkslebens unter Franz dem Ersten: Band 2*, Hartknoch Verlag, 1844

Schorske, Carl, *Fin-De-Siècle Vienna: Politics and Culture*, Random House, 1981

Schnelner, Stefan, *Die Osmanen in Europa – Erinnerungen und Berichte türkischer Geschichtsschreiber*, Verlag Styria, 1985

Schroeder, Paul, *Austria, Great Britain, and the Crimean War: The Destruction of the European Concert*, Cornell University Press, 1972

Schroeder, Paul, 'Bruck versus Buol: The Dispute over Austrian Eastern Policy, 1853–1855', *The Journal of Modern History* Vol 40, No. 2, 1968

Schroeder, Paul, *The Transformation of European Politics, 1763–1848*, Clarendon Press, 1994

Schubert, Peter, *Beruf Kaiser. Geschichte der Familie Habsburg für junge Leser*, Mayer Junior, 1995

Schwinges, Rainer Christoph (ed.), *Gesandtschafts- und Botenwesen im spätmittelalterlichen Europa*, Thorbecke, 2003

Sealsfield, Charles, *Austria as it is; or, Sketches of continental courts, by an Eyewitness*, Hurst, Chance & Co., 1828

Sebag Montefiore, Simon, *Young Stalin*, Orion Books, 2007

Sebag-Montefiore, Simon, *The Romanovs: 1613–1918*, Weidenfeld & Nicolson, 2017

Seidl, Jakob, 'Ein Tagebuch – Wien im Jahre 1809', *Monatsblatt des Vereines für Geschichte der Stadt Wien*, Vol. XVII (52), 1935

Selby, Sir Walford, *Diplomatic Twilight: 1930–1940*, Murray, 1953

Service, Robert, *Lenin – A Biography*, Pan Books, 2005

Sheridan, R.K., *Kurt von Schuschnigg – A Tribute*, English Universities Press, 1942

Shirer, William L., *Berlin Diary – The Journal of a Foreign Correspondent 1934–41*, Hamish Hamilton, 1941

Shirer, William, *The Rise and Fall of the Third Reich*, Pan Books, 1979

Siemann, Wolfram, *Metternich: Stratege und Visionär*, C.H. Beck, 2016

Sked, Alan, *The Decline and Fall of the Habsburg Empire 1815–1918*, Pearson Education Ltd., 2001

Sked, Alan, *Radetzky – Imperial Victor and Military Genius*, Tauris and Co., 2011

Smith, Gillespie, *Memoirs and correspondence of Sir Robert Murray Keith, K.B., envoy extraordinary and minister plenipotentiary at the courts of Dresden, Copenhagen, and Vienna, from 1769–1792*, H. Colburn, 1849

Smith IV, Miles, 'From Savannah to Vienna – William Henry Stiles, the Revolutions of 1848, and Southern Conceptions of Order', *American Nineteenth Century History*, Taylor and Francis, 2013

Sondhaus, Lawrence, *The Naval Policy of Austria-Hungary, 1867–1918 – Navalism, Industrial Development, and the Politics of Dualism*, Purdue University Press, 1994

Spiel, Hilde, *Fanny von Arnstein – A Daughter of the Enlightenment 1758–1818*, Berg Publishers, 1991

Spiel, Hilde, *The Congress of Vienna*, Chilton Book Company, 1968

Spielman, John Philip, *The City & the Crown: Vienna and the Imperial Court, 1600–1740*, Purdue University Press, 1993

Spohr, Louis, *Autobiography*, Longman, Roberts & Green, 1865

Stauber, Reinhard, *Der Wiener Kongress*, Böhlau Verlag, 2014

Stekl, Hannes, 'Der Wiener Hof in der ersten Hälfte des 19. Jahrhunderts', in Möckl, Karl, *Hof und Hofgesellschaft in den deutschen Staaten im 19. und beginnenden 20. Jahrhundert*, De Gruyter, 1990

Sten, Michael, *Schubert – The Great Composers*, Icon, 2014

Steiner, Zara, *The Foreign Office and Foreign Policy 1898–1914*, Cambridge University Press, 1969

Steiner, Zara, *The Lights that Failed – European International History 1919–1933*, Oxford University Press, 2005

Steiner, Zara (ed.), *The Times Survey of Foreign Ministries of the World*, Times Books, 1982

Steiner-Gashi, Ingrid, *Im Dienst des Diktators: Leben und Flucht eines nordkoreanischen Agenten*, Carl Ueberreuter, 2010

Steininger, Rolf, *Austria, Germany, and the Cold War: From the Anschluss to the State Treaty 1938–1955*, Berghahn Books, 2008

Stephanie, Princess of Belgium, Archduchess of Austria-Hungary, *I Was to Be Empress*, Nicholson and Watson, 1937

Stevenson, Struan, *The Course of History*, Birlinn Books, 2017

Stewart, John Hall, *A Documentary Survey of the French Revolution*, Macmillan, 1951

Stiles, William Henry, *Austria in 1848–49 – Being a History of the Late Political Movements in Vienna, Milan, Venice, and Prague: With Details of the Campaigns of Lombardy and Novara: a Full Account of the Revolution in Hungary*, Harper & Brothers, 1852

Stoffel, Oberst Baron von, *Militärische Berichte erstattet aus Berlin 1866–1870*, Janke Verlag, 1872

Stratton, Stephen Samuel, 'Niccolò Paganini – His Life and Work', *The Strad*, 1907

Süleyman, İzzî, *Tarih-i İzzi*, 1785

Sunders, Edith, *The Hundred Days*, Longmans, 1964

Suttner, Bertha von, *Gesammelte Schriften*, Heinrichs, 1886

Suttner, Bertha von, *Die Waffen Nieder*, Jazeebee Verlag, 2016

Suttner, Bertha von, *High Life, Gesammelte Schriften,* Heinrichs, 1886

Swinburne, Henry, *The Courts of Europe at the Close of the Last Century,* Henry Colburn, 1841.

Szeps-Zuckerkandl, Berta, *I Lived Fifty Years of World History,* Bermann-Fischer Verlag, 1939

Szilassy, Sándor, 'America and the Hungarian Revolution of 1848–49', *The Slavonic and East European Review,* Vol. 44, No. 102, January 1966

Tacitus, *Annals,* XII.29.2

Taylor, A.J.P., *The Habsburg Monarchy 1809–1918,* Penguin, 1990

Taylor, A.J.P., *The Struggle for Mastery in Europe 1848–1918,* Oxford University Press, 2013

Thompson, Dorothy, *Let the Record Speak,* Hamish Hamilton, 1939

Thompson, E.A., *Romans and Barbarians: The Decline of the Western Empire,* University of Wisconsin Press, 1982

Thürheim, Ludovika Gräfin von, *Mein Leben – Erinnerungen aus Österreichs grosser Welt,* Georg Müller, 1913

Tietze, Hans, 'Ein Besuch in Wien beim Regierungsantritt Kaiser Leopold I. Nach ein Reisediarium aus dem Jahr 1660', *Berichte und Mitteilungen des Altertums-Vereines zu Wien,* Vol. 50, 1918

Tomenendal, Kerstin, *Das türkische Gesicht Wiens – Auf den Spuren der Türken in Wien,* Böhlau Verlag, 2000

Trollope, Frances Milton, *Vienna and the Austrians,* Bentley, 1838

Trost, Ernst, *Das Blieb vom Doppeladler,* Amalthea, 1984

Trotsky, Leon, *My Life,* Charles Scribner's Sons, 1930

Trotsky, Leon, *Our Revolution,* Hyperion Press, 1973

Tschudy von Glarus, Johann Jakob, *Illustriertes Gedenkbuch,* Schmidbauer und Holzwarth, 1854

Tunstall, Graydon, 'Austria-Hungary and the Brusilov Offensive of 1916', *The Historian,* 70 (1), 2008

Tweddell, John, *Correspondence,* J. Mawman, 1816

Unowsky, Daniel, *The Pomp and Politics of Patriotism – Imperial Celebrations in Habsburg, Austria 1848–1916,* Purdue University Press, 2005

# Bibliography

Usedom, Karl Ludwig Guido von, *Politische Briefe und Charakteristiken aus der deutschen Gegenwart*, Berlin, 1849

Uthmann, Joerg, *Die Diplomaten: Affären und Staatsaffären von den Pharaonen bis zu den Ostverträgen*, Deutsche Verl.-Anst., 1985

Vajda, Stephan, *Felix Austria – Eine Geschichte Österreichs*, Verlag Ueberreuter, 1980

Vehse, Karl Eduard, *Memoires of the Court and Aristocracy of Austria*, Nichols, 1896

Vocelka, Michaela und Karl, *Franz Joseph I – Kaiser von Österreich und König von Ungarn 1830–1916*, Verlag C.H. Beck, 2015

Volek, Tomislav, 'Eines der Probleme – Gottfried van Swieten', *Mozart Studien*, Vol. 25, Hollitzer Verlag, 2018

Voltaire, *Essai sur l'histoire générale et sur les mœurs et l'esprit des nations*, 1756

Wagnleitner, Reinhold, *Understanding Austria: The political reports and analyses of Martin F. Herz, Political Officer of the US Legation in Vienna 1945–48*, Neugebauer, 1984

Walzer, Tina, and Templ, Stephan, *Unser Wien – 'Arisierung' auf Österreichisch*, Aufbau Verlag, 2001

Wandruszka, Adam, *The House of Habsburg*, Sidgwick and Jackson, 1964

Watson, Alexander, *The Fortress – The Great Siege of Przemyśl*, Penguin, 2019

Wawro, Geoffrey, *The Austro-Prussian War – Austria's War with Prussia and Italy in 1866*, Cambridge University Press, 1996

Weiss, David, and Schilddorfer, Gerd, *Die Novara – Österreichs Traum von der Weltmacht*, Amalthea, 2010

Wellesley, F.A., *The Diary and Correspondence of Henry Wellesley, First Lord Cowley 1790–1846*, Hutchinson & Co., 1930

Wertheimer, Eduard von, *The Duke of Reichstadt (Napoleon II): a biography compiled from new sources of information*, J. Lane, 1902

West, Nigel, *The Crown Jewels – The British Secrets Exposed by the KGB Archives*, Yale University Press, 1999

Wheatcroft, Andrew, *The Enemy at the Gate – Habsburgs, Ottomans and the Battle for Europe*, Basic Books, 2009

Wheatcroft, Andrew, *The Habsburgs*, BCA, 1995

Whitman, Sidney, *Austria – The Story of Nations,* Unwin, 1898

*The Wild Geese in Austria – Irish Soldiers and Civilians in the Habsburg Service 1618–1918*, National Museum of Ireland, 2002

Williamson, Samuel, 'Aggressive and Defensive Aims of Political Elites. Austro-Hungarian Policy in 1914', in Afflerbach, H., and Stevenson, D. (eds), *An Improbable War: The Outbreak of World War I and European Political Culture Before 1914*, Berghahn Books, 2007

Wilmot, Martha, *More Letters from Martha Wilmot – Impressions of Vienna 1821–1829*, Macmillan and Co., 1935

Wilson, Peter, *The Holy Roman Empire – A Thousand Years of Europe's History*, Allan Lane Penguin Random House, 2016

Winder, Simon, *Danubia – A Personal History of the Habsburg Empire*, Picador, 2013

Winkelhofer, Martina, *Der Alltag des Kaisers – Franz Joseph und sein Hof,* Haymon Verlag, 2015

Wodak, Ruth, and Pelinka, Anton, *The Haider Phenomenon in Austria*, Routledge, 2001

Worthington, David, *Scots in Hapsburg Service, 1618–1648*, Brill Academic Publishers, 2004

Wraxall, Nathanial, *Memoirs of the Courts of Berlin, Dresden, Warsaw and Vienna*, T. Cadell and W. Davies, 1806

Wührer, Jakob, *Zu Diensten Ihrer Majestät: Hofordnungen und Instruktionsbücher am frühneuzeitlichen Wiener Hof,* Böhlau Verlag, 2011

Zamoyski, Adam, *Rites of Peace – The Fall of Napoleon and the Congress of Vienna*, Harper, 2007

Zweig, Stefan, *Die Welt von Gestern – Erinnerung eines Europäers,* Fischer Taschenbuch Verlag, 1985

# Index

Aargau, Switzerland 10
Absolutism in Austria 150
Adams, John Quincy 120
Adler, Fritz 262
Adler, Max 243
Adler, Viktor 245, 262
Adriatic Sea 101, 168, 235, 256, 259, 315
Aehrenthal, Alois Lexa von 233
AEIOU 10
Agram *See* Zagreb
Albania 249, 264, 280
Albert, Duke of Sachsen-Teschen 60, 62
Albert, Prince of Saxony 196
Albert Edward, Prince of Wales (Edward VII) 196, 210
Alexander, King of Serbia 233,
Alexander I, Tsar of Russia 104, 105, 107, 118, 125, 126, 129, 136
Alfred I, Prince of Windisch-Grätz 126, 155
Alsace-Lorraine 261–2
*Amadeus*, film 86, 110
Andlaw-Birseck, Franz Xaver von 149–50
Androsch, Hannes 341
Arafat, Yasser 343, 347–8
Archchancellor 26

Archduke 10
Argentina 300
Anschluss (1938) x, 74, 205, 2367, 239–40, 271, 286, 289–91, 293–300, 304, 307, 309, 321, 327, 331, 342, 350–1
Anstett, Johann von 119
anti-Semitism/anti-semite 125, 152, 215, 216–19, 222, 239, 244, 283, 296, 301
aristocracy 19, 46, 61, 208, 210, 216
    abolition of 273
Armfelt, Count Gustav Mauritz 91–2
Auckland 174
Augustinian Wing *See* Hofburg Palace
Aulic Council (Reichshofrat) 20, 26–7
Ausgleich See Austria-Hungary 1867 Settlement
Austria-Hungary
    dual monarchy 186, 197, 228, 233, 236, 249, 255, 265, 268, 270, 271, 275, 342
    Settlement/Compromise 1867 186, 249, 266
Austrian Broadcasting Corporation (ORF) xi, 334, 342, 348,
Austrian Civil War *See* wars

Austrian Foreign Ministry x, xii, 37, 108, 153, 194, 221, 248, 264, 295–6, 308–9, 335, 349, 359
Austrian Interior Ministry 108, 111, 153
Austrian National Library (also Imperial Library) *See* Hofburg
Austrian Netherlands 37, 51, 55, 57, 66, 71, 79, 86, 87, 89, 90
Austrian People's Party (ÖVP) 308, 326, 350
Austrian School of Economics 210
Austrian State Treaty 39, 328–9, 332, 349, 354
Austrian War of Succession *See* wars
Avars 6

Baar-Baarenfels, Eduard 296
Babenberg dynasty 6–9
Bach, Alexander von 168
Bach, Johann Sebastian 82, 85, 231
Baden, Grand Duchy 149, 223
Badeni, Count Kasimir 229
Bad Ischl 191, 248
Bagration, Princess Catherine 112, 125, 126
Baillet von Latour, Count Theodor Franz 156
Balkan League 234
Balkan war *See* wars
Balkans 165, 197–200, 202, 232–4, 253, 264, 281, 350–1
Bamberg 6
Banfield, Gottfried Freiherr von 59
Ban Ki-Moon 358
Bartenstein, Johann Christoph von 51
Batavia 173
Batthyány de Némétujvár, Count Lajos 154

battles
Alma River 167
Aspern-Essling ix, 98–9, 365
Austerlitz 98, 117, 148
Balaclava 167
Belgrade 37
Blenheim (2nd battle of Höchstädt) 37
Borodino 103
Cassano 94
Custoza 155, 182
Hohenlinden 94
Inkerman 167
Isonzo 261
Königgrätz 53, 183, 185, 197, 251
Leipzig (Battle of the Nations) xi, 103–4, 114, 118, 171
Lissa (1866) 182, 232
Magnano 94
Marchfeld 10
Marengo 94
Mohács 15
Nile 93
Novi 94
Ostrach 93
Petrovardin 37
Plevna 200
Solforino 171–2
Stalingrad 301–2
Stockach 93
Taku Forts 233
Ulm 94
Vienna (1683) 34–6
Vienna (1945) 306–07
Vittoria 115
Wagram 99, 148, 365
Waterloo ix, 133
White Mountain 19
Zenta 36–7
Znaim 100

Bauer, Otto 243, 284
Baumann, Ludwig 206
Bauermann, Friedrich 140
Bavaria 5, 6, 7, 19, 24, 25, 52, 53,
    57, 71, 90, 94, 95, 97, 101,
    107, 108, 112, 135, 166, 185,
    260
Beethoven, Ludwig van 80, 84, 85,
    91, 92, 94, 97, 112, 115, 116,
    141, 147, 231, 318
Beijing 232–3
Benedek, Ludwig von 170, 182–3
Beneš, Edvard 299
Ben-Natan, Asher 321
Benso, Camillo, Count of Cavour
    170
Benzel-Sternau, Karl 112
Berchtesgaden 286
Berchtold, Count Leopold 221,
    245, 246, 257, 258
Berthier, Louis-Alexandre, Marshal
    102
Best, Robert 278
Béthouart, Antoine 312–3
Bethlen, Gabriel 18
Bethmann-Hollweg, Theobald 246
Beust, Count Friedrich von 197
Bigottini, Emilia 113, 122
Biedermeier era 140–1
Bismarck, Otto von 177, 194, 200
Bittman, Ladislav 335–6
Blücher, Gebhard Leberecht von,
    Prince of Wahlstatt 133
Boieldieu, François Adrien 113
Bohemia ix, 9, 14, 15, 17, 18, 19,
    23, 25, 50, 54, 65, 66, 69, 70,
    71, 103, 104, 107, 113, 125,
    128, 137, 155, 181, 182, 185,
    186, 199, 201, 228, 229, 269,
    270, 271

Bolsheviks 244–5
Borcke, Kasper Wilhelm von 53
Bosnia and Herzegovina 37,
    198–202, 233, 246, 249, 251,
    255, 271, 353
Boxer Rebellion 232
Bradford, William 143
Brahms, Johannes 231
Brandt, Willy 297, 331, 347
Brazil 148–9
Bratislava xii, 54, 145, 289, 302,
    366
Braunbehrens, Volkmar 81
Brest-Litovsk 254, 263
Brixen 23
Bruck, Karl Ludwig von 178
Brusilov, General Aleksei 257
Brusilov offensive 257
Brussels 18, 41, 55, 80, 90, 167,
    204, 352, 354
Buchanan, James 157
Buda/Budapest xii, 44, 172, 186,
    187, 188, 189, 191, 228, 246,
    258, 265, 272, 274, 278, 291,
    301, 330
Bukovina 23, 71, 186, 255, 269,
    271
Bunson, Berta de 247
Bunson, Maurice de 247
Buol-Schauenstein, Count Karl
    Ferdinand von 165–7
Burgenland 315, 321, 341
Burgtheater
    *See* Vienna, theatres
Burschenschaften (student
    fraternities) 137
Butler, Walter 56

Canada 294, 339
Canaris, Wilhelm 296

Cape Town 173

Capo d'Istria, Count Giovanni (Ioannis Kapodistrias) 119, 136

Caporetto (Kobarid) *See* battles (Isonzo)

Capuchin Church, Imperial crypt 150, 192, 215, 231, 260, 268, 364

Carême, Marie-Antoine 122

Carinthia 9, 23, 42, 90, 107, 172, 256, 271, 306, 315

Carlsbad (Karlovy Vary) 137

Carlsbad Decrees 137

Carnuntum 1, 2

Carolingian dynasty 6

Carpathian mountains 1, 253–5, 272

castles

  Buchlau 233

  Buda 189

  Dürnstein 8

  Eckartsau 268

  Habsburg 10

  Klesheim 240

  Laxenburg 12, 44, 72, 261, 339

  Miramare 188

  Neugebäude 30

  Prague 18

  Tata 281

Castlereagh, Robert Stewart, Viscount, 120–1, 123, 128–9, 136

Catherine the Great, Tsarina of Russia vii, 69, 86, 91

Catholic Church

  Eastern Catholic /Uniate Church 250

  Roman Catholic Church 17, 18, 19, 50, 56, 68, 69, 74, 76, 77, 78, 86, 194, 214, 216, 217, 222, 250, 280, 283, 297, 298, 361

Çelebi, Evliya 30–4

censorship 81, 111, 137, 138, 140

Ceylon 173

Chamberlain, Houston Stewart 218–20, 239

Chancellery (Ballhaus, Ballhausplatz) xii, 63–4, 108, 110, 153, 285, 296, 302, 303, 307, 308, 332, 335

Charlemagne 7, 67

Charles, Archduke, Field Marshall 93, 97–9, 102

Charles I (IV), Emperor King (Austria-Hungary) 241, 260–2, 264–5, 267–8, 364

Charles V, Holy Roman Emperor, King of Spain 16–17

Charles VI, Holy Roman Emperor 43, 51

Charles Albert, King of Sardinia 159

Chile 174, 342

China 232, 252, 293, 294, 349, 357

Chotek, Countess Sophie 246

Christian Social Party 217, 229, 275, 280

Churchill, Winston x, 278

Cisleithania 186, 204, 229, 249, 270

Clark, Mark W. 312

Claudius, Emperor 1

Clayton, John M. 160

Clemenceau, Georges 210, 262, 269, 270

coffee houses *See* Vienna

Cold War x, 316–7, 320, 322, 325, 332, 333, 338, 339, 346, 356, 357

Communist Party of Austria (KPÖ) 307, 308, 315, 326

Confederation of the Rhine 96, 104
congresses
  Aix-la-Chapelle (Aachen) 136
  Berlin 200
  Laibach 136
  London 136–7
  Princes (Fürstentag) 179
  Slav Congress 155
  Troppau 137
  Verona 136
  Vienna vii, ix, 104–39, 146, 150, 152, 177, 355, 361, 364
  Westphalia 19–21
  Zionist (First) 223
Conrad von Hötzendorf, Franz 235, 246, 252, 253, 255, 261
Constantinople 16, 39, 44, 56, 165, 200, 202, 261
Consular Academy *See* Vienna
Copenhagen 55
Cowley, Henry Wellesley, First Lord 136
Croatia 14, 15, 23, 37, 56, 74, 154, 156, 158, 161, 182, 187, 228, 245, 250, 253, 272, 274, 300, 321, 353
Czartoryski, Prince Adam 119
Czechoslovakia and Czechs 23, 74, 154, 155, 204, 228, 229,250, 264, 265, 266, 270, 271, 272, 274, 275, 280, 286, 293, 296, 299, 305, 311, 320, 326, 334, 335, 336, 339, 342, 360
Czernin, Count Ottokar 261–2

Daim, Wilfried 298
Dalmatia 90, 95, 186, 187, 271
Danube, River 1, 2, 5, 6, 8, 22, 28, 34, 39, 40, 54, 63, 70, 74, 78, 79, 95, 97, 98, 99, 106,113, 114, 123, 165, 166, 185, 186, 189, 195, 231, 247, 249, 264, 265, 290, 291, 302, 303, 305, 306, 313, 316, 333, 347, 348, 365
Deneuve, Catherine 215
Den Haag 55
Denmark 19, 25, 29, 30, 83, 107, 108, 116, 180, 185, 193, 196, 260
Deriabin, Peter 324
Devereux, Walter 56
Diet of Worms 24
Dietrichstein, Adam von 16
Diplomatic Academy *See* Vienna
Diplomatic Revolution or '*renverse-ment des alliances*' 55, 64
Dollfuss, Engelbert 283, 285, 331
Doron, Lilith-Sylvia 294
Dresden 55, 119, 372, 373, 420
dual monarchy *See* Austria-Hungary
Dubček, Alexander 334, 336
Dubrovnik 23, 174
Dulles, Eleanor Lansing 313–15
Dulles, John Foster 313, 328
Dunant, Jean-Henri 171
Durfort, Almeric Joseph, Marquis de 61
Dutch Republic 20, 51, 52

Edinburgh 210
education 52, 55, 69, 72, 81, 83, 142, 152, 209, 216, 228, 242, 276, 281, 285, 326, 345, 357, 359
Egypt 32, 93, 140, 210, 341, 343, 347
Eichmann, Adolf 295–6, 300–01, 321

Eisenstadt 83, 93, 302
Elba 104, 132
Elisabeth Wittlesbach, Empress (Sisi) 165–7, 172, 187, 191, 209, 230–1
Elliot, Sir Gilbert 92
Elphinstone, Margaret Mercer, Baroness Keith and Nairne 152–3
England viii, 8, 25, 53, 56, 88, 91, 143, 174, 217
Enlightenment 67, 81, 118, 130, 210
Enns 6, 63
Esterházy family 82, 83, 93,
Eugene, Prince of Savoy 36–9, 363, 364
Eugippius 5
Eulenberg, Prince Philipp von 231
European Union (EU) 338, 354
Eynard, Jean Gabriel 117

Fatherland Front 283
Fendi, Peter 140
Ferdinand I, Archduke, Holy Roman Emperor 14–17
Ferdinand I, Austrian Emperor 150–1, 154–5, 163
Ferdinand I, Duke of Bourbon Parma 61
Ferdinand II, Holy Roman Emperor 56
Ferdinand Karl, Archduke 61
Ferdinand, King of Bulgaria 220, 260
Ferdinand, King of the Two Sicilies 61
Ferstel, Heinrich von 205, 239
Fertöd 83
Figl, Leopold 39, 314, 326–8

First World War *See* war
Fischer, Heinz xi, 84, 356
Fischer von Erlach, Johann Bernard 27, 37, 38, 62
Fiume 258, 274
Flahaut, Charles Comte de 152–3
Fodor, Marcel 378, 379
Forman, Miloš 86
France vii, viii, ix, 7, 8, 19, 20, 24, 25, 30 36, 51, 52, 53, 54, 55, 60, 61, 62, 64, 65, 66, 67, 69, 70, 71, 84, 86, 87, 88, 89, 90, 91, 94, 95, 96, 99, 101, 102, 103, 104, 108, 119, 120, 121, 127, 129, 131, 133, 136, 147, 148, 151, 160, 164, 165, 167, 170, 171, 172, 178, 179, 181, 188, 193, 197, 198, 199, 200, 209, 221, 235, 248, 250, 251, 270, 279, 293, 296, 297, 299, 311, 312, 321, 324, 325, 328, 339, 357, 360
Francis I, Holy Roman Emperor, Duke Francis Stephen of Lorraine 52, 53, 54, 57, 58, 61, 62, 68
Francis II, Holy Roman Emperor (Francis I, Austrian emperor) ix, 84, 93, 104, 105, 107, 136, 147, 148
Francis Joseph I, Emperor of Austria vii, xii, 23, 46, 59, 142, 163–9, 171–5, 179–80, 183, 186–8, 191, 194–5, 197–99, 203, 205, 209, 211, 217–18, 224–5, 229–31, 233–4, 236–7, 239, 248, 259, 261, 272, 363, 364
Franz Ferdinand, Archduke xii, 39, 225, 246, 363, 364

Frankfurt am Main 17, 25, 67–8, 178, 181
Frauenfeld, Georg Ritter von 173
Frederick I Barbarossa, Holy Roman Emperor 7, 8
Frederick II (the Great), King of Prussia 52, 53, 65, 66, 67, 69, 70, 71, 72, 80, 83, 91
Frederick II, Duke of Austria 9
Frederick III, Holy Roman Emperor 10, 12
Frederick III, Crown Prince of Prussia
Frederick V, Elector of the Palatine 18
Frederick V, King of Bohemia 18–19
Frederick, Empress of Germany 213–4
Frederick VI Christian, King of Denmark 116
Frederick, King of Württemberg 108
Frederick William III, Prussian king 104, 105, 108
Freedom Party of Austria (FPÖ) 217, 344, 345, 354, 355
Freemasons 83
French Revolution 86–91, 120, 121, 130
Freud, Sigmund 225, 244, 288, 297
Fugger, Princess Nora 244
Fulbright William 279–80
Fux, Johann Joseph 42

Galicia 63, 69, 71, 167, 182, 186, 216, 225, 235, 241, 245, 247, 251, 253, 254, 255, 257, 259, 271, 274, 344

Galimberti, Luigi 214–5
Garampi, Giuseppe 76
Gasperi, Alcide De 204
Gedye, G.E.R. (George) 278, 279, 282, 284, 285
Gentz, Friedrich von 119, 120, 126, 131
German Confederation 129, 130, 137, 155, 178, 179, 180, 181, 184, 185
German empire 185, 216, 236
German Federal Assembly 179
German Foreign Ministry
German language/speaking 26, 32, 107, 127, 175, 224, 227, 228, 229, 250
German National Assembly 155
Germany ix, x, 7, 9, 23 26, 33, 34, 72, 90, 93, 95, 96, 119, 127, 128, 130, 138, 155, 160, 165, 177, 178, 179, 180, 181, 184, 185, 187, 195, 197, 198, 200, 202, 205, 208, 210, 213, 218, 235, 236, 238, 246, 248, 249, 251, 255, 260, 261, 264, 266, 267, 269, 270, 271, 272, 278, 283, 284, 285, 286, 288, 289, 290, 295, 297, 299, 306, 309, 311, 312, 321, 323, 324, 327, 332, 336, 339, 354, 357, 360
Gesellschaft der Associirten Cavaliers (Society of Associated Cavaliers) 82
Gesellschaft der Musikfreunde (Music Association) 85, 142
Ghandi, Indira, 358
Ghiselin, Ogier, de Busbecq 16
Gibraltar 172, 173
Gieslingen, Baron Wladimir Giesl von 247

Glasgow 210, 221
Globočnik, Odilo 301
Gluck, Christoph Ritter von 73
Goebbels, Joseph 291, 304,
Goethe, Johann Wolfgang von vii,
    68, 91, 219
Goldstaub, Eric 294
Golitsyn, Prince Dmitry
    Mikhailovich 82
Gołuchowski, Count Agenor 232
Gordon, Colonel John 56
Göring, Hermann 286, 301
Gorlice–Tarnów offensive 256
Grand Marshall of the Court or
    Obersthofmarshall 55
Grand Master of the Court or
    Obershofmeister 55
Grant, Julia Dent 227–8
Grant, Frederick Dent 227
Gravosa 174
Graz 230
Gray, Sir Edward 247
Grimm, Jacob 108, 125
Great Britain *See* United Kingdom
Greece 119, 137, 200, 234, 264,
    280, 311
Greene, Graham 306, 317
Grillparzer, Franz 140
Gruber, Karl 314, 326
Gunther, John 278
Guteres, António 359
Gyulay de Marosnémethi et
    Nádaska, Ferenc 171

Habsburg
    dynasty viii, ix, 10, 14, 22, 23,
        50, 52, 62, 149, 154, 163, 169,
        231, 236, 249, 361, 363, 364
    empire viii, 11, 23, 25, 94, 154,
        155, 163, 169, 172, 178, 186,

    210, 216, 236, 238, 249, 250,
    251, 254, 259, 266, 270, 275,
    291, 344, 353, 360, 361, 364,
    365
Law 273
Habsburg
    Eduard 360
    Gabriela 360
    Karl 360
    Otto ix, 84, 260, 334, 344, 352,
        364
Habsburg-Este cadet branch 169
Hager, Franz Hager von Allensteig
    111–12
Haider, Jörg 355
Hamilton , Emma, Lady 93
Hamilton, John James 57
Hamilton, Johann Andreas Graf
    von 57
Hamilton, William, Sir 93
Handel, Georg Friedrich 82, 85,
    113
Hansen, Theophil 204
Hardenberg, Karl August von 108,
    119, 126, 136
Haugwitz, Friedrich Wilhelm, Graf
    von 54, 55
Hayek, Friedrich von 358
Haydn, Joseph 63, 80–1, 83–6, 93,
    112, 122, 288
Heiligenkreuz 214
Heinrich vom und zum Stein 118
Heldenplatz *See* Hofburg Palace,
    Heroes' Square
Henry II Jasomirgott, Duke of
    Austria 7
Henry VI, Holy Roman Emperor 9
Herberstein, Siegmund von 14

Herzl, Theodor 221–3, 225

Hildebrandt, Johann Lukas von 26, 64

Hitler, Adolf 148, 205, 216, 218, 219, 220, 236–8, 239, 244, 277, 278, 282, 284–91, 293–4, 298–300 303–4, 309, 311, 354, 364

Hofburg palace, Vienna viii, 2–3, 9, 11–12, 22, 26–7, 34, 44–5, 47–8, 51, 52, 61, 64, 72, 77, 81, 97, 107–111, 113, 115, 116, 125, 126, 129, 139, 147, 164, 166, 203, 204, 205, 215, 221, 227, 230, 231, 234, 236, 259, 266, 318, 332, 333, 346, 347, 359, 360, 364

Ambassadors Stairs (Botschafter Stiege) 12

Alexander Apartments 107

Amalienburg 107

Augustinian Wing 81

Ceremonial Hall 113

Chancellery Wing (Reichskanzeleitrakt) 26–7

Court Chapel (Hofkapelle) 11, 141, 215

Federal Presidency xiv, 12

Imperial Court Chancellery 26–7

Imperial Library 45, 73, 80, 81, 82

Imperial Treasury (Schatzkammer) 11, 45

Inner Castle Court 12

Kaiser Forum 205

Leopoldine Wing 72

New Court (Neue Burg) 205, 332

Old Burgtheater 81, 203

Redoutensaal/Redoute Wing 109, 115, 142, 143, 347

Riding School 45, 109, 110, 113, 115, 365

St Michael's Gate/Square 2, 3, 4, 81, 293, 365

Stallburg mews 110

state rooms 27, 47, 48, 62

Swiss Court (Schweizerhof) 11, 12

Swiss Gate (Schweizertor) 11, 107

Hofer, Andreas 101, 113, 313

Hoffmann, Josef 220

Hofmannsthal, Hugo von 221

Holland *See* Netherlands

Holocaust 295, 300, 321, 344, 345, 365

Holy Alliance 161, 197, 197

Holy League 36

Holy Roman Empire viii, x, 3, 6–7, 9, 11, 16, 17, 19, 22–7, 29, 34, 36, 56, 57, 58, 65, 67, 90, 94, 95, 96, 97, 117, 119, 129, 137, 165, 361, 367

Hong Kong 174

Ho Feng-Shan 293–4

Horn, Gyula 352

Hortense, Queen of Holland 152

Horthy, Miklós 272

Horváth, Ödön von 274

Hötzendorf, Franz Conrad von 235

Hoyos, Count Joseph 212

Hübner, Baron Alexander von 170

Hugo, Victor 210

Humboldt, Wilhelm von 108

Hume, David 210

Hungarian Diet 145

Hungarian language 187, 228, 229, 250

Hungary 1, 9, 14–5, 18, 23, 33, 37, 54, 69–70, 83, 112–3, 145, 154, 156–9, 160–1, 163–5,

172, 179, 186–8, 191, 193, 195, 197–202, 220–1, 227–8, 232–5, 241, 242–5, 249–53, 256–8, 260–3, 265–6, 270–2, 274, 280–1, 293, 296, 299, 301, 325, 329, 334, 339, 352
Huns 4

Île Saint Paul 173
Imperial Court Chancellery (Reichhofkanzlei) *See* Hofburg palace
Imperial Diet (Reichstag) 24–5
Imperial Library *See* Hofburg palace
Imperial Treasury (Schatzkammer) *See* Hofburg palace
Imperial Vice-Chancellor 26–7
India 52, 65, 66, 121, 160
industrialisation 140, 339
Ingestre, Charles, Viscount 145
Innitzer, Cardinal Theodore 297–8
Innsbruck 44, 156, 266
Ireland and the Irish 7, 56–9, 74, 120, 121, 143, 210, 358, 371
Isabella of Parma 60–1
Isabey, Jean Baptiste 122
Israel 221, 223, 224, 297, 300, 321, 342, 343, 344, 358
Italian language 72, 74, 107, 127, 228, 250
Italian peninsula and Italy 90, 137, 154, 155, 159, 170, 172, 179, 181, 182, 249, 256, 257, 258, 260, 265, 266, 270, 271, 312
International Atomic Energy Agency (IAEA) x, 338, 341, 358, 365

International Institute for Applied Systems Analysis (IIASA) 339–40
Izvolsky, Alexander 233

Jagiellonian kingdoms 14
Japan 193–4, 223 251, 253, 293, 339
Jelačić, Count Josip 154, 156–8, 167
Jellinek, Anton 173
Jews 28, 69, 76, 152, 216–9, 221, 222, 244, 250, 255, 274, 29–7, 300, 301, 305, 321, 342, 343, 344, 350, 365
Joanna of Castille 14
John III Sobeiski, King of Poland 34–5
John Paul II, Pope 268
Joseph II, Holy Roman Emperor vii, 55, 60, 62, 68, 69–72, 75–8, 79, 80–1, 86, 87, 91
Jugendstil 206, 209

Kahlenberg vii, 5, 35, 123
Kaltenbrunner, Ernst 301
Kapodistrias, Ioannis *See* Capo d'Istria, Count Giovanni
Karajan, Herbert von 203
Karlsbad/Karlovy Vary 137
Károlyi de Nagykároly, Alajos 202, 266
Kärntnertor 42
Kärntnertortheater 42
Kaunitz-Rietberg, Prince Anton Wenzel 55
Keith, Sir Robert Murray 64, 75, 77, 79
Kendrick, Thomas 295

Kennedy, John F. 62, 332
Khevenhüller-Frankenburg, Hans
    von 16
Khevenhüller-Metsch, Johann
    Joseph von 55
Khrushchev, Nikita 62, 332, 333
King, David 106
King's Dragoon Guards 234, 248
Kirschlager, Rudolf 339
Kissinger, Henry 21, 122, 340,
    341, 343
Klimt, Ernst 205
Klimt, Gustav 39, 203, 205, 220,
    364
Klingemann, Ernst August 113
Koch, Joseph Anton 140
Kohl, Helmut 358
Kokoschka, Oskar 39, 220, 282, 364
Kolowrat-Liebsteinsky, Franz Anton
    von 151
Körner, Theodor 331
Korošec, Anton 204
Kossuth, Lajos 154, 156, 157, 158,
    160, 162, 164
Kraków 253
Kramář, Karel 204
Kraus, Karl 193, 221, 237
Kreisky, Bruno 297, 331, 332, 333,
    339, 340, 343, 348, 350, 363
Kriehuber, Josef 140
Kulczycki, Jerzy Franciszek 35
Kurhessen 108
Kuripečič, Benedikt, von
    Obernburg 16

La Garde-Chambonas, August,
    Count de 106
La Harpe, Frédéric-César de 119
Lacy, Franz Moritz, Graf, Field
    Marshall 57, 58

Lamb, Sir Frederick 125, 151
Lanner, Johann 141, 152
Lansing, Robert 259, 264, 265
Latour, Theodor Franz, Count
    Baillet von 156, 159
Loudon, Ernst Gideon, Baron von,
    59
Le Carré, John 318, 320–1
Lemberg/Lwów/Lviv 241, 253,
    255, 256
Lenin, Vladimir Ilyich 244, 245
Leopold V, Duke of Austria 8
Leopold, Duke of Lorraine 58
Leopold I, Holy Roman Emperor
    28, 31, 32, 34,
Leopold II, Holy Roman Emperor
    55, 61, 70, 77, 87, 88, 89
Leopold II, King of the Belgians 196
Leopoldina, Josepha Carolina,
    Archduchess 148–9
Lerchenfeld 176
Leslie, Count Walter 56
liberalism 181
Lichnowsky, Prince 82
Liechtenstein
    Prince Johann Adam von 41
    Prince Wenzel von 60
Ligne, Charles Joseph, Prince de vii,
    66, 74, 90, 91, 92, 105, 106,
    122, 123, 318
Linz 216, 236, 289, 291, 300, 303
Liszt, Franz 141–2
Ljubljana/Laibach 136, 137
Lloyd George, David 263
Lobanov-Rostovsky, Prince Aleksey
    Borisovich 208
Lombards 6
Lombardy-Venetia 130, 155, 167,
    169, 170, 171, 187
Lombardy 23, 172, 179

London viii, xi, 47, 53, 64, 84,
120, 121, 123, 136, 137, 146,
161, 189, 263, 278, 289, 292,
296, 317, 319, 232, 353
Loos, Alfred 237, 282, 293
Loudon, Gideon von 59
Louis II, King of Hungary,
Bohemia and Croatia 14–15
Louis XIV, King of France 38
Louis XV, King of France 64
Louis XVI, King of France 61, 87,
88, 121
Louis XVII, King of France 121
Louis XVIII, King of France 122
Louis-Philippe, King of France 121,
153
Löwenstern, Otto 117
Lower Austria 6, 18, 22, 113, 223,
247, 268, 315, 322
Ludwig, Archduke 151
Ludwig Victor, Archduke 239, 240,
300
Ludwig, King of Bavaria 260
Lueger, Karl 217, 218, 219, 239,
280
Luther, Martin 17
Lutheranism *See* Protestantism
Lützow, Heinrich von 247

McCreery, Richard Loudon 312
Mackintosh, Charles Rennie 221
Macmillan, Harold 328
Madeira 172, 173, 268
Madras 173
Madrid 16, 37, 44, 70
Maguire, Johann Sigismund Graf
57
Mahler, Gustav 203, 221, 244
Mainz 25, 26, 119
Malvezzi, Giovanni Maria 16

Manila 173
Mann, A. Dudley 160
Maori visit to Vienna, Wiremu
Toetoe and Hemara Te
Rerehau (1859) 174–7
Marcomanni tribe 1
Marcus Aurelius, Emperor 1–3
Margaret, Princess of Babenberg 9
Maria Antonia, Archduchess of
Austria (Marie Antoinette,
Queen of France) vii, 39, 61,
62, 69, 86, 87, 88, 122
Maria Beatrice d'Este, Duchess
61
Maria Carolina of Naples, Queen
61, 93
Maria Christina, Archduchess 60
Maria Isabella of Bourbon Parma
60
Maria Ludovika of Austria-Este,
Archduchess 118
Maria Ludovika, Princess of Spain
61
Maria Theresa, Empress 12, 37,
43, 46, 47, 51, 52, 53, 54, 55,
56–71, 73–77, 80, 93, 340,
363
Order of Maria Theresa 46, 47,
57, 59, 74
Maria Theresa of Naples–Sicily,
Empress 93
Marie Louise, Archduchess,
Empress of France 97, 101,
102, 103, 132, 133, 146, 147,
169
Marlborough, Duke of 37
Marmont, Auguste, Marshal 147–8
*The Marriage of Figaro* (W.A.
Mozart) 83, 85
Marshall Plan 314

Masaryk, Tomáš 204
Marmont, Marshall Auguste
Marx, Karl 158–9
Marxism, Austro-Marxism 243,
    244, 283
Mason, James 215
Mautern 6
Maximilian, Archduke, Emperor of
    Mexico 172, 173, 177, 187–8,
    191–2
Maximilian I, Holy Roman
    Emperor 14, 26
Maximilian, Duke of Bavaria 166
Maximilian, King of Bavaria 108
Maximilian, Johannes, Count of
    Lamberg 20
Maximilian, Count of
    Trauttmansdorff and
    Weinsberg 20
Mayerling 212–15
McElligott, General 57
Mediterranean Sea 52, 92, 104,
    161, 200, 231, 233, 250
Meir, Golda 342–3
Mengei, Carl 210
Metternich, Klemens Wentzel von
    101, 103, 105, 108, 111, 112,
    114, 119–22, 125–9, 133,
    135–40, 143, 145, 147–55,
    206, 209, 230, 308, 355
Metternich System 199
Meyendorff, Peter von 166
Meytens, Martin van 61
Mexico 156, 188, 191
Migration period 4–5
Miklas, Wilhelm 287–8
Milan 76, 188, 170, 155, 170
Minto, Gilbert Elliot, Lord 92
Minto, Harriet, Lady 92, 93
Mock, Alois, 352, 353, 354

Molden, Fritz 298
Molden, Otto 354
Molotov, Vyacheslav 324, 328
Montagu, Lady Mary Wortley
    39–44
Montecuccoli, Count Rudolf, Rear
    Admiral 232
Montmédy 87
Montrond, Comte Casimir de 133
Monts, Count Anton 212
Moravia 18, 23, 50, 69, 71, 95,
    100, 156, 178, 185, 186, 225,
    233, 269, 270, 271
Moresnet 130
Morrit, John 107
Morocco 39, 78
Moser, Koloman 220
Motley, John Lothrop 184, 185
Mozart, Constanze 83
Mozart, Karl 83
Mozart, Leopold 63
Mozart, Wolfgang Amadeus 61, 62,
    63, 80–6, 107, 110, 112, 122,
    141, 152, 317, 333, 346, 365
Mulgrave, Phipps, Henry, Lord 92
Munich 55, 173, 218, 219, 238,
    239, 273, 274, 291, 299, 361
Münster 20
Murray, Joseph Albert, Major-
    General 57
Murray, Joseph Graf, General 57
Musikverein (Music Association) 85
Musil, Robert 297
Muslim 19, 39, 201, 250, 251,
    256, 353, 361
Mussolini, Benito 283
Nagy, Imre 329
Napoleon Bonaparte ix, 36, 62, 87,
    90, 92, 94, 95, 96, 97, 98, 99,
    100, 101, 103, 104, 105, 113,

117, 118, 119, 121, 122, 127, 132, 133, 136, 147, 148, 152, 160
Napoleon II, François Joseph Charles Bonaparte, also Francis, Duke of Reichstadt 102, 146, 147
Napoleon III 170, 171, 188
National Socialism (Nazism) 274, 284, 286
Nelson, Horatio, Admiral 92–3
Nesselrode, Karl, Count 118, 133, 136
Neue Freie Presse *See* Presse
Nestroy, Johann 140
Netherlands 14, 25, 82, 104, 137, 152, 193, 210, 219, 296, 300, 311, 339 *See* also Austrian Netherlands
Neukomm, Sigismund 122
neutrality 103, 118, 130, 131, 165, 197, 258, 327, 329, 334, 340, 346, 358
New Zealand 174, 175, 176, 177
Nicobar Islands 173
Nicholas I, Tsar of Russia 163
Nicholas Orthodox Cathedral, Vienna 208
Nixon, Richard 331, 341
Noailles, Emmanuel Marquis de 89
North America 23, 52, 65, 346
North Atlantic Treaty Organisation (NATO) 327
Novara expedition 173–91
Novikov, Yevgeny 198–9
Nugent, Laval Count von Westmeath 59, 167, 170
Nüll, Eduard van der 203

O5 (Austrian resistance) 303

O'Donnell, Conal Count 371
O'Donnell, Maximilian Count von Tyrconnell 59, 164
O'Kelly, General 371
O'Mahoney, Count Demetrio 57
O'Reilly, Count Andreas 57
Oberste Polizei- und Censurs Hofstelle 111
Olbrich, Joseph Maria 220
Old Burgtheater *See* Hofburg Palace
Olmütz/Olmouc 156, 163, 177–8
orders
  of Elizabeth 46
  of Francis Joseph 46
  of the Golden Fleece 46, 47, 50, 58, 64, 189
  of the Iron Crown 46
  of Leopold 46, 47
  of Maria Theresa 46, 47, 57, 59, 74
  of St Stephen 46, 47
  of the Starry Cross 75
Oriental Academy *See* Vienna, Diplomatic Academy
Organisation for Petroleum Exporting Countries (OPEC) x, 343
Organisation for Security and Cooperation in Europe (OSCE) x, xi, 12, 346, 356, 364

Orthodox Church
  Eastern 164, 165, 199
  Russian 208
Osborne House 214
Osborne, John 318
*Osborne*, Royal Yacht 172
Osbourn, Francis 79
Osnabruck 20

Ostend Company 51
Ostrogoths 4
Ottoman empire 14, 15, 16, 17,
    18, 19, 30,32,33 34, 35, 36,
    37, 28–44, 63. 83, 86, 90,
    137, 164 165, 198, 199, 200,
    201, 202, 233, 234, 235, 256,
    361, 363
Otto, Archduke 240–1
Ottokar II, King of Bohemia 9, 10

Padua Circular 88
Paget, Sir Augustus 207
Paget, Lady Walburga 207, 211,
    214, 226
palaces
    Auersperg 307
    Belvedere 37, 38, 39, 62, 140,
        281, 299, 328, 360, 364
    Budapest 189
    Coburg 357
    Dietrichstein-Ulfeld 107
    Epstein 316
    Esterházy 93
    Eugen Stadtpalais 37
    Favorita 42, 51, 73, 364
    Gödöllő 191
    Hofburg *See* Hofburg palace
    Hohenlohe-Bartenstein 207
    Laxenburg 12, 44, 72, 261, 339
    Liechtenstein 41
    Metternich 114, 206, 209
    Pallavicini 318
    Palm 125
    Questenberg-Kaunitz 108
    Razumovsky 114–15
    Reichstadt 199
    Rosenau 180
    Schönbrunn 12, 41, 44, 62, 63,
        72, 79, 93, 94, 97, 100, 101,

        108, 113, 116, 132, 133, 140,
        148, 180, 197, 215, 236, 244,
        259, 267, 316, 320, 333, 360
Sigray-Saint-Marsan 207
Simon 208
Starhemberg 152
Strelzhof 247
Tuileries 88, 146, 170
Viktor Ludwig 239–40
Palacký, František 154, 155
Palestine 210, 223, 321, 343, 344
Palestinian Liberation Organisation
    (PLO) 343, 347
Palmerston, Henry John Temple,
    3rd Viscount 161, 180
Pannonia 1, 6
Papen, Franz von 286
Paris viii, 61, 64, 67, 70, 80, 88,
    96, 103, 104, 113, 118, 122,
    126, 129, 132, 133, 146, 148,
    153, 168, 170, 178, 181, 182,
    193, 195, 206, 222, 226, 251,
    270, 349
Paris Conference (1919) 129
Passau 5, 13, 40
peace
    of Augsburg 17
    of Nuremberg 17
    of Nikolsburg 20
    of Paris (1856) 168
    of Prague 20
    of Pressburg 117
    of Rome (Pax Romana) 2
    of Westphalia 21
Persia 32, 196
Pest 158, 221
Peter I Karadjordjevic of Serbia 233
Petrushevych, Yevhen 204
Philby, Kim 284, 295, 317, 319
Philip II, King of France 8

Philip I, Duke of Burgundy, King of Spain 14
Piccolomini, Enea Silvio (Pope Pius II) 12–13
Pichler, Karoline 95, 114
Pinay, Antoine 328
Piedmont-Sardinia, Kingdom of 167, 170
Pillnitz, Declaration of 88
Pius VI, Pope 77–8
Plombières 170
Plunkett, Thomas von 57
Podewils, Count Otto Christoph von 54, 59
Poland 14, 34, 35, 71, 118, 128, 129, 163, 197, 204, 256, 270, 271, 279, 296, 299, 300, 301, 311, 334, 339
Pompadour, Madame de 64
Popper, Sir Karl 297, 358
Postl, Carl Anton 138
Pozzo di Borgo, Carlo Andrea 92, 119
Pragmatic Sanction 37, 51, 52, 53
Prague 9, 18, 19, 20, 44, 54, 65, 83, 155, 230, 258, 266, 315, 334, 335, 353
    Defenestration of 18
Prater park *See* Vienna, parks
*Pravda* (newspaper) 242, 243, 244
Pressburg/Posszony *See* Bratislava
*Presse, Die* (*Neue Freie*) 222
Princip, Gavrilo 246
Privy Council 20, 47, 48, 58, 189
*Profil* (magazine) 350
Protestantism and Protestants 19, 29, 56, 69, 77, 78. 131, 250
    Calvinism 17, 18
    Lutheranism 17

Prussia vii, ix, 25, 30, 51, 52, 53, 59, 63, 64, 65, 66, 66, 69, 70, 71, 72, 74, 75, 80, 83, 87, 88, 89, 91, 96, 104, 105, 107, 108, 112, 113, 116, 119, 120, 126, 127, 128, 129, 130, 133, 136, 137, 153, 165, 173, 177, 178, 179, 180, 181, 182, 183, 184, 185, 186, 187, 193, 194, 196, 208, 211, 220, 234, 282, 298
Przemyśl, fortress 253–6
Puynipet Island 174
Quadi tribe 1
'Quadrilateral' fortresses 172
Quadruple Alliance 136

Raab, Julius 314, 326, 327, 329
Rabin, Yitzhak 358
Radetzky von Radetz, Joseph Count 155, 159, 163, 167, 170, 206, 230, 363
*Radetzky March* 141, 159, 234, 274
railways x, 164, 236
Raimund, Ferdinand 140
Razumosky, Andrey, Count 85, 91, 92, 114
Redl, Colonel Alfred 241, 242, 318
refugees 257, 259, 274, 275, 280, 284, 321, 330, 331, 335, 342, 352, 353, 354
Regensburg 20, 24, 25, 39
Renner, Karl 204, 243, 259, 270, 271, 290, 306, 308, 309
Reuss, Prince Heinrich VII 211, 212, 214
revolutions
    1848 vii, 58, 151, 153–64, 167, 169, 186
    American 70, 120, 130

Brabant 86
Czechoslovak (1968) 342
Diplomatic 55, 64, 108
French ix, 86, 87, 88, 89, 90, 91,
    121, 130
Hungarian (1956) 329–31, 331,
    225, 342, 353
Russian 242, 245, 263
Richard I, King of England 8
Richelieu, Louis, 3rd Duke of 136
Ringstrasse *See* Vienna
Rio de Janeiro 148, 173
Robinson, Mary 358
Robinson, Sir Thomas 53
Roman Catholicism *See* Catholic
    Church
Romania 57, 165, 187, 200, 235,
    249, 250, 260, 270, 271, 272,
    293, 325
Römer, Frankfurt 67
Rommel, Erwin 74, 261
Roosvelt, Eleanor 277
Roosevelt, Theodore 225, 297
Roth, Joseph 159, 274
Rothschild, Albert 312
Rousseau, Jean-Jacques vii, 38, 91
Rudolf, Count of Habsburg 9, 10
Rudolf of Austria, Crown Prince
    187, 209–15, 220, 226, 231
Rudolph II, Holy Roman Emperor
    20
Rumbold, Sir Horace, 8th Baronet
    207, 230, 231
Russia and Soviet Union (USSR)
    vii, viii, x, 14, 25, 30, 36, 63,
    64, 65, 66, 69, 71, 79, 82, 85,
    87, 88, 91, 92, 94, 95, 101,
    102, 103, 104, 105, 107, 108,
    112, 114, 118, 125, 126, 127,
    128, 129, 130, 133, 136, 137,
160, 161, 163, 164, 165, 166,
    167, 168, 178, 183, 187, 193,
    197, 198, 199, 200, 207, 208,
    233, 234, 235, 241, 242, 243,
    244, 245, 248, 249, 251, 252,
    253, 254, 255, 256, 257, 258,
    259, 261, 262, 263, 293, 299,
    302, 303, 304, 310, 311, 312,
    314, 317, 318, 320, 322, 324,
    325, 327, 328, 332, 333, 334,
    338, 339, 342, 344, 346, 357
Russian Revolution (1917) *See*
    revolutions
Ruthenian 228, 241, 271

Sacher Hotel 42, 240, 280, 317
Sadat, Anwar 341, 343
Sagan, Wilhemine, Duchess of 125
Salieri, Antonio 110, 112, 141,142
Salzburg 23, 80, 95, 101, 122, 130,
    135, 179, 230, 240, 286, 315,
    318
Sanjak of Novi-Pazar 201, 233
Sarajevo 201, 225, 246, 363
Sardinia, kingdom of 16, 52, 55,
    82, 88, 129, 155, 169
Sarmatian Iazyges tribe 1
Saxony 17, 18, 25, 28, 29, 53, 55,
    60, 65, 66, 104, 107, 128,
    130, 181, 185, 196, 240, 196,
    260, 299
Schärf, Adolf 314, 326, 333
Schattendorf 282
Scherzer, Karl von 173
Schiele, Egon 39, 220, 364
Schindler, Oskar 293
Schleswig-Holstein 30, 180, 181, 185
Schmidt, Heinrich 296
Schnitzler, Arthur 221
Schönberg, Arnold 281, 297

Schönbrunn Convention 197

Schönbrunn Palace *See* palaces

Schöner, Josef 303, 304

Schönerer, Georg von 217–9, 230, 239

Schönholz, Friedrich von 109

Schorske, Carl 220, 221

Schottenkirche 7, 84, 123

Schottenstift 7

Schroeder, Paul 168,

Schubert, Franz 141, 142

Schuschnigg, Kurt 285, 286, 287, 290

Schutzbund 282

Schwarz, Eduard 173

Schwarzenberg, Prince Felix zu 157, 158, 163, 178

Schwarzenberg, Prince Karl Philipp zu 103, 104, 206

Schwarzenberg, Karel 336

Schwarzenberg Plan 178

Schwarzenegger, Arnold 355, 359

Schwechat 157, 322, 332, 338

Schweinitz, Hans Lothar 199, 208

Scotland 7, 52, 56, 295

Scott, Sir Walter 146

Sealsfield, Charles *See* Postl, Carl Anton

Sebag-Montefiore, Simon 244, 361

Secession *See* Vienna

Second World War *See* war

Seipel, Ignaz 280, 281

Selby, Sir Walford 287–8

Serbia 1, 23, 37, 56, 187, 198, 199, 200, 201, 202, 228, 233, 234, 247, 248, 249, 251, 252, 255, 259, 261, 264, 270, 353

Severinus of Noricum, St 4, 5, 6

Seyss-Inquart, Arthur 287, 289, 300

Shanghai 174, 293, 294

Sharif, Omar 215

Shirer, William 278, 289

sieges
  Acre 8
  Belgrade 90
  Breslau 66
  Plevna 200
  Prague 65
  Przemyśl 254
  Santiago de Querétaro 188
  Sevastopol 167
  Stalingrad 301
  Vienna (1529) 15, 30, (1683) 32, 34, 35, 36, 40, 58, 123, 152, 363

Silesia 18, 23, 52, 53, 54, 65, 66, 70, 80, 104, 120, 125 137, 184, 185, 186, 269, 270, 271

Singapore 173

Sixtus of Bourbon-Parma, Prince 261, 262, 268

Skobalev, Matvey 242, 244

Slavs 155, 202, 210, 215, 217, 264, 269, 272

Slavonia 23, 37, 56, 187, 245, 272

Slovakia and Slovakians 83, 154, 187, 228, 250, 270, 271, 271, 272, 299, 360, 366

Slovenia and Slovenians 7, 9, 24, 228, 250, 256, 260, 266, 270, 271, 353

Smith, Adam 210

Sobieski III, John, King 34, 35

Social Democratic Party of Austria (SPÖ) 308, 314, 315, 326, 331, 342, 344, 345

Social Democratic Workers' Party of Austria (SDAP) 269, 275, 276, 280, 282, 284, 287, 297

Society of Associated Cavaliers
(Gesellschaft der Associirten)
82, 84
South Tyrol 186, 256, 271, 355
Sophie, Archduchess 163, 187
Spain viii, 14, 16, 18, 19, 20, 25,
37, 51, 52, 53, 60, 61, 65, 67,
82, 88, 124, 131, 137, 172,
188, 210, 235
Spanish court etiquette 43, 44, 61,
72, 215
Spanish Riding School 45, 109,
110, 113, 115, 365
spies 111, 137, 139, 295, 323,
338
Spiessheimer (Cuspinian), Johannes
14

St Helena 133
St Martin's Cathedral, Pressburg/
Bratislava 155, 145
St Stephen, Hungarian crown,
kingdom and robes of 15, 46,
47, 54, 145, 186, 191
St Vitus Cathedral, Prague 54
Stuckleberg, Gustav-Ernst von 118
Stadion, Johann 120
Ständestaat 283
Stalin, Joseph 243–4, 326
Staps, Friedrich 100–1
Starhemberg, Count Ernst Rüdiger
34,
Starhemberg, Count Johann Georg
Adam 64
State Chancellery *See* Vienna.
State Opera and Court Opera *See*
Vienna
Stewart, Sir Charles, 3rd Marquess
of Londonderry 123, 124,
125, 126

Stewart, Robert, Lord Castlereagh
105, 120, 121
Stewart Island 174
Stifter, Adalbert 140
Stiles, William Henry 155–8,
160–2
Strasbourg 119
Strategic Arms Limitation Talks
(SALT I & II) 345, 346
Strauss, Johann, the Elder 141,
142, 143, 152, 159, 228
Strauss, Johann, the Younger 228,
231
Styria 9–10, 23, 271, 307, 316
suffrage 179, 229
Suleiman the Magnificent, Sultan
14, 15
Suttner, Bertha von 223–5
Suvorov, Alexander 94
Sweden 19, 25, 30, 65, 91, 193,
235, 260, 331, 339, 354
Swieten, Gerard van 54–5
Swieten, Gottfried van 80–6
Switzerland 7, 9, 10, 23, 63, 92,
130, 131, 193, 235, 243, 245,
261, 268
Swiss Guard 11
Sydney 174
Szeps, Moritz 210
Szögyény-Marich, László 246

Taaffe, Eduard Graf, 58, 229
Taafe, Francis, 3rd Earl of
Carlingford 58
Taaffe, Louis Graf 58
Tahiti 174
Talleyrand-Périgord, Prince
Charles-Maurice ix, 105, 109,
110, 119, 121, 122, 126, 128,
129, 133, 152

Tarouca, Count Don Emanuel Telles de Menezes e Castro 54, 55

Taylor, A.J.P. 168

Taylor, Zachary 160

Te Rerehau, Hemara (Samuel) 174–7

Tegetthoff, Wilhelm 182

Temeswar, Banat of 37, 57

Theresian Military Academy 73

Thompson, Dorothy 277, 280

Thunberg, Greta 359

Thürheim, Lulu, Countess von 109

Tisza, István 246, 261

Tito, Josip Broz 244, 245, 253

Toetoe, Wiremu (Wilhelm) 174–7

Trabanten Life Guards viii, 45, 48

Transleithania 186

Transylvania 15, 18, 20, 23, 37, 63, 69, 70, 154, 167, 235, 272

Trapp, Georg Ludwig von 232

Trauttmansdorff-Weinsberg, Prince Ferdinand 110

Trauttmansdorff and Weinsberg, Count Maximilian of 20

Trajan, Emperor 4

treaties
  Aix-la Chapelle (or Treaty of Aachen) 53
  Austrian State 39, 309, 327, 328, 329, 332, 349, 354
  Berlin 201, 202, 233
  Brest–Litovsk 263
  Campo Formio 90, 94
  Hubertusburg 66
  Karlowitz 37
  Lunéville 11
  Paris (1783) 67, (1814) 104
  Passarowitz 37
  Pressburg 95
  Regensburg 20

St Germain-en-Laye 270–1, 289

San Stefano 200

Schönbrunn 100–01

Trianon 272

Versailles (1756) 64, (1919) 130

Vienna (1725) 37, (1864) 181

Trieste 23, 59, 173, 174, 188, 191, 250, 256, 258, 271, 315

Triple Alliance 202

Triple Entente 257, 261, 262

Trollope, Frances (Fanny) 151, 152

Trotsky, Leon 242, 243, 244, 245

Tschudi, Johann Jakob 166–7

Tusar, Vlastimil 204

Twain, Mark 229, 230

Tyrol 23, 71, 95, 101, 113, 130, 135, 172, 186, 256, 266, 271, 313, 315, 334, 354–5, 358

Ungnad, David von Sonnegg 16

United Kingdom (UK) 25, 28, 30, 51, 52, 53, 55, 64, 66, 77, 78, 80, 87, 121, 127, 136 161,164, 165, 167, 168, 193, 199, 200, 234, 235, 248, 295, 311, 312, 317, 328

United Nations (UN) x, xi, 332, 338, 339, 341, 351, 357

United States of America (USA) 79, 120, 156, 157, 160, 225, 227, 235, 259, 280, 278, 311, 322, 333, 337, 351, 353

Upper Austria 18–19, 22, 216, 236, 297, 301, 306, 315, 322

USSR *See* Russia and Soviet Union (USSR)

Valparaíso 174

Vandals 4

Vatican 11, 25, 77, 214

Venezuela 343
Venice 20, 23, 25, 90, 135, 155,
    170, 172
Versailles 62, 64, 87, 130, 272
Vetsera, Baroness Mary 211, 213, 214
Victoria, Princess Royal, German
    Empress and Queen of Prussia
    213
Victoria, Queen 172, 180, 194,
    212, 213, 214, 234
Vélez de Oñate, Don Íñigo 16,
    18–19
Vermeer, Johannes 81, 205
Victor Emanuel II, King of Sardinia
    and Italy 171, 196
Vienna
  architecture
    Art Nouveau 206, 209
    Baroque 27, 37–9, 62, 64,
        125, 152, 364,
    Gothic 11
    Historiciste (Ringstrasse) 2,
        203, 205–7
    Municipal 276
    Neo-gothic 204–5
  Ballhausplatz 64, 129
  balls 43, 45, 49, 106, 110, 112,
      128, 141, 142, 226, 228, 230
  Centralbad 240
  Central Cemetery
      (Zentralfriedhof) 141, 320
  city gates
    Burgtor 139
    Kärntnertor 42
  city wall viii, ix, 4, 6, 7, 9, 12,
      13, 15, 16, 28, 32, 34, 35, 38,
      42, 52, 62, 73, 86, 91, 101,
      105, 116, 122, 139, 143, 144,
      168, 206, 357, 365
  Congress of, *See* congresses

Boys' Choir 11, 333
churches
  Christ Church 208
  Kaputzinerkirche 150, 215, 364
  Karlskirche 38, 364
  Kirche am Hof 97
  St Augustin's 52, 61, 101
  St Peter's 107
  St Rupert's 6, 365
  St Stephen's Cathedral viii, 7,9,
      31, 84, 148, 191, 260, 297,
      307, 333, 360, 365
  Schottenkirche 7, 84, 123, 176,
  Votivkirche 59, 205
coffee houses
  Atlantis 281
  Bräunerhof 293
  Central 243, 245
  Griensteidl 221
  Imperial 279
  Louvre 278, 289
  Mozart 317
Diplomatic Academy xi, 73, 340,
    341, 349, 364
districts
  Favoriten (10th district) 227
  Floridsdorf (21st district) 277
  Landstrasse (3rd district) 114,
      277
  Leopoldstadt (2nd district)
      112, 122, 144, 216, 274,
      365
  Margareten (5th district) 277,
      331
  Mariahilf (6th district) 236,
      316
  Simmering (11th district) 303
Glacis 34, 139, 206
Graben 3, 9, 93, 108, 112, 304,
    365

Gürtel 303
Heroes' Square *See* squares
Herrengasse 111, 266, 269
Hofburg palace *See* Hofburg palace
International Centre (VIC) 347–8
Karl-Marx-Hof 276–7
Kärntnerstrasse 108
Michaelerplatz 3, 4, 293
Minoritenplatz 107, 152
Mölkerbastei 86, 91, 122, 318
museums
 Albertina 302, 307, 360, 364
 Applied Arts 206
 Art History Museum 81, 204, 205, 360, 365
 Austrian Baroque Art 39
 Austrian History 205
 Belvedere Palace 140
 Carriages and Department of Court Uniform 108
 Military History Museum 35, 48, 118, 194, 363
 Museums Quartier (MQ) 365
 Natural History Museum 45, 174, 204, 205, 365
 Third Man 318
 World Museum 174
parks
 Augarten 72, 112
 Burggarten 206
 Prater 50, 72, 114, 144, 145, 195, 197, 225, 293, 317, 365
 Resselpark 310
 Stadtpark 206
 Rathauspark 206
 Volksgarten 139
Philharmonic Orchestra 85, 203, 221, 231, 333, 360, 364

population viii, ix, 4, 6, 13, 22, 28, 97, 106, 216, 275, 310, 360
Rathaus (City Hall) 204, 206, 339
Red Vienna 276–7
Ringstrasse 2, 59, 169, 195, 196, 203, 204, 205, 206, 207, 217, 218, 237, 239, 259, 281, 285, 286, 290, 307, 316, 365
Schönbrunn *See* palaces
Schwartzenbergplatz 206, 209, 239, 312
Secession 206, 220, 221, 364
squares
 Am Hof 4, 7, 77, 156
 Ballhausplatz 64, 129, 285, 308, 309
 Beethovenplatz 294
 Freyung 84
 Heroes' Square (Heldenplatz) 36, 99, 205, 237, 290, 365
 Josefsplatz 318
 Karlsplatz 310, 317, 364
 Lobkowitzplatz 231
 Michaelerplatz 3, 4, 293
 Minoritenplatz 107–8, 152
 Morzinplatz 295
 Nestroyplatz 365
 Otto Wagner Platz 316
 Schwarzenberplatz 206, 209, 231, 239, 312
 Schwedenplatz 365
 Stephansplatz 304
State Chancellery or Federal Chancellery x, xii, 26, 64, 108, 153, 285, 296, 302, 307, 308, 332, 335
State Opera and Court Opera 42, 82, 203, 221, 237, 302, 307, 333, 338, 346, 360, 364

theatres
  Burgtheater 81, 82, 203, 360, 365
  Theater an der Josefstadt 139
  Theater an der Kärntnertor 42, 113, 122, 140
  Theresian Academy or Theresianum 73
  University 12, 13, 59, 205, 218, 225, 269, 319, 331
  Woods 4, 82, 123, 212, 231, 274, 310
  World Fair 195–7
Vienna conventions
  on Diplomatic Relations (1961) 332
  on Consular Relations (1963) 332
  Joint Comprehensive Plan of Action (on the Nuclear Program of Iran) (2015) 357
  on the Law on Treaties (1969) 332
  on Succession of States in respect of Treaties (1978) 332
  on the Law of Treaties between States and International Organisations or between International Organisations (1986) 332
Vindobona viii, 1, 2, 3–7, 365
Visconti, Antonio Eugenio 61–2
Visigoths 4
Vogelweide, Walther von der 8
Vogüé, Melchior de 202
Voltaire, François-Marie Arouet vii, 22, 69, 81, 91
Vollgruber, Alois 296
Volmar, Dr Isaak 20
Vorarlberg 95, 306, 313, 315

Wagner, Otto 26
Wagner, Richard 218
Wagner, Siegfried 219
Waldemar, Prince of Denmark 260
Waldheim, Kurt 73, 309, 335, 348, 349, 350, 351, 352
Waldmüller, Ferdinand Georg 140
Wallachia 37, 165, 167
Wallenberg, Raoul 293
Wallenstein, Albrecht Eusebius 56
Wallis, Count George Olivier, Freiherr von Carrighmain 56
Wallis, Richard of Carrickmines 56
wars
  American Civil War 162, 183, 184, 188
  Austrian Civil War 283–4, 317, 319
  Austrian Succession 52, 54
  Austro-Turkish (1716–18) 57
    (1788–91) 86
  Austro-Prussian (1866) 53, 184, 186, 208
  Balkan 234
  Bavarian Succession 57, 71, 90
  Coalition wars
    First Coalition 90, 93
    Second Coalition 93
    Third Coalition 94
    Fourth Coalition 97
    Fifth Coalition 97
    Sixth Coalition 103, 104
  Crimean 164, 167–8
  First Italian War of Independence 170
  First World War vii, ix, 192, 198, 204, 218, 219, 232, 234, 237, 242, 245, 246–266, 268, 269, 271, 272, 278, 310, 312, 318, 363

Franco-German 185
French Revolutionary 57, 89
Great Turkish 36
Italo-Abyssinian 285
Marcomannic 2
Napoleonic 57, 59, 94, 104, 105, 113, 124, 133, 183, 361
Ottoman–Habsburg 15
Ottoman–Hungarian 15
Peninsular 97
Polish Succession 36, 52
Russian Civil War 245
Russo-Turkish (1877–8) 198, 200, 233
Schleswig 30
Second World War 192, 209, 219
Seven Years' War 57, 64, 74
Silesian 52, 65, 66
Spanish Succession 37, 169, 363
Thirty Years' War 18, 19, 363
Warsaw 55, 80, 101, 130, 163, 256, 301, 315
Warsaw Pact 312, 327, 329, 334, 335, 337
Weimar, Maria, Grand Duchess 116
Welles, Orson 317
Wellesley, Henry 136, 138, 146
Wellington, Duke of 115, 117, 136
West Indies 52, 66
Westminster Convention 64
Wetzlar 25, 26
Wiesenthal, Simon 344, 345, 350
Wilder, Billy 297

Wilhelm, Crown Prince of Germany 260
Wilhelm I, King of Prussia 185,
Wilhelm I, Kaiser of Germany 197
Wilhelm II, Kaiser of Germany 211, 219, 223, 246, 248, 266,
Wilmot, Martha 143, 144, 145, 146
Wilson, Woodrow 129, 263, 264, 269
Windisch-Grätz, Alfred I, Prince of 125, 155, 156, 157, 158, 163, 167
Witos, Wincenty 204
Witt, Graf de 112
Wotton, Sir Henry 17
World Jewish Congress (WJC) 350
Wüllerstorf-Urbair, Bernhard von 173
Württemberg 17, 107, 108, 109, 112, 126
Wylie, Sir James 112, 119

Yad Vashem 294
Young, Terence 215
Yugoslavia xi, 204, 280, 253, 360

Zagreb/Agram 246
Zápolya, John 15
Zichy, Julie, Countess 106, 116
Zichy, Sophie, Countess 126
Zilk, Helmut 334, 336
Zionism 221, 223
Zita, Empress-Queen 260, 268
Zweig, Stefan 218, 221, 241, 297, 318